D1596497

The Rule of Law

FRANZ NEUMANN

The Rule of Law

Political Theory
and the Legal System
in Modern Society

With a Foreword by
MARTIN JAY
and an Introduction by
MATTHIAS RUETE

BERG
Leamington Spa : Heidelberg : Dover, NH

Berg Publishers Ltd
24 Binswood Avenue, Leamington Spa,
Warwickshire CV32 5SQ, UK
Panoramastr. 118, 6900 Heidelberg,
West Germany
51 Washington Street, Dover,
New Hampshire 03820, USA

First published 1986

Original title: The Governance of the Rule of Law.
An investigation into the practical theories, the legal system, and the social background in the competitive society.

British Library Cataloguing in Publication Data

Neumann, Franz
The rule of law:
political theory and the legal system in modern society.
1. Sociological jurisprudence
I. Title
340.115 K370

ISBN 0–907582–36–2

Library of Congress Cataloging in Publication Data

Neumann, Franz, 1935–
The rule of law.

1. Rule of law. 2. Law—Philosophy. 3. Sociological jurisprudence. I. Title.
K3171.N48 1985 340′.11 85–3958
ISBN 0–907582–36–2

Printed in Great Britain by Billings of Worcester

Contents

FOREWORD

Neumann and the Frankfurt School

On 3 September 1954 the car in which Franz Neumann was riding on a country road in Switzerland spun out of control and crashed into a poplar tree. Neumann, then only fifty-four years old and at the height of his career, was killed, along with the driver, Manfred Altmann, and his wife Johanna. The following day, the funeral speech at the small cemetery in Vevey was delivered by Friedrich Pollock, Neumann's old colleague at the Institute of Social Research during its New York exile. Speaking of Neumann as a good friend, Pollock soberly noted that without a belief in a hereafter, the only life after death was that preserved in the memory of the living: 'And this we promise you,' he concluded, 'as long as one of us survives, you will not be forgotten. Good-bye Franz'.

That Franz Neumann has indeed not been forgotten may, in fact, be attributed in part to his association with the Institute, which he joined in 1936 and left in 1942 to work in Washington with the Board of Economic Warfare and the Office of Strategic Services. And yet, his relations with the Institute's central figures, its 'inner circle' around the director Max Horkheimer, which became known as the Frankfurt School, were by no means without certain serious complications. Ironically, the most explicit and public substantive dispute occurred with Pollock over the latter's model of state capitalism, which he introduced in 1939 to explain a new stage in global development, a stage which included liberal democratic, communist and fascist variations. Neumann, more beholden to a traditional Marxist approach during that period, remained convinced that monopoly capitalism had not really been superseded, especially in the Nazi regime he analysed in the work he completed shortly thereafter, *Behemoth: The Structure and Practice of National Socialism* (1st ed., 1942, 2nd. ed., 1944). The extent of the Institute's scepticism about his argument can be judged from the absence of Horkheimer's customary preface and his subsequent refusal to permit a German translation in the Institute's publication series after its return to

Frankfurt in the 1950s. Only, in fact, in 1977, after Horkheimer's death, did the book finally appear, and then in another series, to be followed shortly by several collections of Neumann's essays and a German edition of 'The Governance of the Rule of Law'. More deeply sensitive to the neutralisation of class antagonisms by psychological manipulation than was Neumann, the Institute's inner circle was also convinced that a more general technological, administrative domination was gaining the upper hand over straightforward economic exploitation. Their analysis culminated in the bleak ruminations over the entire course of Western civilisation that appeared in 1947 under the joint authorship of Horkheimer and Theodor Adorno as *Dialectic of Enlightenment*, a work very far removed in tone and inclination from anything in Franz Neumann's corpus.

The ultimate source of these differences is not very difficult to discern. Neumann was born into a lower-middle-class Jewish family in the eastern German town of Kattowicz in 1900, far from the gilded and more culturally sophisticated background of most members of the Frankfurt School. Less drawn than they to aesthetic and cultural issues, untouched by the romantic anti-capitalism that gave their Critical Theory its messianic and apocalyptic edge, resistant to the lure of psychoanalysis until near the end of his life, Neumann represented a very different kind of Weimar intellectual from Horkheimer, Pollock, Adorno, Herbert Marcuse, Walter Benjamin or Leo Lowenthal (even though the last of these had, in fact, been a friend from their student days). Whereas they remained defiantly distant from party politics, unabashed members of the Weimar 'homeless left', Neumann joined the moderate Social Democratic Party after a brief membership in 1918 in a Leipzig workers' and soldiers' council. He lent his considerable legal skills, honed under the direction of the distinguished jurist Hugo Sinzheimer at the University of Frankfurt, to the fight for the reform of the legal status of the German working class. Drawing on the gradualist arguments of the Austro-Marxist Karl Renner, he hoped to exert pressure on the legal system to bring about socialism without a violent collapse of the Weimar Republic. In 1927, Neumann opened a practice in Berlin with Ernst Fraenkel, later himself the author of an important analysis of Nazism, *The Dual State*. Together, they worked vigorously to defend the institutionalisation of trade union rights and in so doing to expand economic democracy. At the same time, Neumann also taught at the celebrated Deutsche Hochschule für Politik, which sought to advance the cause of responsible participation in Weimar politics and undo the traditional disdain of the 'unpolitical German'. Unlike his later colleague at the Institute, Otto Kirchheimer, who was at that time on the left wing of the SPD, Neumann remained interested in more strictly legal and practical questions than in larger theoretical ones.

Thus, in 1933, when both Neumann and the Frankfurt Institute were forced to leave Germany, it would have seemed highly unlikely that their paths would cross only a few years later. 'The Governance of the Rule of Law' is interesting, among many other reasons, for the help it gives us to understand how the connection was made. It was written at the London School of Economics under the direction of Harold Laski, at that time the leading intellectual of the British Labour Party and increasingly attracted to a more explicitly Marxist position. Laski had been one of the supporters of the Institute's London office, which functioned from 1933 to 1936, and was able to exert his personal influence to recommend Neumann for an Institute post in New York, when it became clear that employment opportunities in Britain were extremely limited. But perhaps even more significantly, his training of Neumann had helped lift the latter's horizons from purely legal questions to more broadly theoretical ones, while at the same time moving him in a more radically leftward direction. Bitterly disappointed by the inefficacy of the SPD's reformist strategy, Neumann now kept his distance from emigre political organisations, such as the New Beginning, and applied himself instead to more long-term scholarly questions. Without the hope of a legal career in the Anglo-Saxon world, he set out to remake himself into an academic political theorist by expanding and rethinking the unpublished dissertation he had completed under Sinzheimer in 1923.

The Institute, at that time still pursuing an ambitiously interdisciplinary programme under the guidance of Critical Theory, had need of an expert in political theory. Neumann's political sympathies were congenial, especially now that he had abandoned his moderate pragmatism. Laski's endorsement of his achievement in his new dissertation was sufficient for Horkheimer and his colleagues to invite Neumann to New York. An added inducement seems to have been his practical legal skills, which the Institute quickly put to use in such causes as its unsuccessful effort to persuade the Nazi regime to release its library to the London School of Economics, where Neumann had worked with Laski.

The first scholarly achievement of the new collaboration was the publication of Neumann's essay on 'The Change in the Function of Law in Modern Society' in the *Zeitschrift für Sozialforschung* in 1937. Here a condensed version of many of the arguments of 'The Governance of the Rule of Law' appeared, after having been brought into line with the Institute's general approach through extensive editorial meetings. Neumann's magisterial survey of the history of legal ideas was reduced to a few lines and the more baldly Marxist tone of some of the formulations was sacrificed to the Institute's caution about its emigre status in America. Some of the philosophical dimensions of the work also seem to have been modified or dropped, even though Neumann had drawn on Horkheimer's earlier *Zeitschrift* essay on 'The Rationalism Dispute in Contemporary Philosophy' when writing the English dissertation.

Still, what remained was a genuine Institute product, which reflected many of its most compelling concerns. Neumann's central preoccupation was with the conflict between the universal, formal, impersonal and, most importantly, rational impulse in the Western legal tradition and the countervailing impulse towards the absolute sovereignty of the state. In accord with the Institute's materialist ideology critique of the 1930s, Neumann saw the conflict as both reflecting social trends and in a certain sense transcending them. The rationalising impulse in law, he argued, had to be understood dialectically as the reflection of the bourgeoisie's flawed universalizing mission. Its ethical, transcendent moment derived from its imperative to extend legal equality to all groups in society; its ideological moment came from its mystifying claim to have already provided such formal equality in a society still riven with class divisions. The *Rechtstaat* was thus at once a minimal programme of equality that needed to be preserved rather than merely abandoned and an inadequate mockery of the real equality that only a socialist society could provide.

The second impulse in modern legal theory and practice, its anti-normative acknowledgement of state sovereignty, meant that legal decisions could be made on political rather than rational grounds. Neumann, like Otto Kirchheimer, came to appreciate the importance of this issue from the work of the conservative and later Nazi political theorist Carl Schmitt, who was soon to be a target of abuse in *Behemoth*. But unlike Schmitt, who turned his insight into the cynical conclusion that power could never be challenged by normative claims, Neumann held out hope for an ultimate convergence of the two in a different society, which would be unfractured by irreconcilable class antagonisms.

In the immediate future, however, a very different prospect seemed more likely to the disillusioned emigres in their New York exile. For what Neumann and his colleagues noted was a tendency apparent in Western society as a whole, which was most keenly obvious in Nazi Germany, towards a withering away of the universalist, rational, ethical moment in law. As a result, the decisionist moment had ominously grown, even if under the guise of a supposedly concrete corporate 'institutionalism'. A turning point had been reached, moreover, which could not be reversed, for the social underpinnings of the *Rechtstaat* had been progressively eroded with the passing of classical capitalism. No neo-Kantian legal formalism would be possible and, *a fortiori*, no simple extension of it to the working class would suffice to bring about socialism, as Neumann had naively hoped during the Weimar years. Like Marcuse in his 1934 *Zeitschrift* essay on 'The Struggle Against Liberalism in the Totalitarian View of the State', Neumann now emphasised the fatal lineage between bourgeois and fascist legal and political systems. Like Kirchheimer, whose radical analysis of the terminal crisis of the Republic, *Weimar — And What Then?*, he had once criticised, he came to accept the contention that Weimar could not have been salvaged by reformist means. And like Adorno in his later commentaries on the virtual end of ideology in post-liberal, administered society, he faced the sombre possibility that domination was shedding its legitimating rationalizations, which, for all their ideological untruth, could at least provide the leverage for an immanent critique of the system's inadequacies. It was, in fact, Neumann's appreciation of the disenchantment of the rationalising, normative moment in Nazi law that allowed him as well to question the regime's very status as a traditional state, for there had been a crucial link between reason and the Western state, which Hegel had correctly emphasized. Instead, as he later argued in justifying the title of his great book on Nazism, it had become more of a 'behemoth', a 'non-state, a chaos, a rule of lawlessness and anarchy'.

Behemoth, of course, contained another argument, which emphasised the dependency of that new monster, at least in large measure, on the elites of monopoly capitalism. As such, it contained a potentially explosive economic and social potential that meant internal collapse was still possible. Although after his Institute tenure, Neumann was to abandon his Marxist hopes and move towards a kind of uneasy liberalism, he never felt attracted to the almost meta-historical pessimism of the other Institute members expressed in *Dialectic of Enlightenment*. Like his closest friend at the Institute, Herbert Marcuse, he continued to look for cracks in the one-dimensional facade of modern society. As such, his work has correctly been linked with the most important second generation Frankfurt School theorist, Jürgen Habermas, whose writings on the unresolved crises of capitalism refuse to accept the complete suspension of its potential for radical change.

The later Horkheimer, to be sure, was far less sanguine, as demonstrated by his blockage of the German publication of *Behemoth* and the Institute's failure to bring out a collection of Neumann's work, for which Adorno in fact wrote an unpublished preface. Still, there is sufficient evidence to show that despite this ambivalence, the Institute always considered Neumann one of its own. Thus, after the shock of his sudden death, Horkheimer immediately made Helge Pross, with whom Neumann was then in love, an Institute assistant. According to her own testimony, this gesture was an expression of his respect and gratitude for Neumann's contributions to the Institute. That Neumann himself always felt enormous loyalty and affection for the Institute is shown by the letter he sent Horkheimer in March 1946, when he was leaving government service to take up a position in the Columbia Political Science Department. 'Most of all', he wrote, 'I would like to return to the Institute, in order to work for myself once again.' What Neumann's return would have meant, both for his own work and the Institute's development, we can only speculate. But what is certain is that in his brief time in its ranks, he made a lasting contribution to the still potent legacy for which the Institute has gained international reknown.

MARTIN JAY
History Department,
University of California, Berkeley

STUDIES ON NEUMANN AND THE FRANKFURT SCHOOL

Rainer Erd (ed.), *Reform und Resignation; Gespräche über Franz L. Neumann*, Frankfurt, 1985

H. Stuart Hughes, *The Sea Change; The Migration of Social Thought 1930–1960*, New York, 1975

Martin Jay, *The Dialectical Imagination; A History of the Frankfurt School and the Institute of Social Research, 1923–1950*, Boston, 1973

Alfons Söllner, *Geschichte und Herrschaft; Studien zur materialistischen Sozialwissenschaft*, Frankfurt, 1979

—, *Neumann zur Einführung*, Hanover, 1982

See also the excellent introduction by Söllner to Franz L. Neumann, *Wirtschaft, Staat, Demokratie: Aufsätze 1930–1954* (Frankfurt, 1978), and his informative afterword to the German edition of this text, *Die Herrschaft des Gesetzes. Eine Untersuchung zum Verhältnis von politischer Theorie und Rechtssystem in der Konkurrenzgesellschaft* (Frankfurt, 1980).

INTRODUCTION

Post-Weimar Legal Theory in Exile*

I

Franz L. Neumann is probably best known to the British and American reader for his study of National Socialism, *Behemoth*.[1] Until recently, a German lawyer might have associated his name with the standard textbook on human rights, Bettermann/Neumann/Nipperdey; published in 1954.[2] When, however, a collection of Neumann's essays on *The Democratic and Authoritarian State*[3] was published in West Germany in 1967, a group of students and lecturers of law, political science and sociology eagerly took up some of his ideas, especially those expressed in 'The Change in the Function of Law in Modern Society', in their attempts to understand contemporary West Germany society, its legal system, and its history.

The importance of Neumann's article in (re-)establishing a broad critical legal studies movement in the Federal Republic of Germany can be compared only with the republication of Pashukanis's work in 1966.[4] In this process, those involved began to rediscover the

*I am greatly indebted to Jackie Bennett-Ruete, Leigh Hancher and Robert Millar for comments on earlier drafts.

1. F. Neumann, *Behemoth*, Oxford, 1942; 2nd rev. ed., 1944; repr. 1963 (Octagon Books; pb. ed., Harper & Row, 1966.
2. F. L. Neumann, H. C. Nipperdey and U. Scheuner (eds.), *Die Grundrechte. Handbuch der Theorie und Praxis der Grundrechte*, Berlin, 1954 et seq.
3. F. Neumann, *Demokratischer und autoritärer Staat, Studien zur politischen Theorie*, Frankfurt/Vienna, 1967. American edition: H. Marcuse (ed.), *The Democratic and the Authoritarian State*, New York, 1957; pb. ed., New York/Toronto, 1964. The German edition has a separate introduction by Helge Pross, but leaves out the article on 'Types of Natural Law' contained in the American edition. Some of his Labour Law Texts in T. Ramm (ed.), *Arbeitsrecht und Politik. Quellentexte 1918–1933*, Neuwied, 1966.
4. Eugen Paschukanis, *Allgemeine Rechtslehre und Marxismus*, Vienna/Berlin, 1929; repr., Frankfurt, 1966; transl. as Evgeny Pashukanis, *Law and Marxism: a General Theory*, London, 1978.

critical (democratic) legal tradition of the Weimar Republic which was linked with such names as Otto Kirchheimer,[5] Ernst Fraenkel,[6] Otto Kahn-Freund,[7] Hermann Heller,[8] Hugo Sinzheimer,[9] the journal *Die Justiz-Zeitschrift des Republikanischen Richerbundes*,[10] and, of course, Franz Neumann himself.[11]

It would be foolish, however, to imply that Neumann was only of interest to lawyers; rather it was political scientists who were most active in making Neumann more accessible to German readers. In 1977 Gerd Schäfer translated, introduced and edited the first German version of *Behemoth*;[12] in 1978 Alfons Söllner edited and intro-

5. On Otto Kirchheimer, see K. Tribe, *Introduction to Kirchheimer, Economy and Society*, 66, 1983; M. Jay, *The Dialectical Imagination*, London, 1973, pp. 148ff.; J. H. Herz and E. Hula, 'Otto Kirchheimer: An Introduction to his Life and Work', in *Otto Kirchheimer, Politics, Law and Social Change*, F. S. Burin and K. L. Shell (eds.), Columbia, 1969. For K.'s work, see O. Kirchheimer, *Political Justice*, Princeton, 1961; idem, *Politik und Verfassung*, Frankfurt, 1964; idem, *Politische Herrschaft, Fünf Beiträge zur Lehre vom Staat*, Frankfurt, 1967; idem, *Funktionen des Staats und der Verfassung*, Frankfurt, 1972; idem, *Von der Weimarer Republik zum Faschismus: Die Auflösung der demokratischen Rechtsordnung*, Frankfurt, 1976.
6. Probably best known to the English reader through his analysis of the legal system of National Socialism, *The Dual State*, New York, 1941, repr. New York, 1969 — re-translated; *Der Doppelstaat*, Frankfurt; 1974, whereas Neumann relies heavily on Fraenkel's *Zur Soziologie der Klassenjustiz*, Berlin, 1927, repr. Darmstadt, 1968. In the reprint Fraenkel talks about his time in Berlin when he participated with Neumann, Kirchheimer and Kahn-Freund in producing the SPD journal *Die Gesellschaft*, (ibid., p. viii).
7. A good introduction in Lord Wedderburn, R. Lewis, J. Clark, *Labour Law and Industrial Relations: Building on Kahn-Freund*, Oxford, 1983.
8. Hermann Heller has so far received little attention in English-speaking countries. His collected works were recently republished: H. Heller, *Gesammelte Schriften*, 3 vols., Leiden, 1971. See also C. Müller and I. Staff (eds.), *Der soziale Rechtsstaat — Gedächtnisschrift für Hermann Heller 1891–1933*, Baden Baden, 1984.
9. Sinzheimer was the senior of the group and had taught, amongst others, Neumann and Kahn-Freund. O. Kahn-Freund and T. Ramm edited a collection of Sinzheimer's shorter works in 1976: *Hugo Sinzheimer, Arbeitsrecht und Rechtssoziologie*, 2 vols, Frankfurt/Cologne, 1976, which also contains a good introduction to Sinzheimer by Kahn-Freund (pp. 1–33).
10. *Die Justiz* existed from the autumn of 1925 to April 1933. A selection of legal analyses from *Die Justiz*, mainly by Sinzheimer and Fraenkel appeared in 1968: Sinzheimer and Fraenkel, *Die Justiz in der Weimarer Republik, Eine Chronik*, Ramm (ed.), Berlin/Neuwied, 1968.
11. Bibliographical details and further references in: Jay, *Dialectical Imagination*; A. Söllner, 'Franz L. Neumann — Skizzen zu einer intellektuellen und politischen Bibliographie', in F. L. Neumann, *Wirtschaft, Staat, Demokratie, Aufsätze 1930–1954*, 1978, pp. 7ff.; Marcuse (ed.), preface, *Democratic State*, pp. viiff.; H. Pross, 'Einleitung', in Neumann, *Demokratischer Staat*, pp. 9ff.; K. Tribe, 'Introduction to Neumann: Law and Socialist Political Theory', *Economy and Society*, 10, 1981, p. 316; J. Perels (ed.), *Recht, Demokratie und Kapitalismus, Aktualität und Probleme der Theorie Franz L. Neumanns*, 1984; A. Söllner, 'Leftist Students of the Conservative Revolution: Neumann, Kirchheimer, & Marcuse', *Telos*, 61, 1984, p. 55; R. Erd (ed.), *Reform und Resignation, Gespräche über Franz L. Neumann*, Frankfurt, 1985.
12. F. L. Neumann, *Behemoth*, transl. G. Schäfer, Frankfurt,: 1977.

duced a collection of Neumann's essays[13] and later translated his 1936 LSE thesis on 'The Governance of the Rule of Law'.[14] It was from this thesis that such important articles as 'The Change in the Function of Law'[15] and 'Types of Natural Law'[16] were drawn and on which many of the ideas in *Behemoth* relied. In the meantime, literature on Neumann has mushroomed in West Germany[17] and it seems only appropriate to make his thesis, which was after all written in English, available to a wider English-speaking audience. This seems especially appropriate in the centennial of the publication of Dicey's study on the rule of law[18] which has heralded a multitude of reassessments of the rule of law from a British perspective.[19] Neumann's thesis makes a not insubstantial contribution to that debate, albeit half a century late.

II

'The Governance of the Rule of Law' has as its subtitle 'An Investigation into the Relationship between Political Theories, the Legal System and the Social Background', which more accurately describes the content of the book. In the first part Neumann briefly develops his main conceptual framework, which could be labelled as sociologically informed legal positivism.[20] He relies strongly on the notion of rational law and points to the contrast between state sovereignty and natural law as the key to an understanding of the rule of law. This is followed up in the second part, aptly named the 'disenchantment of the law', by an impressive and stimulating analysis of natural law theorists. The third part then inspects the rule of law in the nineteenth century and the drastic changes with the coming of the interventionist state.

13. F. L. Neumann, *Wirtschaft, Staat und Demokratie. Aufsätze 1930–1954*, A. Söllner (ed.), Frankfurt, 1978.
14. F. L. Neumann, *Die Herrschaft des Gesetzes. Eine Untersuchung zum Verhältnis von politischer Theorie und Rechtssystem in der Konkurrenzgesellschaft*, transl. A. Söllner, Frankfurt, 1980.
15. In German as 'Der Funktionswandel des Gesetzes im Recht der bürgerlichen Gesellschaft', in *6 Zeitschrift für Sozialforschung*, 1937, p. 542.
16. First publ. in *Studies in Philosophy and Social Science*, 8, 1939/40, p. 338.
17. For example, the references in n. 11, above.
18. A. V. Dicey, *Introduction to the Study of the Law of the Constitution*, 1885 et seq.
19. Cf. P. McAuslan and J. McEldowney, *Law, Legitimacy and the Constitution*, London, 1985 (forthcoming); N. Lewis, and I. J. Harden, *The Rule of Law and the British Constitution*, London, 1985 (forthcoming); J. Jowell (ed.) *Essays in Constitutional Law*, Oxford, 1985 (forthcoming).
20. It is interesting to note that Neumann, while refuting the insularity of Kelsen's positivism, in many ways depends quite strongly on this approach in order to show the 'natural law' bias of other theorists.

In developing his analysis Neumann relies on Karl Marx, Max Weber, Karl Renner,[21] Karl Mannheim and Harold Laski, who also supervised his thesis.[22] His main intellectual opponent in his book can be easily identified: Carl Schmitt, constitutional lawyer and outstanding conservative critic of the Weimar Republic,[23] who for a brief period was a staunch supporter of National Socialism and whose work has had a profound impact on modern West German constitutional law. He is probably the author most frequently referred to in the book and can be said to be responsible for its whole layout. When Neumann refutes his claim that the Weimar constitution allowed Parliament to enact only general laws he says of Schmitt: 'For proof of this assertion . . . he has recourse to the ideological history of the notion of law which we have followed up in the second part of our book. . . . We have attempted to prove that the postulate that the State may only rule through general laws is bound up with that of a certain social superstructure; and that it is indefensible to divorce the postulate of the generality of law from the postulated social order' (pp. 273–4).

This in essence is also the major thesis of Neumann's book. He postulates a correlation between the social system of competitive capitalism and its legal system. He describes the liberal legal system — mainly though its theorists — as an ideal-type (in the Weberian sense) which combines generality of legal rules and non-retroactivity of the law with independence of the judiciary. The protection of the (bourgeois) society against the constant threat of intervention by the state is claimed to be guaranteed through this combination. Neither law itself nor those who apply it can be directed to intervene in specific cases and retroactive intervention 'after the event' is equally banned. Neumann attributes three main functions to the generality of law. First, law serves both as an expression of and smoke-screen for the dominance of the bourgeoisie. This in many ways represents a reformulation of Marx's critique of the function of formal equality of law[24] which, as A. France has said, in its magnanimous equality forbids both the rich and poor to sleep under bridges. The second function takes up Max Weber's idea that the role of (general) laws is to provide calculability for the competitive economy. No enterprise

21. K. Renner, *The Institutions of Private Law and their Social Functions*, ed. O. Kahn-Freund, London, 1949.
22. Laski also wrote the preface to Neumann's *Trade Unionism, Democracy, Dictatorship*, London, 1934 and to idem, *European Trade Unionism and Politics*, New York, 1936.
23. On Carl Schmitt's importance for Neumann, see V. Neumann, 'Kompromiß oder Entscheidung? Zur Rezeption der Theorie Carl Schmitts in den Weimarer Arbeiten von Franz L. Neumann', in Perels (ed.), *Kapitalismus*.
24. A good summary in B. Fine, *Democracy and the Rule of Law*, London, 1984.

could function if it did not operate within the framework of predictable rules. The third and most innovating dimension of general laws identified by Neumann is an 'ethical function': 'The generality of the laws, the independence of judges and the doctrine of separation of powers, have . . . functions transcending the needs of competitive capitalism since they secure personal liberty and personal equality (p. 257).[25]

Neumann traces a radical change in the legal system which parallels the transition from competitive to monopoly capitalism: both the structure and function of law are transformed. Generality of law is replaced by a combination of general clauses, vague legal standards and individualised legislation. In (Weimar) Germany, natural law is revived as a conservative weapon against parliamentary sovereignty, the *Freirechtsschule* (school of free discretion) triumphs over positivism, and in Britain, legal standards such as 'reasonableness' are on the increase. Judicial activity, no longer guided by general norms, turns increasingly into substantially administrative activity.

In order to develop this idea, Neumann presents us with an elaborate attempt to combine comparative and historical research with socio-legal study. He undertakes a *horizontal analysis* of a common law and a civil law system[26] which is sensitive to the historical development of these and is combined with a *vertical analysis* of law in (each) society. His starting point is the related but — as he explains (pp. 193–5) — not identical concepts of 'rule of law' and *Rechtsstaat*, which he links with the notion of a societal sphere protected against state intervention by (explicit or implicit) human rights and 'general norms'. Using methods of 'immanent' and 'transcendental critique'[27] he explores the relative weight given to notions of natural law and sovereignty by political thinkers from Aquinus to Hegel and links these to political movements.

III

It is, however, the third part of the book which makes the most fascinating reading. Here Neumann draws on his theoretical expertise as a constitutional and labour lawyer. This was enlarged first by practical experience in the Weimar Republic as legal adviser to the builders' union and to the national executive of the SPD and then by

25. A similar argument is made by E. P. Thompson, *Whigs and Hunters*, Harmondsworth, 1977 and elsewhere. On Thompson see Fine, *Democracy*, pp. 169ff.
26. He concentrates mainly on the English and German legal systems, while also taking sideway looks at France and the United States.
27. Terminology derived from Karl Mannheim.

his encounter with a totally different legal tradition in Britain.

It was the more mechanistic aspect of his thesis which first seemed to offer the greatest attraction to German critical lawyers in the late 1960s and early 1970s. The irretrievably lost paradise of the legal system of competitive capitalism could be contrasted with the irrational use of law under conditions of monopoly capitalism. The use of general clauses, more purposive legislation and generous forms of statutory interpretation had in fact increased dramatically, judicial activism was greater than it had ever been before.[28] Soon, however, it was realised that an evolutionary perspective postulating and equating the decay of monopoly capitalism and its legal system was too far removed from reality to qualify even as an 'ideal type'.[29]

Neumann himself warned against mechanistic and especially reductionist assumptions and attempted to relate law not only to the economic 'sub-system' but also to political, religious, personal and ideological influences. His task, he said, was to 'indicate on the one hand the conditions under which law and state can develop relatively independently and on the other hand the forces which go to destroy this relative autonomy and subject . . . law and . . . state with full force to the stream of realities' (p. 16).

It may be said that he himself did not always measure up to this standard. This should, however, not make us blind to his great achievement which was that he took up and developed Max Weber's hint of the possibility of 'anti-formalist tendencies in modern legal development'[30] and related this to changes in society. Over forty years later this insight is the focus for a debate among legal scholars and sociologists who talk about 'repressive, autonomous and responsive' law (Nonet/Selznick),[31] about 'self-reflexive law' (Teubner),[32] about 'conditional' and 'goal-oriented' programmes (Luhmann),[33] about *Gesellschaft* and 'bureaucratic' types of law (Kamenka/Tay),[34]

28. Analyses can be found in the critical legal journals *Kritische Justiz* (since 1968) and *Demokratie und Recht* (since 1973).
29. One of the earliest criticisms of Neumann was developed by U.K. Preuß, 'Nachträge zur Theorie des Rechtsstaat', *Kritische Justiz*, 16, 1971; a more general critique: K. H. Ladeur, 'Vom Gesetzesvollzug zur Strategischen Rechtsfortbildung', *Leviathan*, 339, 1979; F. Hase and M. Ruete, 'Dekadenz der Rechtsentwicklung?', *Leviathan*, 200, 1983; E. Blankenburg, 'The Poverty of Evolutionism', *Law & Society Review*, 18, 1984, p. 273.
30. M. Rheinstein, 'Max Weber on Law', in *Economy and Society*, Cambridge, Mass., 1954, pp. 303.
31. P. Nonet and P. Selznick, *Law and Society in Transition: Toward Responsive Law*, New York, 1978.
32. G. Teubner, 'Substantive and Reflexive Elements in Modern Law', *Law & Society Review*, 17, 1983, p. 239; idem, 'Autopoiesis in Law and Society: A Rejoinder to Blankenburg', in *Law & Society Review* 18, 1984, p. 291.
33. N. Luhmann, *The Differentiation of Society*, New York, 1982.
34. E. Kamenka, and A. E. S. Tay, 'Social Traditions, Legal Traditions', in *Law and Social Control*, 1980; Kamenka, 'Beyond Bourgeois Individualism: the Con-

about the fourth legalisation thrust of the social welfare state (Habermas).[35]

In the light of this debate, Neumann's ideas appear very modern. There are, however, also obvious limitations. His analysis of the development from competitive to monopoly capitalism is imbued with a notion of decay which was reproduced on the level of the legal system. If 'general law' contained an ethical function, the changing structure of law meant that this ethical function was lost, even that rules could no longer be described as law: 'If general law is the basic form of right, if law is not only *voluntas* but also *ratio*, then we must deny the existence of law in the fascist state'.[36]

Undoubtedly, Neumann's experience of National Socialism led him to this seemingly logical conclusion. The experience of the Weimar Republic had made him distrust natural law theories and their use for political ends, and some of the most interesting parts of this book are his accounts of the sudden revival of natural law as a tool of conservative judges and legal scholars against a democratically elected Parliament.[37] However, faced with the reality of fascism and national socialism the analysis of natural law seems to deprive him of a legal method of critique. Was the fascist system legal? The postulate of the 'generality of law' can in this light be interpreted as an ingenious attempt to develop a critique of National Socialist Germany without reverting to natural law: the 'ethical function' of general law seemed to formalise values such as 'personal liberty and equality' and make them an acceptable point of reference without at the same time abandoning a critique of natural law. Neumann, however, realises the ambivalence of such a notion of generality of law. He criticised Schmitt and others for demanding such laws in Weimar and concluded that such demands were only intended to limit the sovereignty of Parliament: 'By this the generality of the law took the place of a natural law. It was in fact nothing but a hidden natural law' (p. 276) he asserts against conservative lawyers of the Weimar Republic.

Neumann was in the uncomfortable position of having destroyed the ship (of natural law) with which to ride the waves (to criticise the fascist legal system) only to replace the ship with a raft (of the ethical function of law). His discomfort is not dissimilar to the dilemma in which many German critical lawyers found themselves

---

temporary Crisis in Law and Legal Ideology', in Kamenka and Neal (eds.), *Feudalism, Capitalism and Beyond*, 1975.

35. In *Theorie des kommunikativen Handelns*, vol. 2, Frankfurt, 1981, p. 525.
36. Neumann, *Behemoth*, p. 451.
37. On this, F. Hase, *Richterliches Prüfungsrecht und Staatsgerichtsbarkeit*, Gießen, 1980; J. Perels, *Kapitalismus und politische Demokratie*, Frankfurt, 1973.

in the early 1970s. Having developed a radical critique of the natural law approach of the German courts after 1945 and of the bourgeois function of the constitution, the assault on civil liberties represented by *Berufsverbote*[38] and anti-terrorist legislation[39] suddenly made much belittled political freedoms seem important values which were worth defending. Neumann's critique of natural law had helped in developing a sensitivity to natural law theories; he amongst others provided a vessel to return to the safe port of constitutionalism.[40]

Neumann had, by turning his description of the 'ethical dimensions' of general laws into a prescription, secretly become attached to non-positivist *legal* values and thus could be accused of having a natural law bias. By linking formal structures to substantive values he had fashioned a tool for the criticism of fascism which in the long run proved unwieldy. He had poignantly outlined the changing structure of law in the legal system of Germany and — to some extent — of Britain and both systems have developed very much in line with his predictions. Law has become more open-ended and has increasingly been directed in an instrumental fashion at individual problems. Can, however, both the legal system of the United Kingdom and the Federal Republic of Germany be described as non-law, consisting only of *voluntas* and not of *ratio*? This question, absurd as it may seem, echoes some of the views expressed in the recent debate on 'deregulation'[41] and 'crisis of legalisation'.[42] The predominantly American deregulation debate, which is becoming increasingly important in Europe, is based on the liberal theory of a separation of state and society. It is mainly directed at the question of regulating business but also looks at wider issues and — more often than not — comes to the conclusion that regulation has proved irrational, either because the wrong instruments have been employed (mis-match), or because the problem diagnosed was not a problem (false failure).[43]

38. See, as an introduction, G. Brinkmann, 'Militant Democracy and Radicals in the West German Civil Service', in *MLR*, 46, 1983, p. 584.
39. A good summary in S. Cobler, S., *Law, Order and Politics in West Germany*, Harmondsworth, 1978.
40. On this, see F. Hase and M. Ruete, 'Constitutional Court and Constitutional Ideology', *International Journal of Sociology of Law*, 1982, p. 267.
41. A good summary by Reich, 'The Regulatory Crisis: Does it Exist and Can it Be Solved?', 1984 (2) *Government and Policy*, 1984, 177.
42. I. Harden and N. Lewis, *De-Legalisation in Britain in the 1980s*, EUI Working Paper 84/125, Florence, 1984; R. B. Stewart, *Regulation and the Crisis of Legalization in the United States*, EUI Conference Paper, Florence 1985; G. Teubner, *Legalisation — Concepts, Aspects, Limits, Solutions*, EUI Conference Paper, Florence, 1985; R. Voigt (ed.), *Gegentendenzen zur Verrechtlichung*, Opladen, 1983; F. Kübler (ed.), *Verrechtlichung von Wirtschaft, Arbeit und sozialer Solidarität*, Baden Baden, 1984.
43. See S. Breyer, *Regulation and its Reform*, Cambridge, Mass., 1982.

It may seem ironic that this predominantly liberal–conservative debate finds support in a work by a Marxist of the 1930s. However, this is not so surprising when we realise that Neumann worked his way through the writings of liberal political economists to construct his model of the liberal legal system and its correspondence to a competitive capitalist economy and then, in many ways similar to this debate, went on to create his normative ideal out of this 'ideal type'. He is, however, much more ambivalent and even voices scepticism as to the appropriateness of general laws in the age of the monopoly in his concrete analysis of the role of general law in the economic sphere: 'In the economic sphere the postulate of the generality of law becomes absurd if the legislature is no longer concerned with equal competition, but with monopolies violating that principle of equality on the market which we have found to be essential to the theory of classical economy' (p. 275). Neumann realises that a certain type of 'framework' legislation, the era of codes and general rules, has come to an end and at the same time senses the inadequacies of the developing forms of law. Much of his unease is reflected in the debate on the crisis of legalisation which points to the limits of instrumental and purposive regulation of society. The new debate has yet to demonstrate the viability of 'procedural' or 'corporatist'[44] or 'constitutive'[45] responses to the diagnosed crisis of law and many of these solutions will already have been criticised by Neumann.

IV

Any introduction to a work of this breadth and scope has to limit itself to pointing to some essentials. I have stressed the importance of Neumann's work in the development of critical legal studies in Germany and how this book is relevant to contemporary debate. At the same time, I have attempted to develop some critical footnotes to Neumann's main thesis.[46] The idea of this edition has been to preserve the original text, with all its shortcomings, as an important historical document and as a landmark in Neumann's own intellectual development. The reader will find that Neumann's work is full of fascinating and stimulating ideas which have until now not been fully explored. Habermas does not exaggerate when he describes

44. Teubner, *Legalisation.*
45. Stewart, *Crisis of Legalization.*
46. At a later stage Neumann himself voiced some criticism, referring readers to his article on 'The concept of Political Freedom' in idem, *The Democratic and Authoritarian State*, p. 160.

this work as '*bahnbrechende Untersuchung aus den dreißiger Jahren*'[47] (an analysis of the 1930s which broke new ground) and many of Neumann's observations and analyses have again and again proved to provide much food for debate.

Note on the text

Minor changes have been made to the introduction of chapters in the third part, spelling has been corrected and some words replaced or added – the latter changes are clearly marked with square brackets. In a few places I felt that some further explanation would help the reader and have added an editorial footnote, which is indicated by an asterix and can be found on p. 349.

MATTHIAS RUETE
School of Law
University of Warwick

47. Habermas, *Theorie des Handelns*, p. 526.

I

Author's Introduction
The Theoretical Basis

The modern state shows two basic characteristics: the existence of a sphere of sovereignty of the state, and the existence of a sphere of freedom from it.

1.

Only if sovereignty exists can we speak of the state as such. The sovereign state exists independently of the different struggling groups within society. Only the modern state protects the state, guarding its frontiers; it conquers new markets, and produces the inner unity of administration and law; it destroys local and particular powers, squeezes out the Church from the secular sphere, holds the struggling social groups within definite boundaries, or exterminates one of the struggling groups when its extermination seems necessary for the good of the "state".

At the same time modern society recognises in the decisive periods of its existence certain human rights — i.e. guarantees a certain realm of freedom from the state. Thus it has used the idea of freedom in its struggle against feudal powers and against absolutism. It needed economic freedom for the development of the productive forces. Historically and philosophically this freedom was conceived to exist before the state, and the state developed as the means to its realisation. With this conception bourgeois society changed the medieval natural law into secular human rights, serving as a limitation of the power of the state. The conception of such a realm of freedom however, can only be reached by general norms — whether these norms have the character of a divine or secular, natural or general positive law.

The general norm in modern society played and plays however another rôle. In so far as no freedom is granted, or in so far as freedom can be interfered with under extraordinary circumstances, the action of the state must be able to be deduced from general norms, a phenomenon which was postulated by theorists in an absolute form.

Human rights and the imputation of all acts of state intervention to general norms constitutes what is known as the Rule of Law, or, according to German terminology, the *Rechtsstaatscharakter* of the state.

Both sovereignty and the Rule of Law are constitutive elements of the modern state. Both however are irreconcilable with each other, for highest might and highest right cannot be at one and the same time realised in a common sphere. So far as the sovereignty of the state extends there is no place for the Rule of Law. Wherever an attempt at reconciliation is made we come up against insoluble contradictions.

In so far, on the other hand, as the domination of the state is declared synonymous with the Rule of Law it is impossible to conceive of the state as a sovereign and autonomous body, independent of existing social forces. Wherever theorists of the rights of man make this attempt to construct an absolute, sovereign and independent power of the state, they must either abandon the Rule of Law, or they find themselves entangled in insoluble contradictions.

All systems contain both elements, even when they are asserted to be monistic, as for instance, on the one hand Hobbes, and on the other hand Locke.

To the logical antagonism between absolute sovereignty and the Rule of Law, there does not always correspond a factual antagonism between the exercise of state sovereignty and the virtual practice of the Rule of Law: that is to say, there are historical situations in which the exercise of state sovereignty confines itself within such limits as to permit of the virtual exercise of the Rule of Law.

This was true, for example, according to Chapter XIII of Dicey's *Law of the Constitution*, for the period in which he lived. In such a period, that is to say, the highest efficiency of the power of the state is reached just on the basis of political freedom.[1]

There are periods, however, when a real antagonism corresponds to the logical one. This real antagonism leads to a revision of the distribution of spheres between state sovereignty and the Rule of Law in favour of one element or the other, whereby the marginal case on the one hand is state absolutism and on the other hand the cessation of the state as such.

2.

We further attempt to show that a secular and rational[2] justification of state and law: i.e. a human justification, basing itself on the wills or the needs of men, can have under certain historical circumstances revolutionary consequences. This is true as well for the theory of people's sovereignty as for that of enlightened absolutism.[3] So the claims of the bourgeoisie to be the nation is met by a parallel claim on the part of the proletariat constituting itself as the nation. In the same way as the bourgeoisie under the slogan of "Representation of the Will of the People" has brought down the feudal rule and monarchical absolutism, so will the proletariat on its side represent the will of the people by merging the state into the proletariat after it has become the nation. "The weapons with which the bourgeoisie overthrew feudalism are now turned against the bourgeoisie itself." This sentence, intended as valid for the practical sphere, is also valid for the ideological sphere, for the democratic concept only exhausts itself when the proletariat becomes the nation and constitutes itself as the national class. Every modern society is confronted, however, with the well-known dilemma:[4] either to satisfy the claims of the proletariat, or to abolish democracy, i.e. either to abandon its past ideals or to give preference to immediate interests. The choice usually made is well-known. The concept of democracy is abandoned, when the masses, newly awakened and aroused to a political self-consciousness during the period of industrialism and world war, demand this democracy for themselves, and when a society feudalised by monopoly-economy is unable to satisfy that demand.[5]

3.

The third and central thesis is finally to demonstrate the disintegrating effect of the general Rule of Law guaranteeing freedom in a society based upon inequality. We assert that any general norm, whether it be one of natural law, or of positive law, which is intended to set a limit to state activity, necessarily contributes to the disintegration of the status quo. Any such norm is double-edged, is a double-edged sword.

Natural law especially, as Kurt Wolzendorff has shown,[6] is only "a theoretical form for any political idea".[7] The text will show, as the above theses have suggested, that the then valid norms of natural law, as also the general positive laws, correspond to the interests of certain groups, and have the function of legitimising the positions of power to which they have attained. After having attained these positions the representatives of particular classes abandoned the Rule of Law, or only rendered it lip service, so that it only disguised the domination of a class; for, according to theses 2 and 3, it must happen sooner or later, that the further recognition of the Rule of Law becomes dangerous for the power positions or for the stability of the social order. It is therefore attempted to prove that legal theory and legal practice of bourgeois society are, as Carl Schmitt put it, *Situations-Jurisprudenz* — that law is a mere technique for the conquest and maintenance of power.

The abandonment of democracy is accompanied by a reversal in the system of values in the philosophical sphere. The *ratio* is devaluated, because the justification of the state by the wills of men is shown to be immanently revolutionary. The justification on the basis of the needs of men is not realisable because the increasingly obvious contradiction between promise and fulfilment must necessarily disillusion. So, because of the impossibility of reversing the process of secularisation, there remains only the charismatic justification, which is a typical case of an extreme attitude of irrationality. That with which modern vitalist philosophy reproaches rationalism — viz. that thought becomes a fatal influence[8] — is right in so far as thought sets free those forces heading for the destruction of bourgeois society, just as it has contributed to the downfall of the secular domination of the Church and the feudal system, and just as it has contributed to the victory of political rights to freedom.

In so far as this book continues my unpublished doctoral thesis of 1923, it develops what is conceived to be the purely ideological character of natural law on the basis of a criticism of Kantian and Neo-Kantian legal philosophy. The following ten years which I devoted mainly to industrial law, did not leave me the time for a further examination of my thesis. However, my practice during these ten years as a lawyer and a law teacher has in no way contributed to weaken my conviction of the purely ideological character of Natural Law, whatsoever be its structure. My practice has, on the contrary, only strengthened that conviction, which finds expression in the present work.

4.

It is sometimes asserted that the theory of the Social Contract justifies sovereignty, and that the theory of Natural Law justifies the freedom of men from the interference of the state. This is contradicted by the facts, however, for the separation of the Liberal and democratic ideology has taken place only in the nineteenth century. Up to this time both elements were merged in every theory and in practice.[9] The Natural Law theorists also wanted to justify the state, and the democratic theorists of the Social Contract also wanted to justify liberty. Thus was Figgis[10] able to put forward the following thesis in dealing with monarchomachical theories. The *primum mobile* was the religious element: "civil rights are secondary and means to an end". The contract is the basis of the state, therefore natural law must precede the state — which implies that according to his view natural law not only legitimises freedom, but also coercion on the part of the state. Therefore, law is not only a command, but also "the voice of reason". In this formulation of Figgis, both elements are united.

Further, as it appears to me (and in this I agree with C. J. Friedrich), the significance of the juridical category of the contract is easily over-emphasised. What is decisive is not the juridical category of the contract, but its meaning, its secular and rational justification: i.e. a justification deriving from men, their wills and ends. Sometimes in a system the guarantees of liberty are predominant (Grotius and Locke) and sometimes the justification of state coercion (Hobbes and Pufendorf).

Equally unimportant for our investigations are questions which have given much trouble to political theory — viz. whether the natural state was thought to be an historical phenomenon or only a fiction.[11] Even if some theorists of natural law have conceived the natural state to be an historical phenomenon and even if this conception is false — even then, their thesis can be freed from this incorrect basis by maintaining the natural state as a methodological principle only. We have therefore to put the question: How is the natural state to be described in order to justify either the domination of the state, or the freedom from its interference? The answer is, that all absolutistic theorists of natural law (Hobbes) conceived man to be inherently evil in his natural state[12] and the Liberal theorists of natural law (Locke) conceived him as good.

Similarly, for us it is of only minor importance whether the Social Contract is considered as an historical phenomenon, as an ideal to be realised (Rousseau), or as a transcendental idea (Kant).[13]

Even if, which seems to be not certain, no state ever was established by contract, the category of the Social Contract might be a methodological principle necessary for the justification of the state or from freedom from it.

In Part I (The Theoretical Basis) we [are developing] those general principles later to be applied in the analysis of particular instances in the next two parts.

The present work deals with the theory of the relations of law, political science, and economics. In 1.1., The Concept of Law, we make some general remarks on the concept of the validity of law.

Within the theory of law the emphasis of this work is laid on the sociology of law. In 1.2., therefore, we oppose the sociology of law to the exegetic or dogmatic treatment of law, and the central problem of the sociology of law — viz. the problem of the interrelations between law and the legal substructure (*Substrat*), is sketched in its basic features.

Within the sociology of law attention is here directed mainly towards the sociology of the legal structure and the state. In 1.3., therefore, we make some remarks about the concept and the basic structure of the state, and deal with the distinguishing features and essential categories of public and private law.

Within the field of investigation defined above, this work, as its title would indicate, deals mainly with the sociology of the relations of sovereignty and the Rule of Law. In 2.1., therefore, we give a sketch of a theory of sovereignty.

We understand by the Rule of Law a domination through general norms, and consequently through determinate material norms.

As the domination of general norms exercises an important influence upon the character and extent of the rationality of law, we deal with the various types of rationality of law and their interrelationships.

The various norms constituting the Rule of Law are usually either such as guarantee certain liberties or such as guarantee certain legal institutions. Therefore we give a sketch of a theory of liberty and of a system of liberties, and following consistently the theory and the system of legal institutions.

In a further chapter we deal with the relations between liberties and institutions with special reference to the supplementary relations.

Anticipating the sociological investigation of the relation between sovereignty and the Rule of Law, we finally deal in 2.3. with the relations corresponding in law — viz. the dualism of the two concepts of law.

CHAPTER 1

The Place of the Problem within the Legal System

1.1. The Concept of Law

We wish to define law by two 'moments' — that of order and that of coercion.[1] As Hegel says, "the abstract forms reveal themselves not as self-subsistent but as untrue".[2]

By its coercive character law can be distinguished from custom and morality. All attempts at alternative definitions have failed.[3] Since the Renaissance the state, and only the state, has constituted the coercive machinery. But nevertheless the state is not the sole "creator" of law, because the coercive power of the state is only *one* moment of the law and not the law itself. We therefore support the formulation of Wilhelm Dilthey:

> The legal system is the ordering of the aims of society which is maintained by means of coercion exercised by its own external organisation, and the possibility of using force forms the decisive reserve power of the legal system; but external control of wills is seen to be spread throughout the whole of organised society, and that is why not only the state but also other wills have the function of creating and maintaining law. Every concept of law contains the moment of the external society, on the other hand an organisation can be constructed only in legal terms.[4]

So in this way other social groups are able to create *one* moment of the law: i.e. *social* norms which however become *legal* norms only through the coercive power of the state.

All legal norms having sociological validity also possess juridical validity. In order to give these norms *juridical* validity the coercive power of the state must stand potentially at their disposal. The imputation of the coercive power of the state is sufficient for a juridical consideration of the concept of law. For the *sociological* validity of the norm, however, the *potentiality* of its being carried out by the coercive power of the state is insufficient. The fact of its being carried out is essential. The sociological validity of a legal norm is therefore characterised by the fact that "by it is created an expectancy (*Chance*) that one or another economic subject will enjoy a specially emphatic and rarely failing protection of certain of their interests".[5] Sociologically then the legal norm grants an expectancy which is in fact realised by the coercive machinery of the state.[6] Since the Renaissance the state has been the decisive coercive machinery. We have, therefore, in order to be able to decide whether a certain legal norm is sociologically valid, to investigate whether the coercive machinery "state" provides for coercion on behalf of those legal norms, and whether it has such a power that on the average it can be expected that the legal norms will be fulfilled. It is a question, therefore, of typical human behaviour. If we discover that a legal norm is part of the hierarchy of norms, but that it is not fulfilled either because the coercive apparatus is too weak, or because the legal subjects and the legal administrators do not take it seriously, we are no longer able to speak of the sociological validity of that norm. The consent of the legal subject is therefore unessential. The reason for disobedience or acquiescence is not the subject-matter of a sociology of law, although perhaps for a psychology of law.

Law in the philosophical sense is to be defined as a "reality which has as its function the service of the idea of right. The concept of law is directed towards the idea of right".[7]* The idea of right contains on the one hand the demand for justice, and on the other hand the demand for the satisfaction of vital human and state needs in the various spheres of social life. The definition of the idea of justice is here as irrelevant as the extent of its historical realisation.[8] What is here important is the fact that law in the philosophical sense is not identical with the needs of the state or of society. In the dialectical tension between justice and necessity lie the main problems of the philosophy of law.

1.2. The Sociology of Law

1.2.1. *Exegesis and Sociology of Law*

The science of law is just as much a science of norms as of reality. As a science of norms it has as its subject-matter the objective meaning of the legal norms. As a science of reality it investigates the relations between legal norms, the social substructure (*Substrat*), the social behaviour of the legal subjects, and of the legal administrators.

The interpretation of the legal norms can therefore be — like that of all mental structures — a dual one; an immanent and a transcendental one, if we adopt Karl Mannheim's classification of types of interpretation;[9] or, in Marxian terminology, an ideological and a sociological one.

The science of norms has as its subject-matter the legal order as an autonomous mental structure opposed to reality. The pure theory of law of Kelsen is therefore a theory of positive law.[10] Thus far we do not doubt the validity of the pure science of law — as Laski says: "In terms of its axioms, formal jurisprudence is completely justified in the whole of its procedure; in terms of its axioms, neither its method nor its results can be denied. By its own inherent logic, all that makes law, is necessarily legal, all in conflict with it is necessarily illegal. For it cannot continue its sovereignty on any other terms".[11] Normative jurisprudence puts, therefore, the single and exclusive question: which objective meaning is to be attributed to the legal norm?[12] The fundamental difference between "is" and "ought" can be formulated in this way: "From the fact that this is, it follows that that was — or that it will be — but never that something ought to be. Something can be, and yet never has been, nor is it now, nor will it ever be".[13] Normative jurisprudence takes law as a mental structure without reference to social reality or to its ethical justification. Questions such as how law arose, to which social forces it owes its existence, which effects it exercises in social reality, whether it corresponds to an idea or contradicts it — all such questions are for the pure science of law *meta-juridical* problems, juridical mysteries.[14] In this separation of the categories of essence and existence, of ethical norm and legal norm, lies the merit of Kelsen's pure theory of law. By this expurgation of all ethical, natural law, and political evaluations which had found their way into legal science by virtue of the methodological syncretism of the Natural Law period and the nineteenth century, the way is indeed made open for a new ethical evaluation of law and a new genuine relation between law and political science.

In normative jurisprudence state and law are identical.[15] In the last resort law is to be attributed to the state. The finally distinctive characteristic of law is its derivation from the state. If this is the case, and if law and state are both orders, both orders must be identical. The state can legally only be recognised as a phenomenon of law as a hierarchy of norms in which all norms have to be attributed to one basic norm. Every legal norm is therefore a hypothetical judgment on the future behaviour of the state. The essence of a legal norm does not consist in a command but in the statement that if this or that should happen the state shall react in such and such a way. The connection between the legal cause and the legal effect is therefore a normative one. The relation is determined not by the category of causation but by that of norms.

Normative jurisprudence does not reach any concrete positive results. The results reached by it are purely negative ones.

For normative jurisprudence subjective right does not stand before objective law, but is derived from it. Even if, according to the conception of *philosophical* liberalism, the sphere of freedom of the individual is to be considered principally as an unlimited one, in the *legal system* of liberalism this sphere of freedom is only understandable as delegated by the law.

Subjective right is a title, and therefore only a special formation of the process of creation of law. So far the fundamental difference between objective law and subjective rights is abolished.

The legal order can only be conceived as part of a process of a gradual concretisation of law, from a single hypothesis — viz. the basic norm. Law is all that, and only that which can be imputed directly or indirectly to this basic norm. The legal order is a hierarchy (*Stufenbau*). This idea was introduced by Kelsen's disciple Adolf Merkl, who, however, as he himself admitted, derived his idea from Kelsen's work itself.[16] The stages of the hierarchy consist in the constitution, legislation and the administration of justice. The administration of justice does not only consist in the declaration of the law, but also in its creation. The decision of the court creates law because it creates a new norm.[17]

For normative jurisprudence there is no difference between an ethical and a legal person. The natural person is [the] bearer of rights and duties only because the legal system has made him a point of attribution for such legal rights and duties. In the pure science of law there is no difference between administration and the judiciary function, because the unbiased examination of the case which is supposed to distinguish the one from the other is also only a function of the legal system. There is, further, no categorical difference between contract of the legal subjects and the coercive acts of the state. Both kinds of act are individualisations and concretisations of general norms.[18] As for the contract, the state delegates to the legal subjects the power of executing it — i.e. the so-called "private autonomy".

The legal system is closed; genuine gaps do not exist, spheres free from law are inconceivable.

A categorical difference between legal and customary law, state law and autonomous law, case law and statutory law cannot be conceived. For customary law can legally only be conceived as law if one starts from the fact that the state has ascribed to permanent customs the right to create law. This has been very clearly formulated by Hobbes: "When long use obtaineth the authority of law, it is not the length of time that maketh the authority, but the will of the sovereign, signified by silence".[19] Filmer has enunciated this principle even more clearly: "It is not the being of a Custom, that maketh it lawful, for then all Customs, even evil Customs, would be lawful: but it is the approbation of the supreme Power, that gives a legality to the Custom: where there is no supreme power over many nations their Customs can not be made legal".[20]

Autonomous bodies are, according to the pure theory of law, in reality not autonomous because their right to create law is legally conceivable only if it is presupposed that this capacity has been delegated to them by the state. In so far as the pure science of law is also identical with the theories of Hobbes, who could understand canonic law only as a part "of the law of England".[21] Finally, there exists for the pure science of law no difference between case and statute law. Just in the same way as Hobbes has expressed it: "As for the Common law contained in reports, they have force but what the kings give them".[22]

In the system of the pure science of law there is no categorical difference between public and private law, however these are defined; for the legal surplus value* which the public body has as against the private law subject has been granted to the public body only by the legal system itself.

1.2.2. *Law and the Legal Substructure*

Legal science is not only concerned with legal norms, but also with the social substructure (*Substrat*) of the legal system. By the term "social substructure" we understand social reality after the subtraction of the law itself.[1] Social reality is the work of men in society.

The legal norm orders social reality — i.e., in the more exact formulation of Paschukanis,[23] the ordering of social relations takes on under certain conditions a juridical character. Law is the specific order of the social substructure. It seems unnecessary to say that this social substructure is not only an economic substructure. The so-called economic interpretation of legal norms and legal institutions is not a total interpretation. Political, religious and mental ideas as well as family relations are realities to which the legal norm is equally subjected. The exclusively economic interpretation is in no way the Marxist one. Such an assertion would be as essentially un-Marxistic as that history is the development of ideas, or the work of great personalities. Marxism aims at a total interpretation of all social phenomena. Marx was a Hegelian, and Hegel has conceived a law to be "a dependent element in a totality, one of the many others constituting the character of a nation and an epoch, and receiving their meaning and justification from their interdependence".[24] Marxian sociology asserts that law may develop relatively independently of social reality, that autonomous legal forces may drive its development in another direction to that of the social substructure.[25] The independence of the legal system from social forces is, however, as has been indicated by Engels with great firmness, only a relative one.[26] It is, however, a meaningless statement that law and the state are relatively autonomous. The central task of a sociological investigation into the legal system consists in indicating on the one hand the conditions under which law and the state can develop relatively independently, and on the other hand the forces which go to destroy this relative autonomy and subject the law and the state with full force to the stream of social realities. This will be one of the main tasks of the present investigation.

The inter-relationships of legal and social phenomena cannot be contested. It may be perhaps possible to assert that ethical evaluations and styles of art can develop independently of social forces —

i.e. that more or less absolute independence from social reality exists for art and morals. It is, however, impossible to maintain this with regard to law, which is but one aspect of the order of human lives. Nor is law the form taken by human living together. In particular can it not be said that law and the economic system stand in the relationship of form and content erroneously attributed to them by Stammler;[27] law is the structure of human living together in so far as this living together has become the subject of state regulation. A legal order for its own sake is unthinkable. There is no special style of law, as there is no special ethic of law. "Hence, the origin of the conception of right falls outside the science of right."[28]

The legal norm and its social substructure do not always coincide. If we consider their relationship we can state with Karl Renner the following possibilities:[29] (a) the substructure can change while the legal norm itself remains constant; (b) the legal norm can change while the social substructure remains constant.

The legal norm can remain unchanging for years, decades and, under certain circumstances, for centuries while the social substructure suffers in the course of historical events fundamental alterations which reverse the social function of the legal norm. This phenomenon is defined in German literature as a change of the function, a change of the aim, or as a substitution of the basis of the legal norm. The instances are numerous and one hesitates to quote them: one decisive example is offered by the institution of property. The legal norm indicating the characteristics of property domination has remained unchanged ever since Roman times. The same formula covered Roman individualistic private property and Germanic *Ober- und Unter-Eigentum*; the self-same formula was again used for feudal property as well as for industrial property; property in both production and consumption goods has also come under it.

This phenomenon, that legal norms remain unchanged whereas the social structure is subjected to alterations, has induced Max Weber and Kantorowicz[30] to assert that in order to erect a socialist society, not a single word of the civil code need be altered. This assertion assumes a highly improbable possibility. Obviously it is possible, and has been attempted several times. Constituting communal property — i.e. socialist property — by entering into private contracts of sale has not been an uncommon phenomenon. It is quite possible for the state to obtain private property by means of private contracts within the framework of the old contractual law, and then to utilise it for the common good. In this case only the bearer of property would have changed. The legal institution as such would not have been altered. Such a case is of course theoretically possible.

It is, however, not probable, because it is overlooked that a socialist society not only aims at a change of the bearer of the property, but at the attainment of communal property — i.e. at the democratisation of the economic system. This aim could be attained by means of private law contracts only if the society were based on the consent of all citizens — which is an absurd postulate. Therefore, the socialist society, too, will have to take recourse to the institution of the administrative act — i.e. to compulsory regulation belonging to public law. For such a case, however, the thesis of Max Weber makes no provision, for obviously the civil code cannot be dealt with in a socialist society as an isolated phenomenon. The whole legal system must, on the contrary, be considered as a unit, including all auxiliary institutions and auxiliary guarantees, including all those auxiliary norms belonging to the sphere of public law. This being the case, it follows that without a decisive alteration of the legal system the attainment of a socialist society is impossible.

The opposite case, change of the norm while the social substructure remains constant occurs also quite often.

Not every change of the legal norms is socially important. Whether, for instance, social processes such as sale, lease, loan, contract between master and servant, etc. are to be included in juridical exegetic need have no social importance at all. The structural formation of the legal norms keeps itself exclusively within the realm of juridical technique.

On the other hand, it can be the change of the legal norm itself which leads to an alteration of the social substructure. In such a case the change of the legal norm precedes the change of the substructure. This phenomenon has induced many theorists to make the generalisation that a change of the legal system is not only a necessary accompaniment of a change in the social system, but also the only cause of such a change — in particular of such a change in the economic system. This view is mainly adopted by the American Institutionalists, especially John R. Commons[31] and his German follower Karl Diehl.[32] He formulates the possibility of an alteration in a single section of the German Civil Code bringing about socialism. This view, however, is just as incomplete as the opposite one of Max Weber. It is a platitude to assert that a change of the legal system can bring about social changes, but we must not forget that a change in the legal system will only be effected if such a change is demanded by social forces. It is indeed right to assert that a change of the German Civil Code, in the sense that private property be abolished and communal property established, would fundamentally change the economic and property systems. But such an alteration of the Code can only be expected if political and social forces drive in this direction. A socially important change of the legal system does not fall from the blue: it is the product of a social process. It follows, therefore, that both extreme points of view overlook the interdependence of law and social reality, that the first point of view neglects the significance of the legal developments, whereas the second emancipates law from its social basis.

1.3. The Theory of Public Law

1.3.1. *Public and Private Law*

We agree with the pure science of law that the difference between public and private law is no categorical one, but that the sphere of distribution between them is subject to historical changes.

Here we deal with two questions: (a) the concept and the function of public and private law; (b) the legal forms of public and private law.

The dualism of public law and private law is already current in Roman law. The quotation from the Digests: "Publicum ius est quod ad statum rei romanae spectat, privatum quod ad singulorem utilitatem", (Dig. I.I.I.2 Ulpian) is well-known. Some modern authors have followed this quotation and have asserted that private law serves private interests, while public law serves public interests. This delimitation, however, is inadmissible as it confuses the "ought" with the "is". Not everything serving private interests belongs to private law. Some matters are regulated by public law; and not everything which is allocated to public law by the positive law serves public interests.

Unsatisfactory also is the so-called subjective theory according to which public law is given when the state or some other public body comes into action. In the first place this definition pushes the problem on to the question of defining the public body, whose identity in this connection is often extremely doubtful. On the other hand the state sometimes (as the German *Fiskus*) appears as a subject of private law, and sometimes submits itself to private law.

The theory of power — the third theory mentioned above — also confuses the "ought" with the "is". Its contention that public law is to be found wherever power relations exist is contradicted by the fundamental example offered by the existence of property in the means of production and of private monopolies. If this theory is not supposed to be a pure tautology, saying that only where the power relations belong to the public law sphere can public law exist, it must face up to the contradiction offered by the example of private property in the means of production.[33] Private property gives the employers power as against their workers; all monopolies give power in the market; but in spite of this both private property and monopolies are not automatically the objects of public law regulation. One might postulate that this should be so, but it is by no means always so.

The essential difference between public and private law consists in the different legal consequences of regulations in the two spheres. The state delegates to the bearers of public law, as distinct from those of private law, a certain legal surplus value. Public law is the law of domination.

The subject of private law can, apart from original acquisition, or by inheritance, only acquire something by contract — i.e. by mutual agreement between two private law subjects. The state, on the other hand, and the other public bodies, can acquire property by one-sided acts (taxation, or simple expropriation): the private law subject having a claim against another may satisfy his claim only with the assistance of the court and bailiff. Self-help is generally denied him. The state and other public bodies perform, however, the functions of judge and bailiff as well as being at the same time parties to the dispute. Instances can be quoted in profusion. They show that the public law subject, in all those spheres in which the state plays an immediate rôle, enjoys a juridical surplus value as against the private law subject. In the Liberal state, the sole task of which consisted in the protection of private property and the maintenance of bourgeois security, taxation, tariff policy, police, army, and the organisation of administration and justice formed the main spheres of public law; all other spheres come under the jurisdiction of private law, because apart from the limits defined above, human life developed freely and unhampered by state interference.

According as the state penetrates into the realm of its citizens' freedom, and according as the limits between state and society shift in favour of the state, so is the sphere of public law extended. Only an interpretation of the whole legal system can enable us to recognise which spheres the state reserves for its immediate control and which it leaves at the disposal of its citizens; i.e. the boundaries between public and private law follow only *a posteriori*. The notion of order which lies at the bottom of the difference between private and public law can only be the decision of the state itself; the exclusive criterion as to what belongs to public and what to private law is the concrete decision of the state. Any other criterion is impossible.[34]

It is therefore necessary to distinguish the direct from the indirect regulation of the state. The Civil Code is a typically indirect regulation of social relationships by the state. In a civil code the state on the whole only places various legal forms of behaviour at the disposal of the citizen. The State itself does not regulate the social spheres, and this means that the contents of the decision of the state with reference to the respective spheres of public and private law is in this case often difficult to discover. The contents of the decision can only be discovered from a consideration of the legal order in its entirety, and of the relations between state and society.

The typical legal form belonging to private law is the contract, whose perfection depends upon an agreement between two private subjects — although such a mutual agreement may not necessarily be *sufficient* for its perfection.

We shall have to distinguish three different types of contract:

The Exchange Contract — called by Max Weber *Zweckkontrakt.*[35] This is a contract which has as its aim only the realisation of concrete general economic purposes. In such a contract single individuals stand in reciprocal relationship to one another. The contract creates a relationship measuring the degree of permissible interference of either party with the freedom of the other. For instance, the contract of sale or exchange, and the loan, come under this category.

The Power Contract is given when not only performances for mutual fulfilment are stipulated, but when one of the parties to the contract submits to an external power — as for example, when the subject is received into an institution such as a hospital or an asylum. The most important present example of this type of contract is that between master and servant. The power contract constitutes therefore a permanent relationship consisting of the whole sphere of life of the subject, and therefore changing his total legal quality. The power contract becomes a *Status Contract*,[36] if the workers conceive this phenomenon of subjection to an external power not as something to be struggled against, but as something within which to secure their position, either by intervention of the state, the trade union or the workers' council. The distinction between exchange and power contracts appears in the Natural Law system of Samuel Pufendorf as that between "obligations of equality and obligations of inequality".[37] "We call the obligation of inequality that which makes him to whom something is owed by us in virtue of it our superior and brings some authority or command upon us." The contract of inequality is therefore characterised by a power relationship. This contract is, according to Pufendorf, either a "universal obligation" such as our obligation to God, or a "particular obligation" given when "definite men are beholden to definite men". This particular power contract can belong either to public or to private law. The power exercised is either limited, such as that of the husband, the father, or the employer as against the employee, or unlimited as that of the state as against the citizen (unrestricted power contract belonging to public law) or of the master as against the slave (unrestricted power contract belonging to private law).

Finally, a collective act (*Gesamtakt*) is a contract if it has as its object the constitution of a democratic power. The foundation of a corporation, of a joint-stock Company, of a cartel, of a trade union or of a party, by mutual agreements between the members concerned, constitutes such a collective agreement.

In the sphere of public law those legal forms which bring about a legal change are, apart from legislation, the administrative acts (*Acte administratif*). Public law bearers entering into mutual legal relationships may also utilise the public law contract.

There is, further, the one-sided administrative act containing a command from the public law bearers to those subject to them, by which a collective agreement is extended outside the members of the bargaining parties, etc.

We have to separate the administrative act from the governmental act (*Acte gouvernemental*) which is to be attributed to the prerogative; i.e. to a power which has not been bound by law and remains uncontrolled by it. Such an act for example is the declaration of war by the King of England, because the king possesses a genuine residuum of prerogative. On the other hand, an emergency decree of the President of the Reich, according to Art. 48 of the late Weimar Constitution, is only an administrative act and not a governmental act because it is issued only on the fulfilment of certain conditions, which could be controlled by the judiciary. It is, however, not only the head of the state who is entitled to issue a governmental act: in so far as the prerogative lies with Parliament, it can apart from legislating, also issue governmental acts — for example, impeachment.

1.3.2. *The Concept of the State*

I call every sociologically sovereign institution a state.

Therefore the state cannot, according to this definition, be a legal order (Hans Kelsen): neither can it be a fiction, nor an abstraction. For in all these three cases we could not speak of state sovereignty but only of the sovereignty of organs of the state.[38]

In this definition it is further evident that state and society are both quite distinct phenomena.[39] The specific relationship existing between state and society is, formally speaking, that the acts of the sovereign state relate to the society and that these are at the same time caused by social factors operating in that society.

This definition of the state must now be explained. We have defined it as an institution. There belong to this institution "state" the totality of those men who exercise the highest legal power, and that totality of men to whom such legal power is delegated. Therefore, the following categories of persons belong to the institution of the state: the legislative; the executive (police, army, judiciary, bureaucracy); those persons in the service of autonomous public institutions to whom the state has delegated partial legal power (such as municipalities, universities, churches, and corporations); and, finally, those private persons and private corporations to whom the state equally has delegated partial legal powers (such as jurors and lay judges, trade unions and employers' associations). This definition, therefore, contains Laski's identification of state and government, but also transcends it.

We have defined the state as a sovereign institution. Sovereignty contains as a legal moment the original right of the sovereign to issue general norms and individual norms (commands, decisions). In consequence of this dualism of the right of issuing general and individual norms there exists the possibility of an antagonism between the then existing series of general norms and the then issued individual norms. Such conflict between norms is not only possible, but has actually been realised innumerable times in history. Where the state in case of such a conflict has the right in the interests of its "self-maintenance" to break through partially the series of norms by means of individual norms, or even to suspend the whole series, a situation arises which we do not intend to discuss here. Alone important for us here is that state has done this thing, and is continually doing it. In cases the exercise of sovereignty is a power decision in the sense of Carl Schmitt.[40]

Because sovereignty is the highest legal power, in any given territory there can only exist one sovereign and therefore only one state. Lassalle has formulated this idea very well: "Two sovereigns can no more exist in any one state than can two suns shine in the same sky". There is, I think, general agreement here. The sovereign disappears, therefore, in a civil war where the two conflicting parties are equally strong.

But even if one undisputed legal sovereign exists in any given territory, and this sovereign be not strong enough to carry out his legal norms and his individual norms, we can no longer speak of either a sovereign in the real sense or of the state. An example is offered by the impotence of the Italian state power to carry out its norms in certain parts of Southern Italy under the domination of Mafia and Camorra.

We have already declared that the content of a state action referring to society is determined either exclusively or partially by social factors. According to the materialistic interpretation of history, these determining relations are conceived as such that the contents of the state will tend on the whole to coincide with the interests of the economically exploiting class, and that the state is a class state, an apparatus for the maintenance of this relationship of exploitation.

According to Engels' concretisation of this generalisation, under certain historical conditions of class equilibrium the state can place itself above the classes as independent power. Whether such assertions are right can only be verified by empirical investigation. Our own view will be seen from the following chapters.

CHAPTER 2

The Relation of Sovereignty to the Rule of Law

2.1. The Theory of Sovereignty

In a *legal* sense, any institution is called sovereign when it has undelegated and unlimited power to issue general norms and individual commands (decisions).

In a *sociological* sense, an institution is called sovereign if it not only has *legal* rights of this kind, but has also the ability to carry out the norms and commands issued by it. In the sociological sense of sovereignty, therefore, an element of both right and power is included.[1] All analyses of state sovereignty must beware of a syncretism of the subject matter. It is an extraordinarily common phenomenon that all three distinct objects which we have here taken into consideration — viz. the legal, the politico-sociological and the ethical — are permanently confused. The sociologist answers the jurist analysing the concept of sovereignty, and both are answered by the philosopher who raises the question [as to] whether one is *obliged* to obey the sovereign power. The first prerequisite in dealing with the problem of a sovereignty is the unhesitating and callous separation of the three possible statements of the problem.

Sovereign in a sociological sense is therefore not the legal order as asserted by the pure law theorists like Kelsen.[2] Sovereignty according to our definition is not identical with the notion of the essentially undelegated nature of the legal system (*Nicht-weiter-Ableitbarkeit*). According to the pure science of law, all relations of super- and sub-ordination are based upon the fact that either explicitly or implicitly powers are delegated out from the centre. The state is the last point of attribution and at the same time an order itself which cannot be further delegated. What in this connection is the meaning of "point" and how it is possible that a "point" be at the same time an order I have been completely unable to discover even after an exhaustive perusal of all available works by Kelsen.[3]

The pure science of law may indeed be self-contained and self-consistent, but it solves no political problem whatsoever. According to our definition, sovereignty also includes command. Commands and norms can, after all only be issued by men and not by an "order".[4] Equally unsatisfactory is the antinomic theory of Carl Schmitt, expounded before him by Menger.[5] According to Schmitt, he is sovereign who decides what constitutes an emergency situation.[6] This definition has been developed by Schmitt in his book, *Die Diktatur*. There he undertakes to prove that also the natural law theorists of the seventeenth century — above all Pufendorf — understood by sovereignty the decision as to what constitutes an emergency situation. Sovereignty is therefore an essentially marginal conception. The notion covers only the most extreme cases of urgency, when the state itself is in danger. Such cases cannot be subsumed under the legal order. The conditions of the exercise and the contents of the sovereign competence are unlimited because it is impossible to deduce them from an abstract norm. The sovereign, therefore, decides with reference to two things: (a) whether there is such an emergency situation, and (b) by what means it can be overcome. The sovereign is outside the legal order; he is able, therefore, to suspend the constitution in toto as well as to violate it. He alone decides finally when normality is to be resumed.

So much is correct — that for no definition can the exception to the normal be excluded. The exceptional case logically must occupy as important a place as the normal one; and often it is only through the abnormal that the normal comes to be recognised at all. But the abnormal cannot be the unique and essential element in a definition. It must be added that if a constitution grants emergency powers to an organ of the state such as were granted by Art. 48 of the Weimar constitution to the President of the Reich, the question arises as to whether the President is compelled to repeal his dictatorial measures at the demand of another state organ, as for instance the Reichstag? Who in such a case is sovereign? The President of the Reich, Parliament, both together, or the people which is represented by both? The theory of Schmitt does not answer such a question at all clearly. In a state where the principle of "separation of powers" rules, and where the division of function is the rule, Schmitt's definition does not solve the problem; and in a Caesaristic democracy, the question of the bearer of the sovereign power does not arise at all, irrespective of the definition of "sovereignty" adopted.

"The normless will of Schmitt fails equally to solve the problem as the will-less norm of Kelsen" (Hermann Heller).

If we understand by "state" something non-legal (as for example the fellowship theory of Gierke — a naturalistic definition) the state can have power, but not the *legal* power which is required by our sociological definition.[7]

2.2. The Theory of the Rule of Law

2.2.1. *Theory of the Rule of General Norms (Rationality)*

The sociological examination of law is not only concerned with legal norms and their social substructure, but also with the behaviour and activity of men. That law is understood to be the product of social forces means that it is the product of human activity both determined by and determining social forces.

Human behaviour can be rational or irrational. We speak of a rational behaviour, but we do not mean by this a *rationalistic* one.

The noun corresponding to the adjective "rational" is "rationality". The noun corresponding to the adjective "rationalistic" is "rationalism". Perhaps the double concept "rational-rationalistic" corresponds to that of German philosophy "reason-intellect" (*Vernunft-Verstand*). Modern German political theory and the philosophy of law suffers from the fact that these two distinct concepts are made synonymous.

Hence: a rational foundation of the coercive powers of state and law is a justification on the basis of the needs or the wills of men. Such a rational theory does not deny that men, human groups, or classes are driven by motives other than intellectual ones — for instance by superstition, religion, or repressed drives — in short, that these irrational forces play a more or less decisive rôle. The rational approach takes the existence of any irrational elements into account, it attempts to explain them, to show how and why such an irrational sphere exists, and, on an individual basis with the aid of psychology, and with the aid of sociology on the basis of social forces, to explain why the relation between rational and irrational is changing.

A *rationalistic* approach on the other hand (for example, that of natural law and of Kantian philosophy) considers man as a purely intellectual being, as a mere point of attribution.

Whenever we speak of "rational" or "rationality" we mean this kind of rationality and nothing else. When we say that state and law are founded secularly and rationally we mean only that the state and the law are neither creations of God nor institutions of the devil; that they are neither super- nor sub-human institutions, but that they are simply human institutions springing from the wills or the needs of men.

We distinguish with Karl Mannheim between substantial and functional rationality, and correspondingly between substantial and functional irrationality. "We understand by substantial rationality simply the process of thinking and understanding: in short, everything that is cogitative in substance."[8] Substantial irrationality is on the other hand, "all those psychic phenomena which are not cogitative in substance". Substantially rational behaviour can (Max Weber) be either purposive-rational or value-rational (*Zweckrational oder Wertrational*).[9] It is value-rational if the behaviour of the active subject is motivated by its belief in the unique value (ethical, religious, or aesthetic) of a certain type of behaviour as such, independent of its results. If a man wants to realise a certain value through his behaviour, for instance that of brotherly love, and subordinates all his other motives to this central value, we may speak of his behaviour as value-rational.

Purposive-rational, or in Mannheim's terminology functional-rational, is human behaviour for which two criteria are given: the organisation of activities must be directed towards a given end, and there must be given a certain calculability of these activities from the standpoint of the external observer.[10] Or in Max Weber's terminology we can speak of the purposive-rational behaviour, if the behaviour of things and of other men is taken into account as a means to the achievement of one's own desired and calculated ends.[11] The purposive-rationality (functional-rationality) of certain behaviour is therefore a function of a given end. The same behaviour in the same situation can, in relation to another end, be irrational. The aim itself can be an irrational one, and behaviour in an irrational situation can become purposive-rational behaviour. There is, for instance, a purposive-rationalisation of mental contemplation. A theory of the state and law based upon revelation can be rationalised in itself.[12] W. A. Robson has directed our attention to the fact that even in the most unexpected fields, as for example in that of the exercise of the royal prerogative of mercy, which in the last resort is a modification of rational law, the tendency towards "consistency" (only another expression for rationality) is extremely strong.[13]

Rationality in the political and economic spheres is not always produced by the law itself. It can also be achieved by means alien to the law. In the political sphere, for instance, in a transitional situation rationality of political decisions can be reached by extra-legal means. In the totalitarian state which is dominated by a monopoly party, state and party machinery in a transitional situation are opposed to each other. As the instances of Italy and Germany have shown the party machinery at first shows itself stronger than the state. Trotsky, in his *History of the Russian Revolution*, has accurately described the phenomenon of dual rule. In such a situation the monopoly party can transform political decisions into active political reality without the aid of the law, and in a rational manner. This, however, is only possible in a transitional situation which cannot last. During the transition to normality the power position is either relinquished or it is legalised.

In the economic sphere rationality of the exchange process can be achieved by extra-legal means. In a legal system otherwise irrational, for example, or in a system normally rational but temporarily disorganised, the calculability of the behaviour of the state machinery is ensured by corruption of state agents. If the citizen can rely on the possibility of getting every help from the state machinery by bribery, even if this help is legally forbidden him, the expectation that bribery will secure the appropriate action on the part of the state agent — either in doing or refraining from doing — can form under certain circumstances as firm a basis of calculation for the economic subject as the normally functioning rational legal system.

The legal rationality which we are considering is not alien to the law but, on the contrary, is legally relevant. Thus far we base our investigation on Max Weber[14] in that we distinguish two kinds of irrational law. Law can be *formal-irrational* if means other than intellectually controllable ones are applied in the creation and application of law; if, for example, application is made to an oracle. In such a case law is *irrational* because the decision is unpredictable, and it is *formally irrational* because the legal system or custom demands that an oracle be called for the creation or the application of the law. Irrational law can be on the other hand, *material-irrational* if concrete evaluations of the individual cases belong either to the ethical or political spheres, or rely simply on intuition and are then made the basis of individual decisions in place of general norms. So, for example, Kadi justice may be typified as material-irrational; the Kadi bases his decision exclusively on the evaluation of the individual case presented to him, and is neither compelled to base his decision on general norms, nor does he in fact do so.

In the realm of *rational* law we first make a subdivision which does not appear in Max Weber's classification; viz. between adjective and substantive law. The distinction is a simple one. If substantive law is complicated by, for instance, unclear formulation as is often the case where an accurate codification is lacking, calculability of judicial decisions can be ensured by the fact that the organisation of the judicial machinery has a particular structure. A relatively good example is offered by Great Britain. There can be no doubt that the British substantive law is infinitely more complicated and less lucid than the continental ones and that in British private law many irrational elements exist. But there can equally be no doubt that the present English law is to a far greater extent more calculable for the economic subject than was the case with the German law in the period from 1924 to 1932; yet this is in spite of the fact that British law is uncodified. The reasons are that the English judiciary administration is concentrated in the High Court of Justice in which the number of judges is extremely small compared with the highest German courts (*Reichsgericht*, *Oberlandesgerichte*). The small number of judges makes it very easy for the counsel to survey the decisions of the court, thus rendering accurate calculation of the reaction of the judge in any given lawsuit much easier. It must be added that in England the career of judge and counsel are not divorced. The selection of the judges from the members of the Bar, the professional and social connections of the judges and counsels even after the elevation of the judges to the bench (the judges are affiliated to the Counsels' Trade Union) all make possible a far more accurate calculation of the reaction of the judge in individual cases, even allowing for the presence of many irrational elements in substantive law. This idea is very clearly expressed by Sir William Holdsworth,[15] who investigates under which conditions a case law system can function. He puts forward three essential conditions: a centralised judicial system; groups of judges and lawyers bound together by common professional aims and traditions; and an independent well-paid judge who on the whole is more able than the Bar.[16] If we add that there is hardly an important business transaction done in England without taking the advice of a solicitor and counsel, we have in its essential features demonstrated that by purely organisational means it is possible to reach a degree of rationality which is far more efficient than that of the rational substantive law on the Continent. However, we have to add that this blessing of rational law is restricted in its operation to the possessing classes.

Within the rationality of substantive law we distinguish as does Max Weber formal and material rationality. Rationally substantive law is *formally* rational if the legal consequences are either dependent upon characteristics (for instance upon the fulfilment of certain forms like signature, seal or consideration) or on general abstract norms unambiguously defined. Rationally substantive law is *materially* rational when non-logical generalisations, norms belonging to other orders such as the ethical, religious, or political, form the basis of the decisions. The most frequent case of such a material rationality of substantive law is provided by the legal standards of conduct (*Generalklauseln*) such as provisions to the effect that decisions of judges must be made on the basis of "good faith" (*Treu und Glauben* — Sect. 242 of the German Civil Code); or that violation of "good morals" renders liable to damage (Sect. 826); or that a contract is void if it violates good morals (Sect. 138); or that restrictions on free competition which are "unreasonable" or "against public policy" are void and render liable to damages; in all these cases the legal norms represent "blank norms" (*Blankettnormen*) — they refer to general norms which are not legal norms; i.e. to evaluations which can only be elevated to the position of legally relevant clauses by the roundabout method through the legal standards of conduct (*Generalklauseln*).

2.2.2. *Freedom and the Rule of Law*

Freedom in the legal sense is to be defined as the absence of restraint. This definition is most clearly put forward by Hobbes:

"Liberty is . . . the absence of external impediment".[17] For the existence of such legal freedom the factual differences between men are as irrelevant as is the character of the social substructure corresponding to the legal norms. In the economic sphere freedom exists to the same degree, in a contract between two equally strong competitors as in a contract between a monopolist and a non-monopolist; in the same degree between an employer and a worker as between a trade union and an employers' association. In certain legal systems this freedom means the freedom to create as well as to dissolve monopolies. If, for instance, as some well-known German industrial lawyers maintain, "freedom of contract means in fact nothing else than that contracts of *any* content can be concluded so long as they do not violate good faith or the existing law. And we still have such a freedom of contract to-day (i.e. *considered from the point of view of content*)",[18] then that fundamental misunderstanding of the material function of freedom which here takes on a purely formal aspect, becomes fully evident.

In the political sphere legal freedom exists for every type of behaviour not prohibited by the law — law being every norm imputable to the state. Thus is freedom of person, of association, of assembly, or press, of a trade union, etc., "guaranteed within the framework and provisions of the existing legal code". To a well-known English constitutional lawyer the postulate of such a freedom appears as purely tautological, and as the expression of the principle "of the illegality of illegality" in which "the right to personal freedom is not a right to personal freedom, it is a right to so much personal freedom as is given by law".[19]

If we finally add that the concept of "law" is not at all definite, so that by this notion general norms can be meant as well as individual commands, the definition of legal freedom becomes nearly meaningless. By accepting such a definition, text-books on constitutional law can assert the existence of "freedom" even if political freedom in the usual sense of the word does not in fact exist. In spite of this the formalistic conception of legal freedom is extraordinarily politically significant in a positive way.

As we shall show in greater detail in Part III, a *predictable action* of the state, i.e. *its measurable interference, even if oppressive, is to be preferred to immeasurable intervention* (unpredictable, arbitrary action), *even if at one time benevolent*, as such immeasurable state of affairs creates insecurity. A "fair trial", the compulsion of state organs to keep within the limits of the state's own law — even if it can alter the law according to the then existing needs, is preferable to a state of affairs where there is no such compulsion. That is, in truth, the eternal value of the ideas of the "Rule of Law" and of the *Rechtsstaatscharakter* of the State.

Freedom in a sociological sense means something completely different. The approach to the problem is made easier [through the use of] three quotations:

H. J. Laski defines negative liberty thus: "There is no liberty if special privilege restricts the franchise of a portion of the community. There is no liberty if dominant opinion can control the social habits".[20] It is [also] worthwhile mentioning a quotation from a speech made by Edmund Burke [during] his conflict with Pitt over the East India Bill of 1786 in which Burke asked for the control of the East India Company. He said: "The Charter is framed on principles, the very reverse of liberty. It is a Charter to establish monopoly and to create power . . . . Such privileges are all in the strictest sense a trust and it is the essence of every trust to be rendered accountable."[21] Finally we quote from the speech of Senator Sherman; in introducing the Sherman Act he said: "If the concentrated powers of these combinations are entrusted to a single man, it is a kingly prerogative".[22]

We call someone free in a sociological sense if he has the legally free choice between at least two equal opportunities. Freedom depends, therefore, upon the possibility of competition. The statement of J. N. Figgis, "the point to note is that liberty is the result of religious competition",[23] can be supplemented and enlarged by the statement that liberty is as much the result as the condition of competition, not only in the economic or religious spheres but in all spheres of human life. This definition of sociological freedom implies that freedom between mutually competing individuals necessitates in the first place a certain degree of equality, already seen by Rousseau when he maintained liberty and equality as the two fundamental postulates of social life: "La liberté, parce que toute dépendance particulière est autant de force ôtée au corps de l'état; l'égalité, parce que la liberté ne peut subsister sans elle".[24]

The existence of legal freedom is essential to the existence of freedom in the sociological sense. Legal freedom is essential, but it is insufficient. "Negative freedom. . .is one-sided, yet as this one-sidedness contains an essential feature, it is not to be disregarded.

But the defect of the conception is that it exalts its one-sidedness to the unique and highest place."[25]

It seems to us insufficient to define, as does Karl Mannheim, freedom in a sociological sense as given if a person has the possibility of evading the one action by taking another or none.[26] We will attempt to clarify the problem with two examples from the economic and political spheres. If an employer offers his worker inadequate terms of employment, the worker in the liberal system has legally the right to refuse those terms. His decision to accept or to reject is legally a free one. Whether this decision can be called sociologically free, however, depends upon two alternative conditions: the worker is free if he is economically independent enough to allow his labour power to remain idle rather than accept inadequate terms; if this is not the case his decision is only free if he can get a better offer from another employer. Only under such circumstances would the worker have the choice between two equally good opportunities. If both conditions are non-existent and he accepts the work in order to save himself from starving, his labour may be exploited, and although he has the *legal* possibility of evasion he cannot be said to be free.

Similarly in the political sphere; if a citizen under a dictatorship is asked in a plebiscite whether he consents to the rule of the dictator or to a specific law, and he rejects both, his decision is legally free because he is not compelled to consent or to reject. In a sociological sense, however, he is unfree because he has not the choice between two equal opportunities. He cannot nominate another political leader instead of the one presented to him; he cannot give his consent to another law rather than that put before him.[27]

The modern development of law, apart from the more recent Fascist reactionary tendencies, is characterised by ever stronger attempts to realise in practice this sociological conception of law by paying increasing attention to the social differences between men. Here we will give only a few examples in an effort to elucidate a problem which will reappear at several further points in the book. A classic example is presented by Art. 165 of the late Weimar Constitution, in which the freedom of association is guaranteed for everyone in all professions. This guarantee is primarily directed against the police power.[28]* Neither the legislature nor the executive have the power to prevent a worker from joining a trade union or from forming a new one with his fellows. Thus far Article 165 constitutes a legal freedom within a certain sphere of human activity. But the

Constitution took into consideration also the fact that in spite of this constitutional guarantee of freedom an employer might under certain circumstances use the extra social power at his disposal. It therefore added an extra sentence to Art. 165 declaring that all contracts made with the intention of impairing the rights of the worker were void. The constitutional guarantee of freedom of association is therefore directed against both police and private social powers. Thus the legal category of freedom was rendered sociologically valid. In the same way the recognition of collective agreements by Art. 165 was to have led to the realisation of the sociological freedom of the worker in entering into contracts of labour. The legal category by itself in no way guarantees the sociological freedom of the worker entering into contract.[29]

Freedom in a philosophical sense is the real possibility of human self-assertion, the ending of the alienation of man from himself. The realisation of this "concrete conception of freedom"[30] includes the two other notions of freedom.

It is of decisive importance to recognise this hierarchy of concepts of freedom and not to confuse its stages.

Classification of Liberties In the course of historical development a certain number of special liberties have emerged which are described as fundamental rights — as human rights, or as "rights of men". We shall attempt to systematise these theories. We repeat that the so-called pre-state rights of men of philosophical liberalism are also legally intelligible only as rights granted by the state.

It is possible to classify these liberties from two points of view: either from the legal protection which they enjoy, or from the subject-matter which they regulate.[31]

Under the first heading the question arises whether there are fundamental rights which are inalienable even by constitutional methods. It has been asserted both in German and in American literature that there are certain fundamental rights which cannot be alienated even if the constitution permits amendment.[32] Such theorists distinguish between constitutional amendments which leave the "constitution as a fundamental decision" (*Verfassung als Grundentscheidung*) untouched, only altering special provisions considered permissible; and constitutional amendments which aim at the abolition of this constitution and are asserted to be impermissible. We do not want to discuss here the possible political functions of the creation of such a category of inalienable rights of men. We would only remark that in the United States as in Germany, noticeable stress has been laid on such liberties as go to preserve the bourgeois system of property.

Within the inalienable liberties there are, on the one hand, liberties which can only be removed by the legislature in the process of constitutional amendment, and on the other hand, such as can be removed by the simple legislative process; there are fundamental rights which cannot be interfered with by the legislature, and such as can be so interfered with — i.e. those which are equipped with the so-called "reservations of the law" (*Vorbehalt des Gesetzes*); that means granted only within the framework of the legal system. Examples of such "reservations of the law" are to be found in Chapters V–VIII of Dicey's *Law of the Constitution*. There are, finally, fundamental rights which can be withdrawn in exceptional circumstances, and such as cannot even then be touched. In the case of a federal state we have in addition to distinguish between the authority of state legislation and of federal legislation, and between state executive and federal executive.

Apart from these distinctions according to categories of positive constitutional law, we distinguish the fundamental liberties according to their subject matter. From this point of view we have to note the existence of so-called "individual" or "personal" rights to freedom. These are the fundamental rights of the isolated individual, such as the protection from illegal imprisonment, security of dwelling-place and of correspondence, of religion and conscience.

As a second category there appear the so-called political rights to freedom. These are fundamental rights which refer to types of behaviour arising out of the living together of men in the state. To this category belong freedom of association, of the press, of meeting, and secrecy of ballot. They have a dual function: a liberal one in creating directly a sphere free from the state, and a democratic one in serving the integration of the will of the state in a democratic way. It goes without saying that the first group of the rights to personal freedom also serve indirectly the formation of a democratic will of the state because by arbitrary imprisonment or by arbitrary censorship of correspondence the citizens under certain circumstances can be prevented from exercising their political rights. The rights of political freedom are therefore supplementary guarantees of the democratic rights of the citizen. Without freedom of discussion, of press, of association and of meeting, a genuinely freely chosen decision is impossible. The rationalisation of political life by political parties which are based on a formal freedom of propaganda[33] would be impossible without political and personal rights to freedom.

A third category is presented by the rights to economic freedom. The central economic right is property.[34] Property is in the first instance a right. It is a subjective right because it is granted by the legal order. It is an absolute right and not a relative one because it grants rights of defence against everyone and not only — as in the case of the law of contract — against the contracting partner. It is finally a universal right because the power of the owner over the thing is in principle unlimited. We have therefore always to distinguish between the thing over which the right of the owner extends and the subjective right itself of the owner. On the other hand the characteristics of the things are without significance. It is equally irrelevant whether the property consists in consumption or production goods. The supplementary liberties of the right to property are freedom of contract, of trade and of testation.

Finally, in the last category are the rights to social freedom which have developed historically from the rights to economic freedom. They aim at the liberation of the working-class. The primary instance is that of the right of association granted to trade unions — i.e. the freedom of the worker to join with his fellows in a trade union.

From the political rights the rights of *status activus* must be divorced. Democratic rights belong to the citizen, and serve directly to integrate the will of the state in a democratic way. Here belong equal franchise, and the right of equal access to public positions.

One of the central problems of a sociological investigation of law is the question of the relation of these four groups to each other. Modern German constitutional theory takes the view that the first-mentioned three groups — i.e. the rights to individual, political and economic freedom, for the rights to social freedom do not exist for this group of theorists — are children of the modern bourgeois society of free competition. They therefore disappear and as a logical consequence have to be abolished when free competition no longer exists. In the same way the annihilation of the rights to personal, political and social freedom is justified by Fascism, which asserts that all these fundamental rights are the mere offspring of capitalism.

As against this theory we take decisively the view that such a connection between the rights to personal, political and social freedom on the one hand, and the rights to economic freedom which have developed only within a competitive economic system on the other, does not in fact exist. Even a very superficial historical analysis teaches us that at least personal and political rights have existed and even been struggled for long before the competitive economic system arose. It can be proved that the function of these rights is not lost, but tends rather to increase in importance after the disappearance of free competition.

2.2.3. *Institutions and the Rule of Law (Theory of Institutions)*

A legal conception fundamental to the analysis of every legal system is that of the legal institution. We use this term purely descriptively — i.e. the word "institution" does not contain any metaphysical implications. The conception of the institution does not belong either to the pluralistic theory of the state of Gierke, Figgis or Laski, or to the Neo-Thomistic legal philosophy of Hauriou or Lambert. We do not deny that the notion of the legal institution can be absolutised and can therefore be made the basis of a legal philosophy; the conditions under which such a transformation may happen will be shown in Part III. In order to avoid any misunderstanding we therefore repeat that the concept of "institution" is here purely descriptive. We deal first with the notion of the legal institution and then with its relations with freedom.

We understand by a legal institution the establishment of a relationship, intended to endure, either between men, or between properties, or between men and property, for the purpose of regulating social processes, either organised on a hierarchical basis or as a fellowship (*herrschaftlich* or *genossenschaftlich*), and belonging either to public or to private law.

An institution is therefore a complex of rights and duties belonging either to public or to private law — a *jus symbioticum*, which "ex personarum plurium comprehensione corpus constans". The institution can have either a hierarchical basis or be a fellowship as has been defined by Gierke.[35] A hierarchical institution is given when there exists super- and sub-ordinational relationships: power is exercised. A fellowship exists when this is not the case and no power is exercised. The emergence of the character of these relationships is therefore not decisive. A fellowship can be created by power, and domination can be exercised by contract. If, for instance, the public power compulsorily creates a fellowship of fishermen for the construction and preservation of dykes, or if workers are compulsorily joined to a sick-fund, such a bringing together by coercion does not necessarily create a coercive relationship, but in the majority of cases there emerges a genuine fellowship. The legal institution may consist of the bringing together of men alone. That is the case in all human associations whether state, family, church, trade union, political party or cartel.

But specially allocated property can also by itself form an institution. It is created by separating off property and making it independent either virtually or legally. In German law we have the examples of *Anstalt* (belonging to public law) and *Stiftung* (foundation) (belonging to private law).

Finally, men and property can be brought together to form an institution either on an hierarchical or a fellowship basis. The most striking examples of a bringing together of men and things hierarchically is the shop (*Betrieb*),[36]* the undertaking and the combination of undertakings. We understand by a "shop" (*Betrieb*) a hierarchical bringing together of things and men (material and personal means of production). The shop is a technical unit in which economic aims as such are not pursued.

Economic aims find their place in the undertaking. By this we understand a bringing together hierarchically of things and men (material and personal means of production) for the pursuit of *economic* ends. In small units shop and undertaking often coincide. The technical unit is often at the same time the economic one. The spheres for the decision of business policy and the unit for the technical realisation of this business policy are one and the same, although in modern large-scale units they are usually divorced.

The hierarchical combination of undertaking is the *concern*.[37] The concern is a hierarchical bringing together of several legally independent undertakings for the pursuit of economic aims.

We speak of a *trust* when either a hierarchical combination or an individual undertaking exercises monopoly powers. As property in the means of production is a bundle of three functions — possession, administration and profit-making — the concern can either be a hierarchical bringing together of the function of possession (for example, interlocking of share capital), or of that of administration (exchange of members of the managing boards, or the creation of special administrative undertakings for the purpose of controlling dependent undertakings), or of the function of profit-making (the German *Interessengemeinschaft* or the English pool). Finally, all these property functions of combined undertakings can be performed at the same time without in any way destroying the juridical independence of the undertakings concerned.

The legal institution can be defined as a bringing together, intended to endure, for the purpose of regulating the processes of life and for their production and reproduction. All institutions serving the production and reproduction of human relationships and intended to endure are therefore equally legal institutions in so far as they have been the subject-matter of legal regulations. For instance, marriage, serving the reproduction of human life, and on the whole, private property in the means of production.

If property, as we saw above, is a right, property in the means of production is also an institution with a three-fold function:[38] possession, or retention, administration and profit-making. It is unnecessary to mention that from the point of view of the owner the central function of property is profit-making, and that for him all other functions are subordinated to it.

We understand by the function of possession, the physical retention of things or rights by the owner. It will be seen that this function is lost in the case of large-scale property, and is transferred to the workers. In a shop based upon division of labour, the owner loses the factual retention of the means of production.

The function of administration consists in the administration of men, the personal means of production, and of things, the material means of production. The administration of men implies the power to command them.

Property in the means of production necessarily attracts men into its sphere when the society is divided into owners of means of production and "free"[39] workers. Property clearly only possesses this magnetic quality when this collective social relationship exists. The worker cannot escape it if he wants to reproduce his labour power.

The power of command is, on the other hand, potentially exercised by every individual owner of the means of production. Property is a relationship between men through the medium of things. As we have already mentioned, the function of possession and of administration stand, for the owner of the means of production, in the service of the profit-making function even if, from another point of view, they stand in the service of production itself. From his point of view they are only means for the making of profit. At the present stage of development of division of labour the owner of the means of production very often is not the controller of the administrative function. He delegates his exercise to his employees. The invisible principal, the legal employer, has to be distinguished from the visible one, the factual employer.

2.2.4. *The Relations between Liberties and Institutions*

Liberty, (main liberty — *Hauptfreiheit*), may be surrounded for its protection and realisation by other liberties or institutions. We call such liberties and institutions connected, or auxiliary, or supplementary liberties and institutions. Similarly, an institution (*main institution*) can be surrounded by auxiliary institutions and liberties for its protection and realisation.[40]

We understand therefore by *auxiliary institution*, or *liberty*, the guarantee of the main liberty or institution by other liberties or institutions intended to serve its protection. The distinction between a main and auxiliary institution or liberty is of decisive importance not only for any sociological investigation but also for any kind of exegetic interpretation of law. The following instances will demonstrate this.

By the right of association the workers and their employers are given the right to join together for the pursuit of certain ends. This right prevents, as we have already shown, public and private powers from hindering such association. If the legislator grants such a freedom the question will be at once raised, whether those liberties which, for instance, a trade union needs for its successful functioning, and which are only supplementary to the main liberty, are not also guaranteed by the guaranteeing of the main right of association; concretely, whether the rights of the press, of meeting, etc., which at the same time are independent main liberties, do not enjoy the same protection from the law as is granted to the main liberty, the right of association. The question is of decisive significance if, as was the case in the Weimar constitution, the freedom of association has a far stronger legal basis than the rights of the press and of assembly. Whereas the right to associate possessed an absolute fundamental right untouchable by either legislature or executive, the two other liberties were only relative ones coming under the "reservation of the law" (*Vorbehalt des Gesetzes*). Is the legally stronger protection enjoyed by the right of association to be extended to the rights of press and assembly, or must these two be measured by their own constitutional standards?[41]

The right of association does not only possess supplementary liberties, but also supplementary institutions, as for instance the collective agreement which alone can give the trade unions the possibility of carrying out their economic functions.

Marriage as a main institution is also surrounded by auxiliary institutions and liberties such as the social insurance institutions (sick fund, workmen's compensation laws, unemployment insurance), which have become supplementary to marriage in so far as they are benefits differentiated in distribution according to the family circumstances of the person concerned. Another auxiliary institution of marriage is that of testation, which guarantees the bourgeois order of property succession.

Every liberty, therefore, appears both as a main and as an auxiliary one, just as a legal institution appears at the same time supplementary as main. Here, indeed, is an extraordinarily fruitful field for further investigations into the sociology of law.

Property is the means of production, which stands in the centre of our investigation, is surrounded by auxiliary liberties and institutions, all serving the protection and realisation of its profit-making function. In order to be able to carry out the profit-making function the owner must buy and sell, exchange and take loans, enter contracts of labour and, if he is a landowner, conduct contracts of lease and take on mortgages.[42] Freedom of contract is therefore an essential auxiliary liberty of the principle institution of property. The property relationship also necessitates freedom of trade, which at the same time as being a supplementary liberty also has the effect of a natural selection of owners, excluding the uneconomical among them and retaining and strengthening the economical ones. We shall return to this point later in our analysis of classical liberal economic theory.

In certain historical situations both auxiliary liberties, freedom of contract and of trade, have analogous effects. In other situations the two may serve different economic interests; the freedom of contract, for instance, may serve the interests of the monopolists, while freedom of trade serves those of the non-monopolists.[43] It can also happen that liberties and institutions which were previously in the position of supplementing other institutions or liberties, from a certain moment on cease to do so any longer and, on the contrary, exercise an opposing influence to the intended functions of the main liberty or institution they formerly guaranteed. Thus, for instance, do freedom of contract and of trade work against private property in the means of production from the time when a certain degree of monopolisation is introduced. These auxiliary liberties very often suffer infringement or even abolition and are replaced in the legal system by a form of the administrative act belonging to public law. If freedom of trade in a monopolistic economy appears to be leading to diminished profits, the modern twentieth-century state does not hesitate to encroach on these liberties, or even to abolish them by ordering undertakings by administrative act or statute to join cartels, or by prohibiting the floating of new concerns. Regulations belonging to public law then replace supplementary liberties — the administrative act or the statute replace the rights of free contract and trade in their relationship with property in the means of production.

The relation of private property in the means of production to its supplementary institutions and liberties on the one hand, and of the totality of this legal complex to the economic and political dynamic on the other hand, is particularly clearly shown in Marxian sociology. Property in the means of production plus its auxiliary institutions and liberties are called "production relationships" — i.e. "social relationships in which the individuals produce".[44] "This productive relationship is at the same time a legal relationship and a master–servant relationship".[45] Productive relationships are "relationships which are entered into by men in their social processes of life, in the production of their social life", and they have a specifically transitional character".[46] Within the framework of productive relationships, the combination of the different productive forces by which the life of the community is maintained is accomplished. We understand here under "productive forces" the technical knowledge available, the given personal and material means of production (for instance, qualities of land, raw materials, and fixed capital) in society.[47]

The relations between productive relationships and productive forces, according to the Marxian theory, suffers in the course of historical development a typical change of function. When there is a tendency of the productive forces to expand (for example, by virtue of a permanent expansion of technical knowledge) "at a certain stage of their development", it happens that "the material productive forces of society come into contradiction with the given productive relationships" or, "what is only a legal expression for them, with the property relationships within which they have hitherto moved. These relationships, once forms of development of the productive forces, now become fetters hindering the development of those forces".[48] This Marxian theory refers, however, only to the transition from one social order to another, in which each social order, the old and the new, is characterised by one principal institution — for example, capitalism by private property in the means of production, and socialism by communal property in the means of production.

An analogous process occurs also *within* a given social order with regard to the principal institution characterising it and its relations with its auxiliary institutions and liberties. The relationship of such supplementary institutions and liberties to the main institution or liberty can suffer a change of function in a like manner. With a certain degree of development of the productive forces *within* that society, the auxiliary institutions and liberties become fetters on and hinder the aims of the principal institutions they hitherto guaranteed. They lose their supplementary character. In a period of relatively free competition, freedom of contract and of trade are means for the realisation of profit for the owner of the means of production. In this period the state guarantees their existence (by constitutional or simple legal guarantees of the liberties as such) or their function (for instance, by laws relating to unfair competition).

In a period of monopoly economy the relationship is reversed. Freedom of trade facilitates at the same time the rise of competing undertakings undesired by the monopolist: freedom of contract gives outsiders the possibility of keeping themselves alien from the monopolist organisations or to quit them at will. Workers are given the possibility of joining trade unions by freedom of association, and in such circumstances when the profits of the monopolist undertakings tend to diminish, it can very well happen that the auxiliary institutions and liberties are abolished in favour of new supplementary statutes and administrative acts more suited to the monopolist interests.

2.3. The Dual Significance of the Rule of Law

Connected with the conflict between sovereignty and human rights is, in legal terminology, the dual notion of law; the political and the material notion. By the *political* notion of law we understand, therefore, every general norm and every individual command imputable to the state, whether just or unjust, convenient or inconvenient. Every decision of the sovereign state organ is law. Law, therefore, is only *voluntas* and not *ratio*. Freed from all material qualities, this conception of law is to be found most clearly formulated in Hobbes. For him, law is not "counsel", because "counsel is a precept in which the reason for my obeying is taken from the thing itself which is advised". Law is rather command, "which is a precept in which the cause of my obeyance depends on the will of the commander. . . . Law is a command of that person, whether man or court, whose precept contains in itself the reason of obedience".[49] "Law . . . is the word of him, that by right hath command over others".[50] Between the dominance of law in such a sense, and absolute sovereignty no antagonism can exist. If law is nothing else than the will of the state in legal form, then the postulate of the rule of law can offer no limit to the power of the sovereign. Such a dematerialised law does not bind the legislator. The rule of the political notion of law and the existence of absolute state sovereignty are in reality only two different expressions for one and the same thing.

Throughout, this postulate of absolute sovereignty is antagonistic to the postulate of rule of material laws. Material law is to be defined as such norms of the state as are compatible with defined ethical postulates, whether such postulates be those of justice, liberty or equality, or anything else. This notion of law "corresponds" to the conception of law as norms, since the essence of norms is the reasonable principle (*logos*) which it embodies. To this alone it owes its authority, and this principle is wholly transparent to the speculative intelligence. Opaque to reason are only the accidents of its realisation, and these are an inevitable imperfection, not the ground of its authority.[51] Not every *voluntas* is therefore in correspondence with the demand of a certain *ratio*. Material law and absolute sovereignty are clearly mutually exclusive. Absolute sovereignty implies that the legislator is materially unrestricted. This, however, is not the case if the legislator is allowed only to issue general, or just, or reasonable laws — i.e. if a material law (for example,

Natural Law) rules. In such cases, he is no longer sovereign. We can, however, only speak of the rule of a material law if there is a sufficiently great expectation (Chance) that the material law in question will be realised in the positive legal system, or that where a positive law is in contradiction with the material law, the positive is not carried out. The rule of material law cannot be said to exist if — as in the Middle Ages and at the beginning of modern times — the bearers of the state power have subscribed to a natural law justification of state sovereignty. From the bare assertion of a divine or secular natural law standing before positive law, we cannot, however, deduce the rule of material law. Under such circumstances, this would only be realised when this natural law is actually concretised, or when its pre-eminence over positive law is institutionalised (for instance by recognition of the right of resistance or of deposition of the bearer of sovereignty). There must also at the same time be a relative unanimity as to the contents of the natural law.

The conflict between the political and the material notions of law is clearly expressed in the trial of the five knights imprisoned by Charles I on the basis of his prerogative, and who appealed to the Court of Kings Bench for a *habeas corpus*. Selden especially[52] based his pleadings on the provisions of Chapter 39 of the Magna Charta: "No freeman shall be . . . imprisoned . . . except by the lawful judgment of his peer and [or] by the law of the land".[53] But what is meant here by "law of the land"? If "law" means the order of the king for imprisonment, then the freedom guaranteed by the Magna Charta is non-existent. According to Selden's argument, if rights are to be guaranteed in this way, then "law" in this connection must mean "due process of law" — i.e. "law" must be taken in the material and not in the political sense. But as has been clearly shown by McKechnie, in spite of Magna Charta, every king from John Lackland to Charles I had claimed an unlimited right of imprisonment ("protective custody" in modern terminology); and the significance of this clause of Magna Charta has been much over-exaggerated. Attorney-General Heath could well reply to Selden: "The law hath ever allowed this latitude to the king or his Privy Council . . . in extraordinary cases to restrain the persons of such freemen as for reasons of state they find necessary for a time for this present expressing the causes thereof".

II

Sovereignty and the Rule of Law in some Rational Political Theories (The Disenchantment of Law)

The task of the second part of this book is a dual one: first to demonstrate the distribution of spheres between sovereignty and the rule of material law in the most important rational political theories, and second to make clear the connection between the legal theories of the nineteenth and twentieth centuries and divine and secular natural law.

The second part, therefore, is restricted in the first place to *rational* theories. All traditionalistic or charismatic theories remain unconsidered, and are only dealt with in Part III, where the reaction against the rational theories, the transvaluation of values by Fascism, is considered.

In presenting rational theories, it was necessary to choose between two possible alternatives. We could have dealt with *all* theories which have had any influence on the formation of political thought: but such an undertaking would have been synonymous with a history of the whole of political thought, an obviously impossible task, which could only have led to a number of vague and often repeated generalisations. We preferred, therefore, the second alternative, to select *some* of the theories — namely, those which have had an undoubtedly high degree of influence on the development of political thought.

We may be reproached with having made an arbitrary selection, but there appeared to be no other way out of our difficulty.

A second consideration led us to make the choice we did — namely, that we wished to investigate the political theories from one point of view only, from the point of view of the relationship between sovereignty and material law, and that all other problems are for us only incidental and secondary in importance. Until now, this problem has only been dealt with by the way: it has never appeared as a central thesis. We therefore intend to investigate the question, and to ignore the usual problems such as whether a satisfactory solution of the question of obedience to the state has been arrived at, whether the answer of Hobbes is to be preferred to that of Locke, or that of Rousseau to that of Kant. In no case shall we expound the total political system of the theorist concerned, but shall always assume it to be already known. This emphasis laid upon a single problem justifies the monographic character of the work.

We emphasised the necessity of rationalising the political theories with which we are dealing. We have, therefore, avoided dealing with the metaphysical fundamentals of the various theories, which are often in any case incomprehensible. We have tried to divorce the political theory from its metaphysical background, which on the average is very simple, because there usually is very little relationship between the political theory and the metaphysical system. We have also attempted to introduce modern terminology and concepts, in order to make the theories understandable. We have the impression that a simple repetition of words and notions in the theories used by their authors makes any exposition of the theory incomprehensible.

If we go back, in dealing with the relation between sovereignty and material law, to the system of Aquinas, we do not do so for the sake of historical curiosity, but because the Thomistic natural law has indirectly influenced modern liberalism, and because at present we can see a revival of the philosophy, a renaissance, the social and political significance of which will later become evident. Blackstone's terminology has been largely influenced by that of the natural law theory of Thomas Aquinas, and the influence of Scholastic philosophy on Locke has been proved by Telkamp.[1] Further, in Thomistic natural law the disintegrating tendencies which are inherent in any natural law system are especially evident.

CHAPTER 3

Thomist Natural Law

3.1. Cicero's Natural Law

It is well-known that in Thomas Aquinas a number of trends merge together, and in particular the decisive influence of Aristotelian philosophy and of Cicero's theory of law.

The notion of material law was completely alien to Roman jurisprudence. For Republican Rome the statement of Gaius (I. Sect.3) had undisputed validity: "Lex est, quod populus jubet atque constituit". Law was therefore every decision of the *comitia*, which went back to the initiative of the magistrates. It was otherwise in Cicero's theory of law. The acceptance of the notion of material law by Cicero is conditioned by the extraordinarily strong influence which the Stoic philosophy had on him. The Stoics postulated that the state was only allowed to issue general norms in conformity with the ideas of liberty and equality of the Stoic philosophy. To the Stoics all men are brothers. Therefore a universal law should rule with the aim of realising this human equality of brotherhood.[1] In just the same way Cicero postulates the rule of material law, and hereby exercises an extraordinary influence on Thomist natural law, and through this, as well as directly, on secular natural law.

According to the Ciceronian theory all positive laws are nourished by the one divine law.[2] The unwritten law of nature and of divinity is supposed to be the source of statute law. This natural law is eternal and unchangeable, directed towards the realisation of the common good. Positive law, however, has to be adapted to local and temporary conditions, it is particular law, which must not contradict the universal natural law.

Is it possible to say that Cicero postulated the rule of material law in our sense? That is to say: does he allow a sufficiently great expectation (Chance) of the fulfilment of natural law, should it contradict positive law? This question is to be investigated shortly.

In *De Legibus* (I.6.18)[3] he has defined the notion of law as follows: "Lex est ratio summa insita in natura, quae jubet ea, quae facienda sunt, prohibetque contraria. Eadem ratio quom est in hominis mente confirmata et confecta, lex est". In this statement, as in a similar one in *Republica* (III.31–3), obviously nothing is said about our central question, whether the material law has been given a sufficiently high degree of probable fulfilment. In order to prove that Cicero postulates the nullity of positive law in the event of its contradicting natural law, the quotation in *De Legibus* where he asserted that the laws stood above the magistrates, and that they were only the mouthpiece of the laws is often referred to: "Ut enim magistratibus leges ita populo praesunt magistratus vereque dici potest magistratum legem esse loquentem legem autem mutum magistratum" (III.1.2). What does *lex* mean in this connection? Only positive, or only natural law? The question is extraordinarily controversial, and in my opinion at present insoluble.[4] In order to prove that by *lex* in this connection Cicero understood natural law, it is often said that wherever he means positive law he speaks of *jus civile*, and wherever he means natural law, he speaks of *lex*. But the following quotation from his speech *Pro Cluentio* will prove the incorrectness of this assertion (53.146.147): "Mens et animus et consilium et sententia civitatis posita est in legibus. Ut corpora nostra sine mente sic civitas sine lege suis partibus, ut nervis, ac sanguine et membris uti non potest legum ministri magistratus. . . circumspiste omnes rei publicae partes: omnia legum imperio et praescripto fieri videbitis". This speech *Pro Cluentio* is a typical lawyer's speech. In it Cicero first pays homage to the *Lex Sempronia* in order afterwards to prove that his client Cluentios cannot be punished under [it]. He did not at all enter into the question whether the *Lex Sempronia* itself was compatible with natural law according to the principle *non nimis probare*. *Lex*, therefore, can only mean positive and not natural law, and the assertion that in the above quotation from *De Legibus* Cicero was referring to natural law cannot be maintained. In the same speech, *Pro Cluentio*, however, the following sentence is to be found: "Iniquum tibi videtur, Acci, esse non isdem legibus omnes teneri. Primum, ut id iniquissimum esse confitear, eius modi est, ut commutatis eius opus sit legibus, non ut his, quae sunt, non pareamus".[5] Here he demands unconditional submission to the *lex scripta*. This contradicts in itself the assumption that Cicero would postulate the rule of material law: but it provides no solution for our problem which deals with the Ciceronian legal system as a whole. Cicero here appears as an advocate, and by the emphasis he laid on the postulate of the citizen's duty of obedience to the *lex scripta* he hoped to buy the goodwill of the Court. In my view, in the present state of research, a decision as to whether the postulate of the rule of material law is mere lip service rendered by Cicero, or whether he intended to make the fulfilment of natural law highly probable in face of conflicting positive law, is impossible. The impossibility of deciding the problem, however, is of eminent objective significance. If we say with Carlyle that the period between Aristotle and Cicero is the dividing line between "ancient and modern political theory",[6] Cicero then belongs to modern theory in which the conflict between the postulate of sovereignty and that of the rule of material law appears as a typical one.

3.2. Thomas Aquinas[7]

The work of Thomas Aquinas arose in a time when the medieval *ordo* already carried the germs of its dissolution, and his contemporary, Duns Scotus (d.1308) is already a pioneer of an individualism which was determined to disintegrate the unified medieval culture. However, the *Summa* of Thomas is still the expression of this *ordo*, giving adequate place to every phase of human life. In this social system the coincidence of *voluntas* and *ratio*, of intellect and sensibility, and of the legal structure and the strivings of men, provides a happy harmony.

3.2.1.

Thomas Aquinas distinguished between domination bound by the norms of the *lex naturalis* (and therefore of practical reason), and a domination unbound by it. He himself always postulated the first type of domination. The norms of the first type he calls "Laws": "Lex non est ipsum ius proprie loquendo, sed aliqualis ratio iuris" (2.II.57.1–2). Law and concrete legal norms are therefore not identical. Law is the basis, is the standard of measurement, is a regula *artis* with the help of which the just decision is arrived at.

By its relationship to the *lex naturalis* the *lex* is distinguished from the *lex tyrannica* (1.II.92.1–4), and by its *vis coactiva* on the side of a legitimate authority from the mere *admonitio* (2.II.65.2;1.II.90.2–3). Not every norm of the state is therefore law. The *imperium legis* is limited. "The *mensurans* [legislator] is therefore himself again a *mensuratus*. . . law, so to speak, precedes in time its constitution by the legislator in connection with the general order of nature and reason with the concrete historical relations".[8] As the norms of natural law are related to the common good and to the idea of equality, there follow three conditions which have to be fulfilled by a norm of the state in order to be called "law".

Such a norm must first serve the *bonum commune (ratione finis)*, because: "Lex est nullo privato commodo, sed pro communi civium utilitate conscripta" (1.II.90.2). Secondly, the norm must be just — i.e. the burdens put upon subjects must correspond to the principle of proportionate equality (*ratione formae*). Thirdly the norm must be issued by the legislator within the limits of his authority (*ratione auctoritatis*), because: "Lex est quaedam rationis ordinatio ad bonum commune et ab eo qui curam communitatis habet promulgata" (1.II.90.4).

Every norm fulfilling these three conditions is binding *in foro conscientiae*, and *in foro externo*. The postulated attitude of the subject towards such norms as do not conform to these three conditions is differentiated according to the following possibilities.

Firstly, it is possible that positive law contradicts the basic principles of the *lex naturalis* and therefore of the *lex aeterna*, for these basic principles are part of the *lex aeterna*: "Lex aeterna nihil aliud est quam ratio divinae sapientiae, secundum quod est directiva omnium, actuum et motionum" (1.II.93.1). The *lex aeterna* is rooted in God. The order of nature (*justitia naturalis*) and the order of human conscious activities (*ordo iustitiae*) are of the same character. The natural moral law is but a portion of the general law of nature, and the general law of nature but a section of the *lex aeterna*. Man accepts God and therefore also the *lex aeterna*, and therewith necessarily participates in the *lex naturalis*: "Participatio legis aeternae in rationali creatura dicitur lex naturalis" (1.II.91.2); "Omnia participant aliqualiter lege aeterna" (1.II.91.2). The human being is a rational creature endowed with the *lumen naturale*. The supreme principles of the *lex aeterna* are eternal and unchanging (1.II.94.5) even if their recognition and application can be damaged by passion (1.II.91.6).

In the main, their duties involved are, neighbourly love (social duties), maintenance and propagation of life, and love of God (individual rights).[9] If positive law conflicts with these basic principles of the *lex naturalis*, passive resistance on the part of the subject is not only right, but even a duty, for the *lex naturalis* is indispensable — even God cannot dispense with it (1.II.100.8–2). Passive resistance is a duty. So far as positive law and natural law coincide, positive law is compulsory also *in foro conscientiae*. "Si (leges humanae) iustae sunt, habent vim obligando in foro conscientiae a lege aeterna, de qua derivantur" (1.II.96.4).

The second possible case is that positive law [is] not indeed in conflict with the *lex aeterna* and thereby with the basic principles of the *lex naturalis*, but with the secondary natural law. The norms of the secondary natural law derive from the supreme principles of the *lex naturalis*, which of course also derive their power from the *lex aeterna*. They coincide on the whole with the *Decalogue* (1.II.100.1–11). They are not valid in all cases, although in most. They constitute, on the whole, a part from the *Decalogue*, that which the Roman jurist understood by *ius gentium* in the sense of Gaius (*Dig.* I.1.2 and I.1.9): "Quod naturalis ratio inter omnes homines constituit. . .ius gentium, quasi quo iure omnes gentes utuntur". If positive law violates only these derived norms of secondary natural law, the subject is nevertheless compelled to obedience to the positive law. It binds him *in foro externo*, but not *in foro conscientiae* (1.II.95.1–2; 2.II.60.5).

We see, therefore, that the Thomist system, by the partial recognition of the right of passive resistance and the equally partial concretisation of the *lex naturalis*, institutes a factual domination of the rule of material law, at least to a certain degree. The rule of material law is extended even further by the far-reaching coincidence of the material norms of behaviour in the various strata of society.

3.2.2.

The Thomist natural law is on the whole a codification of the feudal order.

There existed in the Middle Ages no schism between a secular and a clerical social sphere. The conflict between church and state was not an antagonism of two societies, but a struggle between two officials — the Pope and the Emperor — within one and the same society.[10] In this feudal society there existed no modern state apart from Frederick II's Sicilian creation. In the secular sphere there was no sovereignty, yet the domination of the Pope in a certain period was genuine sovereignty.[11] The *plenitudo potestatis* is sovereignty. The Pope is the last creator of law. Law is what the Pope determines. Already Gregory VII in his "27 Articles" of the *Dictatus Papae* (1075) postulated the divine origins of papacy, its infallibility, the unlimited and universal authority of the Pope over the whole of human society: he also established the right of deposition of bishops and kings, the right to absolve subjects from their duty of obedience to a secular power. Under Innocent III we find that "the Pope disposes of the income of the Church, he distributes the offices and benefices arbitrarily, he is not only the supreme but the sole law of the Church; the prelates are no longer only his vassals, they are now his officials, and the feudal oath has become the oath of office without any alteration in the wording".[12]

All law in the secular sphere was on the whole private law. All political rights were attached to property in land. The king was always the highest and sometimes the biggest feudal lord. As there was no public law, there could be no statute specifically belonging to this sphere of law. Political relations were therefore contractual relations. The contracts were obviously status contracts as they have been defined above. Society was static. There was no alteration of the hierarchy of estates. Every member of society had a fixed place within this hierarchy of estates from which on the whole he was unable to move. The relation between the estates was hierarchical — a legal relationship of super- and sub-ordination. All this is clearly in contrast with modern society with its constantly fluctuating class-structure and its legal equality.

We have been accustomed since the time of Gierke to distinguish two forms of estate organisation: the authoritarian and the liberal (fellowship) types.[13] It cannot be doubted, and recently it has been reasserted from the Catholic side, that the Middle Ages knew of no liberal order of fellowship. The estates were authoritarian estates[14] comprising nobility, freemen, semi-freemen and serfs. The differences were based on birth, land and power. This authoritarian order was not only not independently changed by the Church; the Church also justified it ideologically, and even made itself a part of it. In the later Middle Ages the rising hierarchy of officials, and the lower ministerials and clerics joined the authoritarian order. By means of a combination of land with office, these new groups became an effective part of the order; the offices remained in their possession and were inherited by their heirs with the land. It is well-known that the Church soon raised itself to the position of the biggest landowner, and from that time on it naturally became interested in the maintenance of serfdom, for the serf was necessary to the successful cultivation of its property. The European social system at the time of Thomas Aquinas was entangled in a complex network of feudal relationships [stretching] from the east to the west and from north to south. Peasants and towndwellers alike were unfree. The peasants were involved in the *Dienstrecht*: the craft guilds of the towns were estates of servitude. Even within the individual estates and their organisations in guilds and corporations only a very limited degree of freedom existed. The medieval estate organisation meant a society based on privilege.

3.2.3.

This authoritarian order found its expression in the *lex naturalis*.[15] The division into estates is justified by Thomas Aquinas. He distinguishes between the *sui* and *alieni iuris* (2.II.183.1), thus recognising the estate of serfdom. The rich had, further, a higher, and the poor a lower place. The hierarchy consisted of the *optimates* standing on the top, the bourgeois middle strata (*populus honorabilis*), and the serving estates (*vilis populus*) at the bottom — and was justified by Thomas in this form: "Una hierarchis est unus principatus id est una multitudo ordinata uno modo sub principis gubernatione, non autem esset multitudo ordinata, sed confusa, si in multitudine diversi ordines non essent" (I.108.2). Slavery is obviously legitimate, even if it is only defined as a necessary evil. Property remains unscathed (I.II.94–105), and is in no way considered as the product of original sin, and the theory of original communism is rejected. Property is a necessary institution.[16]

This justification of the authoritarian order in Aquinas' natural law system corresponded to the conviction of the whole Church, expressed in the literature of his time.[17] Even Augustine had justified slavery with the doctrine of original sin, and his followers have tried to use the analogy of the hierarchy of angels to justify the feudal order.

So long as feudal society was static, and so long as town and country were in equilibrium and the poor could maintain themselves adequately, it was possible that in the mind of the average member of society as well as in the minds of their theorists, norm and will should coincide. But even in the time of Aquinas this was no longer the case; even in his lifetime there were disintegrating tendencies.

To these new conflicts there corresponded the fact that the relations between natural and positive law became problematical — the question of sovereignty was raised. At the same time as the natural order was no longer felt to be identical with human society — i.e. when the feudal hierarchical order was no longer accepted as the obvious social order, and the modern state began to emerge — the divergence between natural law and sovereignty became evident. The process of divorce of positive from natural law, by which positive law became self-sufficient and autonomous, then set in, a process which, from the analogy of Max Weber's famous generalisation of the "disenchantment of the world", we may call a "disenchantment of the law". This process of disenchantment is no unbroken one, progressing uninterrupted through years. Relapses are frequent; law and morals, law and natural law are often confused, but the process finally finds its expression in the Kantian legal theory. The concrete contents of the *bonum commune* to which natural law was related in Aquinas' system became controversial. There arose the question whether this *bonum commune* was really identical with the existing authoritarian order of estates. The process of disenchantment of the law had already begun. When, according to Germanic legal thought and Roman law, the monarch was asserted to be bound by law, any justification on any other basis of the existing monarch necessarily became dubious.

The real ideological conflict hinted at had to break out, and did so in three spheres: in the relation between the Church and secular society; within the Church itself; and, finally, within the secular society itself.

3.3. The Disintegration of the Thomist Natural Law

3.3.1.

In the social and political teachings of the New Testament are already to be found disintegrating elements. The recognition of every man as a rational creature, the recognition of the freedom of the soul and, above all, of human equality before God, were historic acts of Christendom: "There can be neither Jew nor Greek, there can be neither bond nor free, there can be no male and female! for ye all are one man in Christ Jesus". "Every individual by virtue of his eternal destination is at the core somewhat holy and indestructible."[18] It is true that the divine law of human equality had no secular intentions — only the soul was free. But the idea contained a psychological dynamic which had to complete itself in spite of the theory of original sin; this has been formulated by Professor Barker in this way: "If the slave can be treated as a man in any respect, he ought to be treated as a man in all; and the admission, that he can be regarded as a man, destroys that conception of his wholly slavish and non-rational (one might say non-human) character, which was the justification of his being treated as a slave".[19] This is practically our fourth thesis: the recognition of freedom and equality in one sphere leads to the postulate of freedom and equality in others.

The divergence of natural from positive law — of natural law from the social order — occurred when the social substructure was no longer closed, no longer undisturbed, and appeared no longer negative in its function. The conflict between domination and norm, between will and *ratio*, was often not only a theoretical possibility, but a social reality.

The relation of the secular power to the Church and the justification of the secular power at all, became problematical on the basis of the social and political teachings of the New Testament in the new situation. The manifold possibilities of interpretation of the New Testament are well-known: "Let every soul be in subjection to the higher powers, for there is no power but of God; and the powers that be are ordained by God. Therefore, he that resisteth the power withstandeth the ordinance of God" (Romans, 13.1–7). But this statement calling for obedience to the secular power is opposed to other statements such as: "Render unto Caesar the things that are Caesar's": or that commanding more obedience to God than is given to Caesar. All constitute the word of God, which admit of varying interpretations according to the political situation. Fritz Kern,[20] in his fine work on Dante, has expounded the problem in this way: "Is the task of a Christian social theory of forming a community of free individual souls at all possible? Does not the liberty of the individual, itself its own aim, exclude the possibility of subordination under a communal organisation?"

3.3.2.

Not only the inner dynamics of the originally conservative Christian teachings and of the non-secular postulate of equality, but also the interests of the Church itself tend in the same direction. The problem of revolution against the secular power becomes a political problem for the Church as soon as the emperors themselves adopt the Christian faith. The Church then determines not only to recognise the right of resistance, but even the duty of resistance, against heretics and pagans.[21] Further, the Church recognises the right of resistance against such emperors as are neither heretics nor pagans, but who refuse to submit to the will of the Pope. For God, "i.e. the undisputed agent of God's rule",[22] is the sovereign to whom the secular power is subject: subject not because of might, but because, as has been laid down by Boniface VIII in his *Deliberatio*, it is its mission to fulfil God's law, for the liberation of the human soul.

A competing power, however, stood opposed to this claim to supremacy. Society was always conceived and postulated to be a unitarian one.[23] It stands, as we learned from the Thomist philosophy, under one *lex aeterna*. And a unity of execution of the law corresponds to the unity of the law itself (Boniface VIII). The factual superiority of the papal power over the secular[24] had as its consequences that at first the Church society absorbed the secular one.[25] Already under Gregory VII *sacerdocium* and *imperium* were joined hand in hand. The pope held both swords. Under Innocent III, finally, the *plenitudo potestatis* had developed into sovereignty. The claim to sovereignty is deduced from the postulate of the rule of the divine law, which is issued from God himself. For the Church, the king who governs unjustly ceases to be king. *Rex* and *rectum* are indivisible.[26] But who is to decide in each case whether a ruler shall forfeit his power? And what legal consequences follow upon such a forfeiture? The Church, transcending the formless right of resistance, organises the right of resistance and provides for punishments, ranging in severity from voluntary penance to declaratory deposition. These clerical punishments are later operated in the secular sphere.[27] The influence of the conflict around the postulate of a sphere of freedom is a dual one, in which in every phase (from the investiture struggle to Innocent III, and from Marsilius of Padua to the Monarchomachs) the postulate of a natural law guaranteed liberty is put forward by the rising, aggressive institutions.

In the first phase, therefore, the Church determines to carry through its supremacy and its postulate of a sphere of freedom from the secular power as against the already established feudal system. In this period the Church recognised an extraordinarily far-reaching right of resistance, going sometimes even as far as anarchism and fighting, especially in the investiture struggle.[28] Thus, natural law was retained by the Church even after it had achieved its aim. The very attainment of its aim changed the function of this natural law from a revolutionary into a conservative one. It now became conservative, and was faced with two opposing forces: an extra-clerical and an intra-clerical one, both of which were not interested primarily in the liberty of the individual from the state and in the postulate of democratic rights of individuals within the state, but were incidentally forced to support such postulates.

In so far as the sovereignty of the state as against that of the Church was not simply alleged as a *datum* of the divine plan of the world (as in Dante) it was justified by the reduction of the will of the state to the wills of the individuals composing it, the realisation of which came forward as a new value to smash the medieval system of values. The theorists in this category belong almost without exception to the nominalistic party of the Scholastics, especially William of Ockham and Marsilius of Padua. The conflict of the nominalists with the Church is accompanied by the beginnings of the breaking free of secular natural law from the established divine one, which, after having shown its flexibility for a long time, had now reached its limits. Natural law and positive law which coincided in the philosophy of Aquinas, stand unrelated in the nominalist philosophy.[29] The process of dissolution of the feudal order had already reached such a stage that the obvious assertion of the coincidence of natural and positive law, or of material and political law, could be no longer accepted. In the nominalistic philosophy the belief in the existence of a natural law is well maintained, but the political law is emancipated from it. The law becomes a conscious invention, the creation of the whole of human society, and nothing else. The naturality of the feudal hierarchical order can no longer be justified. One way to its negation is opened out by the separation of political from natural law.

3.3.3.

As we are not concerned with the history of ideas we deal now exclusively with a short presentation of those elements of the system of Marsilius of Padua which are relevant to our investigation.[30]

Marsilius of Padua postulates first a certain distribution of spheres between the Church and the State. Here the object of the Church is the morality of the conscience, while that of the state is morality of deed. He declares society to be unitarian, but the Church is incorporated in it and subordinated to it. The postulates of Gregory or Innocent III and of Boniface VIII are, therefore, simply reversed. And in so far as Marsilius fights the exercise of the *vis coactiva* by the Church, he is in full agreement with nearly all Nominalists and with Dante.

The sphere of state sovereignty as defined in this way is now justified by two different arguments.

In the first place he subordinates the secular power to material law — i.e. to natural law (material justification). The legislator, electing the *pars principans* (*Dict.* I.XIV) stands himself under its domination. By this, law becomes a dual command: on the one hand the command of the sovereign, the machinery of coercion (*Dict.* I. X) which can differ as to content from the divine law; and on the other hand law is the science of the just — i.e. a natural law, an eternal and unchanging character standing above the state and limiting it. This natural law is only to a small extent concretised, but it is nevertheless sufficiently institutionalised by giving the courts the power to depose the monarch (*Dict.* I.XV.XVI). By this the right of liberty of the state against the Church is partially based on a right of liberty of the subject against the state.

The sphere of sovereignty of the state against the Church is at the same time based on the liberty of the people within the state, and on the recognition of democratic rights of the people. The usual presentation of Marsilius of Padua's theory is that "with democratic radicalism"[31] he opposed the *universitas civium* to the *pars principans*. Sovereign being, according to such a presentation, the people as legislator (and he understood by "people" all enfranchised citizens), this right of the people to sovereignty is inalienable. The substance of the legislative power lay always with the people or its elected representatives. The will of the state is the will of the people. The legislation institutes a monarch; it binds him; it corrects him; and it deposes him if necessary.

If such an interpretation were right we would have to count Marsilius of Padua as a modern radical democrat. That this is not the case has been convincingly shown by Charles McIlwain. It is true that in the system of Marsilius every form of government is supposed to be created by the legislator, and the best form of government is the constitutional monarchy, under the rule of material law, working for the common good of the community. But who is the legislator? The answer is given by *Dict.* I.XII. Does this chapter contain the recognition of the modern principle of majority rule? Undoubtedly not; for the following statement appears: "I call it *valentiorem partem* having in mind the number and the quality of the citizens".[32] An evaluation of the citizens according to their qualities openly contradicts the democratic majority principle. His Achilles heel, as in so many other theories, even up to the French Revolution and modern Fascism, lies in his definition of "people". "People" is not the modern people of legally and politically free citizens; it is, on the contrary, the *pars valentior* of the Middle Ages.

"People" is therefore a thoroughly anti-democratic concept. It is concerned with the totality of all those groups which, according to the medieval conception, are entitled to represent the genuine people. The anti-democratic character of the system obviously does not exclude its revolutionary dynamic.

We repeat that in the system of Marsilius every command of the state is justified in a dual way: genetically by its origin in the will of the people; materially by its contents — from Natural Law.

3.3.4.

The second attack against natural law, now transformed from a liberal into a conservative factor, and against the Church, arose from the Conciliar Theory. The defeat of the Conciliar Theory influenced the fate of the modern state and its relations with material law in two ways. The attack of the theorists of the Conciliar movement prevented the medieval ideas of natural law and the idea of people's sovereignty from falling into oblivion. The writings of Gerson and of Nicholas of Cusa exercised a far-reaching influence. The victory of Papal sovereignty against the Conciliar Theory paved the way, on the other hand, for modern absolutism, and hereby for the modern centralised state. The political history lying at the roots of the Conciliar Theory, viz: the Babylonian imprisonment of the Church from 1309–76, and the Great Schism — are assumed to be well-known. It is also well-known that this development of the Conciliar Theory arose from the claims of competing Popes for universal domination (with all its consequences, and based on the justification given by Gregory VII in his *Dictatus Papae*) and that Papal absolutism had necessarily to be victorious as soon as the Babylonian imprisonment came to an end and the Great Schism was healed.

Figgis[33] rightly observed that the decree issued by the Council of Constance in 1415, at the suggestion of Gerson, is a revolutionary document of the greatest consequence: "Concilium generale faciens et ecclesiam catholicam representans potestatem a Christo immediate habet, cui quilibet cuiuscunque status vel dignitatis, etiamsi papalis existat, obedire tenetur in his quae pertinent ad fidem".[34] The most accomplished formulation is undoubtedly to be found in the work of Nicholas of Cusa, *De Concordantia Catholica*. Here the inalienable right of the Christian man to freedom from the interference of the state, and to democratic liberties within the state, is recognised as against the Papal claim to sovereignty: "Cum natura omnes sint liberi, tum omnis principatus . . . et a sola concordantia et consensum subjecto" (II.13.). It follows from this recognition of natural law that all constitutions of human society have their roots in natural law — "Omnes constitutio radiatur in jure naturale; et si ei contradicit, constitutio valida esse nequit" (II.14.) — and they are void if they contradict this natural law. It further follows in applying the principles to clerical society that the Papal claim to sovereignty cannot be justified: "Papa non est universalus Episcopus sed super alius primus et sacrorum Conciliorum non in Papa sed in consensu omnium vigorem fundamus" (II.13.). That he does not understand by "omnium" the totality of the people of the Church, but only the clerical aristocracy[35] is of no decisive importance for us, for we are discussing only the immanent revolutionary force of his teachings. The significance of Nicholas of Cusa can hardly be overestimated. Whether it is right to call him the last representative of Thomism, the last great medieval thinker,[36] would appear to be extremely doubtful. The decisive characteristic of the Thomist system, the assertion of the coincidence of natural moral law and the legal order, is in reality completely lacking. Such an assertion would not have been feasible for Nicholas of Cusa; feudal society in his time was already disintegrating. It appears to us to be much more correct to say[37] that in his system justice and the political order are completely divorced. The emphasis laid on individual liberty and on democratic rights within the Church, leads to a sharp differentiation in his work between natural law containing the rules of natural occurrences and morality, and the legal order containing normative commands emanating from the wills of men. Thus he is far away from the Thomist system; in fact he belongs, with Marsilius of Padua, to the modern theorists of natural law.

CHAPTER 4

Sovereignty and the Rule of Material Law: The Monarchomachs and English Natural Law

4.1. The Monarchomachs

4.1.1.

The conception of the Divine Right of Kings in the sense of the seventeenth century, i.e., in the sense of royal irresponsibility, was completely alien to Germanic as well as to medieval law.[1] Bracton conceived the king to be God's "vicar and minister on earth".

Germanic and medieval monarchies were conceived to be neither undelegated by origin nor unlimited in practice. In this conception the Church and Germanic Law were unanimous. The king has to determine a law, the contents of which are already materially conditioned. The sole justification of the state is that it is a means for the realisation of the law: "Not the monarchy but the law shall be sovereign." This law which binds the monarch is according to Germanic and Anglo-Saxon tradition customary law.[2] It is conservative, i.e., it essentially protects existing rights. Any interference of the monarch with existing rights is legitimate only with the *consensus fidelium*.[3] This was generally recognised by the monarchs at the coronation (*tria praecepta*) which contained a genuine *promissio*. The German coronation ceremony of the thirteenth century puts the following question to the monarch: "Are you prepared to administer and to defend the Kingdom which is granted to you by God, according to the justice of your fathers? " Only after the monarch had answered this question in the affirmative were the people asked whether they were prepared to submit themselves to his rule. This *promissio*, however, is no contract, i.e., it is not constitutive but declaratory, because it only declares already existing objective law. To this subordination of the monarch to the law, there corresponds not only a right but even a duty of resistance on the part of the people. Injustice on the part of the sovereign can be opposed with force (*Sachsenspiegel*), consequently the right to murder the king is an integral part of Germanic law. The subject does not own obedience but faith. Faith is a mutual relationship involving mutual rights and duties.[4] If the king violates his duty of keeping faith the people are automatically freed from their duty of keeping faith. This idea is formulated thus by Manegold von Lautenbach: "Only a faithful king has faithful subjects."[5] If one was convinced that the monarch had violated the law, one fought for the monarchy against the monarch. The frequency of medieval revolts, especially in the classical country of revolts, in Saxony between 1060 and 1070, bears out the radicalism of this right of resistance. The Church in its Canonic Law, has, as we have already shown, formalised and organised the formless right of resistance by creating punishments later adopted in the secular sphere.[6]

4.1.2.

But who is entitled to exercise this right of resistance? In order to answer this question it is necessary to refer back to the tradition of Roman law which gave birth to the idea of people's sovereignty, that deadly foe of monarchical absolutism.[7] Manegold von Lautenbach in his *Liber ad Gebehardum* (1083–5) already put forward the theory of people's sovereignty, and postulated the *lex regia* as a contract in which the people appear as master, and the king as servant.[8] For Lupold von Bebenburg[9] the electors were the representatives of the people. They acted for the *universitas ipsa voce et suctoritate*, and are entitled to depose the sovereign.

This theory of people's sovereignty does not, however, stop at the issue of means of repression against wrong-doing, but rather develops preventive means against the commission of such wrong-doing as well; this was especially so in the period of "estates", as is shown by the German law books . The famous example is the judgment against John Lackland in 1202. A special formulation of this idea of the initiation of preventive measures is to be found in the Magna

Charta. It is not decisive in this case that the king himself is bound to the fulfilment of certain aims, and that the right of resistance is recognised as a sort of potential punishment for the king; the characteristic feature is not so much either that the barons are entitled to use force to make the king complete the specified aims; rather is it that the barons are constituted as a permanent organ which has to supervise the performance of the king's duties, and if necessary, to enforce them compulsorily.[10] This, however, is not yet a recognition of the right of *con dominium* of the estates. This new agency did not function, in its place the estates developed and the controlling function of the new organ was transferred to the *con dominium* of the estates. It could not function because, as in every case of control of one state organ by another one, the question at once arose — who controls the controllers? *Quis custodiet ipsos custodes*?[11]

To this development there corresponded a development from the postulate of a responsible secular power to the demand for political rights within the state: i.e., to the postulate of the realisation of people's sovereignty. The claim for domination of the estates is justified with the aid of the technical legal category of the contract. Natural Law, or whatever name one gives the theory, has only secondary functions. This can be shown in French as well as in English legal history. When Laski[12] declares: "For once it is clear that the Prince holds his power upon conditions, it becomes necessary to discover the means through which those conditions may be enforced"; the means justified by natural law for the fulfilment of these conditions become decisive. The *thema probandum* of natural law is generally not a *limitation* of the power of the state, but only the determination of a certain trend and content of its activity. A certain group demands either exclusive control or, [at the least], *con dominium* in the control of the state power. The various systems of natural law are only ideologies of justification which are given up as soon as the postulated political aims are attained. Political democracy — i.e., the integration of the will of the state through the free election of representatives, and the majority principle — and natural law institutionalised by the right of resistance, are two contradictory principles. Natural law disappears. When in a democratic era, natural law has a so-called renaissance, it has nearly always a reactionary end in view — viz., the limitation of the will of the people in so far as it becomes dangerous to the property system.

This thesis, which can only be justified by a social history of natural law, can only be very shortly dealt with here. Its correctness is shown by the instance of the theory of the monarchomachs. Here it can be proved that it was never a question of carrying out the rule of material law, but of carrying out certain political demands.[13]

4.1.3.

The theory of the monarchomachs is undoubtedly rooted in the teachings of Calvin, who has made no original contribution to the theory of state and law. Calvin's theory is not only important in so far as he denies the right of resistance and postulates obedience to the state; it also bears out his statement (1559, *Institutio religionis*) that if there are in a state organs of the people for the limitation of the power of the prince, these organs have not only the right, but even the duty of opposing any excess of the sovereign power. Such organs are, in his view, the estates; and he declares: "Comme sont possible, aujourd'hui en chacun royaume les trois estats, quand ils sont assemblez" (*Institution Chrestienne*, IV, chap. XX, p. 31). This theory of Calvin contains nothing new. It is nothing but the presentation of the positive constitutional law; but just because of his legal realism, his teachings could become the basis of the monarchomachical theory.

The pamphlets of the Huguenots up to the [time of] St Bartholomew's Night, are a clear expression of this constitutionalism, distinguished by an equally strong dislike of absolutism and of anarchism. This constitutional theory is based mainly on French legal history. It is never asserted that one is prepared to fight against the king; it is always alleged that one would fight for him in order to guard him from bad counsel and to protect the throne from the claims of the Pope.

As against this Huguenot theory, the Catholic Front postulated absolute obedience even to heretics.

A change occurs after the Edict of Lonjumeau, which hurt Catholic pride (deposition of the Chancellor Michel de l'Hospital, 1568), and the Catholic Front becomes radicalised. It demands the extermination of the heretics, while the Huguenot Front remains constant until the Night of St Bartholomew destroyed its belief in absolutism and led to a radicalism most clearly expressed by De Mornay: "L'Etat s'est ebranlé depuis la journée de St. Barthélémy, depuis dis-je que la foi du Prince envers le sujet et du sujet envers le Prince, què est le seul ciment qui entretient les états en un, s'est si outrageusement démentie".

In Hotman's *Franco Gallica* (1573), the contents of natural law are very small. He tries to prove that historically the prince's power was always limited by the estates, and he does it on the basis of comparative legal investigations. The result is Calvin — positive law grants the right of resistance to the estates as the representatives of the people. As little "natural-rightly"[14] is Buchanan's *De iure regni apud scotos*; the decisive fact in his work is that he renders Scottish law absolute. The merit of his work is the introduction of the Germanic conception that the ascent to the throne is a genuine contract without regard to whether the monarch is hereditary or elected.

The Night of St Bartholomew made a considerably deeper impression on the author of *Vindicia contra Tyrannos*. Here inductive historical facts stand beside deductive natural law arguments. The positivist exposition of the relation subject and authority, with its denial of the right of individual resistance and its recognition of the right for the magistrate and the optimate, is historically in the same category as that of Hotman. Just as Hotman he introduces comparative legal investigations in order to show that the right of resistance of the estates is an empirical principle and general for all times. But for the first time he transcends Hotman and introduces genuine postulates belonging to natural law: viz. when all *optimas*, or only some of them, exercise tyranny, the right of resistance is transferred automatically to the people. The way in which he argues is interesting. It is decisive that he does in fact base the right of revolution on two arguments to be found in the theory of Marsilius of Padua: genetically by the fact the king appears as the delegate of the people, and materially by the fact that he is bound by natural law. But it is worth while mentioning that the genetical justification has a partially reactionary character:[15] "Though the sovereignty of the people is admitted, nay insisted on, the sovereignty of the majority is tacitly denied, where it might endanger the supposed interest and liberty of a part".

We can sum up by saying that the writings of the Protestant monarchomachs corresponding to their Calvinist origins, show a remarkably small amount of Natural Law apart from du Plessis Mornay, who, however, lived in the free air of the Netherlands. The centre of gravity lies in the working out of the principles of positive law which recognise the right of resistance of the estates.

In 1584, finally, there occurred a last change. With the death of Anjou the Hugenots become conservative. The real power goes over to the *Ligue*, which carries out radically the old theories of the Huguenots.

Boucher, *De iusta Henrici tertii abdicatione e Francorum regno, libir quatuor* (1589), justified in a natural-rightly way the right of deposition of the tyrant. But even he understood by the people entitled to depose him only the estates; and he approached the constitutionalism of the Huguenots again in his attempt to base his theory on historical investigations going back (and rightly) even as far as feudal law.

Rossaeus, *De iusta rei publica christianae in reges impios et haereticos auctoritatae*(1590), takes the *via media* by generalising the principles of positive constitutional law. In the centre of his investigations he puts the duty of the monarch to state and law. From the difference between the state and its highest organ, and the superiority of the ends of the state as against those of the monarch, he deduces the right to depose the heretic monarch, or the summoning of the citizens to refuse to obey him.

Mariana (*Joannis Marianiae Hispani e Societate Jesu de rege et regis institutionae*, III), the famous Spanish Jesuit, worked out a genuine system of natural law; but this construction of natural law only hides his sole aim: viz. to break the power of the heretic monarchs. He also starts from the positive constitutional law, giving the estates the right of deposition; but, just as the work of de Mornay does, he transcends positive law and grants the right of revolution also in the case when a *publici conventus* is impossible. But even in this case, the individual has no right to revolt; he creates a substitute for the meeting of the estates — viz. an emergency meeting of the "men of public standing". We may sum up by saying that the monarchomachical right of resistance is far more justified by positive than by natural law, and therefore is a direct continuation of the corresponding Germanic legal institutions.

Only the actual contents of state activity were of importance for the monarchomachs. The postulate of democratic freedom was equally alien alike to the Protestants and to the Catholics. Charles Labitte was therefore able to say: "La démocratie calvinisme et la démocratie catholique ont donc été une fiction".[16] And this very fact of complete disinterestedness in the basic problems of liberty and democracy has to a large extent contributed to the strengthening of French absolutism. The right of the estates to resistance as an element of positive constitutional law has, in consequence disappeared; it disappeared as soon as the estates were granted *con dominium* by the constitution. With the rise of monarchical absolutism in the seventeenth and eighteenth centuries, the right of resistance arose afresh in the theories of Althusius, Grotius and Locke. Now, however, the importance of the Natural Law ideology became visible, with the same significance in the works of De Mornay and Mariana.

4.2. English Natural Law[17]

4.2.1.

Natural law plays as small a rôle in England. The influence of Roman and Canonic law in medieval England is still a much disputed question. We can assume as probable that their influence was stronger than is usually expected. Investigations such as those by Charles McIlwain and C. G. Haines, in which traces of natural law can be found, seem to us insufficiently formulated; firstly because the subject of the rule of natural law is too broad, and secondly because the relations of natural law to social interests are not sufficiently taken into consideration. We have stressed very often that we understand by natural law a system of norms which is not identical with those rules or norms created by the state, but which is supposed to correct, limit and modify this positive law. We therefore are not able to state with Pollock and Haines[18] that the existence of legal standards of conduct such as "reasonable", or "reasonableness", any more than the existence of equity, necessarily involves the rule of Natural Law. For these norms are not natural law in the sense defined by us above, because the concepts of "reasonableness" and the question of equity are not used for the correction and limitation of the will of the state when that will is clearly and unambiguously expressed. The positive significance of the legal standards of conduct and of equity will be dealt with exhaustively later on. It cannot be doubted that the terminology of the legal standards of conduct, as of the equity principle, has been influenced by Natural Law.[19] They themselves, however, belong exclusively to the sphere of positive law. Only in the case of a court which has expressed its view that an Act of Parliament should be declared void, because it is in contradiction with the principles of "reasonableness" or of public policy or of equity, can we speak of the rule of natural law. But such circumstances have not existed since Bonham's case.

Secondly, in analysing a system of natural law we have to put the question: have political groups used arguments derived from natural law in their attacks on existing power positions, and how have they behaved with regard to Natural Law after their ends have been achieved?

4.2.2.

In the Middle Ages in England, as well as on the Continent, the thesis of the illimitability of the monarchical power was unknown. The monarch was supposed to be bound by customary law.[20] In England as on the Continent, law in feudal times was not enactment but records. The judges' decisions were taken on the basis of custom. The conception of the creation of law as the free deed of man was equally unknown. England and the Continent were alike ruled by this conservative customary law. It was class law directed towards the maintenance of privileges. With this mental unity of law and ethics, customary law had taken on the character of a natural law standing above the king, who dared not violate it. The decisive question, however, is: who is to decide whether this customary law has been violated by the king? And the significance of the Magna Charta in its time does not lie in the recognition of natural law but, as we have already shown, in the creation of a permanent organisation with the function of deciding whether the monarch has fulfilled his obligations. But since that time the political struggle in England has been concentrated in the question of the political *con dominium* of the estates and as soon as this *con dominium* had been realised, natural law disappeared in England. The positive law grants sufficient rights to the estates as against the monarch, and the need for it no longer exists. Only in the seventeenth century, when the rising bourgeoisie had not yet succeeded in winning those political rights for itself, did natural law begin to play a new rôle. In the revolutionary wars it is used by the different groups each for their own conflicting purposes. It was used and dispensed with according to the needs of the moment, just as in the struggles of the monarchomachs theories were changed like shirts. Natural law had no independent significance in those struggles and eventually disappeared from the English scene. Sovereignty of Parliament had been established in the revolutionary wars and it seemed no longer necessary. It is to be noted, however, that this disappearance did not imply that the conception of natural law was never to be revived usefully in the future.

4.2.3.

The best-known case is that of Bonham.[21] Professor Plucknett has, however, clearly shown it to be an isolated one, and the precedents used by Coke to be quite incorrect. I therefore do not think too much can be deduced from it as to the existence of the rule of natural law. The political character of the conflict between Coke and James I is so clear that further discussion of it would be superfluous. It seems inadmissible to maintain on the basis of Coke's witness that natural law played any decisive rôle in legal practice; for Coke was similar in this to Cicero — a pure advocate: "He approached both history and law with the mind of a strenuous advocate. All through his life he never ceased to be an advocate of legal doctrines and political causes".[22] Our theory becomes extremely clear with the instance of the struggle of the revolutionary parties; so clear, that McIlwain himself has to admit the relative character of natural law in this period. He himself proves that natural law was a double-edged weapon.[23]

In Prynne's pamphlet, sovereign power of Parliament,[24] the subject of natural law, and the theory of people's sovereignty are combined. Selden on the other hand, (*Table Talk*, "Law of Nature" and "King") rejects any theory of a natural law guaranteeing liberties; i.e. any theory of the rights of man. But in his political practice, as for instance in the aforementioned case of the five knights, or in Hampden's case, he is compelled to have recourse to natural law. For the "law of the land", the supremacy of which he asserts, is a law distinct from positive law, a historically superseded law which has become in his view absolute. In consequence of his opposition he therefore applied the Natural Law ideology in spite of his theoretical denial of the rights of man.

Similar to the theoretical antagonism between Prynne and Selden is that within the Levellers. Lilburne is at the same time a liberal and a democrat. He postulates Natural Law and sovereignty of the people both at once. In his theory of Natural Law, which appears to his opponents to be a total abrogation of the law, he asks for free trade and the abolition of monopolies and privileges. He stood in opposition to Cromwell, and saw in a system of natural law, not only a limitation of the power of the monarchy, but also an infringement of the authority of parliament. In *The Legall Fundamentall Liberty of the People of England*, he asserts the nullity of acts containing a prolongation of parliament; he bases his proof on Bonham's case. Ireton on the other hand (*Heads of the Proposals*), denied the theory of Natural law because he could see no way of building a state on the basis of such an anarchical theory. But in his comprehensive statement, *The sole foundation of rights is the law of the land*, Natural Law reappears in just the same way as in Selden.

In the writings of the Communalists (John Hare, Hartleb, Chamberlen and Winstanley), a radical natural law ideology is introduced and pursued to its logical conclusion of communalism, especially when, after the abolition of the monarchy, bad harvests, high prices and unstable wages had worsened the position of the people considerably. The principle of natural equality stands in the centre of their propaganda.

Cromwell himself, in his well-known way, takes the *via media*. Theoretically he was an adherent of natural law, as is demonstrated in his often-quoted speech of 9th November 1564, where he declares himself for "a fundamental law, somewhat like a magna carta [*sic*]". He does not realise, however, in practice, this idea of natural law; to him the creation of an efficient sovereign power was far more important.

It is well-known also that natural law was in addition to this a weapon in the hands of the Royalists, who considered it to be a security for the King.

4.2.4.

With the stabilisation of the supremacy of Parliament, natural law definitely ceases to play a rôle in England. Even at the time of Henry VIII, the legislative character of the Acts of Parliament could not be denied: the duty of judges to obey these Acts was uncontestable.[25] Even in the sixteenth century, therefore, the current formula of the supremacy of the law does not in any way mean the supremacy of natural law (of a material law), but exclusively the supremacy of a law created by parliament, a political law. And the premature death of natural law in England, after an ailing life, is due to just this early development of Parliamentarism. English Natural Law occupied a purely secondary position, as is clearly demonstrated by English legal and constitutional history.

It is obvious, however, that the identification of the supremacy of law with the supremacy of parliament in no way excludes the fact that in England certain postulates were maintained with regard to the formal structure and contents of law. There was a very clear conception of the content and structure of law, even if it very often remained unexpressed. We mention this point now in order to return to it later in greater detail. On the Continent as well as in England, since the establishment of the sovereignty of the law in the seventeenth century, "law" has always been understood to mean a general rule issued by Parliament. Natural law is authority by positive general rule. The premature death of natural law, guaranteeing liberties on the basis of the fundamental idea of people's sovereignty, has in fact however, paradoxically enough, contributed to the realisation of those very liberties contained in the natural law ideology. Whereas in Germany the bourgeoisie left the guarantee of its liberties to a pseudo-domination of the law and the courts (*Rechtsstaatsidee*), in England the political struggle in and around Parliament could guard those liberties far better than could the courts and the bureaucracy.[26]

CHAPTER 5

Bodin and Althusius

5.1. Bodin

The antagonism between absolute sovereignty and the rule of material law is very clearly expounded in the works of Bodin.[1] The constitution of both spheres — of sovereignty and of liberty guaranteed by material law — stands side by side in his work because he does not demarcate one from the other.

5.1.1.

Sovereignty is the absolute and perpetual power of the commonwealth which the Romans called *maiestas*.[2]

Sovereignty is the sovereignty of the prince. The state is not yet distinguished from its highest organ, and therefore the question of the highest power of the state is not yet separated from that of the highest power within the state, with very few exceptions.

The absoluteness of the sovereignty implies firstly, the non-existence of a right of resistance; whereas in the theory of the monarchomachs the magistrates were entitled to call upon the troops to fight the illegitimate exercise of state power, Bodin denies the officials this right (III.IV), and they may never forget that their power derives solely from the prince. The absoluteness of the sovereignty implies secondly, the conception of political law. Law is only *voluntas* and not necessarily *ratio*. Every command of the absolute sovereign is law. The sovereign can issue general norms as well as individual commands. The prince can free himself by law from obligations which he himself had undertaken to fulfil earlier in his career; for the prince is the creator and not the subject of positive law.[3] Customary law also derives its validity from the command of the prince standing behind it — its validity from permanent exercise is denied in the same way as in the theories of Hobbes, Filmer and, later, Kelsen (I.X).

From the sovereignty of the prince it follows that all feudal power is derived necessarily from this very sovereignty. It is therefore an original power. In particular, feudal jurisdiction is the outcome of sovereignty and not of feudal domination. (V.II; III.V.) Consequently, the estates general stand under the sovereign prince. They may remonstrate, but they may not oppose the sovereign. In spite of his legal radicalism, however, Bodin does not disturb the factual distribution of power between prince and feudal organisation.

This theory of sovereignty is characterised by two features: it lacks firstly a justification. It is true, as will be shown, that divine and secular natural law stand above sovereignty, but they do not justify it; they merely restrict it, as will be also shown in 5.1.3. Even after the elimination of references to God and to the prince as "God's deputy on earth" from his whole theory of sovereignty, the main content of his system remains unchanged.[4] He intended rather to assert an analogy between the order of nature and the order of society as the basis for justification of his theory of sovereignty. To him nature appeared to be the sum of the relations of super- and sub-ordination — in short, nature was essentially a hierarchy. Political society was to be composed in the same way. But an analogy is never a proof, quite apart from the question of whether it can rightly be maintained.[5]

5.1.2.

On the other hand, sovereignty is not asserted to be an absolute power in all relevant parts of his work. It is limited, at least partially, by the postulate of the rule of the material law, and sometimes even considerably limited. The state was to be a "droit gouvernement".[6] This, however, is a rule of material law. In this connection law is not only *voluntas*, but also *ratio*.

He at first postulates the principle and then proceeds to concretise it.

The aim of the law is justice. Law is the creation of the prince. The prince is the image of God, so human law created by him must necessarily be the image of divine law.[7] According to his second theory, and in contradiction to the first theory, divine and human natural law stand above the prince, who is bound by it and may not act contrary to it; his might does not therefore extend over divine and natural law.[8] This introduction of the idea of right implies a polemical attitude towards Machiavelli; for France, according to the contemporaries of Bodin, was governed "à l'italienne ou à la Florentine".[9] It is doubtful whether Catherine of Medici [had] actually read Machiavelli before the Night of St Bartholomew [in] 1572. Against the all-pervasive influence of Machiavelli Bodin intends to build the state on the idea of right and to limit it by this conception. In the preface to his book Bodin voluntarily attacks: "Macchiavell n'a jamais sondé le gué de la science politique qui ne gist pas en ruses tyranniques". It is, of course, obvious that the external influence of the Machiavellian utilitarianism is apparent on nearly every page of Bodin's work. This principle of the rule of natural law is concretised in three ways.

The basis and essence of the state is the family.[10] The family is "la vraye source et origine de toute République et membre principale d'icelle" (I.II). No state can be called well-administered which is not constructed on the basis of the family.[11] In the constitution of the family he sees reproduced the two characteristic elements of the state: *droit gouvernement*, forbidding the enslavement of the wife and children, and the *patria potestas*, which is considered to be a kind of natural sovereignty. The state is composed of the individual "mesnages".

The recognition of this rôle of the family implies for him the recognition of property, for the family is based on property. Every kind of communistic egalitarianism is completely alien to him. Only the inequality of man can correspond to human nature. The abolition of "mine and thine" ruins the fundamental basis of the state.[12] The sovereign therefore is not able to steal, for he may not transgress the limits which are put upon him by natural law. Only "with just cause" may the sovereign deprive a person of his property — i.e., either by sale or exchange, or by legal taxation, or as reparation against enemies.[13] The protection of property implies the inadmissibility of the levying of taxes without the consent of the people — i.e., of the estates general.[14] Although on the one hand, as we have already mentioned, he denies that the estates general participate in the sovereignty, and in spite of the fact that he subordinates them legally to the prince, he concedes them the right of consent to taxation. Allen, however,[15] rightly denies that from the recognition of this right there must necessarily be implied the acceptance of the theory of people's sovereignty. The two have nothing in common. The prohibition of levying taxes without the consent of the estates general is exclusively an element of the sphere of family liberty, and therefore of private property. The possessing family is an element of the state which may not be touched by the sovereign.

Whereas he, on the one hand [and] as we have mentioned, takes the view that the sovereign is not bound by positive law even in the case of the positive law being good and reasonable,[16] he on the other hand maintains that the prince is bound by his own promises against other princes as well as against his subjects.[17] This obligation to observe contracts follows from the natural equality and from the "foy du prince".[18]

Only the prince who keeps himself within those limits and who esteems divine natural law, who above all does not destroy the family, who does not lay illegal commands upon the property of his subjects, and who does not break his promises, can be termed "roy"; he who does not fulfil these conditions is a tyrant *ex exercitio.*[19] Bodin also recognises in addition to this the tyrant *absque titulo.*[20] As for the family, property and the obligation to fulfil contracts, it is a case of a sphere which belongs to private law and which aims at the constitution of a sphere of freedom from the sovereign power. Bodin also thinks it possible to limit sovereignty by constitutional laws: for instance, by the *legis imperii*, relating to the state and implied in sovereignty.[21] In the case of France he recognises as such limitations the *lex salica* and the prohibition of the sale of state territory; the land belongs to the state — to the republic (VI.II.).[22]

5.1.3.

According to our definition, we can only say that in Bodin's theory the rule of material law is instituted because he concedes to natural law the expectation that it will be carried out even if positive law is antagonistic to its fulfilment. Such an expectation can, as we have shown, be created by the positivisation or institutionalisation of the norms of natural law; this can be achieved either by the recognition of, for example, the right of resistance or, when such a degree of institutionalisation is unattainable, by sufficient concretisation of the norms of natural law. If this is not done, the declaration of the rule of natural law becomes mere lip service paid in the attempt to cover the actual absolute sovereignty of the prince.

Bodin fundamentally denies the right of resistance; but only the active right. He admits in certain ways the existence of a passive right of resistance. The official has to carry out even such commands of the sovereign as violate the norms of natural law, except in the case of those commands involving the infringement of divine natural law. But even in this case the magistrate is only allowed the refusal to obey and has no such right, as in the theory of the monarchomachs, to call upon the troops and to organise resistance with a view to deposing the prince. The same applies to the subjects in their relationship with the magistrates. (III.IV; III.V) Bodin, however is not logical in his working out of the problem, for obviously there arises at once the question: What ought to be done with those magistrates and citizens who appeal to divine natural law in order to justify their passive resistance if the prince demands their punishment?

Bodin has no answer to the question; he has not even seen the problem[23] Bodin therefore gives no room for an adequate institutionalisation of natural law. By the fact that he denies the active right of resistance, that he concedes a passive right for extreme cases, but does not guarantee it by the assurance of freedom from punishment, he has delimited himself from the monarchomachs.

On the other hand, however, we have to admit that the norms of Natural Law are concretised in his work. Family, property, prohibition of levying taxes without consent of the estates general, the recognition of the principle that contracts have to be fulfilled, the recognition of constitutional laws binding the sovereign, all these are undoubtedly adequate concretisations of his rules of natural law.

5.1.4.

Which social function applies to this system of natural law in its relation with the notion of sovereignty? The answer to this question can only be given by treatment of the system on the basis of a sociology of knowledge.

Politically, Bodin belongs to the middle group of the "politicians". He is therefore socially part of the bourgeoisie. The dual face of the theory corresponds to the dual interest of this stratum of society to which he belonged: on the one hand they were interested to establish the strongest coercive state power possible, and on the other hand to canalise the exercise of this coercive power in the direction of their own interests. The emphasis in Bodin's theory is laid on sovereignty; this corresponds to the desire to establish a strong coercive state power; and the current incomplate interpretation of the theory of the state put forward by him bears out the importance of this task. It was essential if the suicidal civil war was to be ended: "To the *Politiques*, the Divine Right of Kings was rather the natural right of the State, it expressed the refusal to ruin the State for the sake of religious questions".[24] The subordination of secular to religious matters was attacked by him, as also by Michel de l'Hôpital — and even more strongly as Bodin rejected all kinds of religious dogmas whether Calvinist, Reformed, Mohammedan or Jesuit. He condemned atheism, it is true, but he was the adherent of a natural religion.[25]

The demand for a strong coercive power of the state could no longer be divinely justified, but only immanently. There were two reasons for this: the idea of the Divine Right of Kings had broken down under the onslaught of the monarchomachs and had already become anachronistic. Bodin therefore replaced the divine justification by the juridical idea of sovereignty. Further, the state could no longer be adequately justified on the basis of its mere existence — as in the theory of the Divine Right of Kings — but only by its performances. We saw that this immanent justification has taken on only a negative character in Bodin's theory, for he fails to admit any behaviour of the state contrary to Natural Law.

This last limitation of state activity did not only correspond to the necessity of an adequate justification of state power, but also to the interests of the social group to which he belonged — i.e., to the bourgeoisie, which needed a limitation of state power. Bodin has laid down his economic beliefs in a pamphlet published in 1568, *Réponse aux Paradoxes de M. de Malecstroixt.* [26] In this pamphlet he objects to the devaluation of money and emphasises the necessity of free trade; he proves the economic determination of foreign political relations.[27] His struggle against equality and collectivism has already been mentioned, as also has his postulate that sovereignty found its limits in the family and in property, and that the sovereign stood under the obligation to keep his promise.

This last limitation which he erects as against sovereignty shows at the same time that he did not want to disturb the feudal hierarchical structure of the state. If his legal radicalism made him assert the juridical subordination of the estates under the crown, this did not correspond to a similar social and political radicalism. The "contract" in his time and in his work is essentially different from the exchange "contract" of the modern bourgeois society; it is the status contract of the feudal society — the society element by which that society was constituted, and by which every contracting partner has his place allocated in the hierarchy of estates. The keeping of these contracts, therefore, implies the maintenance of the feudal order. The recognition of the estates general as organs of taxation and as a means of voicing public grievances, also serves this dual aim of the bourgeoisie — protection of itself at the same time as of the feudal order.

His theory, therefore, has three aspects: it institutes a strong state which grants order and security, and the activity of which is always in harmony with the interests of the estates, and in particular with the interests of the Third Estate, the bourgeoisie, which still finds its place and its subsistence within the feudal order.

Sovereignty and material law therefore stand side by side, and are thereby opposed. The spheres are nearly equally divided between the two constitutive elements of the modern state. The historical position necessitates emphasis on sovereignty. This system of equilibrium, however, could function in social reality only so long as the interests of the crown and of the estates were identical,[28] and so long as the feudal order itself was not disintegrated.

5.2. Althusius

As against the theory of sovereignty put forward by Bodin, that of Althusius signifies an important advance in a direction which we shall attempt to describe below.[29] The fact that his work was an advance does not, however, conflict with the fact that Althusius refuses to use the conception of sovereignty, and constantly polemises against Bodin. Today it is a mere commonplace that he owes much to Bodin and forms a continuation of his work.[30] We can take it for granted that the politics of Althusius are the outcome of the struggle of the Netherlands and of his social situation as *syndic* of the Calvinist Emden — the outcome of his Calvinist conviction and of the struggle against the Lutheran princes. The intention of his politics was to justify the revolt against Spain, a revolt of not only national but of considerable social significance.[31]

Figgis rightly draws attention to the fact that the secession of the Netherlands created the Althusian theory of sovereignty as well as the natural law system of Grotius. What Figgis does not see, however, is that the dualism of the two systems also corresponds to the dualism of the struggle — to the two sides of the struggle, the national and the social sides. In the War of Liberation of the Netherlands the struggle centred around the secular power of the state as well as around the demand for a sphere of freedom from the state. The detailed presentation [here] of Althusius' theory of the state would appear to be superfluous after the works of Gierke, Wolzendorff and the excellent introduction by Friedrich (which has to be ranked even above Gierke's interpretation: except that but for the work of Gierke it is doubtful whether it would have been possible).

5.2.1.

The starting-point of [Althusius'] theory of the state is the necessity and even the sacredness of the state.[32] Individuals have no free choice whether or not they wish to come under the command of a state. Herein lies the difference with Grotius and with all other liberal contract theorists for whom a free choice is possible.

Althusius, in contrast with the monarchomachs, is opposed to the necessity of the dual rule of prince and estates, and postulates with Bodin the existence of a sole bearer of sovereignty: "the people" instead of the prince. This implies the foundation of the state on a social contract by which the sovereign is primarily determined, and followed by another contract of subjection, by which the people delegate their sovereign power to the various organs of the state.

Althusius is a natural law theorist in the sense that we [have] called Hobbes, Spinoza and Pufendorf natural law theorists. Natural law is here no system of norms the validity of which is left undisturbed by the erection of a state. [It constitutes] a theory of the emergence of the state from a pre-supposed state of nature, the laws of which compare with those of external nature.

Man in the state of nature is not just considered to be a wolf — and in this way Althusius is distinguished from Machiavelli — rather has man to be considered as possessing many virtues, although not the perfection assigned to him by Locke. He stands between the two extremes, with a distinct leaning towards a slightly pessimistic view of his characteristics. The state created by the social contract is the property (*proprietas*) of the people.[33] This state owns the *maiestas*. The *corpus symbioticum* is sovereign. The notion of *maiestas* corresponds to that of sovereignty. To the fore of his definition of sovereignty, however, stands the legal power of the state to issue a constitution; this is similar to our definition of sovereignty.[34] In defining this legal power he carefully evades every use of the notion of sovereignty. The state itself is therefore sovereign. The highest magistrate is only the bearer, the administrator , of sovereignty, the property and the usufruct of which lies with the people.

But who [are] "the people"?[35] Here, as in all other bourgeois theories of the contract, lies the real Achilles heel of the argument. Althusius is in no way a democrat. Democracy for him is no "good" form of government, even if he recognises it to be a possible form. In Althusius' work — as also in Hobbes' work — democratic Caesarism after the example of William of Orange is no longer postulated.[36] The totality of citizens elect *ephors*,[37] which, in his Calvinistic terminology are the officials who in their turn elect the highest magistrates — the *summus magistratus* — and influence the exercise of his power by consultation and advice.[38] The exercise of sovereignty lies entirely with the monarch. A monarchy is the best form of government, even if the substance of sovereignty lies with the people represented by the ephors. The mass of the people, the *plebs* (*vulgus*), [are] only an object of rule, since their role as subjects has ceased. As soon as the highest office of magistrate is instituted the theory is therefore one of an absolute monarchy of democratic origin, implying the extermination of all privileged rights of the estates, and even their exclusion from the formation of the political will.

5.2.2.

In open contradiction to this theory of sovereignty stands Althusius' theory of natural law.

On the one hand *lex* and *jus*, law and right, are identified.[39] Law is *voluntas*, and not necessarily *ratio*. Law is the command of the supreme magistrate after the hearing of the representative assembly.[40] As against the absoluteness of the legislature he only gives certain recommendations such as that the legislature should refrain from exercising its legislative power as far as possible, a recommendation which is common to all natural law theorists, and in which Roscoe Pound[41] sees a specifically puritan element.

On the other hand, however, positive law stands under a material law, a natural law consisting essentially of the last six commandments.[42] This natural law, as in Bodin, is concretised by the rights of the property-owning patriarchal family, joined together in communities, in turn joined together in provinces which finally create the state by contract and institute the supreme magistrate. This natural law is institutionalised by the recognition of a corresponding right of resistance.

The tyrant *absque titulo* is a public enemy, [whom] everyone has the right to drive away. Thus far Althusius follows the tradition of the monarchomachs, but it is decisive that he demands a right of resistance against the tyrant *quod exercitium*, and even defines this right exactly and the conditions under which such a forfeiture of the monarchy takes place.[43] He who applies "absolute power" is a tyrant *quod exercitium*. In this case, however, only the *ephors* have an active right of resistance, the subjects have only a passive right.[44] The *ephors* can banish the tyrant, condemn him to death and behead him.

Because of these natural-rightly elements one can hardly agree to Figgis' characterisation of Althusius theory: "All power is concentrated at a single centre, and every form of right or liberty is of the nature of a privilege, tacitly or expressively granted by the central authority, which may be king, nobles, or people". If Althusius postulated an absolute monarchy in this way, the psychological dynamic of his theory, and of its reception, would appear to drive in a revolutionary direction, because of the original democratic institution of the absolute monarchy. The acceptance of the theory would appear to lead to the implication of a right of the people to withdraw legal power delegated by them to the monarch — the more so as Althusius asserts that the substance of sovereignty remains permanently with the people.

This revolutionary dynamic is further nourished by the elements of natural law which contain not only the usually recognised laws of existence but distinctly moral demands. These come finally to mean a sphere of liberty from the sovereign power of the state, and at the same time the canalisation of the exercise of sovereignty in the desired direction. These remnants of natural law, although only partially concretised in the Althusian system, are nevertheless open to interpretation. In these natural law elements, as in the democratic conception of the origin of sovereignty, lies the continuity of development with the monarchomachical theory, which we saw was almost completely based on positive constitutional law, the importance of which necessarily ceases when the feudal system to which it was attached had come to an end. In putting forward the demands of the monarchomachs, justified not only by means of positive law, but even (although in a contradictory way) with the help of natural law, Althusius paved the way for a revival of natural law ideology after the breakdown of the feudal state and the formation of a centralised absolutist system.[45] The union between democratic ideology (the theory of people's sovereignty) and liberal ideology (natural law theory), forms the ideological basis of the revolutions of the eighteenth and nineteenth centuries, just as the Peasants' Revolt in England in 1381, and in Germany in the Reformation period, drew nourishment from the same sources.

CHAPTER 6

Grotius and Pufendorf

6.1. Hugo Grotius

Grotius offers relatively little to the solution of our problem, as his work is mainly devoted to the discussion of international law.[1]

6.1.1.

The social order, and therefore natural law, is to be directed towards the maintenance of an adequate respect of property, the obligation to fulfil promises, and to pay damages where contracts are violated, and towards the just punishment of guilt. (*Prol.* 9, p. 12). Natural law therefore postulates the maintenance of a particular legal system. The idea of a distributive justice is expressly rejected.[2] Law may not differentiate according to the degree of wisdom, or according to the property and birth of a man. It is exclusively concerned with the maintenance of the existing system of property. The basic principle of natural law is the statement, already valid in the state of nature, that contracts have to be fulfilled. This is almost the "mother of municipal law" (*Prol.* 16, p. 15). Grotius sees, as later also Pufendorf with less clarity, that law needs a machinery of sanctions if it is to be maintained valid (*Prol.* 19, p. 16). Nevertheless he asserts that it is, "not entirely void of effect" (*Prol.* 20, p. 16). This effect consists, as will be shown, in the recognition of a right of resistance.

His natural law is a system of moral norms deduced from, and coinciding with rational nature, but containing commands and prohibitions.[3] His starting-point, as well as his later expositions, show that he perpetually confuses law and morals.[4] This natural law has as its contents not only the regulation of things lying outside the domination of the human will, but it is mainly concerned with the human will itself, and especially with property which itself derives from the will of man, and which once introduced, becomes part of natural law (I.I.X, p. 39). This natural law is unchangeable — even God cannot alter it (I.I.X.5, p. 40).

Human nature is directed towards sociation. Man has a definite "appetitus societatis".

Besides this natural law, there also exists *volitional law*, which is either of human or of divine origin (I.I.XIII, p. 44). The main part of human law is the municipal law, which derives from the civil power. Civil power is that "which bears the sway over the state". "The state is a complete association of free men joined together for the enjoyment of rights and for their common interests" (I.I.XIV, p. 44). In addition to the municipal law there is also law which is not directly constituted by the power of the state, but which is subject to it: the commands of the father over the son, or of the master over the servant, for instance, come under this category.

The sovereign is a power "whose actions are not subject to the legal control of another, so that they cannot be rendered void by the operation of another human will" (I.III.VII, p. 102). Therefore the sovereign can alter his own decisions arbitrarily.

Sovereignty does not always lie with the people: for a whole people can give itself into slavery. It is also untrue to say that domination is always exercised in interests of the people (I.III.VIII, pp. 104, 109). A right of resistance against a "bad king" is, however, rejected. Among other reasons, it is rejected because it seems to him extremely difficult to decide whether a certain action of a given king can be considered good or bad (I.III.IX, p. 111).

The difference in private law between property (full proprietary rights, patrimony) and usufruct, corresponds to the distinction in public law between sovereignty itself and the bearer of sovereignty.[5] This is always the presumption that the king, if kingship derives from the will of the people, has only the usufruct of sovereignty, so that in this case, the people [have] the right to prevent the alienation of sovereignty (I.III.XIII, p. 119).

What is, however, the postulated relationship between the eternal and unchanging natural law and the sovereignty which is to be considered as the highest power; between general norms and individual decisions? Grotius postulates that natural law binds all kings

— even the patrimonial ones. This is as compatible with sovereignty as is the fact that the king can bind himself by contracts with his subjects or with God (I.III.VI, p. 121). Thus far the principles are clear. The complications in his exposition begin with the problem of the institutionalisation of his natural law. With this question of the rights of resistance the eternal dilemma of the bourgeois who loves peace, security and order, but does not want interference with his property and his freedom, becomes clearly visible. Grotius starts with the assertion that "if the authorities issue an order that is contrary to the law of nature or to the commandment of God, the order should not be carried out" (I.IV.I, p. 138). In the state of nature obviously every man can rightly resist any wrong. In civil society, however, the principle is reversed. The state has been erected "in order to maintain public tranquillity": therefore the state can limit in the interests of public peace and security, and to such an extent as seems necessary, the right of resistance deriving from natural law. He tries to prove this statement by endless historical surveys and quotations from Sophocles, Euripides, Sallust, Seneca, Tacitus, the Old and the New Testaments (I.IV.II, pp. 139–40). In his view the theory of Junius Brutus is wrong, as the right of resistance which Brutus attributes to the magistrates starts from the incorrect assumption that a subordinate magistrate has more rights than the subject himself. The right of resistance is only alienable by the state in cases "of extreme and imminent peril". He is, however, careful to add that even in such a case of extreme emergency "the person of the King must be spared" (I.IV.II, p. 151). "This law which we are discussing — the law of non-resistance — seems to draw its validity from the will of those who associate together in the first place to form a civil society; from the same source, furthermore, derives the right which passes into the hands of those who govern. If these men could be asked whether they purpose to impose upon all persons the obligation to prefer death rather than under any circumstances to take up arms in order to ward off the violence of those having superior authority, I do not know whether they would answer in the affirmative, unless perhaps, with this qualification, in case resistance could not be made without a very great disturbance in the state, and without the destruction of a great many innocent people" (I.IV.VII, p. 148). As later was the case with Locke, he uses Barclay for the justification of this right of resistance.

6.1.2.

The decisive progress in the system of Grotius lies in the fact that the right of resistance deriving from natural law is sharply distinguished from the right of resistance granted by the constitution itself. In all cases where the constitution delegates to the people a *con dominium* or a right of deposition, or other constitutional rights, one can properly speak of a right of resistance (I.III.VII, p.154). This revolutionary right granted by positive law comprises the following cases: a ruler who is responsible to the people and whose power is delegated from that of the people, and who violates the law, can be punished with death; a king, "who has renounced", or a king, "who alienates his kingdom, or places it in subjection to another", can be punished by a right of resistance belonging to positive law. The positive right of resistance is further given if the constitutional power is distributed between the king and the people, and if the king tries to alter its distribution in his own favour. The right of revolution is constitutionally given against the king, who, "sets out with a truly hostile intent to destroy a whole people", or if a people has expressly reserved to itself the right of resistance. Finally, the people have the right to resist a usurper (Bk. I, C. IV.VIII–XV).

6.1.3.

Grotius' theory of the state and law is the first theory to be almost completely bourgeois. It is almost a secular theory, because natural law is directly founded on reason. Natural law once recognised by reason becomes independent even of God. Divine and human nature are divorced. The break with the Schoolmen has definitely been made. Grotius' theory is further almost completely rational; i.e., it is orientated by the will of man. But the people who create the will of the state are not conceived in a democratic way. Grotius postulates a rule of material law; by this, however, the state has been delivered over to the struggles of the social groups which can destroy it on the basis of the natural-rightly right of resistance. The state is therefore not conceived as an independent autonomous unit; Grotius, unlike Pufendorf, belongs to the Harmonists who believe in a coincidence of common and individual interests (*Prol.* 4). He believes that it might be possible to prevent the dissolution of the state by the simultaneous postulation of the rule of natural law.

The rule of material law is the rule of moral norms, and hi morality is that of the bourgeois, who, however, has to a large exten charitable motives. The postulate of the Rule of Law has therefor not yet taken on the purely disguising function which it late assumes. This can be shown, for instance, in his theory of contracts The contract is based on the equality of the contracting partner (II.VIII, p. 246). The contracting partners must have "the freedon of choice" (II.X, p. 348) which implies in his view an equality of th two mutual performances. "The equality demanded in the principa act of contract is that no more be exacted than is just" (XI, p. 349) Consequently he rejects monopolies; state monopolies, he admits but private monopolies must sell at a fair price and may never us their power to close markets (II.XI.XVI, p. 353).

6.2. Samuel Pufendorf

Pufendorf is often considered as a typical representative of rational istic natural law.[6] If one understands by natural law, a system c material norms guaranteeing the freedom of men from the state then this cannot be applied to Pufendorf. The distinguishing featur of Pufendorf is that he rationally justifies the coercive power of stat with the systematic capability of a Continental jurist, and that h rationally deduces the aims and purposes of the state. There is n place in his system for individual freedom — for *ius naturae*: as w have already emphasised more than once, for the rule of materia law to be a real thing, there must be a sufficiently great expectatio of its fulfilment even if positive law contradicts it.

6.2.1.

The starting-point of Pufendorf's natural law system is the freedon of human action based upon the will and activity of man. Huma action is free because it is based on the freedom of the will. Bu usually these individually free wills do not coincide. They diverg and can only be brought together by law (*De off.* I.1.2, p. 3; II.1, p 3). Law in this sense is a political law — i.e., the command of th sovereign power (*De off.* I.II.2, p. 12).[7] Thus far it is legitimate.

Law is divided into divine and human law, which in turn can b either natural or positive law (*De off.* I.II.16, p. 16).

Natural law contains the fundamental principles and the inferences drawn from them (*Elem.* I. def. XIII.16, p. 159; II. obs. IV.5, p. 242). The two fundamental principles of natural law derive from human nature.[8] According to these principles man is a beast; but he is even worse than a beast because the forces of his intellect put him in a position to commit evil consciously (*De off.* I.III.5, p. 18). Man is malicious and easily impassioned. On the other hand he is helpless, and therefore "adapted to promote mutual interests" (*De off.* I.III.7, p. 19). Man is therefore a genuine political animal. Already in the state of nature he honours God and is thereby distinguished from the animals (*De off.* II.I.3, p. 89). He is free, and his own master. Thus far, the natural state is distinguished from the civil state (*De off.* II.I.5, p. 89). The sole ruler in the state of nature is God. From these two characteristics of man in the natural state, he deduces the two basic principles of his natural law system. Firstly, the law of sociability (*De off.* I.III.8, 9, p. 19). Natural law teaches how the behaviour of man is to make a good member of the community of him. Man has to maintain sociability so far as is within his power, and he must therefore approve the means to the realisation of this sociability.[9]

The second basic principle is the law of self-preservation (*Elem.* II. obs. IV.4, p. 242).[10] This law obliges and entitles man to protect his life and his body and all that belongs to him to the utmost within his power.

These two fundamental principles can, however, conflict. Natural harmony between individual and common interests as it is assumed in the theories of the Physiocrats and the classical economists like Adam Smith, is not only not asserted but, as is shown by his remarks in *De off.* (I.V.5, p. 28), apparently even rejected; although he expresses the hope that such a harmony might arise if man tended his body and soul carefully (*De off.* I.VIII.2, p. 45).[11] This conflict between the law of sociability and the law of self-preservation is resolved in the state of nature by struggle and self-defence; in the civil state, however, such self-defence appears inadmissible (*De off.* I.V.12, p. 32). These two natural laws are unique. All other norms of natural law are rationally deduced from them.

The law of self-preservation has been guaranteed by Pufendorf's assertion of natural equality among men (*Elem.* II. obs. IV.22–3, pp. 259–68; *De off.* I.VII, pp. 42ff). Natural equality does not, however, mean legal, political or even social equality. It means simply that in the state of nature every man possesses the same strength and therefore equal chance of self-preservation. Whether he can realise this chance in civil society is not at all clear.

From the principle of equality he infers the following: the prohibition of bodily injury, [of] the rape of women, of libel and of adultery or the violation of property; the obligation to keep promises and to pay damages where contracts are broken; no man shall be judge in his own case, and the duty of the judge is to give a fair hearing to both parties. Indirectly from the principle of self-preservation and directly from the law of equality follow certain results, which are elucidated further in the *De Officio*. They form in reality, the kernel of Pufendorf's natural law system. They are what English legal science calls jurisprudence, and German legal science, *Allgemeine Rechtslehre*. He rightly sees that the principle of the fulfilment of contracts is a supplementary guarantee of property, and that the statement "pacta sunt servanda" is the basis of the calculations of the exchange process (*De off.* I.IX.3, p. 48).[12] This obligation to keep promises is, however, not an unconditional one, but is conditional upon the legitimacy of the contract concerned (*De off.* I.IX.I, p. 48). As the principle of the necessity for the fulfilment of contracts is deduced from the law of equality, it only operates if the contract itself complies with the principle of equality; i.e., if every contracting partner draws an equal gain from the contract. Pufendorf is of the opinion that a realisation of the principle is only possible where prices are fixed by statute or market custom (*De off.* I.XV.3, p. 74).[13]

Private property is introduced by the will of God and by the expressed or implicit consent of men (*De off.* I.XII.2, p. 62).[14]

Considerably poorer is the system inferred from the principle of sociability. The paramount principle is "that every man promote the advantage of another so far as he conveniently can" (*De off.* I.VIII.1, p. 41), and the obligation not to disturb human society is stressed.[15] He expresses the hope that the advantage of the one might become the advantage of the other (*De off.* I.VIII.2, p. 49). In any case, all the deductions from the principle of self-preservation are equally to be deduced from the law of sociability.

6.2.2.

The decisive progress of Pufendorf's system lies in this thesis of the factual validity of the natural law norms. He alleges that their validity is incomplete and insufficient for the needs of social life (*Elem.* II. obs. V.1, p. 273). Law is only valid if it is fitted out with sanctions. Every valid law comprises two parts: a rule of conduct (what is, and what is not to be done), and the appropriate sanction to this rule of conduct (the punishment to be applied on its infringement) (*De off.* I.II.7, p. 14; ibid., II.XII.4, p. 124).

Natural law, however, does not know of any punishment. It does not know of any law-suit for the fulfilment of contracts. Their fulfilment is "left solely to the divine Judgment Seat". (*Elem.* I, def. XIII, 18, p. 160.) The fear of God and the individual conscience, which operate in the case of natural law to enforce fulfilment of contracts, in no way represent sufficient sanctions (*De off.* II.V.8, p. 104;[16] ibid., I.IV.7, p. 104).[17]

6.2.3.

The inefficiency of natural law in guaranteeing peace resulted in man's being compelled to erect the state. Only in and through the state can peace and security be fully accomplished (*Elem.* II. obs. V.2, p. 274, and 15, p. 286). The state is based on contract, i.e., on two compacts and one decree (*De off.* II.VI.7, p. 107). A contract is first made in which men declare their intention of erecting a state: "all together and singly must agree"; then afterwards the form of government is determined by a decree, and finally a compact is concluded with all those persons to whom the power of the state has been delegated.

The state having arisen, in this way, is now a legal person whose will is to be imputed to all, and whose aim is the maintenance of common peace and security (*De off.* II.VI.10, p. 108,[18] and 5, p. 107).[19] The state organ constituted by the decree can be a monarch, the senate or the people. The forms of government are therefore monarchy, aristocracy, or democracy. All three forms of government are different organisationally, but are really aspects of the one concept of the state (*De off.* II.VIII.3, p. 113). Pufendorf therefore draws a sharp line of demarcation between sovereignty of the state and sovereignty of a state organ.

Monarchies are to be preferred to all other forms of the state because the rapidity of the decisions of state is of great utility, and the monarch can carry out such decisions alone, whereas in democracies and aristocracies assemblies must meet (*De off.* II.IX.6, p. 117). Mixed constitutions are considered unhealthy, although constitutional limitations of absolute power are deemed expedient. "It is wise to circumscribe the exercise of his authority by certain limits" (*De off.* II.IX.6, p. 117). The presumption in every case speaks against a patriarchal type of government (*De off.* II.IX.6, p. 117).

6.2.4.

What are the relations between the state and natural law now? The answer is that no connection between the two exists at all — i.e., that the state is to be conceived sovereign in an absolute sense. The sovereignty of the state is supreme (*Elem.* I. def. IV.1, p. 18); its authority is absolute. (*Elem.* II. obs. V.18, p. 289). It is independent of any other power, and can act according to its own discretion. It is not obliged to render account to anyone.[20] It is not bound by human laws which are its own product.[21] Law is therefore command and not *ratio*.[22] "Laws are actually proceeding from the one who has supreme command" (*Elem.* I. def. XIII. 10, p. 194). The citizen is subject to every command of the state, whether this takes the form of a general norm or of an individual decision: "Finally citizens are bound to obey particular commands of their rulers no less than the general laws" (*De off.* II.XII.9, p. 126). The legitimate sphere of positive law is determined in the same way as in the theory of Spinoza. The legislator can demand everything he has the power to carry out. Therefore, he is only deprived of the power of regulating psychological processes.[23] Forms of freedom such as prevailed before the existence of the state are consequently inadmissable. Even property is granted by the state. From this conception it follows that if the monarch has directly transferred property to a citizen the decision as to the content of the rights of ownership must rest with him. If all property is acquired by "own industry" the owner is subject to state intervention in three ways: the state can prescribe the use of the property in accordance with the interests of the state even to details of amount, quality and method of transference. The state can transfer to itself under normal circumstances a small amount of property — for instance, in the form of taxes — for he who desires protection must pay. Finally, in emergency cases the state may confiscate the whole of the property (*De off.* II.XV.1–4, p. 136). In his absolutist system there is no place for a limitation of the sovereignty of the state.

If laws clash with human natural law, the positive laws of the sovereign have precedence. It is true that the welfare of the people is the raison d'être of the state. The state has been granted the power of the people for this purpose (*De off.* II.XI.3, p. 125), and the character and the extent of its sovereignty are derived from this aim. But as Gierke has conclusively shown this object of the state refers to the state of nature, and therefore, like every natural law in the civil state, is nothing but an *obligatio imperfecta.* It is therefore impossible to speak of the rule of material law because this purpose of the state is not in fact fulfilled.

So far as divine natural law or individual decisions are in conflict with positive law, the gravest difficulties confront Pufendorf, as he himself admits. He rightly sees that the deduction of the state from the will of the subjects implies the admissibility of a right of resistance: "Just as he who confers upon a second person authority over himself, contracts at the same time the obligation not to resist his bidding, since, forsooth, that would imply that someone has the right to command in such a way, however, that the other person retains the authority to resist" (*Elem.* II. obs. V. p. 287). He therefore investigates "how far this obligation not to resist extends". It is in his view a matter for the individual conscience to decide whether to retreat before violence and violate the commands of religion, or whether to offer resistance. If the secular power commits the folly of issuing commands in conflict with human or divine natural law, the blame does not lie with the citizen, but with the sovereign, and in the main the citizen should not revolt. Only if in carrying out such commands the citizen himself would commit a sin, or if he would prefer death to the carrying out of the command, or if the command seems reasonless — then the sovereign becomes "a free enemy" against whom a right of resistance has to be recognised because he himself no longer treats his subjects as subjects but as enemies. But even in such a case the right of resistance is only granted if the citizen finds it impossible to escape or to hide himself (*Elem.* II. obs. V.17, pp. 287–8). In *De Off.* I.II.XII.8, p. 126, the solution to the problem is reduced to a mere formula.[24]

We see, therefore, that the right of resistance unwillingly conceded is practically meaningless, and is in no way institutionalised. In the first place, the motive and the object of the right of resistance are very directly limited. Its exercise depends upon the sovereign issuing a command, the citizen himself carrying out this command, the command violating natural law, and the citizen seeing no possibility of escape or of hiding. A right of resistance against the general misrule of the sovereign which does not prescribe certain remedies to the subject is of little value. Further, an individual right of resistance is only admitted in a very limited sphere. The conception that all power lies with the people, which is entitled to depose and to punish kings, is rejected as a perilous error, in spite of his assertion of the contractual basis of the state (*Elem.* II. obs. V.20, p. 291). There is no right of resistance on the part of the *people* even against a king who degenerates into a tyrant, because it is impossible to decide whether he is actually ruling tyrannically (*Elem.* II. obs. V.21, p. 292). Only the individual concerned has the right of resistance. His fellows are not allowed to help him, because the violation of the rights of one citizen does not absolve the others from their duty of obedience (*Elem.* II. obs. V.22, p. 293). Parties and all intermediate powers between citizens and central authority are inadmissible.

The right of resistance in Pufendorf's system is therefore a *quantité négligible.*

6.2.5.

Pufendorf's system of state and law is one of enlightened despotism. The first element of the bourgeois state, the sovereignty of the state, appears there, but not the second element of the bourgeois state, namely, the sphere of individual freedom. This attitude is politically intelligible. Pufendorf was a bourgeois by descent and education, a jurist by profession, and a state servant in Sweden and Brandenburg. He combined historical training, political experience and legal knowledge to a rare degree. His political confessions appear in his famous book, *De statu imperii Germanici ad Laelium fratrem Dominium Trerzolani liberunus*, appearing under the pseudonym [of] Severinius de Monzanbano, Geneva, 1667. The Holy Roman Empire of the German nation appeared to him as a monster. The constitution of the Empire appeared to contradict entirely all natural demands. Universality of currency, freedom of transport and trade, judicial reform, seemed to him necessary, but their introduction impossible without the establishment of a strong central power of the prince. In order to be able to satisfy the interests of the rising bourgeoisie, he became the jurist of enlightened despotism, and his master, the Grand Elector, had already dealt the final death-blow to the estates, and exterminated the intermediate powers between citizen and state.

CHAPTER 7

Hobbes and Spinoza

7.1. Hobbes

Our fundamental thesis, that the introduction of the postulate of the rule of material law and of a rational and secular justification of the state, necessarily leads to revolutionary consequences, can be demonstrated in Hobbes' system very clearly; although Hobbes is generally considered to be quite immune from any such disintegrating tendencies.[1]

Hobbes appeared to an enlightened period as a second Machiavelli.[2] His one aim was supposed to be the foundation of pure despotism, and all petit-bourgeois looked on him with mixed feelings. It can even be said that the traditional Liberal English political theory is ashamed of Hobbes. Such an interpretation is, at least since Toennies' book, quite out of date, and it is astonishing that it could have arisen at all, because there is hardly another political theory which is formulated with such clarity and accuracy as that of Hobbes.

7.1.1.

In the first part of this work we have already presented the concept of law as it is developed in Hobbes' theory of the state. This notion of law is nothing but the legal formulation of his conception of sovereignty. We have seen that in the quotations cited above law appears only as *voluntas*, and not necessarily as *ratio*: law and right are therefore identical, and law and the state are identical orders. The usual interpretation of Hobbes maintains that there is no law in his system outside the state — that the state is the sole creator of the law, that it can alone decide what is right and what wrong, that it itself can do no wrong, that obedience to the law of the state precedes all duties of the conscience in importance[3] — that, in fact, any form of natural law is lacking.

Such interpretations, however, suffer in that they unduly exaggerate certain tendencies in his system — and it will be our task to show that a genuine natural law does in fact exist in Hobbes' theory, and that the apparently monistic theory is in fact, like all other bourgeois theories, a dual one. In spite of the immediate incoherence of positive law and natural law, in spite of the direct deduction of law from the state, there is a natural law serving to limit the absolute sovereignty of the state, and arising from the fact that the existence of the state itself is justified by natural law, so that the law of the state and natural law are brought into an indirect relationship.

7.1.2.

Hobbes differentiates sharply between natural and positive law: "These dictates of reason, men used to call by the name of laws, but improperly, for they are but conclusions or theorems concerning what conduceth to the conservation and defence of themselves".[4] By this conception of natural law and natural rights, Hobbes is marked off from all other natural law theorists like Grotius, Locke or Aquinas, and because of this it is often questioned whether he should be classed among the natural right theorists at all. In his view, natural law was not a preconceived idea, the validity of which was not to be challenged. Rather does he trace natural law from the basic instincts of man, so that men cannot withdraw from its jurisdiction: "The Law of Nature is a precept or a general rule, found out by reason, by which a man is forbidden to do that which is destructive of his life".[5] That, however, implies that his natural law is materially determined, for its central task is the preservation of man. In conformance with natural law are such measures and actions as serve the realisation of this aim, and in this way the state is at first rationally justified. Only in the state, only through a strong central coercive power machinery can peace and security be guaranteed and human life be secured. In the state of nature men are wolves. The state of nature is the war of all against all. From this justification of the state it follows that there must be some indirect limitation of the sphere of state sovereignty, for natural law demands the preservation of human life and if state law does not conform with such demands which of the two laws is to have precedence — natural or positive law? Hobbes declares himself in favour of the precedence of natural law, thus abandoning implicitly his political concept of law. His first natural law is: "Every man ought to endeavour peace" and if this proves impossible, "by all means we have to defend ourselves". In order to guarantee peace we have to "transfer to another such rights as being retained hinder the peace of mankind".[6] Further, fifteen eternal and immutable natural laws postulate that men are under the obligation to transfer their rights to the state, to keep promises, and so on. But how can these natural laws be realised if men are really wolves? How can the sayings of the New Testament have any validity in such a world? For instance: "Do as ye would be done by"? This objection against Hobbes has already been raised by Rousseau.[7] If these natural law norms have precedence over positive law, is a state law not calculated to aid the preservation of human life, but likely even to operate contrary to this principle, to be considered valid? His answer, which we have already anticipated in a general way is: "Covenants not to defend a man's own body are void".[8] From this basic principle he infers certain concrete consequences. No one "is bound to confess a crime". No one is compelled to kill himself or other people. Universal compulsion to serve in the army is illegitimate.

The way in which Hobbes, in dealing with a problem of the delimitation of the sphere of sovereignty, abandons his usual clarity is characteristic. He clearly postulates the duty of obedience on the part of the citizen to all positive laws. But sometimes he abandons this unconditional obedience and arrives at such vague formulations as for instance: "Law of Nature obliges always in conscience (*in foro interno*) but not always *in foro externo*".[9] The phrase, "not always" implies that natural law obliges even sometimes *in foro externo*, so that the postulate of unconditional obedience is met by the antagonistic postulate of a right of resistance. Those vaguenesses and contradictions within Hobbes' system which have been enumerated in literature on the subject[10] are historically understandable. Although he strongly maintained the creation of a strong state power, it appeared necessary to him almost as strongly to deny the pre-state character of liberty and property which he considered to be only rights granted by the state:[11] he did not want to make the state too much of an all-devouring Leviathan. Further, his ethical and political theory was still strongly influenced by medieval conceptions, although no other man contributed so much to the destruction of the domination of scholasticism. He is, in spite of this, able to use to a very large extent, the very weapons forged by scholasticism to break its own supremacy.[12]

We have therefore to state that his natural law as a system of material norms stands above the state, that its primary content is the preservation of human life, and that consequently the power of the state is limited by the stronger natural law: "If the sovereign commands a man though justly condemned to kill, wound or maim himself; or not to resist those that assault him; or to abstain from the use of food, air, medicine or other things without which he cannot live, yet hath that man the liberty to disobey".[13] He does not answer the question as to what he understands by "other things" which are indispensable to life. Here as with the problem of the validity of natural law Hobbes is deserted by his usual clarity of exposition. The phrase "other things without which he cannot live" would appear to be open to [several] interpretations. It can be interpreted so widely as to include almost socialist elements in the natural law system. Our assertion that the postulate of a restriction of the sphere of sovereignty by material law must necessarily lead to disintegration of the status quo, applies equally to Hobbes.

7.1.3.

In addition to that, the disintegrating function of the rationalistic justification of the coercive power of the state and law, are clearly indicated in Hobbes' system. This phenomenon has often been described. In the struggle around the problem of whether the state is the creation of God or of "human nature", the latter is historically speaking undoubtedly the most progressive; but both answers are equally illusions. Both hide the real cause of the rise of the state.[14] The individualistic justification of the natural law ideology has a psychological dynamic which, as has been demonstrated by Gierke,[15] was already observed by a contemporary of Hobbes, Johann Friedrich Horn, in his book, *Politicorum pars architectorum de civitate* (Traj.a.Rh., 1664).[16] Horn had already undertaken to prove the immanently revolutionary character of the Hobbesian theory. And Friedrich Julius Stahl, who in his book, *Über die gegenwärtigen Parteien in Staat und Kirche* (Berlin, 1883), divides political parties into those desiring conservation, and those desiring revolution, tries to prove that all revolutionary parties have close connections with natural law and are of an individualist character. In contrast he claims that conservative parties recognise something higher than man, something that is unconditionally binding, an order given by God, standing above the will of the people; and he characterises the revolutionary parties as follows: "It is a revolution to oppose civil society to the state of nature, and thereby to set men free from all traditions of law and custom, to reduce the well-ordered society to an original chaos, and to take from this chaos the standards by which social order is measured. It is a revolution to destroy the whole public body of the state, the whole moral order of the nation, and to leave nothing, except the rights and mutual security of individuals. It is, finally, the essence of revolution to deny the authority power in its own right, founding it on the will of the people".

"The natural law Grotius to Kant is a scientific foundation for revolution."[17] Obviously the aim of Hobbes is not to justify absolute monarchy; no one who has ever read his works could come to this conclusion. He intended to constitute the autonomy of the state itself independent of the workings of the social forces and conflicts within it. Whether he stood on the side of the monarchy or of revolution, his aim was nothing but the conquest of the dualism of the monarchomachs. This intention found its clearest expression in the choice of the terms, in the sharp division between sovereignty and the bearer of sovereignty (state equals "commonwealth"). All his definitions provide for the possibility of a non-monarchical state; thus for instance when he defines law as "command of that person whether man or court",[18] or "law is a command of him or them that have sovereign power",[19] he is never deserted by the consciousness of the necessity of justifying the supremacy of the state as such, and not of one of its organs. The possibility of a revolutionary interpretation of Hobbes has induced some scholars[20] to count him from the beginning as a partisan of the Roundheads. That, however, is untrue.[21] Hobbes in reality always put his conscience at the disposal of the strongest political power of the moment.[22] He had experienced the Great Rebellion in which, during the struggle between the parties, the state itself had been in danger of dissolution.[23] It appeared to him, therefore, that a legal order as such was good, independent of its function in the social life of the people, and without regard for the social substructure it preserved. His views, which, however, have not been carried to their logical conclusion, arose in the period which "must have given to lovers of security the same sense of vertigo which has been produced in our own day by Bolshevism".[24]

The sovereignty of the state is based on necessity, that of monarchy, however, only on expediency. The necessity for a strong, central, coercive state machinery consists in the fact that, without the contract of subjection by which the state was created, anarchy would prevail; "for before constitution of sovereign power . . . all men had right to do all things, which necessarily causes war: and therefore this propriety being necessary to peace and depending on sovereign power in order to preserve the public peace".[25] The great advantages and disadvantages of a monarchy based on expediency are, however, "any subject may be deprived of all he possesseth . . . may as well happen, where the sovereign power is in an assembly".[26]

If the state rests on a contract how is it possible, apart from the case of a conflict with natural law, to constitute the duty of obedience on the part of the citizen to prevent a change in the form of government: i.e., how is it possible to exclude a right of resistance based not on natural law but on democracy? Why [are] the people not allowed to repudiate the contract, or at least to deprive the sovereign of his right and might, and to put another in his place? In answering these decisive questions Hobbes falters, as has been clearly shown by Frédéric Atger.[27] In *De Corpore Politico*, and in *De Cive*,[28] Hobbes puts forward the old translation theory, the definite renunciation of the rights of the subjects on the creation of sovereignty. In the *Leviathan*, on the other hand, the contract which established representative state power at the same time definitely instituted that organ of the state which represented it. But even in that case a democratic right of deposition cannot be excluded, as G. P. Gooch rightly observed: "His theory of the contract did not even close the door to rebellion".[29] Hobbes deduces the inadmissibility of a change in the form of government from the contract of subjection which everyone concludes with everyone. He dubs as liars those who claim to justify the right of resistance with reference to a contract with God: "This pretence of a covenant with God is so evident a lie even in the pretenders own conscience, that it is not only an act of an unjust, but of a vile and unable disposition."[30] Those also are wrong who declare that sovereignty can be forfeited; they are wrong because the sovereign "maketh no covenant with his subject beforehand". He cannot conclude any such contract with the people as a whole, because the people as a unit does not exist. In spite of this opposition to a democratic right of resistance the system provides for a degree of democracy, and Hobbes would be the last to deny its rights. The fact that the state is based upon the contract of all with all implies the original existence of democracy: "Those who met together with intention to erect a city were almost in the very act of meeting a democracy, for in that they willingly met they are supposed obliged to this observation of what shall be determined by the major part; which while that covenant lasts or is adjourned to some certain days and places, is a clear democracy; for that convent [*sic*] whose will is a will of all the citizens hath the supreme authority".[31]

Democracy is, therefore, "of necessity" the first form of government, "because an aristocracy and monarchy require nominals of persons agreed upon which agreement must consist . . . in the consent of the major part; and where the votes of the major part involve the votes of the rest, there is actually democracy".[32]

It is, therefore, not surprising that his works, together with those of Bellarmine and Buchanan, were burned in Oxford in 1683. It is not surprising that he was suspected by all political parties in the struggle, and that Clarendon summed him up to Charles II as follows: "I never read a book which contained so much sedition, treason and impiety".

In Hobbes' work are to be found all the constituent elements of the bourgeois state and society. Toennies has shown that free competition corresponds to his theory of the *bellum omnum contra omnes*. However, his notion of a violent and destructive competition is in strong opposition to that type of competition postulated by Adam Smith, although both start from the maxim of competitive equality. Hobbes asserts the approximate equality of all individuals in the state of nature. Only in making such an assumption was it possible for him to develop sovereignty from competition. Just as in Adam Smith's theory of competition between equal competitors, sovereignty could only arise in making this assumption.

Hobbes has created the basic character of the bourgeois *Machtstaat*, a wide sphere of absolute sovereignty. Anyone who believes the bourgeois state to be a negative, a weak state, or a fiction even, will find Hobbes' theory unbourgeois in character — for instance, Fascists, and social reformers. That, however, is incorrect. In postulating a strong central power of the state he also at the same time demands a sphere of economic and cultural freedom for the individual citizen: "The liberty to sell and otherwise contract with one another, to choose their own abode, their own diet, their own trait of life and institute their children as themselves think fit, and the like".[33] This freedom, however, is not conceived to exist before the state; although he sees clearly that without a strong state power, property relationships as he knew them could not be guaranteed.[34]

7.2. Spinoza

Spinoza's theory of the state, especially the relationship between sovereignty and liberty, is the subject-matter of diametrically divergent interpretation.[35] Gierke[36] sees in Spinoza the representative of a pure state-absolutism recognising no sphere of freedom for the individual. The assertion of the existence of such subjective rights is called by him "a series of sophisms". Menzel[37] asserts on the other hand that the rights of men have hardly been more clearly defined than in the *Tractatus Teologico-Politicus*; and Sir Frederick Pollock[38] rejects all assertions which charge Spinoza with state-absolutism, and reaches a conclusion similar to Menzel's. Here and there it is even asserted (for instance in Eckstein's papers) that Spinoza is a genuine theorist of Natural Right, recognising a natural law guaranteeing freedom.

How are such contradictions possible? Menzel's interpretation seems to me to be incorrect. Gierke's is partially right, however only partially; because beside Spinoza's theory of state-absolutism there stands a theory of the legitimacy of the factual which can justify every possible nuance between the extremes of absolutism and anarchism, according to the distribution of factual power between state and society. Moreover, we do not attribute any decisive significance to the changes in Spinoza's theory of the state. In the *TTP* (published [in]1670), the granting of liberty is apparently desirable although not stated to be obligatory. In the *TP* (1676) this is only occasionally mentioned. The reason lies, as Menzel has shown convincingly in various places[39] in the change in the political situation in the Netherlands which had occurred in the meantime. The friendship of Spinoza with Jan de Witt is well-known. He [de Witt] was a member of the Republican party, which mainly represented aristocrat interests, and was hostile to William of Orange and the

Staatholders. In 1672, Louis XIV invaded the Netherlands, the Republican government fell, there was a rising of the mob, and [Spinoza's] friend Jan de Witt was murdered in the neighbourhood of his [own] house. To this murder Menzel attributes the fact that in the *TP* the postulate of the sovereignty of the state is still more emphasised than it was in the *TTP*. But even admitting that, there seems to be no decisive difference between *TTP* and *TP*. On the contrary, all ideas which are expressed in the *TP* are already foreshadowed in the *TTP*, so that the essence of his attitude has not changed.

7.2.1.

His derivation of the absolute sovereignty of the state is similar to that of Hobbes.

The natural state is characterised by the absence of ethical norms. That, however, does not mean that his statements are those of a sociology free from judgments of value, that is to say of a non-normative character. This assertion is generally based on his scientific programme, which he formulates in this way. Whereas others have bewailed or derided the qualities of men, have praised or blamed them, he wanted to understand them with the detachment with which he would contemplate a mathematical problem. He wanted, in his own words, to consider human actions just as if he had to deal with lines, planes, and geometrical bodies. It is true, indeed, that mathematics do not contain statements of an "ought". What one commonly calls natural law does not in itself contain such norms, but statements belonging to the category of existence, namely relating to the character of the natural state, and to the emergence of the State out of it. His theory of the state is, however, not sociology. His laws are, in spite of his assertion, statements belonging to the category of essence and not of existence, so that here no difference can be found between him and Hobbes. For his theory of natural law — better, of the state of nature — which in itself is compounded of statements of the "is", has within his system only the function of showing those presuppositions which must be given in order to justify the coercive power of the state; that is to say, to elicit the consent of men to the form of the state.

7.2.2.

The state of nature is characterised by complete freedom and the factual equality of all men. In the state of nature, men are not bound by laws. It is the natural law of the state of nature that every individual strives to preserve himself, without any consideration except that which he has to take for himself. All men are entitled to act according to their desires and inclinations, whether they are fools, insane, or healthy. Everything which man does, he does by force of a natural law. The state of nature does not prohibit anything, neither fraud nor hatred. For nature is not directed by human reason which aims only at the benefit of man and his preservation. In the cosmos, man is only a *modus*, driven by necessity to act in the way in which he does act.[40]

Men who are in the state of nature typically factually free and equal are not subjected to any other power. They are therefore *sui juris* and not *alienus juris*.[41] He understands by *alieni juris* all those men living under foreign power (*potestas*). But as the state of nature is governed by struggle, and the fight may end in the subjugation of some, in spite of typical autonomy man can already in the state of nature become *alienus juris* in relation to other men.

The need for security drives men in the state, that is to say to the formation of a contract. In so far, his construction is almost entirely identical with that of Hobbes. Against this, it has been asserted that the decisive difference lies in the fact that in Hobbes' theory the contract is the constitutive element of the state, the voluntary deed of men, whereas in Spinoza's theory men are driven into the state by the necessity of natural law, so that the contract only describes an actual happening.[42] This contradiction, however, seems to be wrong, because the drive resulting from the natural law is in Spinoza's theory only motive, whereas the formation of the state itself is a voluntary deed of men. However, the interpretation of the contract is of no decisive significance. The centre of gravity lies in the question which tasks are assigned to the State, and what is to be the relationship between State and individual.

Man receives security only from the state. Only with the help of the state can men obtain their rights. Only the state excludes the blind force of the state of nature.[43] In the contract, therefore, everyone transfers his whole liberty to the state, so that the state receives absolute sovereignty over men. This sovereign power is not limited by any laws whatsoever. Everyone is under obligation to obey the sovereign. In concluding the contract all partners put themselves wholly at the mercy of the state. Therefore having acted as reason and necessity required, they are now absolutely compelled to obey all commands of the sovereign, however absurd they may be. If they refuse to do so, they are public enemies acting against reason.[44]

The sphere of the state comprehends not only secular but also divine matters. The *jus divinum* is law only if it has become positive law, that is to say, part of the law of the state; if not, it is only intuition. The state decides what is just and unjust, what is equitable and inequitable. Justice, reason, and neighbourly love receive therefore validity only through the command of the sovereign. The *dei regnum* can only exist through the medium of the sovereign power. Divine laws are valid not through the commands of God, but only through the medium of the temporal sovereign.[45]

Justice and injustice are, therefore, only possible in the State.[46]

His notion of the law is, therefore, the political notion.[47]

The statement that contracts have to be fulfilled is, therefore, not valid in the state of nature. It is valid only as a part of the positive law of the state. Property is equally only a category of positive law. The state of nature knows no property. In it everyone possesses only what he can conquer by naked force.[48]

The reason of the state has precedence of everything. The highest law of the state is its own good.[49] The state can violate its own principles if the common good demands it.[50] The state, therefore, transforms all men from *sui juris* into *alieni juris*. The state alone is *sui juris*. The state itself is as free as men were free in the state of nature.[51] Thus in the extension of the sphere of state sovereignty Spinoza goes farther than Hobbes. He goes practically to the utmost possible limit. In this he is followed only by Rousseau, with, however, one fundamental difference. Rousseau, as we shall see later, postulates only conditionally absolute sovereignty for the state, that is only if it has a certain political structure (pure democracy); because for Rousseau only the political form of the state and its social substructure guarantee the rightness of the exercise of state sovereignty. Spinoza, however, concedes absolute sovereignty to every state regardless of its political structure and its social substructure.

Spinoza's binding of the citizens to absolute obedience does not, however, imply that he is indifferent to the political structure and to the nature of State activity. On the contrary. In numerous places he gives recommendations as to the content of the exercise of sovereignty, and the form of the State. These, however, as must be asserted again and again, especially against Menzel, are only recommendations, lacking any element of institutionalisation.

Spinoza recommends that the domination of the state should not be its aim. Men should not be kept in terror, but should be freed from terror, so as to live as securely as possible and to be able to realise their freedom; for the true end of the State is freedom. Wherever it is only by terror that the citizen is deterred from insurrection, one can speak negatively of the absence of war, but one cannot speak positively of peace. Peace is not only something negative, but rather the will to fulfil joyfully the commands of the state.[52] A state whose peace depends upon the inertia of its citizens, or upon the fact that the citizens are driven like cattle, may be considered as a solitude rather than a state.[53] Stronger, however, than his enthusiastic desire for a coincidence of the will of the state with those of individuals, is his scepticism as to the possibility of realising this ideal. According to him, no state is secure whose maintenance depends upon faith.[54]

His recommendations with regard to the political structure have undergone a change which has been mentioned by Menzel. In his later years he openly advocated aristocracy. In the *TTP*, however, he gives preference to democracy, and this for two reasons. On the one hand, in a democracy everyone is obedient to himself;[55] "Ut nemo suo aequali servire teneatur"; and on the other hand, democracy is the nearest approach to the state of nature:[56] "Democratia maxime ad statum naturalem accedit". Absolute monarchy is rejected, although in his opinion it is probably more durable than any other form of state.[57] Constitutional monarchy in which the ruler is subject to the law, and the law is the declared will of the king, but not every will of the king is law, is to be preferred to absolute monarchy.[58] The postulate of a share in power by the *concilium* transforms the monarch of his constitutional ideas practically into a shadow king. By aristocracy he understands that form of the state in which the ruling power is exercised by selected people.[59] If domination is based upon law, even if in consequence of a census only few have suffrage, we can speak only of democracy, not of aristocracy. His conception of democracy embraces therefore that form of government which we usually understand by aristocracy, and his praise of democracy corresponds to his political position, and is in fact a panegyric of aristocracy.

His theory of the aims and the form of the state is, however, as must be repeated again and again, only put forward as a recommendation. The passion with which he makes these recommendations does not render them absolute in character.

7.2.3.

The distribution of the spheres of sovereignty and freedom is, according to Spinoza, identical with the distribution of power between state and individual (society). The *potentia* of a person, that is to say the power over the world which confers the natural right, is a function of the actual power which stands at the disposal of that person. Everyone, therefore, has as much right as he has might. The state as exercising the highest might, has, therefore, also the highest right. The individuals possess as much right as they are able to dispose of might.[60]

If, however, right is equal to might, it follows apparently that except within very narrow limits no universally valid statement can be made as to the relation between sovereignty and liberty. This theory fully justifies according to the existing distribution of power every status between the extremes of absolutism and anarchism. The only universal limit of sovereignty, and therefore the only universally existing realm of freedom, is determined by the impossibility of regulating psychic phenomena by any kind of external, and therefore of political, interference. Consequently all those cases which he mentions as limiting the sovereignty of the state fall within this category of the inalienable liberty of thought and of feeling.[61]

If he identifies the limits of the power of the state with the limit of the possibility of carrying out its commands, so that the state has no power where its citizens cannot be compelled to obey either by threats or rewards,[62] this only means that the subjects have essentially the liberty of thought and feeling. If it is possible to compel them in everything else, the frontier which he erects is practically meaningless. This is shown by all his concrete examples, as for instance that no one can be compelled to love a man he hates;[63] or that the soul is free. Thus he can conceive only of a freedom of opinion, not of a freedom to express one's opinion. But according to his theory, even this inner freedom of feeling and thought could be withdrawn, if it were possible to detect by new instruments the physical equivalents of thought and feeling.

This poverty of the recognised sphere of individual freedom is contradicted by his passionate stand for freedom of opinion. He fought against any restrictions of that freedom,[64] and vehemently advocated freedom of religious expression,[65] but in the *TP* dealt only incidentally with these demands.

7.2.4.

As against this interpretation three objections could be raised.

In Chapter IV of the *TTP*, he asserts that it is false to maintain that the positive law of the state, that is the exercise of sovereignty, could be arbitrary, for those men who are the instruments of the state activity are also a part of nature. Therefore he demands that we should not only investigate the nearest causes of their actions, but consider the interdependence of the causes in the whole process of the world. It may be true that the will of the ruler is the nearest cause of the law of the state. But this will of the ruler on its side follows from compelling motives. This assertion, however, does not contain any kind of limitation of the power of the state, unless one imputes to Spinoza a very banal optimism. It is rather a justification of state absolutism, for even tyranny is right because it is a part of nature.

The second objection is usually based upon his famous letter to Jelles.[66] There he writes: "With regard to politics, the difference between Hobbes and me, about which you inquire, consists in this that I ever preserve the natural right intact. So that the Supreme Power in a State has no more right over a subject than is proportionate to the power by which it is superior to the subjects. This is what always takes place in the State of Nature". That he does not understand by natural right a *jus naturae* with an unchangeable content, is clearly shown by this passage. The sentence only confirms that Spinoza did not, and could not, construct any absolute boundary between Sovereignty and liberty.

Finally he considers the construction that man in concluding the contract hands over all his rights to the State, as a mere theory, because no one could transfer so much that he ceased to be a human being.[67]

But what constitutes a human being? The answer is given in Chapter XX of the *TTP*; only freedom of the soul, only freedom of the inner life.For in this chapter he observes that no one could transfer his power to think and to judge freely and independently.

An exception, however, is given in his assertion that no compulsion can be maintained to commit suicide.[68] This is an apparent inconsistency which is, however, irrelevant to European civilization. On the other hand, however, he maintains, in opposition to Hobbes,[69] that conscription is justified. And he himself saw clearly that individual liberty is only a private virtue, but that the virtue of the State is security. Thus it is clear that within Spinoza's theory there is no universally valid limitation of the power of the state; that in some circumstances he sacrifices the freedom of the individual, just as in other circumstances he sacrifices the existence of the State. Vaughan[70] is, therefore, partly right in observing that the right of the individual eventually returns to life, even if through the alias of might. He is only partly right, because the statement that right equals might contains no fixed boundary of the sphere of Sovereignty.

7.2.5.

His theory has, therefore, a dual face; and in this we are in opposition to nearly every interpretation of Spinoza's theory of law in the state. To the dualism of state absolutism on the one hand, and the theory of the legitimacy of the factual on the other, there corresponds the dualism of the interests he represents. The state is absolute in order to [maintain] security, which appears to him as a bourgeois to be the highest good. We saw, however, that he is not indifferent as to the content of the exercise of sovereignty and the political structure of the state. To the recommendations already mentioned may be added some others. We mentioned that there is not the slightest indication of an adherence to the idea of democracy. This can be seen in his treatment of the problem of the *sui* and *alieni juris*, a fact to which Menzel has drawn attention. All men are *alieni juris* in the state because the state is the sole master,[71] but this lack of freedom is only in relation to the state. Nothing is here said as to the mutual relationship of the citizens. In this relationship certain groups of men are always *alieni juris* in relation to other groups, when they live in their physical or psychical power; as for instance the wife and children are subject to the *patria potestas*, and the servants to the *potestas* of the master. Those groups of men living under foreign power are also, as *alieni juris*, not entitled to political equality,[72] so long as they are under foreign power. If they are able to break this domination, they become free and equal.[73] By this proposition the notion of political equality which is the basis of democracy is arbitrarily restricted to certain groups of citizens, in accordance, however, with his social position and with the convictions of his contemporaries. His theory of the political structure of the state is socially the typical construction of the propertied classes. This becomes still clearer when we consider his suggestions as to the exercise of sovereignty. In Chapter V of the *TTP* he describes the ideal society based upon division of labour, exchange of commodities, and mutual help; a society which becomes state by the institution of enforceable legal norms. In this chapter he decisively postulates freedom of trade. This attitude towards the problem of commerce is largely determined by his friendship with the brothers de la Court, whose views are quoted with approval in the *TP*.[74]

The strong state, therefore, implies political domination by the bourgeoisie, and secures the free exchange of commodities. Against a state which does not realise this social and political aim, however, there is in fact a right of revolution following from his proposition of the identity of right with might. This theory of the legitimacy of the factual serves in the first place to crush the power of the people, whom he quite understandably hated. In his view, plebeians should have no protection by the state, as they have already the advantage of their great numbers. On the contrary, the State should protect itself against their great numbers, and it does this best by giving some office to the plebeians.[75] The proposition that right equals might serves in the second place to fight against the danger of monarchy. Generally speaking, the theory of the legitimacy of the factual is the theory of the ruling class, and is a conservative theory; but here it becomes the theory of the opposition, that is of the bourgeoisie and aristocracy united in opposition to the monarchy; an opposition which feels itself powerful and is powerful, and which has not yet played out its rôle, but trusting its power hopes to be able soon to translate its might into right.

CHAPTER 8

John Locke

8.1.

One postulate of Locke's political theory is the securing, as against the state, of the liberty of individuals, which is conceived of as existing before the state.[1] But to present only this element of his political theory is to give an incomplete and one-sided interpretation. As certainly as he extended the realm of individual liberty as against the sphere of state sovereignty, so certainly did he constitute a sphere of state sovereignty which is by no means insignificant. It is true that the word "sovereignty" does not occur in his writings; but this fact must not lead us to assume that he was ignorant of the reality.

His starting-point[2] is the alleged identity of the law of reason with the law of nature, which is asserted to be a part of the divine law. This divine law is perceived by reason: "Reason is natural revelation whereby the Eternal Father of light and fountain of all knowledge communicates to mankind that portion of truth which he has laid within the reach of the natural faculties".[3]

The natural law is binding on everyone. Its content is the prohibition of self-destruction, the equality of all men, and the injunction that no one is to injure his neighbour, neither his life, his liberty, nor his health. He who violates these principles does not live according to the laws of reason and must therefore be punished.[4]

Like all those theorists of natural right who seek to construct a sphere of freedom as against the state, he starts from an optimistic valuation of human nature, and assumes the universal harmony of self-interest and common interest. His description of the natural state contains an implicit criticism of Hobbes. He writes always with an eye on Hobbes.[5] The natural state is a state of peace, goodwill, mutual assistance and preservation.[6] But the question then arises why, in such circumstances, the state is necessary. The state is justified in the same way as in Hobbes' theory; that is to say, it exists in order to exclude the possibility of violent conflicts, to preserve the rights of natural liberty, and to protect property. These are the motives for the formation of the social contract.[7] Property, however, does not only mean a power over things, but it includes also individual liberty and the protection of the body. This property already exists in the state of nature.[8] It is therefore not created by the state, as is the case in the theories of Hobbes, Spinoza, and Rousseau; but is asserted to be a right prior to the state. Thus the principle [sic] elements of the state of nature are maintained even after the creation of the state. The natural state is not entirely replaced by the civil society, as is the case in the Absolutist theories; it is rather only limited by the civil society; and this only in so far as such limitation seems necessary for the protection of the remaining core of the natural state. In terms of legal procedure, this means that there exists a legal presumption for the existence of the state of nature and against the coercive power of the state.

If, however, the aim of the social contract is to preserve the state of nature as far as possible, it seems necessary to limit the sovereignty of the state arising from the social contract, in order to prevent an antagonism to the raison d'être of the social contract. This limitation is achieved by two factors, a material one and an institutional one; that is to say, by the introduction of the rule of a material law on the one hand, and by the separation of powers on the other.

8.2.

In agreement with Hooker, Locke postulates the rule of the material law. Only the law shall rule, and the law is the rule of the people.[9] The rule of the material law implies first that the legislative power cannot dispose arbitrarily of the lives and property of individuals.[10] Applying the old categories of private law, he concludes, from the proposition of Roman law, that no one can transfer more rights than he himself possesses. As the state of nature does not grant to the people the right to affect liberty and property, so they cannot transfer such power to the state.[11] From the above restrictions of the sovereignty of the state as to property, it follows that it is inadmissible to raise taxes without the consent of the people or of the representative organs.[12] The idea of [the] protection of property is so strong that in his view although soldiers are under obligation to obey even the most desperate commands of their superior, he cannot take away even the smallest amount of their property.[13]

It appears to [Locke] that such a limitation of the positive law of the state by natural law can only be realised if the positive law has the character of a general rule.[14] By "standing laws" he understands general rules, as his quotation from Hooker shows.[15]

This obligation of the state to exercise its rule only through general rules reconcilable with *ratio* is valid in his view for every form of government, even for a democracy.[16]

8.3.

Organised security for the rule of the material law as against positive laws is achieved by the institution of the separation of powers, which implies that legislation has precedence of the two other powers.[17] All other elements of his theory of state and law are deduced from these basic principles.

The legislative power is always in the hands of parliament. A delegation of this legislative power to other organs appears to him inadmissible, as the people has not transferred a corresponding right.[18] Executive and federative power are derived from the legislative power, and are legitimately united in one hand, although they are distinct from one another. For both need might, and it is inexpedient to place the power of the state in various hands.[19] Generally the view is held that in Locke's theory there is no real distinction between the executive and the federative power.[20] We shall see later, however, that this objection against Locke is not valid, but that the federative power fulfills a certain distinct function within his system. The rule of the material law is sufficiently institutionalised by the recognition of a right to resistance. We shall deal with it later. What, however, happens when we suddenly discover that not all men are good; that sometimes they are "grasping hucksters, quarrelsome tyrants, rebels"?[21] In general one has to remember, what Locke himself very incautiously admitted, that the positive law is always only a very incomplete image of the natural law.[22]

Finally, the state does not exist in isolation. It exists in a community with other states. It is impossible in face of war to consider the state of nature between the states as a paradise.

8.4.

These three objections are met by Locke by the institution of the prerogative. By prerogative he understands the right of the executive and the federative power to issue individual decisions and commands outside, and even against valid general norms. Prerogative is therefore a discretionary power not bound by laws.[23] The bearer of the prerogative can therefore act without law, even against law. There is not even the need for an Act of Indemnity. The exercise of prerogative is only functionally restricted by his postulate that it is to be used for the public good.

The sovereignty of the state comprises, as we have seen, two things: the right to issue general norms, and the right to issue individual commands. The antagonism which we mentioned [above (2.3)] as a possible one, is excluded by Locke through his affirmation of the precedence of the power of issuing individual commands before the power of promulgating general norms.[24] The additional reasons for the recognition of prerogative power are, according to Locke, the unpredictability of future events by the legislative; the rigidity of general norms, which when applied in their rigidity may often have an inequitable effect; and the fact that the legislative assembly is not always sitting, and works too slowly on account of the great number of its members.

The preeminence of the prerogative over general norms is so great that there is not even conceded to the people a right of resistance against its exercise. There is left to them only the appeal to Heaven.[25] Between the executive which exercises its prerogative, and the legislative power, there is no judge on earth.[26]

8.5.

At this point we must consider [Locke's] theory of the right of resistance. The right is admissible only against a despot. But who is a despot? Despotic power is defined as arbitrary power which deprives a man of his life at the discretion of the despot.[27]

Despotism can firstly be the outcome of conquest. A right of resistance is always given against the robber.[28] Despotism can therefore be the consequence of usurpation (domestic conquest). Finally, the most important case of despotism is tyranny. By tyranny, he understands the exercise of power without corresponding right.[29] This tyrant is therefore a *tyrannus quoad exercitium*. Even James I, whom he quotes in Chapter VII, expressed the view that a king can only act according to law, and becomes a tyrant wherever he abandons the law.[30] Against such a tyrant the right of resistance is thus granted. Violence can only be met by violence.[31] Such a right of revolution is considered to be politically harmless and legally legitimate. It is politically harmless because, if several individual persons offer resistance, their act does not destroy the stability of the state. If, however, the act of the tyrant concerns the majority of the people, or if the injury done to an individual is so important that it is felt by the majority of the people, the revolution becomes an accomplished fact which in any case cannot be prevented.[32]

The legal argument for the right of revolution is based upon the view that he who exercises violence without law puts himself into a state of war with the society: and for the justification of such revolutionary right, even Barclay is quoted, who considers self-defence as a part of the law of nature.[33]

The question now arises how such right of resistance can be reconciled with the recognition of prerogative power. We have already seen that resistance must not be offered to the exercise of the prerogative. Locke himself does not deal expressly with this problem. But we can gather from the structure of his theory that a right of resistance is admissible against the exercise of the prerogative when the prerogative power degenerates into despotism. The decision as to when such degeneration has occurred is left to the conscience of the individual.

We find, therefore, the following distribution of spheres in Locke's political theory.

8.6.

We find first a realm of undisputed state sovereignty, which in the main coincides with the sphere of competence of the federative power. The specific realm of the prerogative is foreign policy, that is, the power of war and peace, the conclusion of leagues and alliances.[34] In spite of the extraordinary significance of foreign policy for the life of the state, its conduct can only to a very limited extent be based on precedents or on general abstract norms; because the carrying out of foreign policy depends to a great extent upon the actions of other countries, and these cannot be predicted.[35] The sphere of foreign policy is thus one of completely free discretion.

The distinction between the federative power, which is dominated by prerogative, and the executive power is thus not only not inexplicable, but conditional on the imperialistic character of Locke's political system. It is well known that the absolutism of Charles II and James II, together with their religious intolerance, had led to a growing conflict with the American colonies; a conflict which reached its climax in 1683, when Massachusetts abolished the Charter. Only the revolution of 1689 made possible a solution of this conflict, and led to the restoration of colonial self-government. Locke himself stands consciously in the imperialist tradition which was initiated by Cromwell, the first conscious imperialist, and which was, moreover, continued in the reactionary period of Charles II and James II. In Locke's lifetime the economic and financial importance of colonies for England as a centre of trade, shipping, and finance became increasingly evident. Locke himself was bound to this imperialistic trend by personal interests and connections. He was for a time partner with Sir W. Colleton in the Bahama Street trade.[36] His friendship with the Earl of Peterborough, the commander of the English fleet, is also well known.[37] His hostility towards France has very often been represented.[38]

To this sphere of undisputed state sovereignty — the sphere of the prerogative — belongs also a part of the executive power; that is, in so far as the executive power seemed necessary for the maintenance of the newly-emerged bourgeois state. We have already seen that commands of the executive not based upon general norms, issued even against the existing legal order, are declared to be admissible when they are directed to the good of the community.[39] Concretely, the good of the community was for him, in its political aspect, the maintenance of the rule of William of Orange and the crushing of all Jacobite attempts at restoration; and socially, the maintenance of the existing order of property. In so far as such individual measures served these two ends, it was in Locke's mind to invest the executive power with the prerogative.

8.7.

Between sovereignty on the one hand, and the rule of law on the other, Locke recognises a second sphere, which we may call the realm of discretion. When the executive acts outside, or against, the positive law, there is always the possibility that it may abuse its power. The extension of this abuse of the executive may lead to despotism, which can be resisted. But if there is no despotism, but only a misuse of the executive power, that is to say, if the actions of the executive are still reconcilable with the good of the community, there remains to the citizen only the appeal to Heaven. The *Staatsraison* requires, however, the admission of such a sphere of discretion; and even if it is desirable that the executive should forbear to interfere arbitrarily with freedom and property, there is no guarantee against such interference. The extension of the executive power must be tolerated for the security of the commonwealth against unpredictable events. Locke could concede such wide powers to the executive because he himself was filled with a strong faith in the new monarch, William of Orange.

8.8.

Finally, we find as a third sphere that of the material law guaranteeing liberty. It is undoubtedly true that this sphere has the widest extent. The content of the material law is sufficiently concretised, and is institutionalised by the right of resistance.

The postulate of the rule of the material law is related to the social sub-structure of a relatively equally distributed small- and medium-scale property. The material law serves the maintenance of this distribution of property. The absence of monopolies, that is to say the relative equality of possessions, alone makes government possible through the medium of general norms. We shall now only touch upon this problem, and shall later deal with it fully. If the legislator is confronted with few monopolies, he is compelled to have recourse to individual regulations. If, however, in an economy of free competition, he is faced with a multitude of relatively uniform units, he must promulgate general rules if he is to deal equally with all these units. By property, Locke understands small- and medium-scale property, and therewith also labour power. By labour power, however, he understands not that of the dependent manual worker, but exclusively that of the capitalist entrepreneur.[40] This capitalist entrepreneur class, together with the nobility, gentry, and clergy, constitutes "the people". The worker has no place in [Locke's] system. Even the interests of the poor receive no consideration; and when he rejects slavery,[41] he hastens to insert in *The Fundamental Constitution of Carolina* (Art. 110) the sentence: "Every free man of Carolina shall have absolute power and authority over his negro slaves of what opinion or religion soever".[42] Larkin has pointed out that "according to Locke's view of the state there should be no propertyless people. But he did not dwell on the full implications of the above statement".[43] The psychological dynamic of the repetition of Locke's theory shows, however, that it could very well become the basis of a petit-bourgeois socialism, and we shall later find an analogous dynamic in the Kantian theory of law.

In Locke's system the postulate of the rule of the material law has thus a threefold function, as later in the whole period of liberalism. We shall now work out these three central aspects of the liberal system of law.

The postulate has in the first place the function of establishing equality. But this equality to which it refers is not any kind of social equality intended to transcend classes, but is limited to the sphere of the possessing class; within this class equality shall exist, and it existed in Locke's time as well as in the following period up to the beginning of monopoly capitalism, anyhow to a certain extent. Even the political antagonisms within the bourgeois class diminished in this period. There were no decisive conflicts between trade and industrial capital on the one hand, and agrarian capital on the other, after 1660. Especially there was, as in Prussia, not only no social antagonism between landed gentry and trade and finance, but, as Guy Miège put it in his *New State of England*, business men and industrialists hastened "to exchange the hurry of trade for the pleasure of country life".[44]

The legislative power is mainly at the disposal of this relatively united class. It is distributed between gentry, merchants, and aristocracy on the one hand, and on the other the king, who in his turn maintains close relations with the city. The composition of the House of Commons [as] presented by Edward and Annie Porritt reflects the composition of the economically ruling classes. After the seventeenth century came the entry of traders, merchants, goldsmiths, and lawyers, who bought cities and boroughs; and this, together with the county franchise still based upon the Forty Shilling Freeholder's Act of 1430, left the House of Commons the monopoly of gentry, merchants, industrialists, and their paid agents, the lawyers; so that the legislative machinery should run in the direction dictated by their interests, or rather be prevented from running.

The second significance of the postulate of the rule of the material law is the function of disguising interests, which perhaps only in the Kantian theory of law is as clear as in Locke's theory. In paying reverence to the "law", one can conceal the fact that the "law" is made by man; one can hide the majority which gives a content to this "law". Rule of law means rule of the bourgeoisie, that is to say, of that part of the people which has at its command property and education; "Besitz und Bildung", to use the Kantian phrase.

The third function of the material law consists in rendering calculable the process of exchange. If the public power may only interfere with liberty and property on the basis of general norms, the economic subject is protected against arbitrary interference carried out without such authority. By this the calculability of the process of exchange is considerable increased.

Locke's is therefore a typically Whig system. It is the expression of a genuine national liberalism. His system, which claims to know no sovereignty, proves to be a typical bourgeois system of state and law, in which sovereignty is not called sovereignty but prerogative. The spheres of prerogative and of discretion make it possible for the state to carry out a strong foreign policy, to maintain order within, to crush political opponents, and especially to prevent the Jacobite restoration. By the sphere of the rule of the material law the position of the economically ruling classes is sanctioned, and the legal foundations of a system of competition are laid.

CHAPTER 9

Rousseau

9.1.

The first modern thinker to see and solve the problem of a synthesis of material law and sovereignty, of liberty and rule, is Rousseau.[1] His problem is the solution of the question [of] how it is possible for the individuals to become members of a community, without giving up their autonomy; that is to say, how it is possible to realise at the same time the state and liberty, to realise material justice within the state.

The interpretations of Rousseau are legion. Sometimes he is regarded as an anarchist, sometimes as an absolutist; sometimes the logical consistency of his system is praised, sometimes his theory is held to consist of a number of irreconcilable contradictions.[2]

We wish to establish at this point that Rousseau is a state-absolutist. He recognises no sphere of individual freedom as against the state. Therefore any interpretation which regards him as belonging to the school of enlightenment, as for instance Gierke's, is wrong. But he is distinguished from all earlier state-absolutists, such as Hobbes, Spinoza, and Pufendorf, by the fact that he makes the surrender of all natural rights of the individual to the state dependent on the fulfilment of two conditions: a political one, the realisation of pure democracy; and a social one, the realisation of economic and social equality. Only if these conditions are fulfilled may, and must, the individual wills be made powerless as against the will of the state. In respect of all states which do not realise these conditions, Rousseau can be considered either as an agnostic, or even to a great extent as a revolutionary. This is shown clearly in the *Contrat Social* (III.10). There he maintains that the state dissolves itself and the citizen recovers his natural liberty, and is no longer bound to obedience, if the prince no longer administers the state in accordance with the law and usurps the sovereignty.[3]

In this case the citizen receives back the right of resistance. Here, Rousseau returns to the monarchomáchs' ideas. The second conception which shows that Rousseau, unlike Spinoza and Hobbes, cannot be regarded as an unconditional state-absolutist, follows from his theory of the people's sovereignty; for the people always dispose of the power of the state, and the institution of the authorities is not a part of the social contract, but of a special collective act.[4] It is just this insertion of social and political factors as constitutive elements, which makes extremely problematical every idealistic interpretation of Rousseau such as those of Franz Haymann, Moritz Liepmann and Paul Natorp, and even that of Ernst Cassirer, who starts from the specific problematics of the Kantian idealism; the antimony between nature and liberty and the solution of this antagonism in the sphere of transcendence.

It cannot, therefore, be decided here whether the Convent was right or wrong in claiming Rousseau's teaching for itself; but there is no doubt that Rousseau exercised over it an enormous influence. However, his hold over the spirit was more important than his influence on the formation of the institutions of the French Revolution.[5]

It is certain that Rousseau spoke of the theory of the *Salut Publique* as a "Maxime Exécrable".[6] But to deduce from this that the Montagne wrongly appealed to Rousseau seems to me unconvincing, because the theory of the *Salut Publique* lies more or less explicitly at the bottom of all political theories, even if it is given another name. One could even add that Rousseau was hostile to any kind of centralisation, especially to the centralisation of public life in the capital. In his *Projet de Constitution pour la Corse*, we find the following passage: "Or, si les villes sont nuisibles, les capitales le sont encore plus; une capitale est un gouffre où la nation presque entière va perdre ses moeurs, ses lois, son courage et sa liberté. De la capitale s'exhale une peste continuelle qui ruine et détruit enfin la nation".[7]

Thus if with Aulard and Hedwig Hintze, we see in the struggle between Montagne and Gironde chiefly the rivalry between Paris and the provinces, it cannot be doubted where Rousseau's sympathies would have stood. Even so, these objections do not seem to me to be decisive. The decision as to the inner relationship between Montagne and Rousseau depends in my view solely upon whether

Robespierre's party desired to realise the two conditions of Rousseau's state-absolutism. It is not possible to decide this question here; it is enough to have put it.

Our interpretation treats the work of Rousseau as an organic whole.

9.1.1.

In the *Discours sur l'Inégalité*, Rousseau gives an analysis of the existing society.[8] I cannot admit that this *Discours* has nothing to do with political theory, as Vaughan asserts.[9] Such a conception would mean the elimination of every sociological analysis from political theory, and the admission only of philosophical speculation as its legitimate task. The *Discours* is certainly negative,[10] as every analysis is negative; but nevertheless, analysis is the indispensable basis, explicit or implicit, of every political theory.

In the *Discours*, the sociological cause of the inequality of man is shown; the reasons why men drift into the civil society. In the *Contrat Social*, on the other hand, he shows the way to a new and a better society.[11] In the *Discours*, Rousseau sets himself the task of discovering the basis of a theory of natural law, that is to say, of determining the nature of men.[12]

In the *Discours*, he rightly distinguishes between the two constitutive elements of the inequality between men, the natural or physical and the moral. Thus he develops an empirical theory of the natural state, in which he rejects both the theory of the *bellum omnium contra omnes* of Hobbes, and the paradisical ideal of Locke, and recognises man as an isolated individual who is neither good nor bad ("ni bon ni méchant");[13] as a neutral which only through society can be made either active or passive. It seems to be clear that this description of the state of nature is more adequate than any of those which preceded it.[14] The *Discours* embodies the conception that property is the basis of society in the famous proposition which Anatole France has used in his *Penguin Island*, that in the very moment in which a man fenced a piece of land and declared "This belongs to me", and found men who were simple enough to believe it, civil society emerged.[15] Finally the *Discours* disposes of all fictitious interpretations of the emergence of the state. Not through conquest, and not through combination of the weak, does the state emerge.[16] He does not indicate the positive cause of its emergence, but he assumes it; the Social Contract.

In the *Discours*, however, he analyses the social function of the state, which consists in laying new burdens on the weak, in giving new power to the rich, in destroying natural liberty, and in creating the right of private property, with the resulting inequalities. The state is a sinister expedient of the rich ("une ruse funeste des riches").[17]

In the *Discours* we already find two conceptions of extraordinary significance; on the one hand, that the group conflicts within human society, and the conflicts of human nature with human society, are empirically caused; and on the other hand, the establishment of a new responsible agent, human society as the causal factor which frees the individual from the natural law.[18] "It is society which makes man a tyrant against nature, and a tyrant against himself". As against all philosophical systems of early bourgeois society (such as the rationalism of Descartes, the metaphysical idealism of Berkeley, and the sensualism of Locke) in which the belief in the absoluteness and indeterminateness of law and the state corresponded to the indeterminateness of external nature, and as against the philosophical conception of early bourgeois systems which transferred the mechanism of natural science to cultural science, that is, to history, Rousseau introduces the notion of the society into the bourgeois system — and thereby destroys it. It is true that Rousseau was a child of the period of enlightenment, and that he accepted its criticism of feudalism and traditionalism; but at the same time his cultural pessimism prohibits his believing in a natural harmony of the world. This cultural pessimism of his is apparent in his two Dijon prize essays.[19] Rousseau therefore does not belong to the school of natural law. Such an interpretation sets us in direct opposition to Gierke, who considers Rousseau to be the final stage in the sequence of natural law theorists.[20] Rousseau's central assumptions, that all conflicts are empirically conditioned and are the work of society, distinguishes him from all other natural theorists. These two assertions have undoubtedly a revolutionary significance. If the human creature is empirically conditioned, if human society is the author of the tyranny of men against themselves and against nature, then it rests with the will of men whether they will abolish this tyranny by a change of the society; for no God helps them. Thus even the *Discours* opens the way for the postulate of the overthrow of the civil society and for the struggle for liberty. We may add, however, that neither his sociology, nor his solution, is that of modern socialism. He has not experienced the industrial revolution, as did Karl Marx after him. He was therefore not in a position to recognise that human liberty is annihilated by certain productive relationships, and is replaced by necessity; and that only the transformation of these relationships makes possible the passage from the sphere of necessity into the realm of liberty. Even after one has read the *Discours*, it remains incomprehensible how the impression could arise that Rousseau postulated a return to nature, inasmuch as he rejected this wrong interpretation.[21]

9.1.2.

Against the actual society examined in the *Discours* and found to be bad, the *Économie Politique* and the *Contrat Social* undertake the task of finding a genuine and true human community, which can dispense with the motives of power, avarice, and vanity, and which is wholly founded on common submission to a law internally recognised as binding and necessary.[22] His aim is a synthesis of Hobbes and Grotius; a society in which individual will and general will coincide, and thus in which only the general will is valid; in which freedom and laws are at once realised; in which right means might, and might means right. To establish this true community in which particular wills and the general will are identical, in which the isolation of the state of nature is overcome in favour of a realisation of morality and humanity, men must enter into the social contract, which is only a social contract, and not one of subjection or domination. By this contract they cede all their natural rights to the state. Each one surrenders his person, his power, and his property, to the general will, and receives in return a new freedom as a part of this whole.[23] Thus individual liberty is undoubtedly given up in Rousseau's system, but not simply annihilated as in the systems of Hobbes, Spinoza, and Pufendorf; it is abolished in a Hegelian sense, that is, annihilated in the sphere of individuality and restored in the collective sphere. The existence of pre-state liberty as a right is inconceivable, whether it be a question of political, economic, or social liberty.[24] Within these limits, it is admissible to speak of Rousseau as the protagonist of a state-absolutism which goes even farther than the conception of Spinoza and Pufendorf. So far, Gierke is right.[25] But we cannot subscribe to Gierke's judgment, that

Rousseau's constructions which aim at limiting and directing this absolute state are nothing but a series of inconsistencies and sophisms.

We have already seen that the negative freedom, liberty as against state, is replaced by political liberty, a freedom within the state; for his aim is to find a structure of society in which each one remains as free as he was before the surrender of the original human rights to the state.[26]

9.1.3.

This is, however, nothing but a pious desire, and it has to be investigated how far his social programme is institutionalised in his system.

We have first to deal with his postulate that a surrender of the natural rights of men to the state takes place only in so far as this surrender has significance for the activities of the state. In this, his theory does not depart from the usual theses of such theorists of natural law as Spinoza and Pufendorf. In the final text of the *Contrat Social*, however, he prudently and realistically adds that the state itself decides whether the surrender of particular individual rights is of significance for the state or not. This sentence was characteristically lacking in the first draft of the *Contrat Social*.[27] It follows, therefore, that he does not indicate a binding limitation of state-absolutism, but only expresses a desire that the state may not assume more natural rights than is necessary for the carrying out of its functions. As, however, this pious desire belongs to the stock of all state-absolutists, and constitutes no binding limitation of state activity, it follows that in this Rousseau differs in no way from a normal state-absolutist.

His second limitation of sovereignty lies in the postulate that the state may only issue general laws. The "general will" is absolute. In the same way as nature gives man absolute power over his limbs, the social contract gives to the state absolute power over its members.[28] This sovereignty is indivisible and inalienable, but it is not arbitrary, for the general will in action is law.[29] This means that the general will may express itself only through general laws. Expression other than through general laws is closed to it. Here lies the decisive divergence from Locke, who by the institution of the prerogative opens the way to the entry of lawless power into his system, which is usually designated as realising the rule of law. In Rousseau's definition of the general will its activity through general laws is implied.[30]

> Par la même raison que la souveraineté est inaliénable, elle est indivisible; car la volonté est générale, ou elle ne l'est pas; elle est celle du Corps du peuple ou seulement d'une partie. Dans le premier cas, cette volonté declarée est un acte de souveraineté et fait loi; dans le second, ce n'est qu'une volonté particulière, ou un acte de magistrature; c'est un décret tout au plus.[31]

There are two propositions in this passage; first, that the generality of the will can only manifest itself through general laws; second, that idea and reality, the categories of essence and of existence, coincide, that is to say, that to quote Christian Morgenstern, what may not be, cannot be: "Le souverain, par cela seul qu'il est, est toujours tout ce qu'il doit être". Rousseau does, however, admit that in practice idea and reality do not always coincide, in so far as he identifies the general will with the will of the majority.[32]

But what is a law? and does the rule of such law really guarantee the freedom of man?

In the *Économie Politique*, the postulate of the rule of law was already the focal point of his doctrine. The law was the author of justice and liberty, the source of material equality. It was "la voix céleste qui dicte à chacun citoyen les préceptes de la raison publique et lui apprend à agir selon les maximes de son propre jugement et à n'être pas en contradiction avec lui-même".[33] There the generality and universal applicability of the law was already stressed, with all its consequences, that the state may bestow honours, but may never grant privileges.[34] In the first draft of the *Contrat Social*, the postulate of the generality of all laws was still deduced from the aim of the state, namely the furtherance of the common good, by the fallacious process of reasoning that because every law should further the common good it must necessarily be general, like the will which is its source.[35] This is obviously a fallacious reasoning, because he never proves that the common good can only be furthered by general laws. The generality of the law thus has reference to its source as well as to its validity. The ultimate formulation is to be found in the final text of the *Contrat Social*.[36] From the postulate of the generality of the law he deduces the inadmissibility of laws with retroactive effect; since every retroactive law is in a real sense individual. The objects of retroactive laws are facts already realised in external nature, and can therefore be enumerated. Thus retroactive laws are not faced with an indefinite, but with a definite, number of already accomplished facts. This proof of his proposition of the inadmissibility of retroaction is, however, not to be found in Rousseau's work; but in his *Projet pour la Constitution de la Corse*, he upheld the proposition in the most rigid manner.[37] Moreover, he found it hard to come to this conclusion, since he wanted to prevent the accumulation of land in one hand; nevertheless, he denied the admissibility of retroaction, even for the sake of the disintegration of large-scale landed property, and only suggests that accumulation should be prevented.

The state exists only if it rules through general laws: "Qu'ils obéissent et que personne ne commande, qu'ils servent et n'aient point de maitre; d'autant plus libre en effet, que sous une apparent sujétion, nul ne perd de sa liberté que ce qui peut nuire à celle d'un autre."[38] But is the generality and universal applicability of the law really a guarantee for the realisation of the desired synthesis between individual and collective wills? The answer can only be that the postulate of the generality of the law guarantees but a little, since he gives to this postulate only a formal character, as is shown by the passage already quoted. The legislator may grant any privilege, may carry out any differentiation, whether just or unjust, equitable or inequitable, provided only that the external form of the generality of the laws is maintained, and that in his law he carefully avoids the mention of individuals.

This rule of the general law is, according to Rousseau, only capable of realisation if no intermediate powers are inserted between the people and the law; if, that is, the legislative power not only rests with the people, but is actually exercised by them. He therefore vehemently rejects political representation; and his characterisation of the British parliamentary system is well-known.[39] But we must admit that he himself hardly believes in the possibility of realising this ideal; and he recommends for Corsica a mixed government and a States-General.[40] The decisive point is, therefore, that the sovereignty of the people actually resides in the people, and not in the representative assembly.

> Whereas earlier writers (the apologists of the right of revolution) considered the sovereignty of the people to be a mere potential (latent) power, which breaks out and puts an end to a tyrannical Government if necessary, it is according to Rousseau a necessary and permanently actual power; the people, all of it, cannot cease for a moment itself to exercise it really and fully. There is thus no further need for a justification of revolution as undertaken by Locke, but the whole conception of revolution becomes obsolete.[41]

Only the administration of the laws does not lie with the people, but in the hands of the government which carries out the general will as the arm of the law, as "force appliquée à la loi".[42] Sovereignty, however, does not lie with the government but with the legislature; that is, with the people, with the general will, which is at bottom nothing but the majority.

It follows, therefore, that none of Rousseau's statements as to the relation between individual and general will, or as to the relation between law and general will, gives the slightest indication that his system is anything but one of naked state-absolutism.

9.2.

9.2.1.

This interpretation has to be fundamentally revised, however, when we keep in view that state-absolutism is only postulated in relation to a certain social substructure, and that the annihilation of the individual wills is made dependent upon the realisation of his social postulates. Rousseau himself did not see the social substructure corresponding to his political system as clearly as he grasped the essence of political democracy. He himself, as has often been emphasised, saw only in a city-state the necessary substructure for the realisation of democracy.[43] A compact territory, simple manners, and simple popular wants, appeared to him to be the necessary conditions for the functioning of such democracy.[44] Even Corsica seemed to him too large, and in his draft for the Corsican Constitution he summed up as follows: "Un gouvernement purement démocratique convient à une petite ville plutôt qu'à une nation".[45] If this were true, one would have to agree to the judgment that

Rousseau's theories do not present any decisive progress.[46]

9.2.2.

Rousseau, however, did postulate the organic structure of society, if not very clearly, even if he denies the admissibility of intermediate powers between the individual and the law. This interpretation of Rousseau will be strenuously opposed, because it is usually asserted that any idea of organic democracy is completely foreign to Rousseau's theory. We find, however, a confirmation of our view in the *Économie Politique*.[47] There he maintains that every larger society is composed of smaller ones of various sizes. Each such immediate society stands in a dual relationship: to its members the society is itself a general will; to the state, it is only a particular will.[48] This theory shows extraordinary progress when considered in relation to atomistic constructions of democracy, since countless conflicts of interests can be solved within each particular organisation.

9.2.3.

Rousseau's second contribution consists in his analysis of the civil society and of the function of private property. Vaughan has shown that his views on private property fluctuated considerably,[49] a sign of uncertainty with regard to this central problem. He has, however, made an essential contribution, a fact which has not yet been adequately appreciated.

In the *Discours*, private property is described as at once the basis, and the curse, of society. The famous passage has already been quoted.

In the *Économie Politique*, private property still remains the basis of society, but it is no longer a curse, and has become a blessing. It is even held to be more important than liberty, because it is the foundation of life, because it can more easily be stolen, and because it is the foundation of true society.[50]

In the *Contrat Social*, as a result of his absolutist conception of the state, he takes the view that man in the state of nature has only possession and no property; that property is first conferred on men by the social contract as a better right.[51] This is not much. This assertion is, as we already know, common stock of all state-absolutists, of Hobbes, Spinoza, and Pufendorf. They all regarded property as a right delegated by the state, without, however, having the slightest intention of altering the existing distribution of property. They were only compelled by the inner logic of their constructions to come to this conclusion, which probably appeared to them extremely undesirable.

Not so Rousseau. Anyone who has read the passage in his *Emile* will know the nature of the social substructure underlying his ideal of the state.[52] Property is to be private, that is to say, derived from labour, which means that it shall be equally distributed. Then alone is it not only not dangerous, but even beneficial. This is also a condition of the rule of the general will and the general laws; if property is equally distributed, then the legislator, if he wishes to realise the idea of social justice as Rousseau demands, can only govern through general laws. But, as will be shown later, if the legislator is faced with monopolies, he must promulgate individual laws, since in this case he is confronted with individual situations. There is also the fact that equally distributed property does not confer power on the owners, invests them with no privileges, and thus prevents a perversion of the rule of the state by monopolists and makes it possible that the general will really contains all individual wills. This proposition of the equal distribution of property has been put forward with the same insistence in his *Lettres de la Montagne*;[53] and in his *Corsican Constitution*.[54]

This is one of the alternatives proposed by Rousseau for the formation of the social substructure of his political system.

The other, which he formulates in an even shorter and more aphoristic way, is also to be found in his draft for the *Corsican Constitution*; "State Property". "Loin de vouloir que l'état soit pauvre, je voudrais au contraire, qu'il eut tout, et chacun n'eut sa part aux biens communs qu'en proportions de ses services."[55]

Thus he postulates either equal distribution of private property, or communal property. In his system there is no place for a property order in which there are differences between rich and poor, between owners of the means of production and dependent workers, between monopolists and non-monopolists. According to his theory, the general will can only be the expression of all the individual wills of which it is composed, if the decisive matter of conflict, the class struggle, is non-existent.

I admit that these conclusions are not fully developed in Rousseau's theory. It may even be doubted whether he was conscious of the implications and logical consequences of his statements; but that they are indicated cannot be doubted.

We find, therefore, that with Rousseau the complete surrender to the state of the individual will and of natural liberty is made dependent upon the realisation of full political democracy, with complete political equality for all citizens without intermediate political powers; upon the organic structure of society; and upon the rule of general laws, in a society in which property is either equally distributed among the citizens or is in the hands of the State. The rule of law has, therefore, an entirely ethical function.

9.2.4.

According to such an interpretation, Rousseau's theory is, in fact, an interpretation of the Marxian theory of the withering away of the state; of the emergence of a society free from external rule which administers itself. This appears at first sight to be an extraordinarily curious result, as no political writer has postulated with such force the absolute sovereignty of the state. Nevertheless, the final result of his theory is that in a society based upon political freedom and on the social substructure which he demands, the state must necessarily become obsolete, because the decisive conflicts are lacking. Rousseau himself has formulated this idea with extraordinary clarity in another way. In his draft of the *Corsican Constitution*, he emphasises that if property really is particular property, that to is say weak and dependent, the Government needs very little force, and can direct the work of government so to speak with a gesture of the hand.[56]

In this, his theory really resembles that of Marx. For Marx, a society without political domination which administers itself is the necessary final stage of a historical process in which the state withers away, after the proletariat has become identical with the nation and has abolished the then-existing property system. Marx has, therefore, filled in Rousseau's logical structure with history. Here Rousseau stands at the frontier of bourgeois thought. German idealism, which is built upon him, has not, with the exception of Hegel, made any significant contribution to the theory of state and law.

CHAPTER 10

Kant and Fichte

10.1. Kant

It is generally agreed that Kant[1] transformed the social contract, which Rousseau regards as an ideal to be realised in history, into a transcendental idea; that is to say, into a rational principle for the judgment of all constitutions.[2] Whether this departure from Rousseau has proved healthy in political practice is an open question. In my view, no philosophy has proved more disastrous for German political thought than the Kantian theory of the state and of the law, which, by banishing the idea of law into the sphere of transcendence, "leaves actual law and actual morals at the mercy of empiricism and the blind forces of tradition".[3] Professor Ginsberg's criticism of Stammler's philosophy of law applies equally to that of Kant, and of all the Idealists with the exception of Hegel. Marx in his criticism of the Hegelian philosophy of law characterised as follows this influence of the German Idealist philosophy: "The Germans have thought in politics what other peoples have done. Germany was their theoretical conscience. The abstraction and unreality of their thought always kept pace with the one-sidedness and inadequacy of their social and political actuality".

10.1.1.

It is doubtful whether Kant linked up his theory of law with his theory of ethics.[4] His is in any case not a love or a power ethic; it is purely legal (*Rechtsethik*).[5] It is secular, which implies the rejection of all ethical theory based upon belief and revelation. It is, however, not based upon the principle of happiness. For whether or not happiness can represent the moral law can only be taught by experience; and the moral law must not be derived from experience, because it would in that case be arbitrary. The moral law must on the contrary be based on a universal law. Finally, the conception of happiness is subjective; that is to say, it is subject to interpretation and is arbitrary. The theories of Eudaemonism and Hedonism are therefore rejected.

Kant seeks, therefore, to discover the "formal" principle of morality which, precisely on the ground of its formality, shall have universal validity. All material principles are empirical and therefore valueless for the determination of the idea of morality. In reality, however, Kant, as has very often been shown, has by no means discovered the formal principle of morality, but like his predecessors has conceived the usual dogmatic material system of ethics.[6]

The formal element in the Kantian theory of ethics is the logical principle of universality and legality. Every human action shall, therefore, appear as an individual case of a universal law. No human action must be an exception to this universal law:

> Because the unvariedness of the laws by which events take place, is the formal notion of what is called Nature, i.e. an order of things determined according to an unvaried universal law, the formula of the ethical imperative might be expressed thus: Act as if the aciom of thy will were to become, by thy adopting it, a universal law of nature.[7]

Human reason, therefore, *produces* in the sphere of human activities formally analogous to those laws which are *discovered* by it in external nature by the process of classification.

If the universality of the law is the objective element of his theory of ethics, its subjective elements are morality and legality. The subjective element is called legality if man obeys the objective order of the law, not for its own sake, but for external motives such as fear. The subjective element is called morality if he considers it as his moral duty to fulfil a legal obligation. This discrimination between morality and legality seems at first to be clear, but it is inconceivable how it is compatible with his premise of the universality and formality of the ethical law.

10.1.2.

The content of his ethical theory is very clearly shown in the four instances which he gives in his *Grundlegung der Metaphysik der Sitten*, and which he reaches on the basis of a classification of duties under perfect duties, whose non-performance is unthinkable, and imperfect duties; and further under inner duties, or duties to myself, and external duties, or duties to others.[8] Thus he regards suicide as unthinkable because it cannot be thought of as a universal law of mankind. The other three instances are famous. They all show that his duties are mainly concerned with the maintenance of the existing state, the guaranteeing of existing rights. In the further expositions in his *Metaphysics* he expressly deduces the prohibition of interference with liberty and property from this principle of reason.[9]

All these negative duties of non-interference are perfect duties, that is to say their non-existence is unthinkable. The positive duties, however, such as the promotion of culture and of happiness, are only imperfect duties, whose non-performance may indeed be conceivable, but may not be willed. All the elements of a love ethic are completely absent. He even deals contemptuously with such ethics.[10]

10.1.3.

The separation of internal and external duties, however, is of far-reaching significance. This distinction is in no sense new, but it is carried impressively further by him. The duties towards oneself are construed as legal claims of the *homo noumenon* (humanity) against the *homo phänomenon*. They are derived "from the right of humanity in our own person", as Kant explains when dealing with the famous formula of Ulpian, "honeste vive, neminem laede, suum cuuique tribue".[11] By this separation of internal and external duties, and by the divorce of legality and morality, his ethic is completely separated from law. Law has become autonomous. Consequently he distinguishes two kinds of legislation, an ethical and a juridical.[12] The juridical legislation, being the norms of legality, has the characteristic that it lays stress upon the factual performance of duties, even if such performance has been under compulsion. As for the ethical legislation, the norms of morality, the decisive question is the motive of the performance of duties. "The science of law holds the essentials of those duties which exist independently of all motives of their performance; the science of morality, the essentials of all duties which themselves constitute motives."[13] Further, "ethical legislation is that which *cannot* be external, although the duties it prescribes *may* be external as well as internal. Juridical legislation is that which may also be external. Thus it is an external duty to keep a promise entered into by contract; but the injunction to do this merely because it is a duty, without regard to any other motive, belongs exclusively to the internal legislation."[14] We must add that the legal duties are of unconditional validity, whereas the ethical duties are only of conditional validity. The reason is that a right or a claim only corresponds to the genuine, the legal, title: "To all duty there corresponds a right considered as a title (*facultas moralis generatim*) but all duties do not impose rights of another (*facultas juridica*) to compel someone. These are especially called legal duties".[15] At bottom this distinction is nothing else but a very complicated formulation of the old antagonism between the natural law, valid for the inner consciousness, and the binding positive law valid externally.

However, the process of the disenchantment of the law, of the rigid divorce of law and morality, of positive and natural law, is here complete. Only positive law is valid. Any kind of extra- or supra-positive law, which could bind or correct positive law, is excluded. His theory is, therefore, the justification of a pure positivism. Law is nothing but the right to compulsion.

10.1.4

But how is this compulsion of the law to be justified?

The central idea of his theory of law and ethics is the conception of liberty. This liberty, however, is negative, it is the juridical notion of liberty. This conception aims at the maintenance of the existing legal situation. It does not aim at a furtherance of alien purposes: "And there is the like contradiction in saying that we ought to design the perfection of another and to hold ourselves obliged to further it; for the perfectness of another, when considered as a person, consists in this, that he can impose upon himself his own end, agreeably to his own understanding of his duty; and it is in repugnancy to impose on me as a duty the doing that which singly the other person can accomplish."[16]

The primary duty is only and exclusively the maintenance of rights, of my own rights as well as of those of others. All other duties such as neighbourly love or care for the moral perfection of others are either secondary, or are even inconceivable. Liberty consists, therefore, in forbearing to disturb the legal order, and in the compulsory performance of duties imposed by this order. The primary idea is everyone for himself and God for all. Everyone has the greatest liberty; but this liberty is not arbitrariness, for it is restricted by universal laws which make calculable any interference with these liberties. The best society is, therefore, that which has the highest degree of freedom and therefore [an all-pervasive] antagonism of its members, and yet the most exact determination and security of the limits of this freedom, so that the freedom of each member can co-exist with the freedom of all others.[17] In this formulation we find the postulate of freedom of competition on the one hand, the postulate that any interference with this freedom is only tolerated on the basis of universal laws on the other hand. Here the basic elements of the modern bourgeois state, of the German *Rechtsstaat*, are already visible, which is asserted to be the idea of the state as such.

How is the relationship between law and the state determined? His theory of the state diverges in one point from that of the theorists of natural law. His state of nature is already a legal relationship, namely the sum of all relations under private law, that is the structure of a competitive society working on a basis of co-ordination. Therefore the state of nature owns "juridical forms of society, such as Marriage, Parental Authority, the Household, and such like".[18] The state of civil society (*status civilis*) is distinguished from the natural state only by the absence of public law which realises the idea of distributive justice. "The non-juridical state is that condition of society in which there is no distributive justice. It is commonly called the Natural state."[19] The state of nature is, therefore, a state which already knows property, even if it is only provisional, and in which contracts can be concluded;[20] but in which legal protection is lacking. It is, therefore, a state of lawlessness but not necessarily of injustice. It is a state of potential *bellum omnium contra omnes*.

The idea of right which aims at the maintenance of law postulates categorically that men leave the state of nature and of mere private law, and enter the civil society, that is, the state of public law — the state as such: "A Civil Constitution is objectively necessary as a Duty, although subjectively its reality is contingent. Hence, there is connected with a real natural Law, a Right, to which all external Acquisition is subjected".[21]

By this statement the state has become the logical postulate of private law, and as private law is essentially the law of private property and of freedom of contract, the state has become the categorical postulate of private property. By the raising of private property to the rank of the supreme principle of the state, his beautiful logical construction, his transcendental justification of the state, collapses. His arguments comprise a genuine vicious circle. In order to be able to construct the law and the legal duties, he has to assert the existence of provisional private property in the state of nature. This provisional property becomes with the help of the state a permanent institution. But no reason is given why the state of nature must necessarily and originally know provisional private property. His theory of law and state is simply a dogmatic assertion of the same type as those of all Natural Law theorists. He himself gives a very clear formulation: "From the condition of private right in the natural state, there arises the postulate of public right. It may thus be expressed: In the relation of inevitable co-existence with others, thou shalt pass from the state of nature into a juridical union constituted under the condition of a distributive justice. The principle of this postulate may be unfolded analytically from the conception of right in the external relation, contradistinguished from mere might as violence".[22]

The logical act and at the same time the transcendental idea for the evaluation of all states is the social contract. The social contract is the source of all law, not historically but systematically; it is therefore the origin, not the beginning, of all law;[23] and it is also the criterion of all law. Therefore "the act by which a people is represented as constituting itself into a State, is termed the original contract. This is properly only an outward mode of representing the idea by which the rightfulness of the process of organising the Constitution, may be made conceivable. According to this representation, all and each of the people give up their external freedom in order to receive it immediately again as members of a commonwealth". The liberty which the citizen receives back is that of a "regulated order of dependence".[24]

10.1.5.

The state constructed in such a way "is the union of a number of men under juridical laws. These laws, as such, are to be regarded as necessary *a priori* — that is, as following of themselves from the conceptions of external right generally — and not as merely established by statute. The form of the statute is thus involved in the idea of the State, viewed as it ought to be according to pure principles of right".[25] By this, Kant fundamentally accepts Rousseau's construction, but whereas Rousseau, by this political principle of pure democracy and his social postulate of economic equality, offers a genuine chance that the individual wills might be merged in the general will in a true unity, and thereby the natural liberty is only formally transformed into political liberty and is nevertheless equally maintained; in Kant's theory nothing is left but the postulate that the State ought to realise the idea of right. "Freedom is independence of the compulsory will of another, and in so far as it can co-exist with the freedom of all according to a universal law, it is the one sole, original, inborn right, belonging to every man by virtue of his humanity."[26] This formula reveals that the natural liberty of men is completely lost in the state; *for the decision whether my freedom can co-exist with that of the other members lies with the sovereign State alone*. The conception of the social contract implies, therefore, a complete surrender of liberty. The reservations which Kant makes with regard to individual liberty are nothing but a repetition of the banalities of the natural law theory of Spinoza and Pufendorf. They contain nothing but the creed of freedom of thought and feeling; for instance, such assertions as that no one can compel me to be happy in his way, or that the state cannot decide that the people shall make no progress in enlightenment.

The decision of the sovereign state is absolute; there is no appeal against it. The subjects may complain, but in no case may they oppose the decisions of the state. A right of resistance is inconceivable, and cannot have a place in any constitution whatsoever:

> For, whoever would restrict the supreme power of the State must have more, or at least equal power, as compared with the power that is so restricted; and if competent to command the subjects to resist, such a one would also have to be able to protect them, and if he is to be considered capable of judging what is right in every case, he may also publicly order resistance. But such a one, and not the actual authority, would then be the supreme power; which is contradictory.[27]

The right of resistance is on the whole denied because there can be no arbiter between people and sovereign. Kant's attitude towards revolution is, therefore, clearly defined, although his contemporaries regarded him as a partisan of the French Revolution.[28]

By this construction, the existing sovereign power is glorified with the aid of the idea of right. If, however, the revolution has succeeded, Kant is realist enough to recommend obedience to the newly-emerged sovereign power.[29]

10.1.6. *Is there no limit to this state-absolutism?*

The idea of right does not offer any restriction of the activity of the sovereign state. Either the idea of right is formal, in which case nothing concrete can be deduced from it; the derivation of anything concrete from this idea of right would be possible only through arbitrary insertions during the process of deduction. We shall attempt to make this clear, from the example of Kant's justification of the death penalty. He distinguishes the "judicial or juridical punishment (*poena forensis*). . . from natural punishment (*poena naturalis*), in which crime as vice punishes itself, and does not come within the cognisance of the legislator. Juridical punishment can never be administered merely as a means for promoting another good either with regard to the criminal himself or to civil society, but must in all cases be imposed only because the individual on whom it is inflicted has committed a crime . . . . The penal law is a categorical imperative".[30] Punishment is, therefore, justified by the idea of justice: "For if justice and righteousness perish, human life would no longer have any value in the world". Retaliation also demands the death penalty; "even if a civil society resolved to dissolve itself with the consent of all its members. . .the last murderer lying in prison ought to be executed before the resolution was carried out. The murderer must die". From this idea of retaliation he deduces the impossibility of any mercy:

> But whoever has committed murder, must die. There is in this case no juridical substitute or surrogate, that can be given or taken for the satisfaction of justice. There is no likeness nor proportion between life, however painful, and death; and therefore, there is no equality between the crime of the murder and the retaliation of it but what is juridically accomplished by the execution of the criminal.[31]

Is it, however, really true that his rigorous theory of punishment follows logically from his idea of the state, that is, from the social contract? It is well-known that Beccaria came to the opposite conclusion. According to him, the death penalty is irreconcilable with the idea of the social contract, as that punishment must go beyond the portion of natural liberty which the individual surrendered in entering the state. Radbruch likewise deduces from the theory of the social contract the conceptual impossibility of the death penalty.[32] "The individual *cannot* be thought of as consenting to the death penalty. One could prove the consent of one's own reason for every kind of punishment which leaves to the punished his life, in however miserable a form. The death penalty, however, cannot be proved to serve the interests of the criminal, as it annihilates the subject of this interest." All these deductions are arbitrary, because from the principle of the social contract no concrete conclusion can be derived. Kant himself dealt contemptuously with Beccaria's deductions, and maintained that he reached this result through the "compassionate sentimentality of a humane feeling", and he continues: "The individual who, as a co-legislator, enacts penal law, cannot possibly be the same person who, as a subject, is punished according to the law; for quâ criminal, he cannot possibly be regarded as having a voice in the legislation, the legislator being rationally viewed as just and holy".[33] By this kind of logic, as F. J. Stahl has shown, it is possible to prove the illegality, not only of the death penalty, but of every kind of punishment. For if the criminal is conceived of as rationally as Radbruch desires, then it is impossible to see why he should consent to imprisonment.[34] If, however, one conceives of the criminal as rational in the Kantian sense, it would even be possible to prove the impossibility of crime. A rational man does not commit crimes. But just as one can prove the conceptual necessity of the death penalty, so to speak as a logical catharsis, so also one can prove a genuine claim on the part of the murderer to be executed. Thus just as little as from the idea of the social contract, can a way be found from Kant's ethic to his idea of retaliation, even if one asserts such a relation between law and ethics.[35] The reason for such arbitrary deductions has often been shown. The transcendental method makes any concrete result impossible. F. J. Stahl, and in recent times Erich Kaufmann, Max Ernst Mayer, and Morris Ginsberg, have all shown this. Stahl himself said that Kant's theory of retaliation was impossible to understand. Feuerbach believed on account of this theory of retaliation that Kant was senile when he wrote his philosophy of law. But the real reason seems to be that the conception of freedom represents a mere negative principle of speculative reason, and that consequently the notion of the individual and that of freedom are purely rationalistic conceptions which have nothing to do with the sociological notions of personality and liberty. The individual in the Kantian system is a universal man, who is at the same time an individual.[36] This is that natural man whose core, stripped of all individual qualities, is always the same. The consciousness of this individual is nothing more than the general feeling of mere existence. He is that infinitely perfect being, a mere logical being. Thus it is understandable why as an individualist Kant attributed so extraordinarily strong an individuality to the State. If he assigned to the creative activity of man an unheard-of sphere of power,[37] this in no way prejudiced the sovereignty of the state, nor did it lead to anarchy, since a pre-established harmony of all individuals was assumed; and could be assumed, since these individuals are mere logical points of attribution.

It follows, therefore, that the introduction of the idea of law constitutes no limitation of the sovereignty of the State.

Is a limitation of the sovereignty of the state to be found in the introduction of the general law? As with Rousseau, the general or universal law is the central point of Kant's legal theory. His postulate that the state should only rule through general laws goes so far as to exclude the application of the principles of equity and of pardon. Equity is in his view a law without sanction, "a dumb goddess who cannot claim a hearing of right. Hence it follows that a Court of Equity, for the decision of disputed questions of right, would involve a contradiction".[38]

But the generality of law guarantees but little. The general law can have a twofold significance. Its generality can as in Rousseau's system, have a merely nominal significance; that is to say, its content may be any arbitrary, any individual, any unjust regulation, provided only that the legislator avoids mentioning individuals or individual conditions. Such a general law, which only demands a certain dexterity on the part of the legislator, constitutes only a slight limitation of the state's activity, as will be shown in the last part of this book.

Alternatively, the general law can have a material content. If this is the case, Hegel's criticism at once becomes relevant. In his early work, *Über die wissenschaftlichen Behandlungsarten des Naturrechts* (p. 22), which unfortunately has not been translated into English, the concept of the generality or universality of the law is considered to be not only useless, but also from its consequences immoral, and this idea is further developed in his *Phenomenology* and his *Philosophy of Right*. Hegel refers to the passage in the *Critique of Practical Reason* in which Kant investigates the problem [of] whether we are at liberty to embezzle a deposit, if the depositor cannot prove that he has made the deposit. Kant asks whether such prohibition to embezzle a deposit can be thought of as a universal law, and he answers that if such a provision could be thought of as a universal law, no deposits would any longer be made.[39] As against this, Hegel replies, if there were no deposits at all, what contradiction would be present? The fact that there are no deposits, will contradict other necessary determinants . . . and he goes on to say [that] whether an aim may be raised to the rank of a universal law can only be answered if we already know whether an aim is worthy of being thus exalted. It is possible to regard every aim as a universal law, and there is nothing which cannot be transformed into a moral law by such elevation; and as the aims of men necessarily collide, the existence of colliding general laws is conceivable. Hegel concludes that if Kant raises the institution of private property to the rank of a universal law, he assumes that his interest in private property is shared by all men. But everyone is free to repudiate private property and can thereby arrive at entirely different universal laws. That is the reason why Hegel considers the conceptions of the universal law in the Kantian theory to be immoral; for whenever a desire is powerful enough, no objection can be raised against its being elevated to the rank of a moral obligation. Every drive of men can be given the validity of law. Kant thus accepts state and property as facts which he does not question, and he only investigates with his transcendental method the conditions of the possible existence of state and property, and he finds as the main condition the duty to fulfil contracts. Hegel's criticism is in the main identical with our assertion that the transcendental method makes it impossible to reach any concrete results. Therefore the introduction of the notion of the universal or general law through which the state should rule has either if it is formal no decisive function of limiting the activity of the State, or if the notion is given a concrete content it has a purely disguising function. The instances of Kant's theory show that his universal law is in fact materially filled, and that the main material is the maintenance of private property. In Kant's theory, therefore, the notion of the general law has mainly a disguising function; that of conferring on the existing property system the dignity of a moral principle.

Finally, the last question is how far the political organisation of the state as suggested by Kant gives any guarantee for the realisation of the idea of law and the limitation of state sovereignty. Kant postulates the separation of powers, with the precedence of the legislative power, and the subordination of administration and justice to the universal law.[40] The combination of the three powers in one hand appears to him as despotic. A government cannot promulgate legislation, it can only issue decrees which concern decisions in particular cases and are alterable. The administration of justice lies in the hands of judges who are subject to the law alone. Their office is merely the application of laws. The legislative power belongs to the united will of the people. "The people" are the citizens (*cives*) who enjoy legal freedom, civil equality, and civil independence, and therefore alone have the franchise. They are thus the *sui juris* of Spinoza, who alone are active citizens, whereas all the others are called passive citizens.

> The apprentice. . , a servant who is not in the employ of the State, a minor (*naturaliter vel civiliter*), all women and, generally, every one who is compelled to maintain himself not according to his own industry, but as it is arranged by others (the State excepted), are without civil personality, and their existence is only, as it were, incidentally included in the State.[41]

Only the property owner has the franchise; and Kant's theory of property is as compared with that of Locke a Prussian reactionary one. His theory of right shows that only the landed proprietor is to control the political destiny of the State: "It is a question as to how far the right of taking possession of the soil extends? The answer is, so far as the capability of having it under one's power extends, that is just as far as he who wills to appropriate it can defend it, as if the soil were to say: 'If you cannot protect me, neither can you command me' ".[42]

Kant, as Marx recognised, wrote the German theory of the French Revolution. His theory, provided that theories have any political influence at all, is responsible for the defeat of the German bourgeoisie in 1813, 1848 and 1860, and prevented the political emancipation of the bourgeoisie. It is the typical liberal theory of the *Rechtsstaat*, which was operative in the state from 1812 to 1918, with its monarch who based his strength on landed property and education, on a bourgeoisie which is politically in a state of subjection and is content with making money; whose property is protected by the separation of powers, the independence of judges, and the exercise of sovereignty through the medium of general laws which perpetuate the existing property order and veil the political domination. The natural law has disappeared; but with it, democracy also. Kant's original contribution is, however, the principle that the maximum of liberty is guaranteed only if every state activity which interferes with freedom and property can be attributed to a general law. The natural law has by this been changed to general laws.

10.2. Fichte

Fichte develops the two constitutive elements of the theory of the state and the law, sovereignty and freedom, with basic completeness, and indeed one after the other.[43] In his first period, he evolved a system of freedom as against the state; in the second a system of absolute freedom of the state. Between the two periods there can be found various attempts at a synthesis, in which the two elements stand unreconciled side by side. Fichte belongs to the transitional period between rationalism and romanticism. He has often been called the last rationalist and the first romanticist. His influence is due not to the originality of his system, nor to the clarity of his theory, nor to the depth of his ideas, but to the extraordinary vigour which his personality, entirely devoid of compromise, lent to his philosophical outlook.

10.2.1.

The antagonism of the two systems is already visible in his ethic. This ethic knows two values, the self and the others; the realisation of the individual personality, and its sacrifice for the community. Whereas Kant — without success, as we have seen — only arranged the given aims in order of priority, Fichte seeks to show in his ethic the ultimate and absolute value: the development of man towards absolute perfection.[44] He describes this process as a continuous progress from a limited to a less limited condition,[45] until the end appears as absolute freedom from all restraint;[46] as absolute independence and self-activity,[47] so that the development is the becoming God in an endless process.[48]

This idea is clearly expressed in his revolutionary pamphlet,[49] and in his lectures of 1794.[50] The ultimate purpose of human life is to subdue every irrationality and to rule according to its own laws . In his *Sittenlehre* of 1798 this idea finds the following formulation:[51]

> Independence, our ultimate aim, consists. . . in this, that everything is dependent upon me, and I am not dependent upon anything; that in my whole world of sense there happens what I will; absolutely, and only because I will it. . . . The world must become to me what my body is. This aim however is unattainable, but I shall approximate to it. . . . This approximation is my final aim.

Fichte, however, sees that man lives in society, and therefore as early as 1794 he begins to construct accordingly: "Man is appointed to live in society; he shall live in society; he is incomplete as man and contradicts himself if he lives in isolation".[52] And in 1798 he declares that: "Everyone shall live in society".[53]

But how can the sovereignty of the individual be reconciled with the necessity of social life?

The recognition of the freedom of the individual implies according to Fichte the recognition of others. Other individuals are not external nature which is to be conquered by men; so the apparent antagonism of the moral law to itself[54] is solved by what can be called a system of coordinating morals.[55] This theory does not represent any progress. At bottom it is nothing but an exposition of the natural law theory that all men are free and equal, and superior to external nature. In spite of this system of coordinating morals, the individual man is considered as isolated, even if, unlike Kant, Fichte early recognised as an ethical aim care for the moral perfection of others.

In 1798 there occurs the first change. After that time, the self is only a means and the others become the end: "To each one, all except himself are the end. No one is an end to himself".[56] All, however, are only means in the service of the realisation of reason.

A second change is to be found in his *Lectures*,[57] which now in an open polemic against the period of Enlightenment assert that "the species alone really exists".

Here he undertakes a complete reversal of his ethic, and declares that in reality the individual does not exist.[58] He demands the sacrifice of the individual for the species, and states that "the individual should forget himself in the species, and should merge his life in the life of the whole".[59]

In his ethic three different systems can be distinguished: that of absolute individualism, from which there is no way to the state; that of coordinating morals, which can lead to the foundation of the state only if a pre-established harmony of all individuals is accepted; and finally, that of an ethic of the species, in which the freedom of the individual disappears.

10.2.2.

To this changed ethic there correspond various changes in the theory of law and the state. Fichte, indeed, ruthlessly separated law and ethics; but this phase is preceded by a general theory of natural law, in which his Jacobin ethic finds expression in a Jacobin theory of the state.

In his *Contribution for the Rectification of the Judgements of the Public on the French Revolution*[60] the state finds no place at all. This pamphlet is a confession to the ideals of the French Revolution, which was acclaimed with enthusiasm by Schiller and Goethe, Klopstock and

Herder, by historians and jurists, and even by Kant. They were all profoundly influenced by the Revolution, which divided the whole of European civilisation into two camps. Fichte's pamphlet is a defence of the principles of the French Revolution as against the literary reaction begun by Burke, who had found disciples in Germany. In this pamphlet, man lives always in the state of nature. The state is superfluous. It is in no way distinguished from a private association.

In his theory of law Fichte distinguishes between innate and acquired rights. The former are inalienable and comprise those actions which are enjoined on me. The acquired rights are alienable, and consist of those actions which are only permitted to me. Of the innate rights he says: "No man can be bound save by himself; to no man can a law be given, save by himself. If he permits a foreign will to impose a law upon him, he waives his humanity and makes himself a beast; and this he may not do".[61]

But what are the innate as opposed to the acquired rights? He distinguishes between the rights of "unchangeable spirituality" ("unveränderlichen Geistigkeit") and those of "changeable sensuality" ("veränderlichen Sinnlichkeit"). It is impossible to alienate the former, even if one should wish to do so. The latter are divided into internal and external rights. The internal are inalienable; of the external (the capacity to act on external nature and persons), a minimum is equally inalienable, for everyone must live.[62] The rest of the external rights can be alienated by means of a contract. All legal changes must take the form of contracts, which are either contracts of exchange or of gift. It is, however, an inalienable right of man to break any contract. Thus those who are oppressed can at any time dissolve the contract by which they have sold themselves into dependence and slavery: "It is an inalienable right of man, even on one side, and as soon as he desires, to annul any of his contracts; immutability and eternal validity of any contract is the ultimate violation of the essential rights of humanity".[63] Therefore anyone can leave the state at any time; anyone can establish a new state within the territory of the state. Decisions of the majority have no validity.

Curiously enough, property belongs to the innate and inalienable rights. It is, however, a right conferred not by occupation but by labour. He accepts, therefore, Locke's cultural property theory, as against the reactionary theory of Kant. The original property consists of our physical and intellectual forces. His theory of property, with the possible swing to the right for the full product of labour has therefore socialistic implications.

This pamphlet also contains, however, a confession of faith in free competition. "Give freedom to trade, with the natural heritage of man, with his powers", and it will be found that social problems can be solved without state intervention, without "drastic agricultural laws". But he demands free competition on the basis of equality of property, and, obviously influenced by Momoro, he asserts "that all men have a legal title to an equal portion of land, and that the soil is to be distributed in equal portions".[64]

This system of Fichte's realises the rule of the material law. Man is under a dual law, that of his nature on the one hand and that of the contract, i.e. the positive law, on the other. The latter is, however, entirely under the natural law; and here he is in opposition to Spinoza and Pufendorf. In a passionate polemic against Hobbes, he takes Locke's positions and carries it to its logical conclusion, by maintaining that the state of nature does not cease, but continues to exist in the state.[65] The state has no place in his system. "No one is cultivated, but everyone has to cultivate himself".[66] The task of Fichte's state is to render itself superfluous: "The State, like all human institutions, which are mere means, has as aim its own annihilation: the end of all government is to make government superfluous".[67] As with Rousseau who reduces state activity to a "mouvement du doigt", and as later with Marx and Engels, the final aim of the State is its abolition.

One can therefore consider Fichte's theory of 1793 as the German physiocratic theory.

Between this early system and the late system of 1812 and 1813, there occur some intermediate systems, which in the main are characterised by the fact that Fichte discovers the political concept of the law, and finds himself confronted with the task of reconciling it with the conception of the material law.[68]

As early as 1796, in order to escape the implications of the social contract conception, he asserts the existence of an objective Reason. This mediatory theory is logically based upon a divorce of the form and content of the social contract. At this period the contract for him is characterised as to its form by the free submission of the citizens.[69] Its content, however, "the positive law", is determined "by the nature of the thing". He even arrives at a categorical denial of the rights of men, equal in dogmatic certainty to his earlier assertion of their existence. "There is no condition of original rights, and no original rights of men. . . . Original right is therefore a mere fiction."[70] Having in the meantime become sceptical of the liberal democratic conception — democracy for him is now an "absolutely illegal constitution"[71] — he leaves the decision as to what is consistent with the nature of things to the executive. He now rejects the separation of powers. He even contests the possibility of distinguishing the executive from the judiciary; but his mistrust of the executive leads him to suggest instituting an ephorate, which is to control the executive.[72] But the conflict between the executive and the people as to the "nature of things" is in this intermediate system decided in favour of the people by granting to them a right of resistance. This right, however, contrary to his theory of 1793, is denied to the individual, and only granted to the people as a whole; for the characteristic reason that "The people [are] never [rebels], and the term 'rebellion' used in relation to [them], is the most extreme absurdity which has ever been uttered".[73]

Let us leave out his further attempts at compromise, and turn immediately to his final system, his *Rechtslehre* of 1812 and his *Staatslehre* of 1813.

The final break with the period of Enlightenment appears in his lectures of 1804 and 1805 on the *Grundzüge des gegenwärtigen Zeitalters*.[74] The period of Enlightenment appears to him as that of "complete sinfulness". Consequently his conception of law and state changes. The idea of the *Raison d'Etat* and of the sovereignty of the state makes its appearance. The state is now recognised as a coercive power, and characterised as domination.[75] It is no longer regarded as a private association, but it is an "indivisible organic whole". Neither is the state an economic unit, nor a legal category; it is, or should be, a cultural state, combating barbarism, subduing nature to men, and furthering the arts.[76] It is now a unity, an organic natural product.[77] It now becomes "an absolute duty dictated by the conscience to unite with others to form a State".[78] On the other hand, he still maintains the existence of [the] rights of men, especially of freedom of religion and freedom of science. The state has, however, a right to mobilise all the forces of the citizens, but always with the final aim of rendering itself superfluous.

Assisted by the impression made upon him by his flight from the French in 1807, the dual conception, state and nation, gains an ever stronger hold over him. His many small works of this period[79] show his attempt to construct a strong state on the basis of the free nation. All his theories are anti-monarchical; they represent in short the anti-liberal side of Jacobinism. Above all, however, he discovers Machiavelli,[80] but at first only with regard to foreign policy. The ideal of the self-sufficient state becomes, under the influence of the Napoleonic wars, the central conception. On this basis he now constructs a system of state socialism, which, however, is mainly individualistic; a system which is the logical consequence of his altered political conception on the one hand, and of his cultural theory of property on the other. In 1807 his ideas were summarised as follows:

> Since the French Revolution the doctrine of the Rights of Man and of Freedom and of the original equality of all — which are certainly the eternal and indestructible basis of all social organisation against which no State dare offend, but with which alone no State can be erected or administered — have been accentuated too much by some of our own philosophers in the heat of the battle . . . .[81]

He denies now that property is a right preceding the state. The validity of contracts depends now upon the will of the state, that is, on positive law.[82] There remains only the postulate of the sanctity of the home; the rest is a centralised police state, a "geschlossener Handelsstaat", in which there is no room for chance, for genius, or for luxury; which is ruled by the purest rationalism.[83] Now it is "the object of the state to give everyone his due, to invest him with his property and then to protect him in it".[84] A synthesis of this "content" of the state with the "form" of reason, as in Machiavellianism and Idealism, to use Meinecke's expression[85] is indeed, attempted only in 1813, and in this connection we wish to emphasise that his solution is based rather on impulse than on ratiocination.[86] It is decisively important that Fichte now abandons the rational justification of the state. It is true that in his *Grundzüge des gegenwärtigen Zeitalters*, a rational justification is still to be found. The state has the task of abolishing feudal privileges, of liberating the peasants, of restoring legal equality, of becoming a cultural, and not only an economic or a legal, state.[87] On the other hand, Fichte always takes the view that religion, science and virtue must never become aims of the state.[88] Under the influence of the Napoleonic oppression, the species which is to be realised by the state becomes for him the nation. The nation now becomes the means of regenerating the world. His conception of the nation, however, is only applied in the field of foreign policy. Fichte is far from identifying the existing reactionary state with the nation. For him, the concept of the nation is still the Jacobin conception.[89] This nation of free and equal citizens is the substructure which creates the state, and which the state must dominate in order to be able to live. In this relationship between state and nation there is, however, an intellectual indecision, which Fichte has not solved because it was impossible to reconcile his two postulates, the absolute state and the free democratic nation. It was important to create German unity; to weld together into a nation the various peoples on the basis of freedom, and to confront the family with this free nation; but as important as the creation of the nation was the reconstruction of an efficient state machinery, as it had broken down in and after the Napoleonic wars. The ultimate task seems even in Fichte's theory to be constant: "The State as the supreme administrator of human affairs and the guardian of those who are under age, which in the exercise of its powers, is answerable only to God, has the absolute right to coerce them — that is, the children — for their good".[90] The relation between this state and the nation is similar to that in the ideology of Italian Fascism. Meinecke[91] considers Fichte's conception of the nation to be merely a rational and not a historical conception. It seems, however, to be more important to emphasise the fact that in Fichte's theory the nation is moulded by the state. The motive which led Italian Fascism, in contrast to German National Socialism, to put the state above the nation and to make the nation the object of the state — namely, the inefficiency of the pre-Fascist State — was equally decisive in Fichte's case. He thus becomes the herald of state-absolutism, just as it is of Italian Fascism.

His last works are an attempt to justify this new Machiavellianism of the state. In his *Rechtslehre* of 1812,[92] law and morality, positive law and natural law, are sharply distinguished, and any relation between positive and natural law is denied. Every law is now positive law. "Outside the State there is no law; there is no natural law, but only the law of the State."[93] Consequently law is now related to might; "Might is the condition of law".[94] By this is postulated the absolute sovereignty of the state, that is to say the formal rule of the political law. All rights are delegated by the state; and therefore also property. The state is the sole owner of land.[95] Trade is a monopoly of the state; the merchants are officials of the State.[96]

How is this system of complete absolutism reconcilable with his individualistic starting-point, which he has never completely abandoned? It would be idle to recapitulate here all his metaphysics, to present his fallacious arguments and the logical plunges he takes in order to prove the necessary identity of the will of the individual with that of the State.

He finally reaches no other conclusion than Spinoza's; that only the spirit is free.[97] Two institutional ways of escape are provided for a limitation of the state activity, namely educational institutes, which the state is to set up for the education to liberty,[98] and the rule of the best.[99] "In theory the judgment of the people is correct, because there is no higher judge. But what of practice? One can trust a select group of wise men far more than a majority which was constituted God knows how."[100] But how these wise men are to be found does not become clear. We may be spared the examination of his *Staatslehre* of 1813.[101] Here he again attempts to restore reason, after having enthroned pure might (*voluntas*). He now suggests that an areopagus of teachers and instructors of the people should select the ruler.[102]

We have not dealt with Fichte's theory because it contains any original contribution. State-absolutism has been far more clearly presented by Hobbes and Spinoza, Pufendorf and Kant; the natural law theory, far more convincingly by Grotius and Locke. We have only considered Fichte's theories because his work comprises every conceivable rational theory of law and the state, from a pure natural law system whose sole aim is liberty, via all possible compromises, to state-absolutism; and because it clearly demonstrates the dependence of political theory on political reality.

CHAPTER 11

Hegel

In Hegel's theory of state and law there stand irreconcilably side by side the rights of men and state sovereignty, the rational justification of state and law and state-absolutism.[1] The dialectical synthesis of sovereignty and the rights of men is with him a mere postulate or metaphysical concept. By this assertion we say nothing against the dialectical method, especially nothing against materialistic dialectics.

In Hegel's paper, which has already been mentioned, on the scientific treatment of natural law (*Über die wissenschaftlichen Behandlungsarten des Naturrechts*, 1802–3), he deals with and criticises in the first part the empirical, that is to say, the pre-Kantian, natural law. He rightly shows the dogmatic character of this natural law, especially in the instance of Hobbes' theory of the state of nature. This theory is dogmatic because only one factor, be it impulse or human will, makes absolute, and from this, state and law are deduced; and because there is no criterion as to "where lies the frontier between the incidental and the necessary, which must thus remain in the chaos of the natural state, or in the realm of human abstraction, and which has to be omitted".[2] Hegel, however, uses an even stronger criticism of the critical natural law of Kant and Fichte, of the divorce of legality and morality, and of Fichte's idea of the ephorate, which idea, however, Fichte later abandoned, as we have already seen. The third part of this paper, the positive part need not be dealt with here, as we have to consider it later in dealing with his Philosophy of Right. It is, however, decisive for the third part that private property and the state become the destiny of men, whereas still in 1798 Hegel praised the wisdom of the Solonic legislation, and saw in private property a perversion of liberty.[3]

11.1.

The decisive change in Hegel's theory begins in 1805.[4]

11.1.1.

After that, the free will of man is the primary principle of the state. In his *System der Sittlichkeit* of 1802,[5] he still identified negative freedom, and crime. Now, however, the free man who realises himself appears as the fundamental maxim of the state. His is not the negative juridical conception of freedom which we find in Kant's system, but the philosophical conception. Man shall not only, as the Kantian ethic demands, emancipate himself from his desires; rather he shall fulfil them. In so far as Hegel bases the state upon the free will of men, he accepts the rationalist principle of the natural law.[6] Thus the individual man must not disappear within the state. "Free will reconciles all. And in this way the reconciliation takes place as well through the individual advantage as through general interests. Individuality shall no longer be sacrificed."[7]

Hegel, therefore, sets himself the same problem as did Rousseau, Kant and Fichte; that is, the problem of how the individual will and the will of the state can be made identical; of how the state and individual liberty can be realised at one and the same time, and in the same spheres of life. We have already considered Rousseau's solution, which presupposes the fulfilment of certain political and economic conditions. Kant and Fichte transfer the solution — if any — to the sphere of transcendence.

Obviously such a synchronisation of the individual will with that of the state is possible only if the interests of all those men who found the state are parallel; that is to say if a certain homogeneity of interests is either given or guaranteed.

11.1.2.

For the solution of this problem, Hegel introduces the second principle of the state,which one could perhaps call Montesquieu's principle, that is, history,[8] in which the objective spirit, the spirit of the people, realises itself. As against this objective spirit, the individuals are to some extent accidentals: "Whether the individual exists or not, is a matter of indifference to the objective ethical order, which alone is steadfast. It is a power, by which the life of individuals is ruled".[9] The individual working for his own ends and his own interests furthers at the same time universal purposes. He acts not only for himself; not against " the order of the universe but for it; for it is the cunning of the Idea, that it allows the passions to work for it".[10] In isolation the individual is nothing. The individual can enjoy his freedom only in the state.

The conception of the spirit of the people is, however, not that of romanticism and of the historical school. It is known that Hegel rejected both, and that he designated as barbarism the conception that men are governed by instincts, feelings, and customs, without a consciousness of whether these are good or bad.[11] The spirit of the people is a self-conscious moral substance ("die selbst-bewusste sittliche Substanz"). What that means, I do not know. I am not in a position rationally to understand this conception, I can only feel it.

Hegel, however, meant by this and similar formulae to transcend the natural law, and the dissolution of the state by natural law thinking. On the other hand, he clearly recognised the historical significance of natural law. He saw in the struggle for the negative, juridical, freedom, by the natural law theory, a necessary historical process. Accordingly the French Revolution appeared to him as a glorious sunrise.[12]

Finally he arrives at the famous formula: "The state is the realised ethical idea or ethical spirit".[13] And "the ethical system is thus the conception of freedom, developed into a present world and also into the nature of selfconsciousness".[14]

11.2.

If I am unable rationally to understand the assertion of a coincidence of freedom and the spirit of the people in the state, just as little as I am able rationally to understand similar formulations in Kant, Fichte, and Rousseau, then it seems to me more fruitful to present the relation of liberty and state sovereignty in various instances.

11.2.1.

Starting from the conception of Roman Law, Hegel develops first the conception of the person, and reaches, in agreement with the natural law, the postulate of the legal equality of men. His postulate is: "A person must give to his freedom an external sphere in order that he may reach the completeness implied in the idea".[15] To his repudiation of the separation of legality and morality, corresponds the introduction of the philosophical conception of freedom into the postulate of the freedom of the person; so that his conception comprises both the juridical and the philosophical liberty.

11.2.2.

From these basic principles of liberty and the person, he deduces the theory of property. Each personal right is a property right, and only in and through property can the idea of the person be realised. Manifestly influenced by Adam Smith, he develops a cultural theory of property; use and labour, and not only possession and legal title, constitute property. Thus the concept of property, just as that of the person, has a dual content: negatively, property confers rights of defence and positively, rights of use. Hegel, therefore, implies in the notions of person and property a system of political and economic rights of freedom: "It is fully 1500 years since through the influence of Christianity the freedom of the person began to flourish, and at least in a small section of the human rank as an universal principle. But the recognition here and there of the principle of the freedom of the property is, as it were, a thing of yesterday".[16] Thus free property makes possible free initiative.

One essential perception is, however, lacking; and in this Hegel is behind the Physiocrats and Adam Smith. He lacks the perception that only equality of property makes free initiative possible for all; that only in a given state, one of equally distributed property, can sovereignty emerge from competition; and that only this state of equal property distribution guarantees the parallelism of individual wills. He himself rejects the postulate of equality.[17]

Beside the postulate of freedom of property, and in connection with it, there stand those of freedom of trade, of contract, of religion, of the press, and of the equal access of all to all public offices. He even demands the recognition of the rights of minorities, such as the right of conscientious objection for the Quakers.[18] These political and economic liberties are, however, not conceived as existing before the state; they are only granted by the state. They are for Hegel products of a historical process, children of the civil society. In long discussions,[19] he explains that freedom does not mean freedom to do, and especially to write, what one wants: "These views belong to the undeveloped crudity and superficiality of fanciful theorising".[20] Rather, freedom implies restraint. The state limits freedom, and action against the state before courts or administrative tribunals was to him unthinkable; so that a guarantee for the rights of freedom is only given if the interests of the state and those of the civil society are identical. If they diverge, the same dilemma occurs as in all rational theories: the state either abolishes the rights of freedom, or the civil society abolishes the state.

11.3.

11.3.1.

Here we are faced with the theory of the civil society. This civil society is distinct from the state. It is the society which the individual enters after having left the family. It is "the realm of difference, intermediate between the family and the State".[21] The notion of the civil society is thus a historical conception. It denotes the society which emerged in the seventeenth and eighteenth centuries, especially in England and France, after the collapse of the mediaeval order.

The civil society is the society of egoism; but it is an egoism, however, which through the interdependence of social men becomes a link in the working of society itself: "The individuals in the civic communities are private persons, who pursue their own interests, as these interests are occasioned by the universal, which appears as a means, they can be obtained only in so far as individuals in their desire, will and conduct, conform to the universal and become a link in the chain of the whole".[22]

The civil society has three functions: the satisfaction of needs in a society based upon division of labour, "the recanting of want and the satisfaction of the individual through his work, through the work of all others and through the satisfaction of their wants"; the realisation of the necessary freedom by protection of property and the administration of justice; and, finally, the necessary intervention in such freedom against possible mischances, and care for the common interests by means of police and corporation.

The civil society is, like that of Kant's theory, a society of private law, having as its main function the protection of property. Work is sacred. "Industry and trade have now become moral."[23] "Through the dependence and cooperation involved in labour, subjective self-seeking is converted into a contribution towards the satisfaction of wants of all others. The universal so penetrates the particular by its dialectic movement, that the individual, while acquiring, producing, and enjoying for himself, at the same time produces and acquires for the enjoyment of others."[24] This theory places Hegel among the true harmonists such as the Physiocrats and Adam Smith. He himself often speaks with approval of Adam Smith, Jean-Baptiste Say, and David Ricardo.

11.3.2.

Society is divided into estates according to the activities of man. But this estate order, which he proclaims in his Philosophy of Right, has practically no connection with the mediaeval order of estates. Hegel not only recognises free access to professions, but expressly demands it.[25] The first estate, the universal estate, comprises officials, teachers, and officers; the second and third, peasants and trades respectively. He does not recognise a fourth estate of dependent workers. Obviously the phenomenon of poverty did not escape his notice; he even saw that accumulation of riches on the one side produces poverty on the other.[26] He had even seen the phenomenon of the replacement of men by machinery; and he acclaimed this process, because he saw in it the progress of history. He objected to the unhistorical conception of the natural law, which praised the happy state of nature which had been destroyed by the civil society. Hegel has even been called the founder of modern German economic theory;[27] but concede to the fourth estate of workers a place in his system of estates he could not. Had he done so, he would not have been able to construct the state; for it cannot be too often repeated, that such a rational construction of the state is only possible if harmony of the interests of all those groups which form the state is presupposed. To introduce the fourth estate into his system without abandoning this presupposition, it would have been necessary to accept the proposition that the interests of dependent workers and those of landed property and capital are identical. This assumption, however, he could not make without doing violence to reality; consequently, the fourth estate is missing. What remains is his belief in the identity of interest of the other three estates, from whose competition and collaboration sovereignty emerges. The centre of gravity lies so essentially in the first estate, that in reality this universal estate of the bureaucracy and army becomes the bearer of the state, and the realisation of the ethical will.[28]

11.3.3.

This civil society, based upon property, freedom of contract, and freedom of trade, is guaranteed as to its fundamental institutions and supplementary liberties by the legal order. The law serves to punish injuries to property, and to ensure undisturbed personal security.[29] The passage in section 188 of his *Philosophy of Right*, in which he enumerates the three elements of the civil society, shows very clearly that he considers private property to be the principal institution, whereas the liberties are regarded as supplementary; that is, as serving the institution of property. Consequently "right enters into being only because it is serviceable for wants".[30] The law is general, irrespective of whether it is statutory or customary. For "the right of the subject to economic freedom is secured by the condition that the determination of law by reason shall stop short of the particular detail of execution".[31] The generality of the law is in his view the essential guarantee of freedom. But he gives the preference to statutory law, so as to exclude arbitrary decisions of the judges.[32] The only law is positive law emanating from the authority of the state (section 212). The administration of justice is the bringing of a concrete case under the general norm (section 214). But this is not all; the activity of the judge is not merely the activity of a machine, (section 211, addition). Even the will of the judge, controlled by positive law, has decisive significance (section 214). The courts must be independent. They must administer the law "without the subjective instigation of private interest".[33] Considerations of equity must find no place in the decisions of the judges (section 223). The administration of justice must be publicly carried out (section 224).

11.3.4.

This society, based upon property, freedom of contract, and of trade, and protected by the legal order, must, however, be subject to state interference in such matters as the war against crime (section 232), the repulsing of disturbances of the external order, and so on. This is the task of the police (section 231), which also has authority to create the external conditions for the functioning of free competition by lighting the streets, building bridges and roads, and taking measures for the protection of public health (section 236, addition). The police has the further task of keeping in check poverty (section 241), which grows through the accumulation of capital. Consequently checks must be provided, and the country must be colonised. The corporations, which, together with the family constitute the moral root of the State (section 255), are to unite the estates and undertake the care of their members. They are, however, not autonomous bodies, but are under the control of the state (section 255, addition). Police and corporations are thus corrective and supplementary institutions of free competition.

11.4.

Individuals, the family, corporations, the civil society — this is the sequence which leads to the state.

11.4.1.

The state is distinct from the civil society, which is only one of its elements, as Hegel repeatedly emphasises. The state has an existence of its own. In the state as an idea the antagonisms of needs are solved in a higher sphere. The state as an idea stands above the civil society. The family and society are the two structures in which man lives, and through which he prepares himself for the state. But in reality it is true that the only bearer of the state is the civil society.[34] The civil society is not only one element of the state; it is in truth the state. It subordinates it, makes it its servant. According to Hegel, the state is in relation to the family and civil society a higher power, for both shall be subordinated to it, but at the same time the state is their "indwelling end" (section 261). It goes without saying that the state does not rest on a contract. Its subjective basis is patriotism (section 268), that is to say the free consent of the citizens; because, in the spirit of Freiherr von Stein's thought, genuine patriotism can only grow out of free consent. It is possible also that the historical example of England may have been effective. English democracy, as against French absolutism, had shown that an efficient organisation of state activity is possible also in a state dependent on free consent; and that it can be successful even in great wars. The French revolutionary wars had confirmed this experience, and taught that patriotism is indissolubly bound to liberty.

The state is the organisation of the general interests of society through the medium of its particular interests. One could perhaps formulate in this way the Hegelian theory of the state (sect. 270, addition).

11.4.2.

Hegel adheres to the principle of the separation of powers as a guarantee of freedom (section 272). But this distinction between the three powers must never lead to their estrangement, any more than it is the meaning of the principle that the three powers should be mutually restrictive; for this would lead in his view to the destruction of the state. Thus for him the unity of the purposes of the state is of decisive importance; and distinction between the powers is for him as for Max Weber only a necessary consequence of the increasing complexity of state activity. The three powers are the legislative, that is, "the power to fix and establish the universal"; the executive, that is, "the power which brings particular spheres and individual cases under the universal"; and the monarchical, the power of final decision — "In this function the other two are brought into an individual unity. It is at once the culmination and beginning of the whole. This is a constitutional monarchy".[35]

11.4.3.

This formulation could lead us to conclude that Hegel identifies sovereignty of the state with sovereignty of the state organs; this, however, is not the case, as section 279 shows. "The monarch is not sovereign: only the state is sovereign; but sovereignty is monarchical: the sovereign state demands the monarchical individual."[36] Thus the power of the state is identified with that of the prince; for the monarchical power has, as section 275 shows, received all the moments of totality. It comprises the right to promulgate general norms as well as to issue individual decisions. We may be spared the extremely complicated justification of this theory. The decisive point is that sovereignty does not mean only the right to issue general norms, but also individual decisions; and that these can only be made by a person.

11.4.4.

In Hegel's theory no institutional limits to the exercise of monarchical sovereignty are to be found. For if the state is integrated by the monarchy, if the majesty of the monarch is the sole guarantee of unity, then limitations of the power of the monarch are inconceivable. Here in reality is the key to Hegel's theory. By the rationally unproved identity of the "ethical will . . . with the will of the ruler" it becomes true that "the State is the necessary condition of its exercise", but it will be true also that its exercise is confined to a limited body of men. In their will alone absolute *Sittlichkeit* will be realised and the possession of this freedom and the realisation of this *Sittlichkeit* will presuppose the existence of another body of men excluded from participation in either.[37] Neither property nor political freedom nor the postulate that the state rules through general norms constitute in Hegel's system limitations of the monarchical power, although he himself asserts the existence of a subjective limitation in the conscience of the ruler, and an objective one in law and the constitution (section 285). But the content of the law is itself determined by the sovereign. To this power of the monarch belongs the right of pardon (section 284), the right to appoint officials (section 283), and the right to issue commands to subordinate officials (section 284).

11.4.5.

In contrast to the monarchical power which is decisive, the executive power has merely to apply already established decisions of the monarch. Its function is administrative (section 287). The monarchical and the executive power stand to each other in the relation of *actes gouvernementaux* to *actes administratifs*. The function of the executive embraces the administration of justice. Government and the administration of justice both involve the application of norms. In this, Hegel is distinguished from Montesquieu, who knew no internal administration, as his attention was centred upon England where internal administration was concentrated in Parliament and therefore did not present itself to him as a distinct function. Hegel, however, had the Prussian bureaucracy before his eyes, and therefore, as we have already shown, and as sections 290 [to] 294 prove, bureaucracy as the first and universal estate plays a decisive rôle in his construction of the state. Only the bureaucracy can guarantee the freedom of the citizens. This assertion proves the sureness of Hegel's historical insight. Legality of administration is guaranteed, not by the right of resistance, but by permanent institutions such as the bureaucracy; and the interaction which, in spite of their separation, takes place between the state and the civil society. This guarantee is strengthened by the distinction between the three powers (section 290), and by self-government (section 295). Self-government "supplements from below the control from above".[38]

11.4.6.

The merging of civil society and state takes place in the sphere of legislation as well as in that of self-government. Legislation is the creation of general norms, that is to say, of "those internal affairs, whose content is universal".[39] As for foreign policy, its conduct on the basis of general norms appears to him impossible (sections 321, 322), and here he is in agreement with Locke. The definition of general norms is a true liberal one — interferences with liberty and property — as may be gathered from the very complicated section 299. They create duties and rights.

Legislation does not rest with a parliament; he knows no parliament. He always repudiated universal and equal suffrage, precisely because parliament considers the citizens only as isolated atoms. His praise of the system of estates, which in relation to the legislative process have only an advisory function, is well-known. He is conscious that, by the recognition of such advisory rights for the estates, the state is drawn into the civil society (section 311). For the estate of landed proprietors is "a support at once to the throne and to the community" (section 307). The third estate comprises the "fluctuating side of the civic community".

11.5.

11.5.1.

In Hegel's system two elements can be discerned: the rational justification of the state on the one hand, and history as a datum on the other, that is to say the coercive machinery of the state as represented by the monarch and the bureaucracy. His rational arguments are not carried to their logical conclusion. "Hegel is guilty of indecision, in explaining the philosophy as the existence of the Absolute Spirit, and at the same time refusing to allow himself to accept the real philosophic individual as the Absolute Spirit."[40]

Freedom of the citizens is guaranteed neither by the right of resistance, nor by admission to a share in political power, nor by the separation of powers. Protection is transferred exclusively to the civil society, which by its free consent justifies the state.

Thus Hegel's conception of the state is not that of the *Machtstaat* (as it is presented by Heller); and this neither with regard to the internal nor to the external policy of the state. Even if the decision of the monarch is considered to be the constitutive element of the State, the remnants of natural law are still preserved intact. As far as foreign policy is concerned, Hegel never glorifies war, as is shown especially by his criticism of Heller (section 258). He rejects Machiavellian methods in foreign policy, and emphasises the importance of keeping international treaties (section 333). If he expresses the view that war is the last resort for a decision as between states (section 334), and rejects the Kantian assertion of the possibility of eternal peace (section 333, note), he rendered to the science of politics a far greater service than did Kant, because he recognised the forces driving towards war and, unlike Kant, did not veil them.

His ideal state was, as has been shown definitely by Franz Rosenzweig,[41] the Prussian state of the reforms of Freiherr von Stein. Liberation of the peasants, freedom of trade, local self-government, the recognition of the existence of a bourgeoisie, with the correctives of corporations and police; these were the foundations of the state which he accepted as obvious. Rudolph Haym[42] has already drawn attention to the fact that Hegel's state could appeal to Stein and Humbolt.

11.5.2.

His solution of the problem of a synthesis of liberty and sovereignty, of the rights of men and the state, depends, therefore, on a series of assumptions which must be analysed briefly.

The first, a philosophical, problem, is how far the dialectic philosophy of history is compatible with the assertion that the state is the realisation of the ethical idea. It is only possible because for Hegel history ends with the attainment of the "modern" epoch, just as for the Marxist theory history ends with the realisation of the classless society.

Identity of liberty and the state is only possible if the interests of the civil society and of the state, that is to say of the monarch and the bureaucracy on the one hand, and of landed property, industry, and trade, on the other, are basically identical. This in turn presupposes that the civil society itself has a common and united interest. Hegel assumes this. For him, as a harmonist who has studied and accepted Adam Smith and J.-B. Say, the competitors who pursue their own interests realise, by virtue of a world plan, the common interest. The Hegelian theory, in its acceptance of an identity of the interests of landed proprietors and of industry and trade, is pre-Ricardian; and it implies that no account is taken of the existence of a working class as a social and political reality.

It is true that the problem of the fourth estate did not in Hegel's time present any difficulty; but an identity of the interests of landed proprietors and industry and trade within the civil society certainly did not exist.

11.5.3.

If one accepted the Hegelian theory of the state without reference to the two assumptions upon which it is based, it could become a weapon in the hand of reaction, and could be transformed into the theory of the *Machtstaat* which it has become. It is undoubtedly true that Hegel himself is guilty of this interpretation. In the preface to his *Philosophy of Right*, 25th June 1820, he praised the Prussian state; the state of broken promises, of disappointed hopes; a state which cared nothing for free institutions. One cannot excuse Hegel on the ground that he was not realist enough to recognise the true character of the Prussian state.[43] At all events, his theory served first the state of the Restoration, and afterwards that of Bismarck. It was made to serve the cause of absolutism, as the young Hegelians already observed. But his conception could just as easily become the revolutionary theory of Marxism, if one took into account the existence of the fourth estate of workers, and proves the theory of the harmonists to be a false doctrine. This has been done by Marxism.

III

The Verification of the Theory: The Rule of Law in the Nineteenth and Twentieth Centuries

INTRODUCTION

The Totalitarian State's Criticism of the Liberal Theory of Law

It belongs to the commonest tricks of a certain type of political science to confront the idea of one type of state with the reality of another; to confront the ideology of a political idea with the sociology of an antagonistic theory. We do not assert that this trick is always consciously applied; very often it is applied with such nonchalance that it might be supposed that the authors are quite unconscious of the inadmissibility of such proceedings. In this way, Italian Fascism confronts the idea of the corporate state with the reality of liberal capitalism; National Socialism, the idea of a leadership state with the alleged sociology of Parliamentary democracy; Bolshevism, the idea of the Soviet system with the sombre reality of bourgeois democracy. This is not only done in pamphlets published by the propaganda ministeries of the countries concerned, but it is part of the habitual equipment of their theorists. Victories won by such methods are easily won. The beautiful and enticing pictures painted of the proffered state theory appear of course preferable to a conception of the state whose functioning is depicted in the darkest colours. This struggle with unequal weapons is as regards the public always won by the stronger weapon, the more if this Utopia is helped forward by more or less gentle coercion.

It must be obvious for a science of politics that an idea can only be confronted with an idea, and a reality only with another reality.

The outstanding example of the above type of pseudo-science of politics is the fight of the present-day German political science against liberalism and democracy and for the ideology of the National Socialist leadership state. In spite of the diversity of conceptions of the constitutive elements of the National Socialist ideology, there exists a complete harmony of the whole of German political science with regard to the wickedness of liberalism and democracy. Hundreds of pamphlets and works which have only the remotest connection with politics paint the devilish picture of liberal democracy, very often only to procure for themselves an alibi towards the new master.

From the abundance of the National Socialist pamphlets and works only a few specimens of the vilification of liberalism and democracy shall be given here. "The blood rises against formal reason, the race against rational purposive action, honour against profit, union ("Bindung") against arbitrariness which is called liberty, organic totality against individualistic dissolution, readiness to fight ("Wehrhaftigkeit") against bourgeois security, politics against the supremacy of economy, state against society, people against individual and mass." This quotation from the pamphlet of the philosopher Ernst Krieck,[1] the successor of Heinrich Rickert, can be regarded as an epitome of the National Socialist criticism of the liberal system. All other criticism concerns certain specific phenomena of the liberal system, its economic theory, its theory of society, and its conception of the state and of the law.

The liberal state is considered to be "neutral",[2] "negative", a "fictitious state, a mere machinery",[3] and Lassalle's description of the liberal State as a "night-watchman state" is now generally admitted.[4] This negative state is alleged to be without substance,[5] without the capacity to reach decisions, unable to determine whether anything is good or bad, beautiful or ugly, just or unjust. Liberalism is a mere degeneration of the idea of freedom. It leads to anarchy. It is dissolving, materialistic, and this applies also to Marxian socialism, which is considered to be a mere variety of liberalism. Democracy is the rule of the unorganised mass.[6] It knows no people, but only a mass of Robinson Crusoes. Fundamentally, democracy is without political domination, or the domination is anonymous.[7] The principle of democracy is that of the "direct counting of noses".[8] Parliament is the stage for unrestricted competition, for the most naked battle of interests, for the hunger for power. It is dominated by pluralistic private organisations.[9] The law of liberalism is mechanistic. It serves only private interests. It is merely static.[10] Under the influence of Franz von Liszt, crime has been regarded as a mere natural phenomenon. The penal code has been regarded as the Magna Carta of the criminal.[11] Fundamentally liberalism and law are mutually exclusive. Their alliance is only based upon necessity.[12] The judge is only a machine for the administration of justice. The liberal theory of the state and law has been created especially under the influence of "racially alien" theorists ("artfremder Theoretiker").[13] The state of the Weimar Constitution is described as a state of pluralistic parties. Trade unions and masters' organisations; Churches and political parties; the federal states; the policracy, that is to say, the domination of the public works undertaken by the state; and the state bureaucracy; all shared in the exercise of state power. This is only a very modest selection from National Socialist criticism of the essence and function of liberalism and parliamentary democracy. Both appear as monsters whose — negative — force is considered to be so powerful that it has corrupted all ideas and all institutions. This negative Leviathan has ruined all German racial institutions and ideas.

These attacks are by no means new. They are as old as liberalism and democracy. But what distinguishes Fascists from Catholic counter-revolutionaries and Marxian socialists is the universality and the vehemence of the attacks against liberalism, and especially the fact that Fascism completely denies any degree of liberty; whereas Marxian socialism at least believes in the restoration of liberty in a classless society. One has only to read for instance the criticism of Donoso Cortes, the Spanish Catholic counter-revolutionary:[14] "Dissolution of all continuity, of honour and glory, destruction of love for family and home, finally complete annihilation of the family and the nation. Neither family nor nation can exist, and can as little be understood, without the connection with past and future, without the bond of honour and glory, and without that great dual love, love for the home and for the father's house, which are the two firm bases". That is the picture which the Spanish counter-revolutionary gives of liberalism and of Proudhon's socialism.

We have, therefore, to re-state the liberal theory of society of the law and the state.

CHAPTER 12

The *Rechtsstaat* and the Rule of Law (The Problem Stated)

12.1. The German Theory of the *Rechtsstaat*

The legal form of a system based upon political and economic freedom differs in Germany and in England. The specific German phenomenon is the so-called *Rechtsstaat.*[1] The specific English creation is the unison of the two notions of the supremacy of Parliament and the rule of law.

By *Rechtsstaat*, two different things can be understood. For the pure science of law every state is a *Rechtsstaat*, be it democracy or dictatorship, be it a Fascist or a Bolshevist state. Even absolute monarchy and Fascist dictatorship are *Rechtsstaaten*, since they become objects of the pure theory of law only because we are compelled to conceive of the unlimited power of the monarch or of the dictator as derived from a basic norm. In this sense the idea of the *Rechtsstaat* is interpreted by Laski:[2]

> But the idea of a *Rechtsstaat* is a purely conceptual notion. It is a category of essence and not of reality. It makes the rulers of the state bound by the law they make; but it still leaves them free, through the use of the appropriate organs, to make the law. The Hitlerite state, equally with that of Great Britain or France or Czecho-Slovakia is a *Rechtsstaat* in the sense that dictatorial power has been transferred to the Führer by the legal order . . . . The idea of a *Rechtsstaat* is always qualified by the fact that the state is able, through its sovereignty, to change the substance of the law.

Such a conception of the *Rechsstaat* makes it possible for us to make every phenomenon called "state" the subject of normative jurisprudence. Such a conception is neither right nor wrong; it is simply meaningless.

From a historical point of view, the notion of the *Rechtsstaat* is a political one, and therefore, like every political conception, a polemical one. The word itself, but not the substance, is, according to Rudolph Gneist,[3] due to Robert von Mohl.[4] Lorenz von Stein already declared: "For it is clear that properly speaking there is no State without law. In a certain sense, every State is a *Rechtsstaat*. We, however, attach a special meaning to this word".[5]

We must, therefore, first determine clearly this special meaning. The notion of the *Rechtsstaat* appears already completed in the Kantian system. The *Rechtsstaat* is the creation of the bourgeoisie as an economically rising but politically stagnant class. This class identifies its state with the state as such, and thereby denies the character of *Rechtsstaat* to every other state, characterising it as a non-*Rechtsstaat*, even as a state of wrong (*Unrechtsstaat*).

The essence of the *Rechtsstaat* consists in the divorce of the political structure of the state from its legal organisation, which alone, that is to say independently of the political structure, is to guarantee freedom and security. In this separation consists the difference between the German *Rechtsstaat* and the English doctrine of the relation between the supremacy of Parliament and the rule of law.

The *Rechtsstaat* is, therefore, not the specific legal form of democracy, but it is neutral as regards the political structure. This radical separation of the form of the state from the legal structure is completed in the work of Friedrich Julius Stahl:

> The State is to be a *Rechtsstaat*; that is the watchword, and expresses what is in reality the trend of modern development. It shall exactly define and inviolably secure the direction and the limits of its operations, as well as the sphere of freedom of its citizens, by means of law; thus it shall realise directly nothing but that which belongs to the sphere of law. This is the conception of the *Rechtsstaat*, and not that the State shall only apply the legal order without administrative aims, or even only secure the rights of the individuals. It signifies above all not the aim and content of the State, but only the method and the nature of their realisation.[6]

It is characteristic that not only the liberals such as Rudolf Gneist, Lorenz von Stein, and Otto Bähr reached this formulation, but even

Stahl, the author of the Christian conservative theory of the state; and that Gneist[7] as well as Bähr[8] gave to it his assent. The postulate that the state has to have the character of a *Rechtsstaat* was developed by Stahl in a series of biting polemics against de Maistre and Bonald, in a criticism culminating in a denial that the monarch is the representative of God on earth,[9] and ending with the statement that the monarch "may not rule against the law, but only through the medium of the bureaucracy, and only with representation of the people".[10] It may be noted that Stahl, who had been appointed to Hegel's chair in Berlin University in order to combat Hegel's influence, himself shows clearly in this formulation the influence of the Hegelian philosophy of law. Similar formulations are to be found in Otto Bähr's work. According to him, a *Rechtsstaat* is given if the postulate is fulfilled that the state makes the law the fundamental condition of its existence, and that all life within its boundaries, of the individual as well as of the state in relation to its members, must move within the limits of the law. "In the realisation of the law the State realises the first germ of its own Idea."[11] For Rudolf Gneist, a state is a *Rechtsstat* if it fulfils four conditions: everyone must know exactly his duties; no citizen must bear more burdens than his fellows; private law must carry out the protection of the person and of property insistently, jealously, and energetically in the various spheres of its functioning; and, finally, the relation between citizen and state must be subject to the control of administrative tribunals.[12]

This praise of the idea of the *Rechtsstaat*, which in Welcker's words belongs to the highest grade of culture, belongs as has been shown by Dietrich Schindler, to the period of early liberalism. In this period, however, the *Rechtsstaat* theory does not merely stress the negative character of the state, that is to say the protection of liberty and the maintenance of the legal order; on the contrary, in opposition to Stahl, the idea of the *Rechtsstaat* was made to serve the cultural and welfare activities of the State.[13] This aspect of the *Rechtsstaat* was especially stressed by Robert von Mohl in his *Encyklopädie* of 1859:[14]

> Its essence consists in that it protects and furthers all natural aims recognised by the people as the life aims of the individuals, as well as that of the community. For this purpose it takes care that all activities of its citizens and that of the governing power are carried out within the limits of an all-embracing legal system; and that in the aggregate of life within

> its boundaries, in the relation of the individuals to each other as well as in the relation of the whole to its parts, the law is not violated. On the other hand, it furthers the various powers of its citizens and the interests resulting from them, in so far as their own powers are insufficient and in so far as the object justifies the application of the total power. The establishment and maintenance of the legal order is therefore not its sole, not even its most important aim, but is the dominant character, the inviolable negative side of all its operations.

The characteristics of the *Rechtsstaat* are in Mohl's theory equality before the law, care for the maintenance of individuals in all suitable cases, equal access of all competent citizens to all public offices, and finally, personal liberty. This material conception of the *Rechtsstaat*, which has been called by Heller the social *Rechtsstaat*, is however lost after the débâcle of the revolution of 1848. In the later development, the relation of the *Rechtsstaat* to the cultural and welfare aims of the state comes last. In the succeeding period of liberalism, only the negative aspect is understood by *Rechtsstaat*. In this period the already mentioned differentiation between the changeable aims of the state on the one hand, and the equal and unalterable form through which every state must realise its aims on the other, becomes constitutional reality. In this theory the strange alliance between throne and altar on the one hand, and the competitive economic system on the other, is consummated.[15]

After this, the essentials of the *Rechtsstaat* are therefore as follows. The fundamental principle is the legality of administration,[16] that is to say, the postulate that the administration of the state is bound by its own laws, and that every interference of the state must be reducible to such laws. This implies the supremacy of the law and only of the law; but of a certain type of law, namely of the general laws. From this it follows that the relation between the state and individuals must be determined in advance by formal rational law. The interference of the state with liberty and property must be predictable and calculable; in Stahl's words, it must be exactly defined. From this it follows that those interferences must be controllable, and indeed by independent judges.

This idea of the *Rechtsstaat* is indifferent in the first place as to the aims pursued by the state, and secondly — and this is decisive — as to the form of the state. Whether it be republic or monarchy, democracy or aristocracy, is without significance, provided only that these essentials of the *Rechtsstaat* are fulfilled.

12.2. The Rule of Law and the Supremacy of Parliament

By this indifference as to the political structure, by this irrelevance of the genesis of the law, the concept of the *Rechtsstaat* is clearly distinguished from the English doctrine of the Rule of Law; but from the Rule of Law in its relation to the doctrine of the supremacy of Parliament. This correlation of the two doctrines is to be found clearly in Blackstone's *Commentaries*, and is the consequence of the disappearance of a genuine natural law during and after the Great Revolution. For Blackstone, the supremacy of Parliament is the keystone of the constitutional system. Parliament can do anything which is not naturally impossible.[17] This supremacy of Parliament shall realise at the same time the rule of law. The correlation of the two doctrines is dated by Roscoe Pound[18] from the 10th November 1612, when Coke, on the occasion of the Case of Prohibitions opposed the claim of King James I to be himself a judge; and this identity of the two doctrines is clearly established in the Petition of Rights of 1628. Here Natural Law finally ceases, and the supremacy of the law becomes the supremacy of Parliament. The correlation of the two doctrines has been conclusively established in Dicey's famous book. In our view chapter XIII, which deals with the relation between parliamentary sovereignty and the rule of law seems to be decisive. Dicey clearly recognises the logical antagonism between the two fundamental conceptions; but as an essentially political thinker he comes to the conclusion that "this appearance is delusive; the sovereignty of Parliament as contrasted with other forms of sovereign power, favours the supremacy of the law, whilst the predominance of rigid legality throughout our institutions evokes the exercises, and thus increases the authority of parliamentary sovereignty".[19]

It is just the coordination of the genetic determination of the content of the law by Parliament with a certain structure of the legal system which appears to him as a secure guarantee for the maintenance of political freedom.

His first thesis is, therefore, that the sovereignty of Parliament furthers the rule of the law of the land. The fact that the commands of Parliament "can be uttered only through the combined action of its three constituent parts . . . prevents those inroads upon the law of the land which a despotic monarch such as Louis XIV, Napoleon I, or Napoleon III might effect by ordinances or decrees or which the different constituent assemblies of France and, above all, the famous Convention, carried out by sudden resolutions".[20] The monopoly of legislation by Parliament, with the balance between the House of Commons, the House of Lords, and the king, also strengthens the power of the judges, who up till now have always refused to interpret an Act of Parliament in another way than is necessitated by the wording of the Act; and, finally, explains the absence of administrative law.

His second thesis is that the supremacy of the law strengthens the sovereignty of Parliament.[21] The law is rigid and by its rigidity very often hinders the activities of the executive. If the executive power desires to act efficiently and purposefully, it must be freed in certain circumstances from the rigidity of the law. This exemption, however, can only be granted by Parliament, either in advance or by an Act of Indemnity. "A statute of this kind is the last and supreme exercise of Parliamentary sovereignty. It legalises illegality."[22]

This solution does not appear to him as merely formal, for the fact that the wide discretionary powers of the executive always necessitates a parliamentary delegation introduces the control of judges. "Parliament is the supreme legislator, but for the moment Parliament has uttered its will as lawgiver, that will becomes subject to the interpretation put upon it by the judges of the land."[23]

The supremacy of the law means, therefore, the supremacy of that law enacted by Parliament, that is to say, of statutory law, which is historically and politically opposed to the supremacy of the Common Law. This doctrine of the supremacy of enacted law arises historically in the very period when the creative power of the Common Law was denied. The seventeenth century, which brings the triumph of the bourgeoisie, brings at the same time that of Parliament and of the supremacy of parliamentary legislation. From then on, statute law is dominant, although the Common Law was more fully developed. This idea has been clearly formulated by Blackstone.[24]

The contradictions and inefficiencies of Dicey's constructions have been conclusively proved by Mr. Jennings' book. But this criticism does not concern the decisive sociological problem, for it cannot be denied that Dicey's construction has functioned, and is even operating now. It is undeniable that parliamentary sovereignty and the rule of law, that is to say sovereignty and material law, or the political and the material conceptions of law, had the same meaning in Dicey's day. It has therefore to be investigated why no social antagonism corresponded to the logical one which Dicey himself recognised. Dicey's formulation also shows clearly the fundamental difference between the English and the German doctrines. In the British doctrine, the centre of gravity lies in the determination of the content of the laws by Parliament. The German theory is uninterested in the genesis of the law, and is immediately concerned with the interpretation of a positive law, somehow and somewhere arisen. The German theory is liberal-constitutional; the English, democratic-constitutional. This difference explains the existence of a fully developed science of law in Germany, and the non-existence of such a science in England. The English bourgeoisie translated its will into law through the medium of Parliament; the German bourgeoisie found given laws which were systematised and interpreted in a very refined way in order to secure the maximum of liberty against a more or less absolute state. The social causes of these two divergent theories on the function of law in political and social life are to be dealt with in the following chapters.

12.3. Theses on the Construction of the Legal System in a Competitive Society

The legal system of that period centres around [the following:]

12.3.1.

The conception of personal political and economic liberty, which implied a presumption for liberty against the right of the state to intervene (the so-called pre-state character of freedom).

12.3.2.

This freedom is guaranteed by formal rational laws. This means: by general laws; and by the application of general laws by independent judges (*the formal structure of the legal system*).

12.3.3.

The legal system was related:

economically, to a system of free competition which found its legal expression in freedom of contract and freedom of trade (*the material structure of the legal system*).

It was *socially* related to a state of affairs in which a working class as an independent movement did not exist, in which therefore the existence of class conflicts was simply ignored (*the social structure of the legal system*).

It was *politically* related to a system of separation and distribution of powers; in Germany, to a system in which the bourgeoisie did not play a decisive political rôle; in England, to a system in which the bourgeoisie determined the content of the law, and political power was shared between Crown, nobility, and bourgeoisie (*the political structure of the legal system*).

12.3.4.

The force which integrated that society, based upon personal, political, and economic freedom, into a State, was the conception of the nation (*the irrational basis of society*).

These are the theses, which ought to stand at the end of this chapter, but with which, for didactic reasons, we begin, and which shall be interpreted in the following pages.

We shall proceed as follows: first we shall analyse the economic substructure upon which the legal system is erected; then we shall turn our attention to the political substructure and deal exclusively with the German development, as the corresponding English political history is well-known. In this connection we have to define the concept of the nation, and the function it performs as an integrating factor in the modern competitive society. Finally, we shall analyse the various elements of the liberal legal system, and lay stress on its formal structure; because its material elements, such as freedom of contract and freedom of trade, have been dealt with so often that they need no emphasis here.

CHAPTER 13

The Substructure of the Legal System of Liberalism

13.1. The Economic Substructure and the Material Structure of the Law

The presentation of the legal system of liberalism and of the economic structure adequate to it offers extraordinary methodological difficulties, which will be indicated here without being developed. In the first place the presentation of the legal system of liberalism alone is a task beyond the powers of a single man; and certainly one which would demand a long period of preparatory work, and which cannot be completed in a few pages. This preparatory work has not yet been fully done. The following pages offer, therefore, only a sketch which endeavours to present the ideal-type of liberal legal system. By an ideal-type, is to be understood, according to Max Weber, "one of those syntheses which one usually designates as ideas of historical phenomena. . . . This mental picture unites certain relations and processes of historical life in a cosmos of relations which is considered to be consistent".[1] The ideal-types are therefore "structures in which we construct relations in violation of objective reality, which our fantasy, trained by reality, considers as adequate".[2] The ideal-type "is a mental structure which is not itself a reality, but with which reality is measured and with which it is compared". If, however, the ideal-type does not describe reality, it is on the other hand not an *a priori* concept. It derives on the contrary from reality, it stands therefore between the transcendental *a priori* notions and an individualising historical description. It is attained by the elimination of certain individual features, and by the emphasising of others which appear as essential for the constitution of the ideal type.

But why may we neglect certain historical phenomena, and consider others as essential? Is it not true that every selection is arbitrary? Is not, therefore, the very notion of the ideal-type a purely arbitrary one? Is there any standard of measurement indicating which individual historical features are necessary for the constitution of the ideal-type, and which are only incidental? The justification on the basis of Max Weber's theory of knowledge, namely the basing of his methodology on the philosophical relativism of the South-West Kantian School of Germany, is undoubtedly inadequate. Another answer can, however, not be given here. It may suffice to assert that the rightness of the construction of the ideal-type can be proved by the convincingness of the results of the investigations.[3]

The second methodological difficulty which presents itself here lies in the coordination of various partial types and of various partial structures into a structural whole. What gives us the right to say that the ideally-typical construction of the liberal *Rechtsstaat* is related to the ideally-typical construction of the liberal economic system? The problem of coordinating phenomena from various spheres has already been stated by John Stuart Mill,[4] as Morris Ginsberg observes:

> When states of societies and the causes which produce them are spoken as the subject of science, it is implied that there exists a natural correlation among their different elements. That not every variety of combination of these general facts is possible, but only certain combinations; that, in short, there exist Uniformities of Co-existence between the states of the various social phenomena. And such is the truth. . . .

They are the *axiomata media*, the middle principles which, in John Stuart Mill's theory, justify the coordination of the various partial structures of various special relationships into a total structure and into a total relationship, and which then in their turn can be made fruitful for further sociological investigations.

13.1.1. *The Social System of Adam Smith and the Material Structure of the Law*

The general law which, as we saw, became increasingly the central consideration of the liberal system of law, was related to the economic theory of classical liberalism; this, however, was not only an abstract theory, but at the same time the description of a reality.

This liberal theory was from its beginnings based upon metaphysics. It consisted of a combination of experience and belief. The characteristic expression of this reconciliation theory is to be found in Bolingbroke's works. For him, the identity of self-interest and common interest is an obvious and undeniable fact — "That true self-love and social are the same"[5] and the two noblest gifts to mankind are "natural reason and supernatural revelation".[6] "The revelation of the instincts of self-love through reason to benevolence", that is for Bolingbroke the golden rule of life. God rules in his theory, as generally in the Deism of the eighteenth century, through the medium of general laws which can be learnt by experience.

The classical expression, however, is to be found, apart from the writings of the Physiocrats, in the system of Adam Smith.[7]

Adam Smith belongs undoubtedly to the school of natural law. His *Wealth of Nations* is but a part of a total system which, as his *Theory of Moral Sentiments* shows, should provide a complete theory of society. The world is ruled by one natural law, and is developing according to that natural law. Adam Smith, as his *Theory of Moral Sentiments* shows,[8] accepts the ideas of Hutcheson and Mandeville, and attempts to combine the fundamental elements of both theories and to merge them into unity. Hutcheson is rejected in so far as he denies the motive of egoism to human activities. The benevolence which was asserted by Hutcheson to be the sole motive of all human actions "may, perhaps, be the sole principle of action of the Deity" (p. 296), but not that of men. He, however, accepts from this "amiable system" the view that human egoism must be limited; that therefore economic and social activities must have an ethical basis, and that this ethical foundation must never be abandoned. From Mandeville, on the other hand, he adopts the conception that egoism is the central motive of human activities, without, however, accepting the view of the social function of vice.

Consequently, Adam Smith divides human drives into the selfish and the benevolent, and thereby, like all theorists of natural law and later Hegel, is confronted with the question of how it is possible to construct a society in which self-interest and common interest stand side by side; in which, therefore, sovereignty emerges from competition. The solution of this problem he finds in the belief that the pursuit of individual egoistic interests leads automatically, by reason of a world plan, to a realisation of the common interest; that, therefore, because of the coincidence of all human interests, sovereignty must necessarily arise from competition, provided, however, that this natural law which realises the world plan is not disturbed by external interferences. It must, therefore, be pointed out, with all possible emphasis, that the system of Adam Smith is based upon two assumptions: that the individual interest is embodied in the common interest; and that therefore the aim of the society is the realisation of the common and not of the individual interest which is only one means — or better, the only means — for the realisation of this aim. Thus far, classical liberalism stands in the tradition of mercantilism, with the decisive difference that the method for the attainment of the idea of welfare is basically distinguished from that of mercantilism.

All these ideas are clearly expressed in Adam Smith's works.

> As every individual endeavours so much as he can, both to apply his capital in the support of domestic industry and so to direct this industry that its produce may be of the greatest value, every individual necessarily labours to render the annual revenue of the society as great as he can. He generally, indeed, never intends to promote the public interests, nor knows how much promoting it . . . he intends only his own gain, and he is in this, as in many other cases, led by an invisible hand to promote an end which was no part of his intention.[9]

His belief that nature, "which is the polite term for God",[10] leads to a realisation of this identity is so strong, his conviction that "whatever is, is right" is so deep, that he thinks it better that the individual should not even know that he pursues communal interests by acting egoistically.

> The Happiness of mankind. . . seems to have been the original purpose intended by the author of nature when he brought them into existence. . . . The rich only select from the heap what is most precious and agreeable. They consume little more than the poor and in spite of their natural selfishness and rapacity though they mean only their own conveniency, they divide with the poor the produce of all their improvements. They are led by an invisible hand to make nearly the same distribution of the necessities of life which would have been made, had the earth been divided into equal portions. . . and thus, without intending it, without knowing it, advance the interest of the society and afford means for all the multiplication of the species.[11]

This asserted harmony is in the first place a harmony on the commodity market, in the sense of a coincidence of demand and production. In his view, only that can be produced perpetually which encounters effective demand; whereby he assumes an ever greater surplus.[12]

It is now of decisive importance to indicate the realistic conditions for the functioning of this harmonic system, that is to say, for the emergence of sovereignty from competition. For only if we know what conditions must exist in historical reality in order that the struggle of the competitors may not degenerate into the *bellum omnium contra omnes* of Hobbes, can we guard against the temptation to divorce the postulate of free competition from the social system as a whole; that is, to absolutise the postulate of free competition and to transfer it to a social system for which it never was intended, as was done soon after Ricardo. For the generalisations of classical economy are nothing else than a system of sociology *sui generis*.[13]

Competition means struggle; but this struggle is to move within ordered limits. Adam Smith's picture of competition has nothing to do with the description which Hobbes gives of the natural state. Competition must never lead to the ruin of a fellow-competitor. The individual advantage must never be attained by the injury of a brother competitor: "One individual must never prefer himself so much even to any other individual as to hurt or injure that other in order to benefit himself, though the benefit of the one should be much greater than the hurt or injury to the other".[14] This more ethical formulation is now clearly applied to competition in the economic sphere: "In the race for wealth and honours and preferment, each may run as hard as he can and strain every nerve and every muscle, in order to outstrip all his competitors. But if he should jostle, or throw down any of them the indulgence of the spectator is entirely at an end. It is a violation of fair play, which they cannot admit of".[15]

Thus there is to be found in Adam Smith the rudiments of a theory of competition which has since been developed by German jurisprudence, namely the distinction between competition in efficiency (*Leistungswettbewerb*), and restrictive competition (*Behinderungswettbewerb*).[16] The difference between the two kinds of competition is in the first place in the aim of the struggle. The competitors in a free market fight for existence or for economic improvement. The monopolist fights either to abolish the freedom of the market, or, when he has succeeded in doing this, to fortify or to complete the monopolistic position. By a monopolist — this is a marginal definition — we understand anyone who succeeds in obtaining from his customers better terms than those he would receive under conditions of free competition. Consequently, not only the aim of the struggle, but also the methods, are different. A competitor in a free market seeks to realise his own economic success. He therefore engages in such activity as is not in itself combative, but which becomes so only by the fact that everyone seeks to attain identical aims. The monopolist, however, fights in order to frustrate the aims of others, but not necessarily in order to attain for himself economic success which he often realises only after the struggle is over.

Competition serves according to the classical theory the purpose of selecting the competitors. In this it has institutional significance. Competition is an instrument of the economic system, and not only a means to the attainment of profits. This selection is brought about on the demand side by the choice of the customers between the offers of various competitors. The consumer becomes the umpire.[17] Disturbances are only of short duration. Equilibrium is assumed always to re-establish itself automatically.[18]

Only the first type of competition was recognised by classical economy as legitimate, as the above quotations show. Restrictive competition, the struggle of monopolists against non-monopolists, is not included in the classical theory of competition.

This competition finds its legal form in freedom of contract and trade, in the institution of private property in the instruments of production, and in the principle of the non-intervention of the state in the natural course of economic processes. In a free market where competition is not restrictive, freedom of trade realises not only the juridical but also the sociological freedom, because equal parties struggle against one another, and each consumer has actual and not only formal freedom of choice. Freedom of trade, like freedom of contract, is a necessary supplement to the institution of property, as both together render possible the natural selection among undertakings.

It must, however, be stressed that this conception of competition was developed by classical economy only for the commodity and not for the labour market. It is true that for Adam Smith, as for his successors, the trend of development appeared to be necessarily advantageous for all classes of society. For progressive division of labour "was taken as permanently increasing real return. . . by stimulating accumulation of money capital, the same technical progress was constantly to raise the wage-level. In this way, the autonomous forces of the market were ultimately to indemnify those classes which came off badly in the early stages".[19]

From this sole legitimation of competition there follows his rejection of monopolies.[20] His repudiation of all monopolies and privileges is of decisive significance for the evaluation not only of his economic but of his social theory as such. It is well-known that he admits of exceptions only for colonies, and even there, only for a transitional period.[21] The reason for his hostility to monopolies is the fact that his theory is concerned with the needs of the community as a whole. Monopolies were characteristic of mercantilism. The laws of mercantilism for the protection of monopolies were "like the laws of Draco; these laws may be said to be written in blood".[22]

His negative attitude towards monopolies is implemented by certain positive postulates which relate to an economic condition in which privileges and monopolies exist. In his *Lectures*, as later in his *Wealth of Nations*, he first expressly asserted that monopolies and privileges such as the [bakers' and butchers' guilds] "destroyed public opulence. On this account there is always required a magistrate to fix the prices. For any free commodity . . . there is no occasion for this, but it is necessary with bakers who may agree among themselves to make the quantity and prices what they please".[23] In other words, the juridical category of freedom of contract is a sociological freedom only in the case of absence of monopolies. In the same way, the political principle of non-intervention is desirable only if the market is a stage for the struggle of equal competitors. Therefore wherever monopolies exist, the principle of freedom of contract and of non-intervention ceases to be applicable. This view, that the difference between intervention and non-intervention entirely depends upon the social conditions, has been very cynically expressed by Talleyrand with regard to foreign policy: "Madame," he said, "non-intervention est un mot diplomatique et énigmatique, qui signifie à peu près la même chose qu'intervention".[24] In monopolistic situations, Adam Smith, like Pufendorf, clearly sees that the supplementary liberty of the freedom of contract must necessarily be replaced by that of the supplementary institution of the administrative act belonging to public law. The demand for a control of monopolies is not only reconcilable with

Adam Smith's theory, it is rather a direct consequence of it.

The repudiation of monopolies implies the equality of competitors, and, in addition, a certain type of entrepreneur. It is known that Adam Smith rejected the institution of the joint-stock company, and admitted it only for four economic activities — banking, insurance, the building and navigation of canals, and the water supply of great cities;[25] and it is characteristic of his profound sociological insight that joint-stock companies are considered legitimate in those fields of economic activity in which the element of the initiative of the entrepreneur is unessential — in which the economic activity is mainly a matter of routine. The entrepreneur is, therefore, the capitalist who risks his capital and his labour power for an uncertain aim, in short, that capitalist who combines all three functions of property, not only legally but actually. Administration *and* utilisation of capital make the entrepreneur. A divorce of the functions, a splitting of "diffused ownership and concentrated control",[26] a division of the three property functions and their allocation to various hands is completely foreign to him. The entrepreneur is for him not a functionary of society but an entrepreneur. The entrepreneur of classical economy had "cut out his own task to fit his own measure of himself and set himself at it", whereas the functionary of a corporation, the hired manager, has had "his task cut for him by others and been set to perform it".[27]

From this conception of the entrepreneur Adam Smith infers that he has to bear the risk of the undertaking and that every shifting of the risk to others, especially to the state, be it through direct or indirect subsidies, cannot be justified to the society.

Only if these conditions exist in reality does Adam Smith believe in the realisation of the pre-established harmony of individual and common interests. Only under these conditions is his statement valid that: "All systems, either of preference or restraint, therefore, being taken away, the obvious and simple system of natural liberty establishes itself at its own accord".[28]

We have already mentioned that this system of a democracy of small-scale undertakings is applied only to the commodity market. On the labour market, in so far as there exists no trade union, typical monopolists and non-monopolists stand in opposition to each other. The employer as the owner of the means of production is typically the stronger. In the relation between employer and employed, freedom of contract does not guarantee sociological but only juridical freedom, which hides the fact of social dependence. It is true that Adam Smith, as well as Ricardo, enjoined some measure of welfare for the workers, but contrary to their theory of the commodity market,[29] they did not make institutional provision against a possible exploitation of the non-monopolist by the monopolist, and for a restitution of the competition in efficiency. In addition we must emphasise the sociological principle which Max Weber has called the "advantage of small numbers".[30] The small number of the entrepreneurs gives them always a certain superiority as against the large number of the workers; and even their organisations share in this advantage, because the small number of members makes it always possible for their deliberations to be kept secret, and because there is greater solidarity of interest among the employers than among the workers; so that even in the case of two-sided organisation there is always a relative superiority of the entrepreneur. If Adam Smith's theory of competition was applied to the labour market, it would follow that freedom of the worker in a sociological sense begins only with collective organisation. This means that the trade union corresponds to the individual employer. Even the entrepreneur, who in the commodity market is not a monopolist, is always one in the labour market if trade unions are absent.

From this it follows that the postulate which is constantly repeated — that trade unions are cartels because they monopolise the commodity labour power in the same way as cartels monopolise commodities and services; and that therefore wherever control of cartels is instituted, that control must necessarily be applied to trade unions also — is inadmissible. The German legislation, in view of the structural difference between commodity and labour market, has clearly differentiated between them. This differentiation culminated in the establishment of a control of cartels and monopolies on the one hand, and in the institution of a complete freedom of trade unions on the other hand. In England, on the other hand, in legal theory as well as in legislative practice, no distinction is drawn between cartels and Trade Unions. Cartels also come under the Trade Union [Amendment] Act of 1876.[31] As against this, we have only to state here that trade unions certainly fulfil cartel functions by endeavouring to sell the labour power as dearly as possible, but they also have inner trade union functions (mutual help, training for members, legal assistance, cultural activities), and certain political functions.[32] This functional difference between labour and commodity market appears also in the distinction in the legal forms which are used by the respective organisations. The cartel as the commodity monopoly fixes its prices in the legal form of the one-sided decision. The trade union, however, fixes wages only in the form of a mutual collective agreement in which the antagonistic wills have already reached a compromise.

13.1.2. *The Classification of State Interferences*

In the free economic system thus constituted, state intervention is the exception. The function of the state is exhausted in the "individualistic minimum",[33] that is to say, in the establishment of personal security, in the protection of private property, and in the provision of means to enforce the fulfilment of contracts. The organisations for the fulfilment of this individualistic minimum are justice, police, the army, and taxes, as has been set forth in Adam Smith's *Lectures*. In attempting to classify state intervention with a view to recognising, on the basis of such classification, the aim of the general law, we shall discriminate between the classification of motives and that of the social functions of the various forms of state intervention. We determine the notion of the social function much as R. H. Tawney has defined the social function of property.[34] We admit that state intervention does not always attain the aim whose realisation was its motive. The economic subjects are often able to evade state intervention by structural and functional changes which immediately confront the state with new problems (e.g. the influence of the Turnover Tax on the concentration of capital in the form of mergers of undertakings).

The classification according to motives can only be undertaken if we keep in mind the social strata which are concerned by the interventionist measures. We therefore distinguish intervention in favour of the state as such; for example, taxes which are to provide the costs of state administration. Obviously, the motive given need not be the sole motive. The financing of the state's expenditure in this or in that way can be, and usually is, motivated also by the consideration of certain group interests. Intervention can take place in the interests of the nation as a whole, for example, health and food control. It can be motivated also by the interests of the class of industrial, financial, or agrarian capitalists, as in the case of tariffs, compulsory cartels, prohibition to establish new undertakings, and so on; it can be in the interests of consumers (control of cartels and monopolies, anti-trust legislation); or in the interests of the working class, as in the case of unemployment insurance, the eight-hour day, and so on.

This classification, however, is not so important for us as that according to the function of intervention; that is to say, on the basis of its influence on the structure of the economic system. For instance, intervention may have the object of maintaining the functioning of a competitive economic system, as in the case of the German law against unfair competition, which prohibits the use of unfair methods by competitors; or, in England, the individual prohibitions of slander to goods;[35] or of the deliberate spreading of inaccurate statements for the purpose of damaging the business;[36] or the prohibition of inducement to break contracts.[37] All these rules will not interfere with the processes of free competition, they will not disturb its harmonious working; on the contrary, they are intended to protect its working, and to secure fulfilment of the rules of the game of free competition. These rules have, therefore, the task of moralising competition, of making competition real.[38] They are intended to secure and guarantee the equality of the competitors.

To these rules there also belongs a certain type of social reform; those measures which are necessary for the social security of the working of the economic system.[39] A certain, even if modest, number of measures for the protection of the working class is necessary in the interests of productivity. Even the recognition of trade unions may be necessary for the maintenance of free competition, for the restoration of industrial peace, and the establishment of a certain amount of calculability in the relations between workers and employers.

Interventions of the state may consciously aim at altering the economic structure, or they may functionally lead to such transformation. A law forbidding unfair competition will undoubtedly perform fundamentally different functions in a competitive and in a monopolistic society. In the latter, the fairness of the methods used in the economic struggle is not determined by competition but by the monopolists themselves. The binding of the wholesale and retail dealer in the selling of trademarked articles, and the protection of these contracts by injunction and even fines and damages, changes the law against unfair competition from an instrument for the maintenance of free competition into an organ of its destruction. If the state, as happened in Germany, defends the obligation imposed upon wholesalers and retailers by the monopolists by means of the law against unfair competition, the result is legal protection of monopoly, whose commands become commands of the state itself. To this realm of state-interventionist measures there belong all those provisions which recognise cartels and which abolish the freedom of trade; but to it belongs also that kind of social reform which no more serves the maintenance of free competition, but consciously aims at a change of the economic structure; as for example the recognition of rights of collaboration of the working class, whether it be in the shop (works' councils); or on the labour market (trade unions and industrial arbitrations); or on the commodity market (participation in the control of monopolies and the establishment of estate organisation beside the political organisation, as for instance the *Reichswirtschaftsrat*).

To summarise: only under the conditions which classical economy holds desirable for the structure of a liberal economic system is the liberal principle of non-intervention of the state justified. Such a state is to be what we are accustomed to call a negative state. If by this expression we mean only a factual relationship, and if no value judgment is implied, no objection can be raised against the use of the term. If, however, we mean to express, as do Fascist and social-reformist critics of the non-interventionist state, that this state is a weak one, and that the positive state is an interventionist state in every case preferable to it; if therefore the term negative implies a value judgment; we must energetically protest against its use. The non-interventionist state of liberalism was certainly negative but it was never weak; it was, rather, just as strong as its economic and social structure made necessary. Whenever it was a question of conquering or of defending new markets, of subduing inner unrest, of protecting the bourgeois order, the liberal non-interventionist state proved itself strong enough in the decisive periods of its existence. Classical economy never thought of sacrificing an efficient state machinery to the needs of [a] free market economy; on the contrary, when Nassau-Senior describes the tyrannies of the African tribes, he says: "But they are trifles compared to those which are felt in the absence of government. . . there is no tyranny which man will not eagerly embrace if anarchy is to be the alternative".[40]

13.2. The Political Substructure

13.2.1.

The liberal legal system is not only functionally related to the economic structure as developed by classical economy, but also to a particular political structure.[41] As economic theory, political theory centres around the idea of the harmony of society, of the identity of self- and common-interest, of the equilibrium of all social forces, of a balance between the state and the society. This idea has been clearly formulated by Bolingbroke,[42] who as a typical eclectic accepted all decisive trends, the rationalism of Voltaire as well as the Deism of his period, and who applied the harmonistic theory to the political sphere.

> A King of Great Britain is that supreme magistrate who has a negative voice in the legislature, and several other powers and privileges, which we call prerogatives, are annexed to this trust. The two Houses of Parliament have their rights and privileges, some of which are common to both, others particular to each. They prepare, they pass bills, or they refuse to pass such as are sent to them. They address, represent, advise, concentrate. The supreme judicature resides in the Lords. The Commons are the grand inquest of the nation; and to them it belongs likewise to judge of national expenses, and to give supplies accordingly.
>
> If the legislature as well as the executive power was wholly in the King, he would be absolute; if in the Lords, our Government would be an aristocracy . . . ; if in the Commons, a democracy. It is division of powers . . . which constitutes a limited monarchy. . . . If any of the three . . . should at any time usurp more power than the law gives, or make ill use of a legal power, the other two parts may . . . by exerting their strength, reduce this power into its proper bounds. This is that balance which has been so much talked of . . . . This proposition is therefore true; that, in a constitution like ours, the safety of the whole depends on the balance of the parts.[43]

This balance has been called by Walter Sichel "independent interdependence".[44]

13.2.2.

The dissimilarity of the English theory centering around the relationship of the two doctrines of the Sovereignty of Parliament and the Rule of Law, and the German theory of the *Rechtsstaat*, is only to be understood in the light of the dissimilarity of the political structure of the two countries, and especially of the different rôle played by the German bourgeoisie in constitutional development. We do not, of course, deny that the political history is in its turn determined by economic considerations. But this economic determination is so evident that it seems superfluous to mention it here. We shall refrain from following the course of English nineteenth-century constitutional history; but it seems necessary to say something about nineteenth-century German Prussian constitutional history in order to [reach an] understanding of German constitutional theory.

13.2.3.

In the battles of Jena and Auerstädt the creation of Frederick the Great disintegrated, because free participation of its citizens was not only unknown to the enlightened absolutism of Frederick's state, but was even consciously repudiated by it. The examples of England and France, the Spanish wars against Napoleon, the Tyrolese risings, which proved that a democratic integration of the state could produce a more efficient state machinery than had till then been brought about by absolutism, had little influence in Prussia.

The liberal development began only after the defeat of the Napoleonic wars, and became visible in the Edict of 9th October, 1807, which for the first time shows clearly the break with the police-state tradition. The liberation of the peasants promulgated in this decree is undoubtedly traceable to the Napoleonic liberation of the peasants, in the kingdom of Westphalia, and especially in the Duchy of Warsaw. The Prussian liberation of the peasants was, however, only juridical and not economic. They became free in a dual sense. Their feudal subjection was ended, but so also was their connection with their land. Stein himself was compelled to sacrifice his friendly feeling towards the peasants. In this decree, Prussia only decided "to abolish everything which up till now has hindered the individual from attaining the prosperity which, according to the measure of his powers, was within his reach". The bourgeois professions were opened to the nobility, the privileges of the estates were abolished, especially the exclusive title of the nobility to the posts of officers in the army (Decree of 6th August, 1808). Conscription was introduced on 9th February, 1813, but even then only for the duration of the war, after the great democratic reformers of the army — with the exception of Scharnhorst — frustrated by the stupidity of Frederick William III, had been compelled to seek foreign service.

Theodore von Schön — the disciple of Kant and collaborator with Stein — Altenstein, and Hardenberg, all of them true disciples of Adam Smith, proceeded along the lines laid down by the Edict of 9th October, 1807. On the 14th November, 1811, the peasant acquired full property rights over his land, only, however, after ceding a part of it to the landed aristocracy, and after waiving the protection which till then he had enjoyed. If economically the system was relatively progressive, socially it was the more reactionary. Stein, probably the only liberal minister who dared seriously to oppose the Prussian Junkers, and who was a genius in character even if not intellectually of the first rank, was never able, with his social reformist views, to assert himself successfully. His successor Hardenberg was socially a pure reactionary. He did not carry out the abolition of the exemption of the landed property owners from taxation, which had been planned by Stein. He introduced a feudal regulation for domestic and agricultural workers (*Gesindeordnung* of 8th November, 1810), which, in spite of the postulate of legal equality in the later Prussian Constitution of 1850, remained untouched. "Rather three battles of Auerstädt than one October Edict", was the motto of the Prussian Junkers, and consequently that of Prussian policy.

Apart from this foundation of the state on economic liberty and social reaction, the state machinery was itself reorganised and modernised. On the 24th November, 1808, a ministry was created for the first time. On the 19th November, 1808, local government for towns was introduced; an idea, indeed, to which Hardenberg — a true disciple of Napoleonic centralism — was entirely opposed. The decisive political problem, namely that of the participation of the liberal bourgeoisie in the formation of the will of the state, was however never attacked and never solved.

It is true that on the 22nd May 1815, Frederick William III promised to the "Prussian Nation" rights of *con dominium*. It is equally true that he repeated this promise on the 17th January, 1820, and promised in addition to contract debts only with the consent of the estates. But he never kept these promises. By an order of the Cabinet of 11th June, 1821, the settlement of the constitutional problem was postponed to an indefinite date. Nobility and landed property, led by the Crown Prince, had successfully sabotaged the constitutional reform. This sabotage of the promises of Frederick William III is inseparably linked with the name and the system of Metternich who, jointly with the Russian Czar, did his utmost to change Frederick's mind; a task which was made comparatively easy by the King's mean and suspicious character. Metternich's two memoranda, in which he enumerated the reasons against the constitutional reform, belong to the most repulsive documents of Prussian history. What remained of the constitutional promises were the provincial diets (*Provinziallandtage*), which could be convoked by the government at its discretion, and which deliberated behind locked doors. The government appointed an official who presided over their meetings, and who could prevent any undesired discussion. The estates had only an advisory voice, only the right to remonstrate and to bring forward requests. The diet consisted of 584 members, of whom 278 were noblemen, 182 representatives of towns, and 124 peasants. In order to exclude the influence of the urban intelligentsia, only urban property owners of at least ten years' standing could be elected. The election of any kind of official could be annulled by the government. Only in 1840, after the death of Frederick William III, did the bourgeoisie again begin to take courage. The bourgeoisie of the Rhineland, led by Beckerath, Camphausen, and Hansemann, and the East Prussian bourgeoisie under the leadership of Theodor von Schön, claimed anew the fulfilment of the constitutional promises. It is known that they were partly fulfilled only under pressure of the revolution of 1848, by the Camphausen–Hansemann March Ministry. A National Convention was summoned, which was entrusted with the task of drafting a constitution on the model of the Belgian. We assume that the course of the Revolution is known. Its failure is attributable not so much to the strength of the reaction as to the cowardice of the bourgeoisie, which after 18th March, 1848, played into the hands of the reaction, because of its fear of the proletariat which had been victorious at the barricades. The fear of king and Junkers in face of this revolution did not last long. The reaction organised itself in the conservative party, and began the connection with the king through the famous *Camarilla* founded by Ludwig von Gerlach. It established the reactionary ministry of Brandenburg, which, after the crushing of the Revolution in Vienna, performed the "saving deed" of adjourning, of transferring, and finally of dissolving, the National Convention. The king imposed a new constitution on 5th December, 1848; abolished universal, equal, and secret, suffrage; and introduced the famous three-class suffrage, in order to secure the consent of the new Parliament to the imposed constitution, in which he was naturally successful.

The succeeding period is on the whole one of reaction on the part of the landed aristocracy. The reintroduction of the police powers of the manorial lord; entailed landed property (*Fideikomisse*); the restriction of freedom of meeting by a reactionary statute; [and] the transformation of the second chamber into a House of Lords (*Herrenhaus*) are characteristic of this period. Karl Marx rightly pointed out that Germany in 1848 had hardly reached the condition of France in 1789, [or], as we may add, which England had already attained in 1688. Frederick the Great had said that the condition of Prussia in his youth corresponded roughly to that of France under Francis I.

It is obvious that this political reaction could not hinder the economic and social rise of the bourgeoisie; and, to a modest extent, the strengthening of its social position must have a political effect. The "new era" of liberalism begins in 1858, when the so-called liberal Hohenzollern–Auerswald ministry succeeded the reactionary Manteuffel ministry. The liberalism of the regent, later King and Emperor, William I, who appointed this ministry, was conditioned mainly by the fact that he needed money for the reform of the army and the increasing of its numerical strength, and was therefore compelled to abolish the taxation privileges of the landed aristocracy. For this he needed a liberal ministry. The bourgeoisie rejoiced; it discontinued its opposition to the three-class Parliament, and resigned itself merely in order to raise no difficulties for the new ministry. This reign of liberalism lasted only a short time. It ended with the famous struggle over the army reforms, which began in 1860 and which expanded into a constitutional conflict. The progressive liberal party, which insisted upon the budgetary right of Parliament, won 250 seats in the election of 5th May, 1862; an extraordinary success, of which, however, full use was not made. It is true that Parliament rejected the military budget. But Bismarck, who was called upon as a saviour, ruled without budget, in virtue of Art. 99 of the Prussian Constitution, and of a constitutional theory devised by him for the purpose. The same progressive party, which had rejected the military budget, assented to the rest of the budget, negotiated with the government, and contented itself with deploring the violation of the Constitution by the regime. In this way, political liberalism disgraced itself in the eyes of the petty bourgeoisie, which very soon, especially after the victorious wars, was driven into the arms of Bismarck. The right wing of liberalism, which had constituted itself as an independent national liberal party, even made formal peace with the regime.

As a result of this series of defeats, the Parliamentary system was abandoned, and the monarchical principle, as advocated by Friedrich Julius Stahl, was realised in political practice. All decisions were made by the monarch, who was identical with the army, the landed property-owners, and the bureaucracy. The influence of the nobility in the officer corps was extremely strong. The internal administration of Prussia was the domain of the nobility. In 1906, eleven out of twelve provincial presidents were noblemen; twenty-three out of thirty-six district presidents (*Regierungspräsidenten*) were noblemen; while for the famous post of *Landrat*, the title of count was even necessary.[45]

The rights of the bourgeoisie were, therefore, not secured by participation in the formation of political decisions, that is to say, not genetically, but only materially, by the rule of general laws as enacted by Parliament and as applied by independent judges. This distribution of powers between the various strata of the ruling classes was not materially altered after the formation of the empire. This formation as such, and the victory of the unitarian tendencies, corresponded to the economic interests of the bourgeoisie. The legislation of the Empire fulfilled all the demands of economic liberalism. Politically, however, the bourgeoisie did not play a rôle in any way corresponding to its economic and social significance. In the decisive question of conflict, namely that of whether the government was under obligation to secure annually the consent of Parliament to the budget, it was defeated. The compromise reached by Bismarck, that the strength of the army and the army expenditure should be approved by Parliament only every seven years (from 1893, every five years), was in fact a victory for him. This compromise lasted until 1914. Bismarck crushed liberalism, but he created a political catholicism by his *Kulturkampf*. He needed the Catholic party for his economic policy, and this party knew how to use its key position with energy and recklessness for its own interest, without attempting to establish a parliamentary system. At the same time, by his law against socialism, Bismarck practically created social democracy; which, however, owing to the three-class suffrage, had no parliamentary influence in Prussia. The semi-parliamentarism of Bülow in the Block period strengthened the parliamentary groups, but did not substantially change the distribution of power. In Prussia, the three-class suffrage remained. In his address to Parliament on 20th November, 1908, William II promised "an organic development of the suffrage"; but he remained faithful to his Hohenzollern tradition, in not keeping his promise, and in preferring to come to an understanding with the Junker reaction in the summer of 1909. The permanent influence of the East Prussian Junkers was made possible by the compromise with the Catholic centre party in the Reichstag in 1909, on the occasion of the estate tax. The conservative parliamentary group in the *Reichstag* was entirely dominated by nobility and estate owners; for instance, in 1909, out of sixty conservative deputies, thirty-eight were estate owners and twenty-eight noblemen; and in the Prussian Parliament, out of 152 conservative deputies, ninety-eight were estate owners and eighty-eight noblemen. Their domination was secured by the three-class suffrage. In the Reich, although the suffrage was general, it was only nominally so on account of a reactionary division of the constituencies.[46] The liberal socialist majority, which factually existed in the *Reichstag* of 1912 was without political importance.

13.3. The Nation as the Integrating Factor of the Competitive Society

13.3.1. *The Concept of the Nation*

The nation is the integrating principle of the modern state.[47] It is the unifying link between the individual and the state in the nineteenth and twentieth centuries. The modern state needs a legitimation. The rational legitimation lies in the foundation of sovereignty on political and economic liberty, that is, in the reduction of the will of the State to those of the individuals; but these individual wills collide. Each man represents the sum of various interests, and belongs through each of his interests to a different group. He is a member of a municipality, a member of the State; he belongs to economic organisations, and to social circles; to religious units, and to political parties.[48] The unification of these divergent desires and interests takes place in the nation, which thus becomes, so to speak, the irrational substructure of the state.

The concept of the nation must be confronted with that of the people; and the latter is a cultural as well as a natural phenomenon. The naturalistic interpretation of the people is based upon natural properties, and especially upon race, in the sense in which this concept is understood by anthropologists: "By race, anthropologists understand a group of individuals who, within given limits of variation, possess in common a combination of hereditary traits sufficient to mark them off from other groups".[49] Whether such natural differences can be objectively determinable, whether they arise by themselves, or are to a greater extent culturally and spiritually conditioned, lies outside the limits of our discussion. Especially we need not investigate the problem of whether a way leads from the concept of the race to that of the state. The social and political significance of the race theory of National Socialism will be considered later.

The people as a cultural formation, however, [are] constituted as a sociological unit by an abundance of natural and cultural factors. Common descent, common geographical position, language, religion, customs, science; all these objective factors play a rôle, and their individual significance varies according to the historical-political situation.[50] But these objective elements do not suffice to constitute the people as a unit. The inadequacy of the objective theory is alleged to be met by the subjective theory, which found expression in Renan's famous formula; that the people [are] "un plébiscite de tous les jours".[51] Here, therefore, not existence but consciousness, the conscious decision of the individual to belong to a people, is considered to be decisive. It is obvious that this theory does not stand the test of experience.[52] Conscious decision in itself does not normally constitute a man a member of a people; nor can membership be lost by a reverse decision. The cultural conception of the nation is, therefore, an inextricable coil of objective and subjective; and within the objective, of natural and cultural factors.

The concept of the nation can only be reached through its connection with that of the state. A people becomes a nation if it has the consciousness of individual and common political aims, if it is capable of achieving and maintaining a relatively united political will.[53] As we understand by "political" everything which is directed to the acquisition and maintenance of power in and over the state, the concept of the nation is inseparably linked with that of the state.

13.3.2. *State and Nation*

The modern state is, however, not the work of the nation; it is rather the child of commodity production. Only when the product of labour has become a commodity, and has been converted into money, can a part of that money be used through taxation to finance the modern centralised state, and to create a machinery for influencing the society, especially an army and bureaucracy. Capitalistic commodity production is older than the nation. Consequently it is in the Italian city-states that we find the first modern states. These states were not the work of nations, but of rich capitalists who bought soldiers and with their help were able to establish tyrannies. The capitalist thus used his military power, which was based upon money, to exploit the mass of the people by new taxes. These many tyrannies lacked any kind of legitimation. Domination was justified by naked force. A national ideology was completely lacking;[54] but the modern state was there.

The decisive function of the nation consists in rendering possible the unification of a multitude of individual energies, in a period in which the bourgeoisie attains consciousness of its own political value; in making universally binding its political and cultural decisions. The nation, therefore, supersedes in the first place every non-secular legitimation, and is thus in antagonism to the conception of the state as a divine institution. Secondly, it provides a justification of every state, and stands therefore in opposition to the universalism of the Middle Ages. Thirdly — and this is decisive — it supersedes the dynastic legitimation. The modern state in France and Germany develops from the organisation of the feudal state. Kingship, whose bearer was the supreme feudal lord, changed the feudal state into a modern state by making use of the new means of commodity production, and, with the help of bought soldiers and officials, crushed the feudal lords. This development begins in France with Philip VI, it is effective under Louis XI, and comes to an end under Louis XIV. In Germany the same development leads to the formation of territorial states, mainly because the German Emperors were more interested in the higher profits of the Italian commodity production than in the lower profits of German urban production, and therefore left this field to the German territorial princes.

In all these periods of feudalism, of estate absolutism, and of monarchical absolutism, the concept of the nation in the modern sense is not to be found.[55] In this period, the state has been created, but not the nation; the legitimation of the state is either divine, or by natural law.

On the Continent, the nation first appears as an independent factor in the French Revolution, and only after that time becomes the subject of sociological analysis.[56] The objective factors which constitute the nation obviously emerged long before; but in this period the subjective factors, which, together with the objective, make a nation, first become visible.[57] In this period, one class constitutes itself a nation. The nation becomes so to speak the property of the bourgeoisie. Via the nation, the bourgeois conquers culture, and by its character as nation legitimises the centralised rule of the state.

The French Revolution resumes the development which had been interrupted in 1615, and which culminated in the proposal of the Third Estate in the Estates-General to abjure the monarchical principles and to establish the sovereignty of the crown, but which replaces the dynastic by the national principle.[58] The idea of the nation gains a revolutionary force by its synthesis with the concept of the sovereignty of the people.[59] Here is found the unifying principle which makes it possible to integrate the essentially secular competitive society, and to declare universally binding its social and political decisions.

All these ideas have been clearly expressed by Sieyès. According to him, only the Third Estate is productive; the hitherto privileged Estates are negative, and stand therefore "hors de la nation". For him, the nation is the aggregate of those individuals who stand under a common law and are represented by the same legislative assembly. The nation is sovereign; its being is the functional justification of its existence; its will is the supreme law, and finds legal expression in the *pouvoir constituent*. The state stands in the service of the nation. Its power is justified only if legitimised by the nation. This conception of the nation is revolutionary, and is directed against monarchy and aristocracy. The French aristocracy clearly saw the implications of this new conception, and replied to Sieyès (de Montlosier and de Maistre), that the aristocracy alone, or the aristocracy and the monarch together, represent the nation.[60] It is the democratic nation of free and equal citizens, the Jacobin concept of the French Revolution.

This new polemical-political concept has certain concrete social functions. In the first place, modern democratic development presses towards the recognition of the new nation.[61] The necessity for large thickly-populated economic territories necessitates the creation of the state, in which particular local and non-secular powers are annihilated, and in which a common currency, a unified taxation, and a common system of transport, prevail. Therefore the Constitution of 1791 (Tit. III, *Préambule*, Art. 1er), and the Constitution of 1793 (*Declarations des Droits*, Art. 25), and that of 1848 Art. I), state that the sovereignty of the nation is "indivisible, imprescriptible et inaliènable".[62] The nation watches jealously over its rights. The deputies are elected in its name, and not in that of Estates, of territorial powers, or of social groups. No one may interpose himself between the individual and the nation, as was pointed out by the deputy le Chapelier, when he moved his famous law of 14th June, 1791, forbidding the association of workers; "the individual", he said on this occasion, "owes allegiance solely and exclusively to the state, and to no one else".

Thus far capitalism is imperialistic; national feeling becomes nationalism and thereby the servant of economic interests.[63] The idea of the nation mobilises the nations for war. The nation therefore creates for capitalism the efficient State.

The nation has also a sociological, as distinct from its economic, function. If a society desires to be distinguished from others, it must be marked off from these other groups. The integration of a society into a unit is possible only if this society is confronted with others, and if the integrating factor is efficient enough to invest this society with particular characteristics by which it can be distinguished from others. This process of individualisation was performed, after the breakdown of mediaeval universalism, by the dynastic principle. But the divine right of kings became obsolete. The state as such could not serve as an integrating factor for the liberal society, as according to the liberal ideology the state has purely negative functions: the functions of guaranteeing liberty and security, of preserving the state of nature, of protecting liberty and property. Therefore the integrating function is taken over by the nation. The French nation, for instance, is alleged to be different and distinguishable from other nations. The constitutive element of the civil society is found. The nation has become "an effective body of adherents united by a sense of common interest".[64]

The English development deviates from the continental[65] in that the concept of the nation, though known, plays no decisive rôle. Even Richard I used to ask, when he wished contemptuously to refuse some unreasonable demand; "Do you take me for an Englishman?" The English state very early becomes centralised, and overcomes the feudal powers much earlier than the feudal states. In political literature, the concept of the nation is very often to be found in Bacon's works; for instance, in his Essay XXIX (*Of True Greatness of Kingdoms and of States*) where he contrasts people and nation. The people is the mass of the workers and of the middle class: "The middle people of England make good soldiers". The nation is represented by the nobility and gentry, which bear the power and the greatness of the state. In the Great Rebellion, the nation plays, of course, a greater rôle. The Rump Parliament appeals to the nation. The House of Lords is abolished by referring to the supreme authority of the nation. But in Cromwell's *Instrument of Government* there appears as the justifying basis of the state "the people", which is represented in Parliament and comprises the three nations. In contrast to the French development, "the people" becomes, because of the plurality of nations, the unifying bond. After this, the concept of the nation does not play a great rôle in England; in the first place, because of its insular position; then because Tudor absolutism was incomparably milder and more popular than its continental equivalent; and further because England did not know a bureaucracy to the same extent as did the continent, so that the antagonism between the state and society was never so strong; and finally because of the existence of a colonial empire, which naturally tended to lay more stress on the integrating force of the monarchy than on that of the English nation.

In pre-war Germany, the concept of the nation in the Jacobin sense does not play any rôle; just as the idea of the *Rechtsstaat* is divorced from the political structure, the concept of the nation is completely separated from that of the sovereignty of the people; in the works of Wilhelm von Humboldt,[66] the sovereignty of the nation is expressly denied. During Bismarck's period, the whole conception of the nation is refuted, especially by Treitschke.[67]

In this period of the rise of the bourgeoisie, it is socially and politically undeniably identical with the nation. The bourgeoisie is in this period the historically progressive class. In the very moment, however, that the bourgeoisie has fulfilled its historical mission, and when, therefore, a politically self-conscious labour movement appears, there necessarily begins the struggle over the question to whom the concept of the nation belongs. In this moment the nation loses its integrating force. The claim of the bourgeoisie to be the nation becomes a privilege which on the continent is used to denounce every non-bourgeois group as non-national, even as inimical to the fatherland. In such a situation two nations in reality exist. Paul Viénot in his book *Incertitudes Allemandes* has formulated the problem in this way; "Besides the Germany of Weimar and the Germany of Potsdam, there exists an industrial and an agrarian Germany, a proletarian Germany and a Germany of the propertied classes, a Catholic and a Lutheran Germany, a Germany of the federal states and a Germany of the Reich, a Germany of the youth and one of the old age and, above all, a democratic and an anti-democratic Germany".

CHAPTER 14

The Legal System of the Competitive Society

14.1. The Generality of the Law

14.1.1. *The Concept of Generality*

We have, therefore, arrived at the conclusion that the central idea of the liberal legal system is that of the generality of the law. This law is in the first place the positive law of the state, and not any kind of natural law as distinguished from it. Since Kant and Rousseau, the liberal legal theory has been entirely based upon the view that law is only valid if it can be imputed to the sovereign state.

But the tradition of scholastic and secular natural law is not completely lost; it is still alive in the postulate of the generality of the law. The general law as a new material law is thus confronted with law in a formal sense. We have, therefore, very briefly to state the essentials of the concept of the generality of the law. The general law is opposed to any kind of individual command. The difference is a relative one. It is certain that every command of a superior authority to an inferior organ to perform a certain act is, in relation to the execution of the command, always general and abstract; "that is to say, that it can never comprehend the whole detail of the act in which it is to be fulfilled".[1] So far, it is undoubtedly true that the execution of any command leaves to the commanded person a certain kind of initiative. From this point of view, the individual command can be regarded as a general one.

But it is equally true that the fact cannot be overlooked that the amount of initiative left to that person in carrying out an individual order is so little that it can sociologically be neglected. The borderline, therefore, between general laws and individual commands runs through the various types of commands. By a general law, we understand, therefore, with Carré de Malberg, an abstract rule which does not mention particular cases or individually nominated persons, but which is issued in advance to apply to all cases and all persons in the abstract.[2] Thus only two things are relevant. In the first place, according to Rousseau, the law is nominally general ("nommément générale") without regard to the content; but this formal structure of the law contains at the same time a material element, namely the prohibition of retroaction.

The relation between this formal structure of the law and the social substructure falls, as is to be proved, into three divisions:

(a) the general law has a socially and politically protective function. It is equalising. In this lies the ethical value of the generality of the law;

(b) the general law has a disguising function. In a class society and in a competitive economic system, a general law conceals the realities. By the postulate that the state may rule only through general laws, the competitive economic system is invested with the dignity of a moral value;

(c) the general law in a competitive economic system has finally the function of rendering the exchange processes calculable and predictable. This function has been stressed especially in the works of Max Weber, and was indicated earlier by Pufendorf and Bentham.[3]

The conception that the general law, as the material law, is distinct from law in a formal sense is decisively influenced by Montesquieu's theory of the separation of powers, which assumes that it is possible materially to distinguish various functions of the state. His theory presupposes, therefore, that legislation, jurisdiction, and administration are not only distinguishable by the performance of these three functions by three different organs of the state, but that the three functions are themselves substantially different. His theory further assumes the existence of a sphere of freedom of the individual which is fundamentally unlimited, so that any intervention of the state must be based upon general laws and must be controlled by independent judges, who do not create, but only declare, the law. The elements of the system are, therefore, pre-state liberty, interference with this liberty by material laws and execution of the laws by independent judges; with the consequence of the separation of powers.

14.1.2. *The French Doctrine*

The French theory was developed under the influence of Rousseau and Montesquieu. Both stress the generality of the law. But they are distinguished by the fact that in Rousseau's system the generality of the law is related to a material value, whereas in Montesquieu's doctrine this ethical basis is absent, and is replaced by his theory of the separation of powers. The postulate of the generality of the law can undoubtedly be traced to the influence of Descartes and Malebranche. Montesquieu himself speaks of Descartes with admiration and respect, and Malebranche's influence upon him has been clearly proved.[4] In Montesquieu's theory, as with Descartes, the world is based upon the general law of mechanics, which even God cannot alter because any individual utterance is alien to him; so that God withdraws from the centre of the universe and becomes "immense, spirituel, et infini". The law of the state is equally general; general as regards its origin as well as its content. Two ideas are, therefore, contained in this postulate; the supremacy of the law, that is, the exclusive governance of the rule of law; and its generality.

Both ideas, with all their implications and consequences, are clearly to be seen in the French Revolution. Mirabeau, as chairman of the Committee for the Drafting of the Rights of Men, proposed on 17th August, 1789, a motion which was verbally identical with Rousseau's fallacious conclusion that "la loi étant l'expression de la volonté générale doit être générale dans son objet". Consequently Art. 6 of the Declaration of 1789 contained the provision that the law is the expression of the general will, which is repeated in Art. 6 of the Declaration of 1793, and in Art. 6 of the Constitution of the Year III.

But beside this notion of the general law there appears simultaneously a second concept [of] law in a formal sense. The king had still the power to carry out certain legislative acts; so that the National Assembly was compelled to take into account this legislative activity of the monarch, and to sanction it by the law of October 12th–November 6th, 1789. "Les décrets [of the National Assembly] sanctionnés par le Roi portaront le nom et l'intitulé de lois"; a formulation whose author was Robespierre. The Constitution of 3rd September, 1791, (Titre III, Chap. III, Sect. III, Art. 6) contains the following passage: "Les décrets sanctionnés par le Roi, et ceux qui lui auront été présentés par trois législatures consécutives ont force de loi, et portent le nom et l'intitulé de lois". Here the legislator was more cautious. He did not conceive of a formal law as a law, but only gave to the formal law the name and the force of law.

The Jacobin Constitution of 24th June, 1793, which, however never came into operation, divides the decisions of the legislative council into two groups, "lois" and "décrets". The latter are mainly administrative acts, the former must be submitted to the people. We clearly see in this distinction the all-pervasive influence of Rousseau.

The decisive influence emanates from the Draft of the Gironde Constitution of 1793, where in Sect. II, Art. 4, the following distinction is made: "les caractères qui distinguent les lois sont leur généralité et leur durée indéfinie". Apart from this, the Draft recognises at the same time "décrets" which are either locally or materially individualised; and finally, it recognises the "mesures" (Art. 7) in a state of emergency. The Constitution of the Directorate of the 5th Fructidor of the Year III discriminates sharply between laws and any other kind of legislative act, by speaking of "les lois et les autres actes du corps législatif"; but in Art. 92, it is clearly expressed that every resolution of the Council of Five Hundred which has been adopted by the Council of Elders, is designated as a law. In the consular Constitution of the 22nd Frimaire of the Year VIII, however, this distinction is no longer maintained. Now all decisions of the legislative power, the issuing of the budget, the declaration of war and peace, the conclusion of alliances and of trade agreements, are "lois" (Arts. 45, 50); but at the time, the law becomes no longer an act of the tribunate or of the legislative body, but of the government. In the "Chartes" of Louis XVIII and Louis Philippe, the distinction is equally lacking, and in the Constitution of 1875 (Law of 25th February, 1875) no definition of law is to be found; the law simply states that the legislative power is exercised jointly by the two Chambers.

In French constitutional theory — with the exception of Carré de Malberg — the separation of the two kinds of law is still maintained. It appears clearly for the first time in Merlin's *Répertoire universel et raisonné de jurisprudence.*[5] He puts the question, whether every act of the legislative power can be called a law; and he answers no. Duguit, Esmein, and Barthélmy all still maintain the distinction between the general law as law in a material sense, and non-general laws which are law in a formal sense. A general law is an act of the legislative power creating a general legal situation, which is impersonal and abstract and which is intended to govern categories of individuals and series of cases.[6] No proof whatsoever is given by the representatives of contemporary opinion as to the justifiability of the distinction between the two kinds of law. Duguit invokes Aristotle, Thomas Aquinas, Rousseau, Montesquieu; but he fails to prove that the positive constitutional law of France recognises this distinction.

Neither Art. 6 of the Declaration of 1789, nor the corresponding provisions of the Declaration of 1793 and of the Year III, give the slightest evidence that the legislature can only issue general laws. These passages can only mean, what the Constitution of 1791 (Titre III, Chap. II, Sect. I er, Art. 3) clearly expressed: "Il n'y a point en France d'autorité supérieure à celle de la loi". The centre of gravity lies, therefore, in the genesis and not in the content of the law. That the Constitution of 1875 does not give the slightest indication that a distinction is to be drawn between the two different kinds of laws, has been convincingly proved by Carré de Malberg. He has shown that the Constitution of 1875 sought only to make good the degradation of Parliament under Napoléon, so that it laid decisive stress on the democratic legitimation of the law and not on its content.

"La domaine de la loi est sans bornes, comme celui de la volonté générale."[7] He has equally proved that French constitutional practice has never factually recognised the two types of law.[8] As we are not concerned with a discussion of the merits of the various French theories, it may be sufficient to refer to the works of Carré de Malberg. The assertion of representatives of contemporary French opinion, such as Duguit, that law is only a general rule, and that an individual command is not a law even if issued by a "prétendu souverain", is a mere assertion which in fact represents a relapse into natural law theory. French constitutional practice knows in fact a number of individual laws.[9] It cannot be doubted that in a competitive society law is typically general; but the postulate that every law must be necessarily and exclusively general is nothing but an attempt to absolutise a certain historical situation. The great importance which is usually attached to the generality of the law is decisively conditioned by the fact that the monarchs in the middle of the nineteenth century imposed constitutions and thereby, by their own wills, limited their sovereignty; but only in so far as they committed the right to make law jointly to Parliament and to themselves. In such a situation it became, of course, necessary to mark off those subjects for which a law — that is, a joint decision of monarch and Parliament — was necessary, from those for which the monarch was still the sole authority. The decisive characteristic for such distinction was the notion of the generality of the law, which seemed also to be a necessary inference from Montesquieu's doctrine of the separation of powers and from the distinction between the material functions of the State involved therein.

14.1.3. *The German Doctrine*

The German doctrine is deeply indebted to the French, but at the end of the nineteenth century it diverges decisively from it. In the Germany of the mid-nineteenth century, constitutional doctrine was entirely dominated by the above-mentioned distinction between general (material) and individual (formal) laws. Only the general law is law. Individual laws are in contravention of the postulate of equality. If a set of concrete facts has already been realised historically, and is only then regulated by law, such law is merely an arbitrary act. If the realisation of the set of facts is not yet historically accomplished, its individual regulation is in any case objectionable.[10] Law, according to Robert von Mohl, is, therefore, a promulgation of the legislative authority, intended to endure and characterised by its generality.[11] Lorenz von Stein accepts Hegel's formulation: the law emerges from the consciousness of the state and has, therefore, to attain two ends; to regulate similarities of the factual life, and to establish the differences between them.[12] Klüber, like Blackstone, takes as his basis the natural law theory of Burlamaqui, whose book appeared in a German translation in 1848; and postulates the generality of the law and equal rights and equal duties of all citizens in similar situations.[13] The same applies to Gneist, Rotteck, and many others. The German theory, however, rejects Montesquieu's doctrine of the separation of powers. Christian Wolff and Kant accepted it, but it was rejected by the majority of constitutional lawyers; as for instance, by Bluntschli and F. J. Stahl.

The postulate of the generality of the law is, however, in itself sufficient to guarantee a minimum of separation of powers; it is on the whole sufficient to establish the independence of the judges. A judge who may only apply general rules is for that very reason not subject to individual commands of the government.

A constitution such as the Prussian Constitution of 1805 (Art. 62), and the Bismarck Constitution (Art. 5), can offer not the slightest evidence for the existence of the dualistic theory of law. Both constitutions are concerned only with the origin of law, not with its content. Both simply state that law is any statute enacted by the two Chambers.

Under the influence, however, of Paul Laband[14] the assertion of the general character of the law is abandoned. Laband admits that the laws enacted by Parliament are typically general, but he denies that generality is an essential characteristic of the law. He introduces, however, another distinction between formal and material law. For him, formal law is simply the form in which the will of the state is declared, irrespective of its content. Material law, on the other hand, is essentially the promulgation of a rule creating a right (*Rechtssatz* or *règle de droit*).* These are two entirely different conceptions of law. The consequence of the distinction is that a law may be a formal law (as for instance the budget) because it has been enacted in accordance with Art. 5 of the Bismarck Constitution; but nevertheless it is not a material law, because a formal law such as the budget does not promulgate rules creating rights of individuals. On the other hand, an executive order may contain rules creating rights — as for instance, an order by the police regulating the traffic — and is therefore a law in a material sense, but not a law in a formal sense because it is not enacted according to Art. 5 of the Constitution. This distinction between law in a formal and law in a material sense, as developed by Laband, was universally accepted by German constitutional lawyers. It was repeated by every text-book on constitutional law and by every University teacher.[15]

But what is the rule creating a right, which is the basis of the dualistic theory? One searches Laband's works vainly for a definition. He gives only an approximative definition by distinguishing the rule creating a right from the contract which contains duties and claims.[16] That is to say, it is practically the difference between objective and subjective law; so that material law is only given if an action of the state directly concerns the individuals in their mutual relations and thus creates claims of one individual against another, with the corresponding duties. Any action of the state which only affects the relation between state and individuals, or which only indirectly affects the individuals in their mutual relations, is therefore not law in a material sense.

Anschütz, a more liberal interpreter of Laband's theory, has extended the realm of the law in a material sense. At first, he understood by material law all those rules whose immediate aim was the delimitation of the spheres of activity of individuals.[17] By this conclusion he altered Laband's theory by bringing the relations between state and individual within the conception of the material law. Still, however, the indirect influencing of the legal status of the individuals was left outside the realm of the material law. Later, however,[18] he understood by the material law all those norms which either directly or indirectly affect the liberty or property of the citizens. By this extension he practically abandoned the dualistic theory. For can we conceive of any activity of the state which does not directly concern the citizens? To-day we recognise more and more the interdependence of all social phenomena, and we are, therefore, unable to conceive of any activity of the state which in the last resort does not affect the status of the individual; whether it be the organisation of administrative bodies, or of Courts of Law, or the creation of public enterprises.

14.1.4. *The English Doctrine*

In view of the English theory of the relation between the sovereignty of Parliament and the rule of law, which we have considered above, it is not surprising that the dualistic theory is practically unknown in present-day England. This, however, was not the case in earlier theories.

Blackstone in the first place confesses his faith in the existence of a natural law. In this, as has been shown by C.K. Allen and W.A. Robson, he simply adopted the theory of Burlamaqui,[19] whose work had been translated into English in 1748. By this confession Blackstone, however, only renders lip-service to natural law, which has no practical significance for his theory. This natural law is neither concretised nor institutionalised.[20] Even Bentham pointed out the inconsistencies of Blackstone's theory of natural law; "He sinks into a compromise which involves all the absurdities of the tenets he discovers".[21] Whereas Blackstone, on the one hand, postulates the supremacy of the *lex naturalis* over the *lex humana*,[22] on the other, he postulates far more insistently the supremacy of Parliament which can do what it likes, and recognises no remedy against it.

But this criticism of Bentham's also applies to Blackstone's distinction between the various types of the *lex humana*. Law is for Blackstone "a rule of action dictated by some superior being", and municipal law (civil law) is "a rule of civil conduct prescribed by the superior power in a State, commanding what is right and prohibiting what is wrong".[23] Legislation is "the greatest act of superiority that can be conceived that can be exercised by one being over another. Sovereignty and legislature are indeed convertible terms; one cannot exist without the other".[24] But this sovereignty is not to be unlimited. No individual laws are to be issued by the sovereign. Individual laws are inadmissible. An individual law is not law at all. It "does not enter into the idea of a municipal law! it is rather a sentence than a law".[25] Therefore the state may not order by law the confiscation of the property of one particular or of several particular persons. Laws must, therefore, be general for moral reasons in that individual laws are unjust; and for utilitarian reasons, in that the state cannot give injunctions to every individual. General laws serve, therefore, the "perpetual information and direction of all persons in all points whether of positive or negative duty".[26] Blackstone, however, does not draw any practical conclusions from this dualistic theory. The postulate of the sovereignty of Parliament stands side by side with the postulate that the state may rule only through general laws; and the former postulate is far stronger than this latter one. Blackstone's theory is, therefore, nothing more than a recommendation to the legislative power to issue only general laws. Generality is not an essential of his conception of law.

The same discord can be found in Austin's *Lectures*.[27] He distinguishes law, or rules, from "occasional or particular commands". "Now where it obliges generally to acts or forbearances of a class, a command is a law or a rule." If, however, the legislative sovereign issues a particular command, Austin is compelled to admit that this command is also law. The legislative authority of Parliament is in his theory entirely unrestricted, so that the dualistic theory is without practical significance.

The distinction between the two conceptions of law can also be found in Walter Bagehot's *English Constitution* (V): "A law is a general command applicable to many cases. The 'special acts' which crowd the statute book and weary parliamentary commentators are applicable to one case only". He, too, attaches no practical significance to this dualism.

The distinction between general and individual law must not be confused with the public and private bills of English constitutional practice. Although the private bill always provides for one individual case, the public bill need not necessarily have a general content. The two notions, therefore, do not coincide. A private bill might be defined as "a measure for the interest of some person or class of persons, whether an individual or corporation, or the inhabitants of a county, town, parish, or other locality, and originates on the petition of the person or persons interested"; whereas a public bill "is introduced as a measure of public policy in which the whole community is interested, and originates on the notion of some member of the House in which the Bill is introduced".[28] The difference is, therefore, one of interests. And the final statement of Sir Courtenay Ilbert, that the subject-matter of a private bill is a *privilegium*, an "exception from the general law", must not be understood as meaning that a public law may not deal with one particular case.

In the decisions of the courts, I have been able to find only one case in which the distinction between individual and general laws was thoroughly discussed: *Re v. Crewe* (*ex parte Sekgome*).[29] The Court had to deal with the validity of a Proclamation of a colonial High Commissioner for detention of a native made under an Order in Council of 9th May, 1891, and based upon the Foreign Jurisdiction Act, 1890 (53 and 54 Vict. c. 37), by which the Habeas Corpus Act was suspended. Farwell, L. J., in giving his judgment, began with the following sociological statement: "The truth is that in countries inhabited by native tribes who largely outnumber the white population such acts, although bulwarks of liberty in the United Kingdom, might, if applied there, well prove the death warrant of the whites"; which means that the general law guaranteeing liberty has a disintegrating force if applied in a society based on inequality. He, therefore, admits an abrogation of the Habeas Corpus Act, either generally, or "in respect of a particular individual"; and Kennedy, L. J., adds that the Proclamation is a *privilegium*, "legislation directed against a particular person, and generally, as I hope and believe, such legislation commends itself as little to British legislators as it did to the legislators of ancient Rome"; and Rowlett (for the defendant) rightly pointed out the relationship between such Proclamation and the Bill of Attainder.

From this it follows that however undesirable individual laws may be according to present English constitutional theory, they are not prohibited; and its generality is not recognised as being the essential characteristic of a law.

14.1.5. *The Doctrine of the Non-retroactivity of the Law*[30]

> "La rétroactivité est le plus grand attentat que la loi puisse commettre; elle est le déchirement du pacte social, elle est l'annullation des conditions en vertu desquelles la société a le droit d'éxiger l'obéissance de l'individu; car elle lui ravit les guaranties qu'elle lui assurait, en échange de cette obéissance qui est un sacrifice. La rétroactivité ôte à la loi son caractère; la loi rétroacit n'est pas une loi."[31]

In these words Benjamin Constant characterises the retroactivity of the law. Its general character and its non-retroactivity are mutually linked. If law provides for an indefinite number of future individual cases, a retroactive law cannot possibly be law; because those facts already realised are computable, and therefore the law is confronted with a definite number of particular cases. We have already drawn attention to Rousseau's theory which also in this respect found its way into the Revolutionary French legislation. Art. 8 of the Declaration of 1789, and Art. 14 of that of 1793, forbade penal laws having retroactive effect; "l'effet rétroactif donné à la loi serait un crime". Merlin, however, during the Thermidor reaction, asserted that this principle had equally to be applied to civil law. Consequently Art. 14 of the Constitution of the 5th Fructidor of the Year III prohibited any kind of retroaction; "aucune loi, ni criminelle, ni civile, ne peut avoir d'effet rétroactif". Art. 2 of the *Code civil* states that the law can only provide for future cases, and a similar provision is to be found in Art. 4 of the *Code pénal*. There is, however, in spite of the high esteem in which the principle of non-retroactivity is held by liberal constitutional theory, no doubt that the prohibition is only addressed to judges and not to the legislative body itself.[32] Since the statute of 13th April, 1908, however, it is clear that the legislative body is entitled to promulgate laws with retroactive effect.[33]

The development in Germany takes a similar course. Sect. VIII of the order by which the *Allgemeine Landrecht* of February 5, 1794, was published, as well as Sect. 14 of the introduction to the *Allgemeine Landrecht*, prohibited retroaction, but only to the judge; whereas the legislature was at liberty to issue retroactive laws, but did so only in exceptional cases. An exception, however, is to be found in penal law. Here the prohibition of retroaction has also an ethical function, which finds expression in the two principles, *nullum crimen sine lege*, and *nulla poena sine lege*. Sect. 2 of the German penal code, valid until 28th June, 1935, has formulated these principles in the following way: "A crime can only be punished if the punishment was determined by law before the crime was committed". This prohibition has been rigorously applied in German practice; so rigorously that even an analogous application of provisions of the penal law was considered to be in contravention of this principle.[34] The *Reichsgericht* decided that the theft of electricity could not be punished as a theft under Sect. 242 of the penal law, as that section provided only for the punishment of a theft of things; and electricity cannot be considered as a thing. In order to make it possible to punish the illegal appropriation of electricity, a special statute had to be enacted by Parliament. The Weimar Constitution raised this principle even to the rank of a constitutional guarantee.[35] National Socialist lawyers have asserted that the principle *nulla poena sine lege* derives from Roman law and for that reason is inapplicable to a Germanic system of law.[36] This assertion of the non-Germanic character of the principle of non-retroaction was intended to justify the famous *lex* van der Lubbe (of 29th March, 1933, *Reichsgesetzblatt*, I, p. 151), which introduced retroactively the death penalty for certain crimes. Every legal historian knows, however, that it is nonsense to allege that the principle of non-retroactivity belongs to Roman law. Roman law never embodied such a principle. The Latin formulation of the principle, which derives from Feuerbach, is as little proof of its Roman origin, as the Latin or Greek designation of a disease proves that it was discovered by Roman or Greek doctors. With this principle, *nulla poena sine lege*, there was linked a second postulate, namely the application of the milder penal law, if between the commission of the crime and the trial the punishment had been mitigated by statute. This postulate can already be found in Merlin's report on the retroactive effect of penal laws,[37] in Arts. 1 and 4 of the law of 3rd September, 1792, of the Constituent Assembly; in Sect. 18 of the introduction to the *Allgemeine Landrecht*; in Art. VII of the Prussian penal code of 1851; as well as in the German penal code.

The attitude of English legal theory and practice is similar to that of the continent. Blackstone postulates that "all laws should be, therefore, made to commence in futuro".[38] But practice applies retroactive laws if a statute expressly and clearly demands its retroactive application.[39] Whenever a judge is by the express words of a statute compelled to apply it to past cases, he expresses his indignation in very strong words; thus Parke: "It seems a strong thing to hold . . ."[40], or Vaughan-Williams, L. J.: "It is impossible, I think, to believe".[41]

14.2. The Law and the Judge

14.2.1. *The Presentation of the Theory and Practice*

The extraordinary significance of the general law in the liberal legal system places the problem of the application of the law in the centre of the discussion. If law, and law alone, provides regulations for the relations between individuals and between individuals and the state; if enacted law is the sole means of social change; this naturally does not mean that the written words produce these changes, but that the application of these words by organs of the state, in the sphere of social relations, fulfils those tasks which are attributed to the law. The attitude of the judges towards the law, and their position in the state, is therefore the crux of the liberal legal system.

Much has been written on this problem; but, in spite of the esteem in which I hold the theories which have been developed, I cannot see that the problem has been solved. One of the main reasons for the inadequacy of the solutions is the unhistorical and unsociological treatment of this problem, and the complete neglect of the interdependence of all social phenomena. The other main reason seems to be a syncretism of the methods with which this problem has been attacked.

Let us begin with the answer which the *pure science of law* gives to the question of the relation between judge and law. In that theory, the judge not only performs an act of recognition, but also an act of will. The function of the judicial decision is to create "an individual legal norm, an individualisation and a concretisation of the abstract legal norm".[42] This individual norm, however, stands as we have already seen in a relation of regulation and determination. It stands under the general norm, just as the general norm stands under the Constitution. The general norm determines not only the procedure but the content of the decision too. But this determination is never complete, so that there always is a certain amount of discretion for the judge. The distinction between the function of creating and of concretising the law is thus only a quantitative one, and therefore irrelevant for the pure science of law.[43] The judge is relatively free, that is, within the framework of the general norm.[44]

Similar conclusions are drawn by Hermann Heller, from totally different premisses. He is unable to determine substantively different functions of the state. All activities of the state have substantially, therefore, the same character. They are only distinguished by the different forms in which those acts are performed, and by the superior validity of one activity of the state in relation to others.[45] The conclusions reached by Jennings are similar to those of Heller. He, too, is unable to make a distinction between administration and justice, because every decision, be it one of an administrative body or of a judge "involves . . . the general rule, the ascertainment of facts, the exercise of discretion".[46] One difference, however, he sees in the "rule of precedent". Wherever a higher court interprets general rules, this court always makes new law; an administrative body, however, whose precedents can subsequently be disregarded at any time, does not make such law; as nobody has the right that "departmental practice shall be followed".

By these conclusions, the pure science of law seems to contradict the *orthodox theory of Montesquieu*. In that theory, the judge only performs an act of recognition. The judgment expresses only those ideas which are already contained in the general norm in an abstract way. The function of the judge is that of making a mere logical subsumption, in which the law is the major premiss, the facts of the case the minor premiss, and the decision of the judge nothing but the application of this major premiss to the minor premiss. This "phonograph theory", as Morris R. Cohen[47] called it, has been clearly formulated by Condorcet.[48] The classical expression is found in Montesquieu's *Esprit des Lois*; "Les juges de la nation ne sont . . . que la bouche qui prononce les paroles de la loi des êtres inanimés, qui n'en peuvent modérer ni la force, ni la rigeur". Because of this alleged insignificance of judicial acts they are "en quelque façon nul";[49] but only if, as in England, the judges are drawn from the body of the people at certain times of the year. The connection between this phonograph theory and the distinction of substantially different functions of the state has been clearly formulated by Cazalès:[50] "Dans toute société politique, il n'y a que deux pouvoirs, celui qui fait la loi et celui qui la fait exécuter. Le pouvoir judiciaire, quo qu'en aient dit plusieurs publicistes, n'est qu'une simple fonction, puisqu'il consiste dans l'application pure et simple de la loi. L'application de la loi est une dépendance du pouvoir exécutif".[51] The same idea is expressed in the *Federalist.*[52] There, invoking Montesquieu, Hamilton considers [this] to be "the weakest of the three departments of power". "The courts must declare the sense of the law." Hobbes also accepts this theory by saying: "For every Judge of right or wrong, is not Judge of what is commodious or incommodious to the Commonwealth",[53] and even Hale, in his *History of the Common Law*,[54] asserts "yet they do not make the law, properly so called, for that only the king and Parliament can do". Jurisdiction* is called a process of "deduction and illation upon those laws". In this phonograph theory, "the law was taken to be complete and self-sufficient, without antinomies and without gaps, wanting only arrangement, logical development of the implications of its several rules and conceptions and systematic exposition of its several parts".[55] Modern English legal theory accepts in practice this orthodox theory; "there is, in fact, no such thing as judge-made law, for the judges do not make the law, though they frequently apply existing law to circumstances as to which it has not previously been authoritatively laid down that such law is applicable".[56] "It is in my opinion impossible for us to create any new doctrine of common law."[57] And Lord Shaw, a member of the Judicial Committee of the Privy Council, has given to that idea the final formulation; "the legislator is free and the judiciary bound".[58]

Bentham[59] argued the preferability of a codification in the following words: "A code. . . would not require schools for its explanation, would not require casuists to unravel its subtleties. It would speak a language familiar to everybody; each one might consult it at his need. . . . Judges should not make new Law. . . . Commentaries, if written, should not be cited. . . . If a judge or advocate thinks he sees an error or omission, let him certify his opinion to the Legislature".

French doctrinairism carried Bentham's postulate to its logical perfection, and even transformed it into a reality. The Constituent Assembly accepted Montesquieu's theory.[60] Robespierre declared: "Ce mot de jurisprudence des tribuneaux. . . doit être effacé de notre langue. Dans un état qui a une constitution, une législation, la jurisprudence des tribuneaux n'est autre chose que la loi".[61] Consequently the decree of 16th and 24th August, 1790, which carried out the doctrine of the separation of powers, prohibited the judge from interpreting a law. If the judge has doubts as to how a statute is to be interpreted, he must apply for help to the legislative power. The law says: "Les tribuneaux s'adresseront au corps législatif toutes les fois qu'ils croient nécessaire d'interpréter une loi". The functions of this *référé legislatif* were later taken over by the Tribunal de Cassation (later, Court de Cassation), which had the task of controlling every judgment as to whether it contained an express contravention of the wording of the law. But it must be kept in mind that this tribunal was not conceived to be a court, but a mandatory of the legislative power, as is shown by the Constitution of 1791 (Titre III, Chap. V. Arts. 21 and 19): "Il y aura un tribunal de cassation, établi auprès du corps législatif". The *référé au législateur* [was] abolished by Art. 4 of the Civil Code, and the Tribunal de Cassation changed its functions; it had now no longer to look only for a formal violation of the wording of the law, but also for wrong interpretations.[62] By this, the admissibility of interpretation was implicitly admitted. Portalis, who exercised a decisive influence on the drafting of the Civil Code by his *Discours Préliminaire*, expressly gave to the judge the right to interpret law and to fill its gaps; "Nous reconnaissons dans les juges l'autorité de statuer sur les choses qui ne sont pas déterminées par les lois".[63] According to Portalis, it is impossible for the legislator to foresee all possible cases. Therefore the judge has to fill the gaps "par les lumières naturelles de la droiture et du bon sens" (Vol. I, p. 467). This idea of Portalis, which found its way into the *Code civil*, has, however, not prevailed in French legal theory and practice. On the contrary, the *Ecole de l'Exégèse* was completely victorious.[64]

Bonnecase mentions the characteristic fact that the turning point in the history of French legal thought is the year 1830; from then on, for half a century, this doctrine prevailed practically unchallenged.

The *Référé legislatif* has been formally abolished by the laws of 30th August, 1828, and 1st April, 1837.

The decisive significance of this institution is the attempt to carry the supremacy of Parliament to its logical conclusion, and to prevent the establishment of a rule of judges veiled by the phonograph theory. These attempts, however ridiculous they may appear to us today, distinguish that period from the nineteenth and twentieth centuries, when the orthodox theory of Montesquieu prevailed without finding its corrective in such institutions. Today the orthodox theory is a doctrine hiding the power of the judges. The French revolutionary period, however, by establishing the *Référé legislatif*, really attempted to reduce the power of the judges as much as possible.

Similar developments took place in Germany. A decree of Frederick the Great, of 14th April, 1780, also forbade to judges the interpretation of laws;[65] and this decree was only repealed by his successor, by means of another of 8th March, 1798. Sect. 4 of the Introduction to the *Allgemeine Landrecht* forbade judges to interpret laws against the wording of the law and the context of the words of a law. Paul Johann Anselm Feuerbach, the founder of the German science of penal law, was as much opposed to any kind of commentary as was Bentham. He declared it to be absurd to interpret penal laws by books, and it is probable that the Bavarian Instruction of 19th October, 1813, which prohibited officials and private scholars from writing a commentary on the Bavarian penal code of 1813, was due to his influence.[66] But Feuerbach's great opponent, Savigny, took practically the same line.[67] He sees in statutes and customary law the only sources of law. The judge has only the function of recognising law in its truth. Even the filling of gaps is to be done by positive law. Therefore any attempt to make Savigny a forerunner of the School of Free Discretion must fail.

With the victory of juridical positivism about the middle of the nineteenth century, the triumph of Montesquieu's theory is complete. The law is a dogma, the interpretation, therefore, dogmatic. The difference between the historical school and the dogmatic school is not great. For the historical school was convinced of the prejudicial existence of the law, and whereas for the dogmatic school law was only realised in statutes and codes, for the historical school it was to be found in codified and customary law. Both repudiated the right of the judge to entertain considerations of equity or morality.[68]

The absolute subjection of the judge under the law is supplemented by complete denial of the right *of judicial review.** From the logical definition of the conception of the separation of powers nothing can be deduced as to whether such judicial review follows from that notion or is incompatible with it. One can, of course, argue, with Hamilton in the *Federalist* (No. LXXVIII), that: "There is no position which depends on clearer principles than that every act of a delegated authority, contrary to the tenor of the commission under which it is exercised, is void. No legislative act, therefore, contrary to the Constitution, can be valid". With equal logic one can deduce from the superiority of the legislative power the exact opposite of Hamilton's theory. The decision as to whether judicial review is compatible with the idea of the separation of powers has nothing to do with logic, but everything to do with politics.

The problem was practical in Germany for the first time in Hessen in 1849, when the judges declared void an emergency Taxation Decree of the Government. In consequence of this conflict, German constitutional theory was divided into two camps. The liberals[69] advocated the right of judicial review; the conservatives, of course, repudiated it.[70] Although the fourth meeting of the German Jurists in 1863 declared itself in favour of judicial review, the number of the adherents of this principle dwindled rapidly during the Bismarck period, so that at the end of the nineteenth century, theory and practice were nearly unanimous in rejecting the controlling right of judges. The German Courts recognised such right only with regard to decrees, and allowed judges only the right to examine whether such executive decree was covered by delegation by a statute. The Supreme Court further admitted the authority of the judges to examine laws of the federal states as to their compatibility with the law of the Reich.[71] The admissibility of judicial review of statutes of the *Reich* and of the federal states as to their compatibility with the constitutions concerned was clearly and unmistakably denied.[72]

Almost the same views are held by English theory and practice.[73]

The other radical position is taken by the American Realists.[74] Whereas for the pure science of law, law is the sum of constitution, general norms, decisions, and administrative acts; and whereas for dogmatic jurisprudence, the only law is codified and statutory law; for realistic jurisprudence law is but the sum of judicial decisions: "The law of the state . . . is composed of the rules which the courts, that is the judicial organs of that body, lay down for the determination of legal rights and duties".[75] The judge is not only the discoverer but the author of the law.[76] The reason that the judges do not like to admit this simple proposition lies in the fact that they want to veil their power. Consequently, realistic jurisprudence suggests that students should turn from the study of material law to that of judicial behaviour.[77] Frank, for instance, denies any certainty of the law. He admits that public opinion asks for certainty, but the assertion that the law is certain is for him a mere myth. Law is "largely vague and uncertain" even in a relatively static society.[78] He attempts to give a partial interpretation of this drive for certainty, and he finds it psycho-analytically in the fact that man as a child always regards his father as the infallible judge. Man, however, always remains the victim of his childish desires. In the substitute of law, he rediscovers his father, and he ascribes to the law those qualities which he ascribed to his father when he was a child. Although Frank in many places asserts his interpretation to be only a partial one, the fact that he expressly rejects the constitutive character of religious, aesthetic, and economic factors, and all other psychological factors such as "a partial interest in peace and quietness", "imitation", "inertia", "laziness", "stupidity", shows that his partial interpretation becomes a complete one. His definition of law consequently goes even farther than that of Gray:

> For any particular lay person the law with respect to any particular set of facts, is a decision of a court with respect to those facts so far as that decision affects that particular person. Until a court has passed on those facts no law on that subject is yet in existence. Prior to such a decision, the only law available is the opinion of the lawyers relating to that person and to those facts. Such opinion is not actual law but only a guess as to what the court will decide.[79]

He, therefore, distinguishes between actual law, consisting of already reached decisions, and probable law, containing a guess as to future decisions. His final thesis is that the jurist has to "catch the spirit of a creative scientist which yearns not for safety but for risk, not for certainty but for adventure which thrives on experimentation, invention and novelty and not on nostalgia for the absolute, which devotes itself to new ways of manipulating protean particulars and not to the quest of undeviating universals".[80] The process of application of the law begins, therefore, with the "hunch" of the judge, which is only subsequently rationalised. The traditional theory that the application of law is no more than an act of recognition, is a mere veil. Rules only have the task formally to justify the judge, and sometimes even hinder a good decision.[81]

> At their best, when properly employed, they have undeniable value. The conscientious judge, having tentatively arrived at a conclusion can check up to see whether such a conclusion . . . . can be linked up with the generalised points of view . . . If none such are discoverable, he is forced

> to consider more acutely whether his tentative conclusion is wise, both with respect to the case before him and with respect to possible implications for future cases.

Rules are, therefore, nothing but "formal clothes" for the judge. In the second part, he applies his theory to the doctrines of "certain brilliant legal thinkers".[82] He demands adult judges such as Mr. Justice Oliver Wendell Holmes, who have compensated for their father-complexes.

> If the search for the father-judge is ended, if the authority-ridden mode of regarding law is eliminated, if men see law as a human adjustment and not as a gift or mandate from some external source, no violent transformation need or will occur. The relief from fear of chance might not result in the adoption of a policy of incessant hectic change, but will lead to a policy of healthy and vital growth.[83]

The continental reaction against dogmatic jurisprudence is expressed in the theory of the School of Free Discretion.[84] The School of Free Discretion is decisively based upon the theory of François Gény; according to which law is not only contained in statutes, as the legal system is not closed and complete but has gaps which must be filled. And they can only be filled with legal rules; therefore the decision of the judge must be a legal one. These rules must be general in order to fulfil the demands of the principle of equality. These rules are found by the judge, who is, therefore, not a mere "slot-machine", but has creative functions.

To this theory of the sources of the law there are attached certain postulates of the reform of the legal system, which are best expressed in the famous pamphlet of Gnaeus Flavius (Hermann Kantorowicz), and in the pamphlets of Ernst Fuchs, and which are directed to the revision of the relation between law and the judge. These two parts, the theoretical observations on the sources of the law, and the postulated political theory, must be rigidly separated. In so far as the School of Free Discretion represents a political theory, it demands the supersession of formal rational law by legal standards of conduct. Whereas Kantorowicz, the German founder of the school, in his later works laid more stress on the theoretical aspects of the teaching of the School of Free Discussion, his successors have mainly underlined its political postulates as it is, for instance, expressed by Ernst Fuchs:[85]

> The civil code is good only in one place, namely, where it abandons abstract casuistries, and only puts up a finger-post. It bears the inscription: "Entrance to the Free State of Law of the Needs of Exchange". It is the section 242. This regal paragraph proved subsequently to be the Archimedic point, from which the old legal world could be shaken to its foundations.

14.2.2. *The Theoretical Evaluation of the Doctrines*

This plethora of doctrines must not prevent us from recognising clearly some fundamental facts. For us, indeed, there stands in the centre of the discussion, not the theoretical problem of whether this or that theory is right or wrong, but rather the politico-sociological problem of why in a certain historical period a certain theory became prevalent, and of what social function it performed.

It cannot be doubted that the function of the judge does not consist in a mere act of recognition. Hegel already drew attention to this fact.[86] The judicial process is, therefore, an indistinguishable mixture of theoretical and practical, recognising and creative, reproductive and productive, scientific and supra-scientific, objective and subjective elements.[87] Since Karl Mannheim raised the sociology of knowledge to the rank of science, we have been in possession of a technique, even if not fully developed, enabling us to distinguish the existential determination of thought.[88]

> The existential determination of thought must be supposed to be a proven fact, in those spheres in which we succeed in showing (a) that the process of *recognition* does not historically develop itself according to "immanent laws of development"; that is in no way determined by the "nature of things" and by "pure logical possibilities", in no way by an "immanent spiritual dialectic"; but that decisively extra-theoretical factors of a totally different kind, which we are accustomed to call factors of existence, arise and determine the process of thought; and (b) that the emergence of those factors of existence which determine the concrete content of knowledge are not only of a peripheral significance, but determine it in content and form, in structure and way of formulation.

This existential determination of the judicial process happens in the first place when the judge tries to discover the concrete facts of the case. The distinction between material and immaterial facts, the evaluation of statements of the parties and of witnesses, in so far as rigid laws of evidence do not exclude the possibility of such interpretation, is to a large extent the work of the will of the judge and not a mere logical process. The evaluation of evidence is, so to speak, dependent upon the mental climate of the judge. The second sphere in which the mental climate of the judge becomes operative is the interpretation of the legal rules, be they contained in a code, in a statute, or in precedents. An abundance of legal norms are open to interpretation. Whether the judge prefers this or that interpretation, whether he applies a precedent or disregards it with the help of the art of distinguishing, is entirely a matter of free will.

Whoever, therefore, begins a book on the judicial process with the proof that this process does not consist of a mere act of recognition, is proving the obvious.

Given this basic assumption, the pure science of law is right in maintaining that the concept of law-making cannot be identified with that of legislation, and must not be confused with the activity of certain organs of the state; and that, therefore, the concept of law (*Recht*) cannot be identified with that of statutory law (*Gesetz*);[89] but this conclusion of the pure theory of law, that there is no qualitative difference between legislation and jurisdiction, has no great significance. However the theoretically unassailable position, that there is no theoretical distinction between legislation and jurisdiction, is important for the refutation of all those doctrines which assert the existence of an unbridgeable gulf between legislation and the application of law, such as, for instance, the decision of the U.S. Supreme Court in the recent [1930s] Schechter case.

From this basic position, however, the contribution made by American realism, although significant, appears in no way decisive. Let us choose Frank's book. Frank asserts several times that his is only a partial interpretation. Partial interpretations, however, have a merely illusory character if one omits to state the relation of this part to the others. On this point, Frank remains silent. He repeatedly asserts that the father-as-judge theory does not represent the whole truth. But the passion with which he rejects any other interpretation shows that this partial interpretation transforms itself in his hand into a complete one. His incapacity to determine its relation to the various facts is clearly shown when he deals with the function of rules. He cannot ignore them, but he asserts them to be only formal clothes of the judge. But they are more even in his theory. It is true that the decision starts with the "hunch", but in his view the judge has to give up the "hunch" if this intuition of his is in open contradiction to the rule or to the case. So that practically the rule, as distinguished from the decision of the judge, has a reality of its own. His mistake, like that of all other realists, is that he does not see the real existence of the rules. The rule is a means for human adjustment, as is the decision of the judge, which in his view is the sole means. And the rule is as little a gift or mandate from some external power as is the judicial decision. It is as much the work of man as is the judgment of a Court. His merit, however, consists in having demonstrated that the quest for certainty, for absolute security, is a phenomenon of bourgeois society. The bourgeois, in spite of the fact that in his philosophy the individual moves in the centre of the universe, always clings to something absolute; and this absolute is since Descartes the universal law. But Frank simply substitutes for the absolute law the absolute judge, who assumes the rôle of the absolute unrestricted leader. It is, therefore, true when Professor Goodhart says that the doctrines of the realist school itself are due to an inferiority complex. His psycho-analytical interpretation of law is as much a bourgeois theory as is the orthodox theory of Montesquieu.

His theory in no way explains why a judge decides in this or in that way, and why we have current opinions as to interpretation of rules.

This problem can only be solved by the method of sociology.

The thinking of the judge is determined by two sets of factors. In the first place, by individual dominants; by his dislike or liking for certain lawyers or parties, or of males or females, or of Catholics or Protestants, or Jews. These individual dominants are indeterminable. They can only be rationalised if they have become typical habits and can, therefore, be observed and taken into account.

Far more important, however, is that the social structure conditions mentality.[90] The manner in which he regards a thing, what he grasps, and how he mentally transforms it, is determined basically by his social position. The existential determination of thought differs in the various stages of the judicial process. We follow Mannheim's distinction between the various stages of thought.[91] The first stage is that of intuition (*Finden*). Here the judge waits for the intuition, the "hunch". It is the most primitive stage of thought, and is realised in the Kadi justice, or in the activity of the jury. In this stage, the part played by thinking is relatively small, or is non-existent. The decision is mainly an unconscious reaction.

But the judge does not stop short at this stage. He ascends to the stage of inventive thought (*Erfinden*). The process of subsumption begins. The judge is not allowed to be satisfied with an intuition; he is compelled to produce arguments, that is, to rationalise the intuition. At this stage of inventive thought, the share of thought is large, but the existence determines the thought. If the judge now begins to think sociologically, he ascends to the third stage, that of planned thought (*planendes Denken*). Sociologically, this means — from the judge's point of view — that he makes himself conscious of the fact that his thinking is existentially determined. This sociological self-analysis is in my view the first task of the judge. This problem was presented in a very interesting way in Germany on the occasion of a controversy between the former President of the Supreme Court, Dr. Simons, and Radbruch, the former *Reich* Minister of Justice and Professor of the Philosophy of Law. Dr. Simons asserted that no Marxist could possibly become a judge, as every Marxist is biassed by his conception of class struggle; as against which, Radbruch replied that only a Marxist can possibly be a judge, as he is able consciously to see the determination of his judicial process by his existence and by that of the parties to the litigation. "Planned" thought means materially — according to its function — the fitting of the judge's decision not only into a logical system of rules, but into a social system which is determined by the constitution.

Marxism fills materially this methodological conclusion of the sociology of knowledge, by the assertion that the attitude of the judge towards the law is conditioned by the class relationship upon which it is dependent.[92] The principal assertion of Marxism is that in a class society justice must necessarily be class justice, but it does not seek to indite the judge, but only to explain the function of the judge in modern society. Marxism, therefore, distinguishes the phenomenon of class justice from that of political justice; whereas class justice is an unconscious existential determination of the judicial process, political justice is a conscious misuse of the law for political purposes, mainly for the destruction of political opponents. The phenomenon of class justice has been admirably described by Lord Justice Scrutton:[93] "Impartiality is rather difficult to attain in any system. I am not speaking of conscious impartiality; but the habits you are trained in, the people with whom you mix, lead to your having a certain class of ideas of such nature that when you have to deal with other ideas, you do not give as sound and accurate judgements as you would wish". And for labour disputes, he adds: "It is very difficult sometimes to be sure that you have put yourself into a thoroughly impartial position between the two disputants, one of your own class, and one not of your class". He even reaches the surprising statement that whereas commercial courts are advisable because they have to deal with litigation in the same stratum of society, industrial courts are extremely precarious as the parties belong to antagonistic classes with antagonistic convictions.

The great German liberal Gneist,[94] who was far from being a Marxist, regarded law as the sediment of settled class conflicts of society, and he added that the judge shares the feeling, the interests, and the ideas of the educated class to which he belongs.

It is obvious that only by special investigations can it be proved whether or not the existential determination of the judicial process, in the sense that the judicial process is essentially conditioned by the class relationships, is valid or not.

The sociological investigations on these two bases — the sociology of knowledge and the sociology of ideologies — have to deal with the following problems.

In theory and practice a distinction is drawn between legislation and the application of law. It is asserted that there exists a substantial difference between these two types of state activity. It is as true that jurisdiction involves law-making, as it is that there are differences between legislation and the activity of the judge. Those differences are not of a categorical nature. They are historically, politically, and socially conditioned. As such, they are without interest for the pure science of law and for American realism; but for any sociology of law their significance is decisive. We are on the whole in agreement with the careful evaluation of Mr. Justice Cardozo,[95] and Professor Goodhart.[96] We agree with him that in spite of the great importance of the subconscious factors in the judicial process, the importance of the conscious factors must not be under-estimated;[97] but that the logical method leads only to a certain point, after which the sociological method has to be applied.[98] As against the exaggerations of the doctrine which emphasises the creative activity of the judge, Mr. Justice Cardozo stresses especially the fact that although there are enumerable cases, yet in the majority the law is clear, and not open to interpretation. Every practical lawyer knows this. The quantitative over-evaluation in the United States of the creative activity of the judge derives especially from the fact that interest is centred on constitutional disputes, and that the constitution consists not at all of abstract legal norms, but of undefined legal standards of conduct, which either have no content whatever, or whose content is indeterminable. These constitutional provisions are not legal rules; rather, they are legal principles. The quantitative over-evaluation is generally conditioned by the fact that legal theory deals exclusively with decisions, and not with those legal disputes which never reach the stage of litigation. Finally, it is conditioned by the fact that legal theory concerns itself with reported decisions, but hardly ever takes into account the unreported judgments, whose number is far greater.

Within the application of law, we have to attempt a distinction between jurisdiction and administration. We have no intention of adding a new investigation to those already in existence; we aim only at giving an outline of that problem which seems to us decisive.[99] According to the pure science of law, there is no formal difference between jurisdiction and administration; as administration, like jurisdiction, is nothing but the individualisation and concretisation of general norms. The differentiation of justice and administration is in this connection "in a greater or less degree, historical arbitrariness".[100]

But what is irrelevant from the point of view of the pure science of law, is decisive from that of sociology.

It is generally agreed that we may speak of administration wherever "the executive arm of government interferes with individuals of its own motion, prior to and apart from the existence of any controversy between them".[101] It is similarly agreed that the administrative activity of the state includes the organisation of any kind of body. In these cases, the state realises its aim directly, for instance by building hospitals, controlling the traffic, and running banks, postal services, and so on; whereas in all other cases, the state provides for the subjects certain patterns of behaviour, through which it only indirectly realises its aims.

But the state deals not only with relations between itself and the citizens, but also with conflicts between citizens. These disputes are on the whole decided by courts, and are the subject of jurisdiction. But this is not necessarily so; and in any case, the fact that they are decided by ordinary courts tells us nothing as to the nature of these conflicts. The positive law can obviously allocate any dispute to the sphere of the ordinary courts. It can even appoint administrative tribunals for the decision of genuine civil conflicts. The decision as to whether the decision of a legal dispute is sociologically jurisdiction or administration does not depend upon the decision of the positive law, but on material criteria. One must, however, ask whether it is useful to discover such material criteria, if the positive law has already given a decision as to whether a dispute is one of civil or of administrative jurisdiction. The answer to this objection is that the sociological analysis is preparatory to a reform of the law. If we discover by a sociological analysis that a certain activity of the state is structurally and functionally administration and not justice, we might postulate in certain circumstances the allocation of this matter to administration or to administrative tribunals, and not to ordinary courts. From this point of view, the analysis must be regarded as justified.

We define as administrative disputes those disputes between individuals which are *exclusively or overwhelmingly decided on the basis of legal standards of conduct; that is to say, by free discretion.* We are conscious of the fact that there is no categorical distinction between free discretion and the binding of the judge by the law; as free discretion is obviously granted by the legal order. In that sense, acts of free discretion are legal acts. We are further conscious of the fact that even the activity of the ordinary courts is to a great extent discretionary activity. Notions such as negligence, malice, and so on, are discretionary notions.[102]

The distinction between discretionary notions and exactly defined legal concepts is no formal one; it represents a material and sociological difference. The boundary is to be found where disputes are exclusively or overwhelmingly decided on the basis of legal standards of conduct, such as good faith, good morals, public policy, or reasonableness. In such cases, the activity of the ordinary courts is in fact administrative activity. Legal standards of conduct, and the free discretion which is the realisation of such standards, serve the reconciliation of colliding interests, and not the determination of conflicting rights. Such standards make it possible to consider questions of conveniency and not only questions of law. If for instance a Court dissolves a marriage because of "any facts by which the marital relation owing to any grave breach of marital duty or dishonorable or immoral conduct on the respondent's part, is disturbed to such an extent that the petitioner cannot fairly be expected to continue the marriage" (Sect. 1568 of the German Civil Code); if the Court decides the legality of a strike or of a lock-out, entirely with regard to its morality (Sect. 826 of the German Civil Code); if an industrial cartel can be dissolved, "if any agreement or convention . . . shall endanger the economic life of the community as a whole" (Sect. 4 of the Decree against the abuse of economic power of 2nd November, 1923); if English or American courts decide the legality of a combination in restraint of trade entirely on the basis of whether such restraint is reasonable or not; then the courts, even if their decision has the form of an ordinary judgment, are in fact reconciling conflicting interests and thereby exercising administrative power.

The distinction is important because administrative acts and administrative decisions are essentially more political than those of the ordinary courts.

14.3. The Doubt Raised by the English Law

14.3.1.

Before, however, we approach the politico-sociological problem, one central question has to be discussed, namely, whether the formal structure of English law, and above all, common law and equity, are compatible with the needs of the liberal legal system for rationality, certainty, calculability and predictability.[103] We have already seen that the generality of the law, its non-retroactivity, and the position of the judge, are typical structural phenomena of the liberal legal system in the period of free competition. The question which is of sociological relevance is now whether or not these characteristics are constitutive elements of every legal system in an age of free competition and of political liberalism, or whether they are merely accidental. If we come to the conclusion that the formal structure of English law differs fundamentally from that of Continental law, then we cannot assert that there is any necessary connection between the competitive economic system and the above-mentioned legal structure. If, however, we are able to prove that the structure of English law, in spite of many differences from the Continental legal system, has so much in common with it that its essential features are identical, then we have evidence that there corresponds to the competitive economic system one particular type of legal system, finding its expression in the generality of the law, in its rationality, and in the merely declaratory function of the judge.

For this purpose, the analysis of the English legal system is one possible test of the validity of our thesis. We are conscious of the difficulties which a Continental jurist has to overcome in presenting an analysis of the English legal system. We are fortunate, however, in that in recent Anglo-American literature the problem has already been dealt with, so that we are able to build upon the results of these investigations.

The decisive difference between Continental and English legal theory lies in the fact that English legal theory denies the law to be a closed system expressing a logical, consistent body of rules. It is not the lack of codification which makes the approach of a Continental jurist to the problem of English law so difficult; it is rather the conviction of English lawyers that the law does not present a system. This conviction has been expressed, for instance, by Lord Halsbury: "A case is only an authority for what it actually decides. I entirely deny that it can be quoted for a proposition that may seem to follow logically from it. Such a mode of reasoning assumes that the law is necessarily a logical code, whereas as every lawyer must acknowledge, the law is not always logical at all". [104] This is a formulation which a Continental jurist is simply unable to understand. The theory of the logical consistency of law prevalent on the Continent is replaced in English law by that of its historical continuity.[105] The "law of the land" is a collection of principles which is in permanent development. There is no breach with tradition. It is otherwise in Germany; the dissolution of the old *Reich* in 1806 interrupted German legal history also. The old *Reichskammergericht* had no connection with the new *Reichsgericht*. The differences between the English and the Continental legal systems are conditioned, as we have already noted, by the differences in economic and political history. The main technical reason lies in the existence of strong corporations of lawyers in England[106] which opposed the reception of Roman law, thereby preventing a synchronisation with Continental legal development.

But these differences must not lead us to overlook the fundamental structural similarity of the two legal systems, a similarity which is so great that from a sociological point of view the differences lose their significance.

14.3.2.

We begin with the first thesis: that the general law in the Continental legal system is replaced by the *ratio decidendi* of the case in English law. The modern law as to the binding force of precedent is: every judge of the High Court is bound by the decisions of the Court of Appeal and of the House of Lords, but not by those of other members of the High Court. The Court of Appeal is bound by its own decisions and by those of the House of Lords. The House of Lords is subject to its own prior decisions. The Judicial Committee of the Privy Council is technically not a court in this sense, but as its personnel is nominally identical with that of the House of Lords, its judgments, though not legally binding, are of high value. The position of the Court of Criminal Appeal is doubtful; it is likely that it is bound by its own decisions, but its relation to the Court of Appeal is undefined.[107]

The following questions have, therefore, to be examined:

(a) What is understood by the binding force of precedent?

(b) What is the distinction between the *ratio decidendi* and the *obiter dicta*?

(c) And to what extent is this theory used?

(d) What is the rôle of equity in the English legal system?

(e) What is the social function of the binding force of precedent and of equity?

We begin with the statement that the principle of the binding force of precedent, as such, has nothing to do with the case-law system.[108] The doctrine of the binding force of precedent is perfectly compatible with a codified legal system as well as with the common law. And it is characteristic of the English law that this doctrine is applied not only to common law but is superimposed on statutory law.

According to modern theory, a precedent contains a principle, a rule which has to be distinguished from the binding force which a decision exercises between the two parties of the litigation. This principle, the *ratio decidendi*, has a power which transcends the binding force between the parties. The determination of the rule is extremely complicated. The technique has been fully developed by Goodhart.[109] The complications are due to the fact that the principle is embedded in the facts of the case, so that "every judgement must be read as applicable to the particular facts proved, or assumed to be proved, since the generality of the expressions which may be found there are not intended to be expressions of the whole law, but are governed and qualified by the particular facts of the case in which such expressions are to be found".[110] Another difficulty arises from the fact that very often judges who concur in a decision give divergent reasons for so doing. The close connection between the *ratio decidendi* and the facts of the case makes it necessary, therefore, in the first place to determine the facts of the case, secondly to distinguish the material from the immaterial facts, and finally, to follow the conclusions of the judge who built upon those facts. It is extremely difficult to state the rule of a case; but difficult as it may be, there is no doubt that the rule is identical with the abstract general law of a formal rational norm. The *ratio decidendi*, therefore, is as much the object of subsumption by a later judge as is the provision of a statute or of a code.[111] It cannot be doubted that this inductive and pragmatic approach presents to the finding of the general principle difficulties far greater than those involved in finding the appropriate provision in a code or in a statute. However, the dissimilarity between the two systems, although great, does not affect their fundamental likeness; the more so, as the belief that an appropriate clause in a statute or in a code can easily be found and as easily determined, is obviously a myth,[112] as everyone knows who is even slightly conversant with Continental law.

The art of distinguishing, that is, "to prove a case cited as applicable, inapplicable", can be found in Continental as well as in English law. A comparison between the highly-developed technique of distinguishing in English law and the decisions to Sect. 137 of the German *Gerichtsverfassungsgesetz* (law relating to the constitution of courts), show this art to be very highly developed in the German legal system also. According to that section, a plenary decision of either the combined civil senates or of the combined penal senates of the *Reichsgericht* was necessary when one senate intended to deviate from a known decision of another senate. And a plenary decision of the combined penal and civil senates of the *Reichsgericht* was necessary when a penal senate intended to deviate from a decision of a civil senate, and vice versa. But the "horror pleni", as the aversion to such plenary decisions was called, was always so strong that the *Reichsgericht* developed to perfection the technique of distinguishing, so that the application of Sect. 137 was avoided as often as possible.

In England, "it is only under a system of binding precedents that the necessary continuity and certainty inherent in the conception of law can be achieved on the basis of judicial decisions".[113]

It is, therefore, of vital significance to ascertain when the negation of creative activity on the part of common law courts first occurred and when the binding force of precedent first prevailed. This question is a subject of controversy, and when high authorities differ, it is impossible for an outsider to make a decision.[114] Before the end of the nineteenth century, Allen asserts, "the application of precedent was powerful and constant, but no judge would be found to admit that he was absolutely bound by any decision of any tribunal".[115] Allen quotes as general proof the decisions of Lord Mansfield,[116] who maintained that

> the law of England would be a strange science if, indeed, it were decided upon precedents only. Precedents served to illustrate principles and to give them a fixed certainty, but the law of England, which is exclusive of positive law and enacted by statutes, depends upon principles, and those principles run through all the cases according as the particular circumstances of each case have been found to fall within the one or the other of them.

We are not able finally to decide the controversy. But we may draw attention to the following problem.

The theory of the binding force of precedent has to be distinguished from the doctrine that the judge does not make law but only applies it.[117] The English law could — theoretically at least — accept the doctrine of *stare decisis* and yet repudiate the orthodox theory of Montesquieu. That is to say, it could maintain that in so far as judgments have already created objective law, judges are bound by it. But in so far as such law is not to be found in previous decisions, the judges are at liberty — and are even compelled — to create it. Such a state of affairs would presuppose that Lord Halsbury's view in Quinn v. Leather is correct; that, in other words, the legal system is not closed and final but in a permanent state of development, and full of gaps.

We have, however, found that the English judges adhere to the phonograph theory.[118]

It is, therefore, not a valid objection to the theory of Sir William Holdsworth and Professor Goodhart that every decision makes law. This is the very same objection which is being raised against the universally binding character of enacted law and against the phonograph theory in any legal system. The objection does not apply only to the English law. In order to do justice to English legal theory, we must reason on the basis of the orthodox theory.

We want to point out that in accepting the view that any decision is a mere expression of what already created objective law contains and in view of the fact that the common law is to be found in previous decisions, the doctrine of the binding force of precedent must have arisen at the time when the orthodox theory became prevalent. If the legal system is closed and final and judgments, therefore, mere declarations of what the law is; and if that law exists only in decisions; then the only possible consequence is that any later decision has to follow a previous one, as a later decision cannot create law but can only apply it. There is, therefore, in spite of the distinction between the two doctrines, a close, even a necessary, relation between them.

If we discover that the declaratory theory was fully developed and universally accepted before the end of the nineteenth century, we have a probability that the doctrine of *stare decisis* must have emerged at about the same time.

The declaratory theory, together with that of *stare decisis*, is clearly developed by Blackstone,[119] who asserted the pre-judicial existence of the common law, so that every decision is merely an "evidence of what is common law".[120] That this theory is wrong has been proved by Bentham and Austin; but their criticism does not concern us here. It is true that the present theory of the merely declaratory character of the activity of the judge is not based upon the assumption of the pre-judicial validity of common law, but upon the entirely different assumption that the common law has already been fully developed by judicial decisions, and has, therefore, been transformed by them into a complete body of rules, so that after the completion of that body, every decision of a common law court is a mere application of rules found in previous decisions. We, therefore, argue thus: Sir W. Holdsworth, who sees clearly the dependence of the doctrine of *stare decisis* on the phonograph theory of Blackstone, infers that "the adoption of this point of view, gives the Courts power to mould as they please the condition in which they will accept a decided case or a series of decided cases as authoritative".[121] But as Blackstone's evidence theory is rejected and replaced by the theory that the common law is only to be found in decided cases, it follows that Professor Goodhart must be right, and that, therefore, the combination of the two doctrines makes for the highest possible degree of rigidity.[122]

This, however, also implies that in spite of the lack of systemisation of English law, there must lie at the bottom of the doctrine of the binding force precedent, the conception of the logical closeness of the law. If all decisions are only to be reached on the basis of decisions already made, then the implication is that the legal system is complete, closed and logically consistent, so that any change in that system can be made only by way of legislation. This idea is stated with clarity by Georg Jäger.[123] He has proved that the common law is considered to be a system of objective law which is without gaps, closed in space and time, and which is therefore unchangeable. Any change can consist only in a transfer of existing rights from one individual to another. The land, however, is distributed. All land must have an owner. Somewhere the ownership must rest. Property cannot be in a state of abeyance — an idea which has been expressed by Blackstone[124] in this way: "But when once it was agreed that everything capable of ownership should have an owner, natural reason suggested that he who could first declare his intention of appropriating anything to his own use, and, in consequence of such intention, actually took it into possession, should thereby gain the absolute property of it". Or, in another connection he maintained that "the fee-simple of all land must abide somewhere", and even chattels "can never be in abeyance or without an owner". Original acquisition does not play a decisive rôle. Chapters XXVI and XXVII ("Title by Prerogative" and "Forfeiture") show that his whole theory of common law is based upon the assumption of the finality of that law; new customary law is no longer formed. The theory of the finality and closeness of the legal system is closely related to the rejection of the labour theory of value and the acceptance of the property theory, for instance, as it is developed by Kant. If the labour theory of value is accepted, it is difficult to affirm the finality of the legal system. If property is "being grounded on labour and invention",[125] new property must constantly arise; the legal system cannot, therefore, be thought of as being without gaps. If, however, property is being based solely on "the right of occupancy",[126] and any other method of acquiring property is derived from that primary method; if therefore the earth is divided, the legal system must necessarily be considered to be closed, since in the liberal theory objective law follows subjective rights. Consequently, Blackstone was compelled to repudiate Locke's labour theory of value and to assert that property "grounded on labour and invention is more properly reducible to the head of occupancy than any other; since the right of occupancy itself is supposed by Mr. Locke, and many others, to be founded on the personal labour of the occupant".[127] It is not our task to deal with the rightness either of the labour theory of property or of the finality of the law. We seek only to stress the following points: the repudiation of Locke's property theory; the constant affirmation by English judges that they do not make, but only apply, law; the doctrine of the binding force of precedent; must all necessarily imply that the common law is a closed system, a final body of rules, without gaps, so that any decision must be reached — in so far as statute law does not apply — on the basis of previously made decisions.

A structural dissimilarity to the Continental law has, therefore, to be denied, as the Continental doctrine similarly assumes that the legal system is closed and that every decision is a mere application of a code, a statute, or of customary law.

The doctrine of the binding force of precedent pervades, in consequence of these assumptions, the whole of the English law; its application is not restricted to those realms of the law where authority by precedent is necessary for the protection of subjective rights, especially of property, but is "founded on the broader theory that it is essential for the law to be certain".[128]

The conviction that the theory of the binding force of precedent, with that of the finality of the common law, must have arisen earlier than Allen believed, is further strengthened by the constitutional theory of the rule of law in the sense which we have developed; namely the rule of *enacted* law.[129] That doctrine, however, arose in the middle of the seventeenth century, and was finally victorious at the end of that century. We know already that even Blackstone, while repeating Burlamaqui's assertion of the supremacy of natural law, at the same time saw no remedy if Parliament enacts a law "which is unreasonable"; and we have in Part II [above] traced the disappearance of natural law. If, however, "rule of law" means "supremacy of that law enacted by Parliament", then obviously the importance of the common law must have been reduced to such an extent as to make that common law a body of fixed rules.

I may, therefore, sum up: Layman as I am with regard to English legal history, I should like to express my conviction that, by reason of the rejection of the labour theory of property, by reason of the supremacy of enacted over common law, and by reason of the universal recognition of the orthodox theory of Montesquieu, the views put forward by Goodhart are more convincing than those stated by Allen. "The modern theory as to the authority of decided cases was reached substantially by the end of the eighteenth century".[130]

It is nevertheless true that the culmination of the doctrine of authority by precedent is to be found in the fact that the House of Lords considers itself to be bound by its own decisions. This fact is, in Vinogradoff's words,[131] "the keystone of the whole system". This doctrine was formulated only in the second half of the nineteenth century.[132] It is worth noting that this culmination was reached just in that period when in France the "école de l'éxégèse" and in Germany the "dogmatic" school became predominant; in the period of the full development of competitive capitalism.

We now ask if this doctrine admits of exceptions. In answering such a question, two viewpoints have to be considered. In the first place, we have to ask whether courts deviate from clearly expressed precedents. This problem is the subject of a controversy between Holdsworth and Goodhart;[133] and although it is impossible for an outsider to come to a final decision, it seems to follow from this controversy that the attempts made by Lord Mansfield[134] to deviate from the already established, consideration theory of contracts and to merge law and equity, have failed. It also seems that the decision in Drummond v. Drummond[135] which Sir William Holdsworth quotes, can be explained by the fact that it was based upon a statute which had been overlooked; so that in this case, because of enacted law, the court passed over a previous decision. Other deviations can be explained by the various degrees of authority which were attributed to the various reports, and we may conclude that no judge can deviate without abandoning the principle of the binding force of precedent. It seems to follow that the system of *stare decisis* is one which admits of no exceptions.

The second question to be asked is how far, according to their own statements, judges admit to creating new law. Allen's opinion is that they do admit to this,[136] but the cases he quotes[137] do not prove his contention. If we use Allen's formula, they merely show that the judges make law only "in a secondary sense". In all the cases he mentions, the judges either apply legal standards of conduct (such as public policy), or they interpret contracts, or they deal with liability for damages without negligence. This means that they apply all the established principles of common law, even if the principles are not sufficiently concretised. Here, however, no divergence from Continental law can be found.[138]

In order to avoid any misunderstanding, we reiterate: the orthodox theory is undoubtedly wrong, as has been shown above. But we are [not] primarily concerned with the *juris prudentia* problem of whether the phonograph theory is right or wrong, but with the sociological problem of why it arose, to what extra-legal ideology it corresponds, and what social function it fulfils.

From this sociological view-point, we may summarise: there exists neither a structural difference nor a sociologically relevant distinction between English and Continental law; or if they do exist, then only in the sense that the German, for instance, is far less rigid than the English law.[139] The greater freedom of the Continental law is the outcome of the fact that it is codified. The greater rigidity of English law is the consequence of its pragmatic and inductive character. If, for instance, we compare the German law of torts with corresponding English legal provisions, we find that the German law distinguishes between three basic types, in Sect. 823, Para. I; Sect. 823, Para. II; and Sect. 826. All other provisions of the law of torts are deduced from these three basic types, so that in case of difficulty, a German judge can always have recourse to one of them, a fact which gives him a good deal of free discretion. In English law, the question of whether the law of torts knows such fundamental types is still undecided; so that if a judge denies their existence, he must necessarily attempt to bring any case which may arise under one of the established cases.

Alternatively, let us compare the German law relating to unfair competition with the corresponding English rules. In Germany, the statute dealing with this problem contains in Sect. 1 a legal standard of conduct generally prohibiting any kind of unfair competition; so that any unfair behaviour on the part of a competitor, if it cannot be brought under a special provision of that statute, can always be made to fall under this legal standard of conduct. In England, on the contrary, we have only a series of several firmly established provisions (which we have already mentioned on page 197 above) which make it difficult to alter the existing law according to the needs of the changing competitive system of society.

14.3.3.

We have already pointed out that one of the fundamental doctrines of the liberal legal system is that of the prohibition of retroaction. Is this prohibition at all reconcilable with the system of case law? Vinogradoff, who alone deals with this problem, answers the question in the negative.[140] He maintains that "case law cannot be brought under the operation of a famous doctrine proclaimed for enacted law, namely, that it ought not to have retroactive application". For him, this liberal doctrine can only be applied to common law if we have recourse to a fiction.

> For if a case is material for an enunciation of law, the application of this very law to this very case is necessarily retroactive. The parties could not know what the law was before the decision was given, and it is the exact knowledge which makes all the difference in a dispute: no one would willingly expose himself to defeat and heavy costs if he knew for certain that the law was against him.

But this objection of Vinogradoff seems in no way convincing. If the creative function of the common law courts has really ceased, if therefore the body of common law rules is really closed, if the activity of judges is a mere application of already established principles, then the prohibition of retroaction is as applicable to common law as to statutory or to codified law. If, however, we take the line that every decision of a judge as an individualisation and concretisation of a higher norm is necessarily creative, then of course, the prohibition of retroaction is as little applicable to common law as it is to statutory or codified law. A difference between the Continental and the English legal system with regard to the doctrine of non-retroaction cannot therefore be maintained.

14.3.4.

With regard to equity, the question at once arises, whether the existence of equity as such is at all compatible with the need of the liberal legal system for rationality, or whether such equity does not render irrational any system of law. But even that assertion has to be denied. It is true that long ago equity meant the interpreting of the whole law in the spirit of equity. This meaning of equity has been developed by Blackstone, who thus opposes equity to law.

> From this method of interpreting laws by the reason of them, arises what we call equity; which is thus defined by Grotius, as the creation of that wherein the law (by reason of its universality) is deficient. For, since in law, all cases cannot be foreseen or expressed, it is necessary that when general decrees of the law come to be applied to particular cases, there should be somewhere a person vested of defining those circumstances which (had they been foreseen), the legislator himself would have expressed.[141]

Equity in civil law, according to this definition, plays the same rôle as the prerogative does in Locke's theory of constitutional law. The rôle of equity thus as thus defined is essentially identical with that of the legal standards of conduct in the German law after 1919.

Originally, it seemed that equity, in the sense in which Blackstone defined it,[142] was applied in and through the common law courts; without, however, the problem being finally decided.[143] The above conception of equity may be traced directly to Bracton, and indirectly to Aristotle, Ulpian, Thomas Aquinas and Grotius. It is a conception of equity that has completely disappeared, but we must admit the possibility that one day, in changed political circumstances, it may be reborn. Blackstone himself rejected that function of equity[144] in the following words: "Law, without equity, though hard and disagreeable, is much more desirable for the public good than equity without law: which would make every judge a legislator, and introduce most unfortunate confusion". This character of equity, intended to pervade the whole legal system, has entirely disappeared. Since 1875, the only possible definition is that "equity is that body of rules which is administered only by those courts which are known as courts of equity".[145] This means that for a presentation of English law even today we can perhaps reiterate what Maitland maintained to be a postulate for the future and what Lord Mansfield attempted to carry out as Lord Chancellor; that "the day will come when lawyers will cease to enquire whether a given rule be a rule of equity or a rule of common law".[146]

The social function of equity is a dual one. Equity had created legal institutions whose formation was imperatively demanded by economic development, as for instance, a trust (exclusive jurisdiction) or the specified performance and the injunction (concurrent jurisdiction). On the other hand, equity partly fulfils the function of the Continental legal standards of conduct. If, for instance, the statute of limitations is supplemented by the introduction of forfeiture, based upon the legal standard of conduct, then "equity acts the vigilant and not the indolent";[147] this principle is identical with the theory as developed by the German Supreme Court, mainly at the instance of the jurisdiction following on the revaluation of the mark and the forfeiture of wage claims of employees.[148] Or if equity says that the conduct of the parties must be weighed, or that he who seeks equity must do equity, these provisions exactly correspond to those of the German system of law which contain the prohibition of the *venire contra factum proprium*, deduced from the German legal standards of conduct.

It is however sociologically significant that in the decisive period of the rise of the bourgeoisie and of the emergence of the competitive economic system, i.e., from the end of the eighteenth century, equity was converted into a system almost as fixed as that of the common law itself. This transformation occurred in two directions. On the one hand, the equity rules were adjusted to those of the common law. On the other hand, equity became a rigid system and its creative function ceased. It became a closed system, as is common law; or rather, common law and equity together were transformed into final system of law.

This development began with Wolsey's fall and reached its height during the period of Lord Chancellor Nottingham. The injuction, a weapon of monarchic absolutism against the *ius strictum* of common law courts, retarded this development towards rationality which is essential to the law of modern society. It is, therefore, not surprising that the main advocate of rational law, Sir Edward Coke, sharply opposed the use of equity as it was formulated by Thomas Egerton (later Baron Ellesmere, Viscount Brackley) and Francis Bacon. It cannot *be* doubted that Ellesmere's decision in the Earl of Oxford's case,[149] in which Chancery reserved the right to alter by injunction judgments of the common law courts which had been reached by "oppression, wrong and a hard conscience", violated the predictability and calculability of the liberal legal system. The political background of this conflict, which has very often been described, and James I's decision, taken upon Bacon's advice and maintaining the fundamental ideas of the Earl of Oxford's case, were in flat contradiction to the required rationality of law.[150] This irrationality has been explained by Selden in the following way:

Equity is a roguish thing. For law, we have measure, and know what to trust to: equity is according to the conscience of him that is chancellor; and as that is larger or narrower, so is equity. 'Tis all done as if they should make the standard for the measure, a chancellor's foot. What an uncertain measure would this be! One chancellor has a long foot, another a short foot, a third an indifferent foot. It is the same thing with a chancellor's conscience.[151]

This great bourgeois detected with the sure instinct of his class, the vulnerable spot of the legal system of his time. Equity naturally shared the fall of the Stuarts; under Cromwell, the Court of Equity was abolished in 1654. With the Restoration, however, it rose again. But the bourgeois revolution, even if it retained the Court of Equity, decisively changed its social functions. This change brings to mind the [four] famous names of Sir Heneage Finch, Lord Nottingham (1673–82), Lord Hardwicke (1736–56), and especially Lord Eldon (1801–06) and (1807–27), who formulated the completion of this transformation in the following manner:

The doctrines of this court ought to be as well settled and made as uniform almost as those of the common law, laying down fixed principles, but taking care that they are to be applied according to the circumstances of each case. . . . I cannot agree that the doctrines of this court are to be changed by every succeeding judge. Nothing would inflict me greater pain in quitting this place, than the recollection that I had done anything to justify the reproach that the equity of this court varies like the chancellor's foot.[152]

The Chancery Division is no longer a court of conscience.[153] It must, however, be admitted that the doctrine of the binding character of judicial precedents was received in equity later than in the common law.[154] Even in 1879,[155] Jessel, M. R., asserted that

It must not be forgotten that the rules of equity are not, like the rules of the Common Law, supposed to have been established from time immemorial. It is perfectly well-known that they have been established from time to time — altered, improved and refined from time to time. . . . We can name the Chancellors who first invented them, and state the date when they were first introduced into equity jurisprudence, and therefore, in cases of this kind, the older precedents in equity are of very little value. The doctrines are progressive, refined and improved; and if we want to know what the rules in equity are, we must look, of course, rather to the more modern than the more ancient cases.

This deviation is perfectly explainable by the fact that equity deals with legal standards of conduct, which form the inexhaustible resource for alteration of the law in any direction. On the whole, however, authority by precedent is established in equity as well as in the common law.

14.3.5.

The reasons for this transformation are clearly explained in the utterances given by the judges concerned. We have already found that according to Goodhart the system of *stare decisis* pervades the whole law, but we must add that it does so because of the trend towards calculability, rationality, and stability, of property and the exchange processes.[156] The binding force of precedent is, therefore, demanded in order to avoid the endangering of "property and titles".[157] Receding "from authorities unsettles property".[158] A deviation from previous decision would harm promoters and landowners, and endanger the rights of property.[159] It would undermine the confidence necessary for contractual relations,[160] especially if the cases dealt with contracts "in daily use and if the decision had been acted upon throughout the country for a long time".[161] Every deviation, therefore, endangers titles and embarrasses "trade and commerce".[162] Even where there exists no obligation to follow precedents, deviation is avoided as far as possible; for instance, by the House of Lords, with regard to judgments of inferior courts. The rigidity of equity is not only due to the Puritans' dislike of it at this particular period, as has been explained by Roscoe Pound, but results from the need of a competitive economic system for formal rationality of law.

14.4. Sociological Evaluation of the Function of the Law and the Judge

14.4.1.

In England as well as in Germany, and naturally too in France, with which at the moment we are not concerned, the expression in the belief of the rule of enacted law is the expression of the power of the bourgeoisie as well as a confession of its weakness. The supremacy of enacted law, which is stressed again and again, implies in the first place, that social changes can only be brought about by legislation and the supremacy of legislation is emphasised because the bourgeoisie had a large share in the legislative process[163] and because laws are interferences by the state in liberty and property. If such interferences can only be made by law, if that law can only be enacted by parliament, if the bourgeoisie is decisively represented in parliament, then the doctrine of the rule of law implies that that stratum in society which is the object of such interference, inflicts those interferences on itself. And naturally, it has a regard for its own interests.

The doctrine of the rule of enacted law implies in the second place, a veiling of the weakness of the bourgeoisie. For it is clear that the conception that social changes can only be brought about by parliamentary law and that administrative bodies and judges can only declare and not make the law, is an illusion created in order that the power of such administrative bodies over parliament need not be admitted. The law is the absolute to which the bourgeoisie looks for its salvation, although it regards itself self-sufficient and as the centre of the world. Since Descartes, the individualist theory asserted that man — that is the man who has property and education — stands at the centre of the world, and that the universe moves around him; but at the same time, it constantly tries to discover an absolute, whether an absolute law, or an absolute good, or an absolute leader to whom the bourgeoisie may take recourse. The confession to the rule of law is the expression of a weakness which accompanies the economic strength of the bourgeoisie. This weakness is far more visible in Germany than in England. The weaker the bourgeoisie is politically, the more the importance of the rule of law is stressed.

We have, therefore, to note two functions standing in an antagonistic relationship: law is, so to speak, an expressive ideology (*Ausdrucksideologie*) but it is at the same time, a veiling (*Verhüllungsideologie*). The latter function has two aspects. It veils the rule of the bourgeoisie, since the invocation of the rule of law makes it unnecessary to name the real rulers in society; at the same time, the invocation of the rule of law veils the unwillingness of the ruling classes for social reform. "The slowness of the Parliamentary machine transforms the sole means for the alteration of the law into a means of securing its unchangeability".[164] This, however, implies that the emphasis laid upon the rule of enacted law depends upon the fact that Parliament on the whole is a representation of bourgeois interests, that is to say, that the proletariat has not reached the stage of being a political power dangerous to the interests of the bourgeoisie. The functioning of Parliament is normal, only so long as the propertied classes dominate it.[165] At the very moment in which the working class emancipates itself, becomes politically conscious, the bourgeoisie abandons the belief in the rule of enacted law, and either has recourse to a new "natural" law which cannot be changed by Parliamentary legislation and which consists in the main, in the existing property order — this, however, only in a transitional period — or it abolishes Parliament and its legislative function altogether.

The belief in the rule of enacted law is, however, also due to the needs of competitive capitalism for formal rationality of the exchange processes. "The need for calculability and reliability of the functioning of the legal order and of administration, induced the bourgeoisie to restrict the power of patrimonial princes and of the feudal nobility, by the institution of an organisation in which the bourgeoisie played a decisive rôle, and which controlled administration and finance, and collaborated in changes in the legal system."[166] In this way, the fictitious conflict in the attitude of the liberals towards parliamentary legislation, which Roscoe Pound[167] has convincingly shown to exist in the attitude of American Puritans, is solved: the aversion to legislation on the one hand, and the firm belief in enactment on the other. But not only the American Puritan pursued this dual course. It was the attitude of liberalism as such which rejected the principle of legal interference in liberty and property, but which at the same time expressed its conviction of the superiority of Parliamentary legislation, either so that it might prevent such interference, or if this were not possible, adjust it to its own interests.

To the needs of competitive capitalism there corresponds a general law as the highest form of formal rationality or the binding force of precedents and the absolute subjection of the judge under the law, consequently the separation of powers. Competitive capitalism is characterised, as we have already seen, by the existence of a vast number of competitors of approximately equal strength, competing on the free market. For details we refer to Max Weber's presentation of the various elements of the capitalist system:[168] liberty of the commodity market, liberty of the labour market, freedom in the selection of entrepreneurs, freedom of contract, complete calculability of the administration of the law. The outstanding characteristic of capitalism is "the pursuit of profit and of *renewed* profit by means of continuous rational capitalistic enterprise. . . . We will define capitalist economic activity as that which rests on the expectation of profit by the utilisation of commodities for exchange, that is on (formally) peaceful chances of profit".[169] The state has, therefore, to measure the fulfilment of contracts. The expectation that contracts will be performed must always be calculable. The fulfilment of this expectation in a competitive society presupposes, however, general laws; it also presupposes that the legal norms are exactly determined, that is to say, that they are as formal and as rational as possible, so that the judge has as little discretion as possible. In such a society, the judge must not have recourse to legal standards of conduct such as good faith, good morals, reasonableness, or public policy. The state itself, if it interferes at all, must make its interference calculable, that is to say, it must not interfere retroactively, for otherwise it would invalidate created expectations; further, it must not intervene without law, because such intervention is unpredictable. Finally, it must not intervene by individual commands, because any individual intervention violates the principle of equality prevailing between equal competitors.

Consequently the judge must be independent, that is to say, litigation must be decided independently of any commands of a government. The independence of judges is, of course, an essential feature of competitive capitalism. It implies, however, a distinction between various powers in the state. The doctrine of the separation of powers is therefore the organisational element of competitive capitalism, and apart from its political significance, creates competences, clear delimitations between the various activities of the state, and therefore guarantees the rationality of the law and of its administration.[170]

But the general law and the principle of distinction between the powers of the state, has, besides its task of veiling power and of rendering exchange processes calculable, a decisive ethical function which is expressed in Rousseau's theory. The generality of law and the independence of judges are intended to realise personal and political equality. The general law as the basic notion of the legal system of liberalism establishes the personal equality of all men, a postulate which seems to us to be so obvious that it is almost inconceivable that as a maxim it should be questioned to-day. We have already seen that all rights of men stand under the "reservation of the law". Interferences in liberty must be made on the basis of the law. Therefore, the character of the law to which any intervention must be attributed is of decisive significance. Only if such intervention is based upon general law, is liberty guaranteed, because the principle of equality is preserved. In this connection, Voltaire's statement is true, that freedom means to be dependent upon nothing else but the law; but only if the law is a general one; thus it was conceived by Voltaire. If the legislator can issue individual commands, if he can arrest this or that man, if he can confiscate this or that property, we are unable to speak of the real independence of judges. If the judge has to apply individual commands of the state, he becomes a mere bailiff, a mere policeman. True independence, therefore, presupposes the rule of the state through general laws which provide for an indefinite number of future cases. The generality of the law, the independence of judges, and the doctrine of the separation of powers, have, therefore, functions transcending the needs of competitive capitalism, since they secure personal liberty and personal equality. The generality of the law and the independence of judges veil the power of one stratum of society; they render exchange processes calculable and create also personal freedom and security for the poor. All three functions are significant and not only, as is maintained by the critics of liberalism, that of rendering economic processes calculable. We repeat, all three functions are realised in the period of competitive capitalism, but it is of importance to discriminate between them. If one does not draw these distinctions, and sees in the generality of the law, nothing but a requirement of capitalist economy, then of course, one must infer with Carl Schmitt that the general law, the independence of judges, and the separation of powers, must be abolished when capitalism dies.

14.3.2.

Let us now consider from these view-points the social significance of the German doctrine.[171] The stress which is laid upon the generality of the law derives from the fact that in the middle of the nineteenth century the monarchs imposed constitutions which restricted their own legislative power, but only to the extent to which they transferred that power to Parliament. In such a situation, it became necessary to distinguish the subjects which were to be regulated by law, that is to say,those regulated by the joint decision of the monarch and of Parliament, from those controlled by the monarch alone.

A real understanding of the German doctrine is only possible by keeping in mind the defeat of the German bourgeoisie. The introduction by Paul Laband, of law in a material sense, reduced the authority of Parliament. Parliament could only enact laws in a material sense, but laws in a material sense are only such as contain a rule creating a right; that is to say, such as interfere directly with liberty and property. Laws in a formal sense are, therefore, those enactments which either indirectly concern the individual or which regulate the relationship between the individual and the state; they therefore, do not come within the sphere of Parliament. The budget, the organisation of administrative bodies and tribunals, the fixing of salaries of civil servants, the operation of public undertakings — all these are laws in a formal sense. This is the first political significance of the German doctrine. But we must add a second. As the genetic determination of the content of the law is irrelevant, it is possible to maintain the validity of all those laws which were issued before the creation of the Constitution. In Prussia this doctrine led to maintenance of the validity of the pre-Constitutional decrees of the monarch and of the *Allgemeine Landrecht*, especially of the famous II.17. Sect. 10.[172] On the basis of this section the police obtained extraordinary discretionary powers to interfere in liberty and property whenever they thought fit without parliamentary consent. According to this section, the police had to provide the necessary means for maintaining public quiet, security and order, and for the warding off of all dangers which threatened the public or individuals.

In the third place, the German school, with the exception of Gierke and Hänel, adopted a very strange theory as to the character of the legislative process, namely, its separation into logical parts which were called the determination of the content of a statute, and the issuing of the sanction to the statute. The Prussian constitutional theory therefore arrived at the conclusion that the content of a statute was established by Parliament (agreement of the two chambers), whereas the sanction was issued by the king. "Only the assent of the king raises the draft of a statute to the rank of law. The king is . . . the legislator."[173] This strange distribution between the powers of king and Parliament has been deduced from Art. 62 of the Prussian Constitution, which, however, does not say anything about it. For the *Reich*, the same conclusion was drawn from Art. 5 of Bismarck's Constitution. Here the determination of the content of a statute was left to an agreement between the *Reichstag* and the *Bundesrat* (Federal Chamber), whereas the sanction was exclusively the work of the Bundesrat. Art. 5, however, contained nothing but that "the legislation of the *Reich* is exercised by the *Bundesrat* and the *Reichstag*". In spite of this clear formulation, Leband asserted: "The sanction is therefore legislation in the constitutional sense of the word. . . . The question as to the object of the legislative power is identical with the question as to the bearer of the power of the state".[174]

The political defeat of the German bourgeoisie cannot be more clearly demonstrated than in the acceptance of that dualistic theory which on the one hand reduced the extent of the parliamentary legislative power and on the other hand, even within the restricted legislative power, over-stressed the rôle of the king or of the federal monarchs assembled in the *Bundesrat*. This emphasis laid upon enacted law is, as we have pointed out, a veiling of the weakness of the bourgeoisie.

The German bourgeoisie, which never attained political influence and therefore, a controlling interest in the genetic determination of the law, turned more to the cultivation of institutional and organisational security against the intervention of the state, by building up a huge system of legal securities, particularly by concentrating its attention to the position of the judges.

The development towards the independence of judges is a very complicated process. German liberalism fights against the interference of the monarch and against the claim of the monarch to be himself a judge, and for the sole authority of the judge to decide litigations. The victory of Prussian liberalism was made visible for the first time in Sect. 6 of the "Introduction" to the Prussian *Allgemeine Landrecht* which says that the decree of the monarch is no part of the code, but a mere arbitrary decision, and that he is therefore unfitted to settle litigation.[175] Under Suarez' influence, the view was held during the deliberations of the *Allgemeine Landrecht* that in despotic states the despot could be a judge, but not in a monarchy.[176] But in spite of these liberal demands, the interference of the monarch did not cease.[177] It was only in 1804 that Frederick William III renounced his claim to declare a judgment invalid.[178] Finally, the king, by an order dated 6th September, 1815, accepted the doctrine that the judges are subject only to the law.[179] But even in 1842, Savigny complained of continual interferences of the administration in mattters of civil justice.[180] The state of penal justice was even worse. Frederick William III reserved the right even in 1802 to increase a sentence of a penal court,[181] and the Prussian penal code of 1805 retained this right of the king. The king himself could not punish, but he could ratify judgments and increase their severity. This right was superseded on the 29th June, 1840, by the right of mercy.[182]

Parallel with this advance of the idea of the judge's independence, is that of the generality of the law. The postulate of the generality of the law arose in the transitional period, because it was the sole basis of the judge's independence in the absence of institutional means for its protection: that is to say, it was still possible to discharge him or to transfer him to another court. The lack of organised security led also to the institution of special courts which permanently deprived the ordinary courts of their authority and which had to decide according to the will of the monarch.[183]

A decisive change was brought about by the Revolution of 1848, which first secured the absolute independence of judges. There is little doubt that up to this time, in spite of the controversy as to whether the king was entitled to discharge judges at his discretion,[184] he frequently did so. The law of 29th March, 1844, though it represents considerable progress, still, however, left to the government the right to pension judges at any time at its discretion. The Frankfurt Constitution, which as a matter of fact, never came into operation, postulated in Sect. 175.I. the independence of judges; in Sect. 177, the prohibition to discharge them or to transfer them to another court, or to pension them against their will; and in Sect. 175.II. it prohibited exceptional courts. At the same time, the Constitution excluded administrative tribunals and transferred solely to the ordinary courts the power to decide any kind of litigation (Sect. 182.I.). In spite of the failure of the Revolution, its fundamental ideas with regard to the position of the judge became a political reality. They were accepted and further enlarged in the Weimar Constitution of 1919. The Prussian law of 7th May, 1851 realised the fundamental ideas of Sects. 175 and 177 of the Frankfurt Constitution. Judges could then be discharged or pensioned only after disciplinary proceedings.

From 1848 until 1919 the independence of the judge was never problematical, in spite of many attempts by various governments to interfere with their independence. After the formation of the *Reich*, the law of 27th January, 1877, once more recognised this fundamental principle. But this law introduced another guarantee, that of the autonomy of judges — the right to distribute amongst themselves the various offices of a court. Up to that time, the Prussian Minister of Justice distributed such offices himself, that is to say, he determined which judges should sit in the penal and other courts. In the already mentioned "conflict period", the Prussian Minister of Justice misused his authority and so composed the penal courts as to obtain sentences against political enemies.[185] The sections 63ff. leave the selection of the judges for the various courts entirely to the *presidium* of the court, with the exception of the examining magistrates and the presidents of the commercial courts.

In this period, i.e., from 1848 to 1918, formal rationality of the law was developed and realised to an extraordinary degree. Laws were interpreted literally. Questions of equity and convenience were alien to the interpretation of laws. The theory of the school of free discretion and the sociological interpretation was expressly rejected. The right of judicial review was not recognised, although the liberal lawyers demanded it as a corrective against the lack of influence of Parliament. During this period, legal standards of conduct play no part at all. The Supreme Court began its work in 1879. In the first thirty published volumes of its decisions in civil matters, the court only exceptionally referred to the *exceptio doli generalis*.[186]

Even after the Civil Code came into operation on 1st January, 1900, legal standards of conduct did not play a great rôle. Sect. 10.II.17 of the Prussian *Allgemeine Landrecht* was also hardly taken into practical account during the nineteenth century. The leading commentary on the *Allgemeine Landrecht* by Koch (3rd ed., 1863) does not mention a single decision on the basis of that provision.

This period might, therefore, be called the period of normativism or positivism.

The attitude of the judges towards the law during the period of William II is sociologically understandable. The state knew at that time perfectly how to maintain its hold over the independent judges.[187] The social station of a judge was fixed. He began his career as an officer in the reserve. During his military training, he learned the significance of the notions of obedience and discipline. The positions of presidents of courts were almost exclusively occupied by former public prosecutors who were, and are, dependent civil servants of the state, and had, therefore, an exceptionally close relation to the government. They well knew how to fulfil the wishes of the minister, even if they were not verbally expressed, and they knew how to use their power over members of the court. Further, the guarantees of the independence of judges were only valid for those judges who were definitely engaged, and [not] for the large number of auxiliary judges who could be discharged or transferred to other courts according to the discretion of the minister, and who, for their careers, were entirely dependent upon the good will of the superior judges.

Finally, the Prussian judge, especially as compared with his English contemporary, was a badly-paid civil servant, who had to sit for years before he [was] finally engaged, so that only the children of the middle bourgeoisie could afford to enter the profession. The judge of this period possessed all the characteristics of the petty-bourgeois, his resentment against the worker, especially the organised and well-to-do worker, love of throne and altar, desire for the maintenance of property, but also his indifference to finance capital.

The rationality of the law was realised mainly on the commodity market and in the relations between the ruling classes. In the relationship between worker and capitalist, up to 1918 there were still exceptional laws, as is proved by the law relating to the right of association of workers.[188] In France, we [may] mention the law of 14th June, 1791 (*Loi de Chapelier*) and the *Code pénal* (Arts. 414, 416); in England, the corresponding Societies Acts (39 Geo. III, c.79) and the Combination Acts (39 Geo. III c. 81, and 39 and 40 Geo. III c. 106); in Prussia the *Allgemeine Landrecht* (Sect. 8.II.358) and the Prussian Factory Act of 1848 (Sects. 182, and 183) prohibited strikes and the inducement to strike. The law of 24th April, 1854, extended the prohibition to other categories of workers, and the Prussian law of 21st May, 1850, extended it to miners. This period of prohibition of trade unions was justified ideologically by the liberal theory that trade unions were against the liberal rules of the game, and economically by the prevalence of the wage-fund theory.

This period of prohibition was followed by one of toleration o trade unions. In England, the period began with the laws of 1824 (5 Geo. IV, c. 95)and of 1825 (6 Geo. IV, c. 129); in France with the law of 25th May, 1864; in Germany with the factory act of 29th May, 1869. At this time the state no longer dared openly to prohibit trade unions, but rendered any kind of industrial action so difficult that strikers and the strike leaders were constantly caught in the meshes of exceptional provisions (cf. Sect. 152.II. and Sect. 153 of the Factory Act). It is specially worth mentioning that, according to the Factory Act, a member of a trade union could leave the union at any time he desired, and that no legal relationship could be established between member and union. The trade unions were already so strong as to make their prohibition impossible, but they were not yet strong enough to secure recognition by the State.

In Germany, the worker, and especially the socialist worker, was no part of the nation. William II expressed this very candidly when he remarked that "the Socialist worker did not belong to the Fatherland". The nation was represented by Crown, army, bureaucracy, landed aristocracy and bourgeoisie. The judges represented these strata of society. Their interests and those of these sections of the nation were identical; and while the laws corresponded to their interests, why should they interpret them otherwise than literally? The *Rechtsstaat* was decisively a state of the ruling classes. But the generality of the law and the independence of judges contained elements which transcended the function of veiling the power of the ruling classes and of rendering the economic processes calculable. The State was reactionary, but it was not a despotic state. It kept within the bounds of its own laws. The separation of powers was not only a distinction between various functions of the state, but was also a distribution of the power over the State between the various strata of the ruling classes. But this class rule was calculable and predictable, and therefore not despotic. Those elements of the *Rechtsstaat* which we might possibly call eternal, guaranteed security and a certain amount of liberty to the working class.

In England, where the centre of gravity lay in the recognition of political rights, the victory of the rule of law was far swifter and far more thorough than in Germany. The obvious violation of the principles which we consider as constituting the rule of law, is to be found in the establishment of the Court of Star Chamber, which dated from the statute of 1487 (3 Hen. VII c. 1). This court violated the principle of the separation of powers, because "the same body which issues ordinances, which controls the execution of the law and the administration of the State (the King's Council) acts also as a court of justice with a comprehensive penal jurisdiction".[189] This body, established by the statutes of 1487, did nothing to restrict the unlimited authority of jurisdiction of the King's Council. In addition to this committee, there existed still other exceptional courts of a similar character, but by 1641 the Star Chamber was abolished and in 1679 the Habeas Corpus Act was passed (31 Car. II 6. 2). The Acts of Settlement (12 and 13 Will. III C. 2) commissioned judges *quamdiu se bene gesserint*, their salaries were fixed and they were removable only upon the address of both houses of Parliament. This meant that a judge could only be dismissed either in consequence of a conviction for some offence, or on the address of both houses. From a political point of view, the rule of law [was] therefore secured.

In the economic sphere, the rationality of English law reached a very high degree, but only as to relations of the plutocracy. We have already mentioned that among the conditions which Sir William Holdsworth established as indispensable for the functioning of the English legal system, the most important is that the number of litigations should be relatively small. This aim, however, is only attainable if the costs are high and if poor persons have little factual opportunity for litigation; that is to say if the protection of the law is denied to a large section of society. Owing to the defectiveness of English judicial statistics, it is extremely difficult to obtain a correct view of the situation. We therefore only compare some figures for England and Wales with the Prussian figures for 1927. In that year, in England and Wales, the Judicial Committee of the Privy Council decided 165 cases; the House of Lords 58; the Court of Appeal 470; and the High Court of Justice 401 appellate proceedings. In Germany, the *Reichsgericht* decided 2,767 appellate proceedings of Prussian courts in civil matters and 1,197 cases in penal matters. We must add that the appeal decisions of the federal high courts (*Oberlandesgerichte*) in penal matters numbered 6,410, the first appeals to the *Oberlandesgerichte* and the *Landgerichte* in civil matters with 117,279 cases, and the appeal decision in criminal matters of the Landgerichte, numbering 46,331. These figures reveal that the legal protection of large masses of the population is far more effective in Germany than in England; that the boon of the rationality of the law is enjoyed by far larger strata of society in Germany than in England.

The idea of extending the benefits of rational law to the lower-middle classes and to the workers was realised only very slowly. In the seventeenth century, a classification of the various activities of the state, a distinction between justice and administration, was hardly possible.[190] The centralised system of the sixteenth century "pressed hardly upon the poor".[191] The attempts to remedy these deficiencies, such as the Court of Requests, disappeared after the Great Rebellion. At the beginning of the nineteenth century, the English legal system was more centralised than any other in the world. "With the exception of petty criminal business entrusted to the Justices of the Peace, practically all the judicial work of the country was done by the judges of the common law courts, the Chancellor, or the Master of the Rolls, or the Court of Admiralty." Blackstone[192] demanded local courts, and the county courts were only by the end of 1879 (9 & 10 Vict. C. 95) introduced. It cannot be denied that the problem of extending the rationality of the law to the poorer classes has yet to be solved. Bentham's[193] assertion that the common law is a conspiracy because it is irrational, is justified only to a certain extent. The common law is highly rational, but only for the rich. It is still irrational to a large extent, for the poor and for the lower bourgeoisie.

CHAPTER 15

The Rule of Law under the Weimar Constitution (Monopoly Capitalism)

15.1. The Change of the Economic and Social Structure and of the Material Elements of the Legal System

From the competition of pre-war Germany there emerged the concentration of capital; and from the concentration of capital, monopoly capitalism.[1] The post-war period has decisively affected the structure of German economy. The reasons for the divergent course of German and English pre-war development have been shown by Veblen. The beginnings of tendencies were fully developed by the war and during the period after the inflation. The scarcity of raw materials led to the creation of new industries. The division of labour reached a maximum, which was paralleled by a maximum rationalisation of the whole economic machinery. The rationalisation of the individual undertakings is supplemented by the rationalisation of the whole economic system, by standardisation and uniformity.

The needs of the single undertakings for lowering their costs and securing markets press in that direction. These needs, however, cannot legally be fulfilled on the basis of free competition, they can only be realised by cooperation, that is to say in a higher and more conscious form of the cooperation of the producers.

The potential and actual productivity of the post-war period grew rapidly. Technical progress surpassed anything that had been experienced before. But capital accumulation meets boundaries, especially in Germany, in the narrowing of the field of capital expansion. This challenge is met by a shifting of the industrialisation to new industries, but the weight of the stagnant industries, especially of agriculture, is permanently growing. The possibility of evasion gets more and more difficult in the period of crisis, as the composition of capital is changed, and the ratio of fixed capital has grown. Discharging of workers does give some possibility of meeting the needs of the crisis by lowering costs.

The increase of productivity on the one side and the ever greater difficulty of securing markets on the other leads to a waste of capital on a great scale. Production wasted by the war, the closing down of undertakings, the imposing of quotas, the price struggles of monopolies, all increased the *faux-frais* of capitalist production. The monopoly is the tool of organised waste of capital mainly in those industries which are out of date. The monopoly has, therefore, a dual function — a progressive one by increased rationalisation, and a reactionary one of destruction of capital. The monopolist is in no way hostile to technical progress, but he renders the full exploitation of this technical progress more difficult.

The theory that monopolies are always progressive corresponds to the political theory of German Social Democracy and to the views of trade unionists, who see in monopolies the first step towards socialism. To the theory that monopolies hinder the development of capitalist productivity corresponds the Communist political theory of a decay of capitalism.

Both theories are right and wrong at the same time. For whether monopolies, as higher forms of industrial organisation, can be made beneficial to the whole of society or not, depends entirely upon political forces.

The forms in which monopoly capitalism is organised are set out in Professor Levy's book. The significance of monopoly rationalisation can be found in Robert A. Brady's book.

In Germany, capitalism is organised in three different types of organisation: for the domination of the labour market, in the employers' organisation, centralised in one big union; for the domination of the commodity market, in the already mentioned types of the concern and cartel; and for the domination of the state, in a kind of "estate" organisation, such as the *Reichsverband der Deutschen Industrie.* The trade unions on the other hand combine all the three tasks.

The intervention of the state has a dual character. It is on the hand progressive. It aids the development of the productive forces, either directly by its own economic activities (post, railways, water power), or indirectly by a certain amount of social insurance, especially by the taking over of the risk of sickness, health and unemployment insurance.

On the other side the intervention of the state hinders the development of the productive forces, by subsidies which prevent the natural capitalistic selection, by tariffs, by the prevention of imports, by prohibiting the establishment of new undertakings, and by compulsory creation of cartels. The importance of the state is increased not only functionally but also by the increased number of its officials. Owing to the increased amount of state intervention the number of those persons who form the state, as defined in Part I above, increases rapidly.

This changed economic structure changes the functions of the entrepreneur. The free entrepreneur disappears. The entrepreneur of to-day is more or less a mere functionary of the undertaking. The property owners (see Part I above) all disappear. Hilferding had already said in 1909 that the joint-stock company is distinguished from the entrepreneur not only by the different organisational form, but by the fact that it divests the capitalist of the function of the entrepreneur. This transformation is clearly described, apart from Hilferding's book, in those of Renner, and Berle and Means.

The change of the economic structure also produces a decisive transformation of the social stratification of society. Technical progress creates considerable structural unemployment. For the capitalist stratum the ratio of those who live simply from rentier incomes increases. Still more important is the change in the composition of the working class. The number of office workers, clerks, and officials increases. The introduction of scientific methods, mass production and standardisation, reduces the number of skilled workers, while at the same time it increases the number of technical superintendents on the one hand and of unskilled and semi-skilled workers, especially women, on the other. As markets contract and competition intensifies, the distributive apparatus grows. Consequently the number of those engaged in the distributive process is increased. Instances may be found in Brady's book. This changed composition of the working class changes also the functions of the trade unions. Their aim was the restriction of the competition of the labour market by collective organisation and collective agreements. Insurances for health, sickness and unemployment acted in this connection as supplementary institutions to a free labour market by relieving the pressure exercised upon the labour market by the groups of workers concerned. But by this very development, which was essentially progressive, the workers forged themselves golden fetters, as Karl Marx has observed.[2] The power of the trade unions decreases, in proportion *as ratio* that of the monopolist organisations increases. Unskilled workers, supervisors, administrative officials, shop assistants and women are extremely difficult to organise. The arbitration systems, the regulation of wages by the state, and the increased importance of social insurance, reduced the significance of the trade unions in the life of the workers. But the decisive fact is that the power of the trade unions is greater the smaller the size of the undertaking.[3]

15.2. The Change of the Political Structure[4]

The constitutions of the post-war period, whether written or not, are all based upon the political principles of pluralism, that is to say, the distribution of the power of the state among socially free organisations. This pluralistic conception was specifically transformed into the idea of parity between the two classes of society.[5] Whereas liberalism ignored the existence of a class conflict, and felt the recognition of legal freedom and legal equality to be sufficient, this period of collectivist democracy recognised the existence of a class conflict, but attempted to transform the conflict into cooperation of the classes on the basis of parity. The period after the war is characterised by the fact that the labour movement became politically self-conscious, that it separated itself from the liberal movement of the bourgeoisie, that it constituted itself as an autonomous political organisation, and attempted to transform the whole of society according to its own philosophy of life. This tendency, the self-consciousness of the labour movement, has been speeded up by the war, which led to the transformation of the liberal state into a mass democracy.

The idea of parity between various strata of society is a theory visible in the formation of the Weimar Constitution. The history of the Weimar Constitution shows that the conception of a social contract is not a mere ideal or a mere methodological device for the justification of the state, but even sometimes a historical reality. It is strange that nobody ever observed that the Weimar Constitution was in fact the work of various social contracts concluded between various groups of society.

The first decisive contract is that between the late *Reichspräsiden* Ebert and General Gröner on the 10th November, 1918. Gröner, a witness in the libel action in Munich, told the story of how thi contract was concluded.[6]

> We have allied ourselves in order to fight Bolshevism. The restoration o the monarchy was unthinkable. Our aim on the 10th of November wa the introduction of an ordered Government which is supported by a army, and the National Assembly, as soon as possible. I have advised th Field-Marshal [von Hindenburg] not to fight the Revolution. . . . I hav proposed to him that the Supreme Army Command might make a alliance with the Social Democratic Party only in order to restor together with the Supreme Army Command an ordered Governmen The parties of the Right had completely vanished.

This alliance between Ebert on the one hand and Gröner on th other was confirmed by a letter, which Hindenburg wrote to Eber on the 8th December, 1918.

The second decisive contract on which the Constitution was base was that between the central organisations of the employers and o the trade unions of the 15th November, 1918, the so-called Stinnes Legien agreement. By this the employers' organisations recognise exclusively the independent trade unions, and abandoned the "yel low" unions, which were till then financed by the employers. The promised to the trade unions the right of cooperation in industria affairs, and they consented to the regulation of employment con ditions by collective agreements. This agreement as well as the firs one, implies not only the rejection of Bolshevism, but also that of a socialist state.

The third decisive contract upon which the new State was buil was that of 4th March, 1919, between the government and the Socia Democratic Party of Berlin, as the representative of the revolution ary Soviet movement. This covenant contained on the side of th government the promise to introduce works councils, but of a typ completely distinct from the Russian Soviets. A result of this agree ment was Art. 165 of the Weimar Constitution which recognise works councils and promised them a share in the management of th economic system.

The fourth covenant was that between the *Reich* and the Federa States on the 26th January, 1919, which implied the abandonmen of the old aim of achieving a unified Germany, and the recognition of the continued existence of federal states.

The fifth and final contract, which practically included all the previous ones, was that between the three coalition parties, the Social Democratic Party, the Centre Party, and the Democratic Party; the so-called Weimar Parties. The main content of this contract was the maintenance of the old bureaucracy and judiciary, the rejection of the Soviet system, the maintenance of the influence of the Church, the introduction of parliamentary democracy, and consequently the rejection of socialism.

This whole system of parity ought to be called a system of collectivist democracy,[7] which means that the state for the fulfilment of its tasks uses private organisations, and gives them a share in political power. The state acts between the two negotiating and collaborating parties as a neutral third, which should interfere only if the social opponents do not reach agreement. Similar developments can be traced in Austria,[8] France,[9] and England.[10] This constitutional system has been called a social *Rechtsstaat.*[11]

It seems obvious that such a system not only did not reduce the influence of the state, but increased it. Free agreements of the partners concerned can only be reached if the economic conflicts do not become decisive political conflicts. Understanding between employers and workers above all is only possible if the employer is able to make concessions. Such free agreements practically ceased in 1931, when the economic crisis made further concessions impossible. From then on the free agreements of the social partners disappeared, and compulsory enforcements by the state, the "neutral third", which should only intervene in exceptional cases, became the rule.

The political structure is characterised by mass democracy, or in Mannheim's terms, by a fundamental democratisation of the whole of society. The period is then one "of the reintegration of large groups in which the individuals, who until now had been increasingly separated from one another, are compelled to renounce their private interests and subordinate themselves to the interests of larger social units".[12] It is characterised by the fact that the bulk of the population now got political rights, and was no longer passively detached from the ruling élite.[13] But in such a society until the large mass of the working class has become politically conscious, cooperation or coordination on the part of the society is possible only if there is a balance of forces between the classes; that is to say, if neither class is strong enough to subdue the other, or to rule without its help. This balance of the forces was expressed in the constitutional institutions.

The function of the suffrage changed. The universal suffrage with the Parliamentary system is an expression of the fact that the idyllic period of the bourgeoisie has gone. The Parliaments are no longer places where the representatives of the privileged parts of the nation deliberate. They have rather become the stage where compromises are reached between the various partners in the class struggle.[14]

The balance of forces between the classes is legally introduced in the second part of the Weimar Constitution, which deals with the fundamental rights. The interpretation of this, the second part, was the subject of heated controversies. Whereas the first part of the Constitution provides for the organisation of the state, president, parliament, *Reichsrat*, and so on, the second part contains the decision as to the future activities of the state. The predominant view was that the Constitution contained nothing but the expression of the old liberal principles of freedom of contract, guarantee of property, freedom of trade, and so on. The view usually taken was that the fundamental decision reached in this second part was for constitutional democracy and the bourgeois *Rechtsstaat*.[15]

But it cannot be denied that the historical rise of the constitution, the various contracts which formed its basis, had found expression in the second part of the constitution not only by the recognition of the old liberal principles, but by the introduction of new social principles, which are mainly to be found in Art. 165 (promise of industrial democracy), Art. 159 (recognition of the freedom of the trade unions) and Art. 156 (promise of the socialisation of certain industries).

The system of pluralism, and the changed structure of the economic system, naturally strengthened the power of the government as against that of Parliament. Although Parliament was formally sovereign, its power subsequently decreased in proportion as that of the government, or better, that of the ministerial bureaucracy, increased. This process has been admirably set out in Harold J. Laski's *Democracy in Crisis*. The results are equally applicable to the German post-war development, only with the difference that the decrease of Parliamentary power is even more discernible in Germany than in England. The German development is characterised by the fact that Parliament, by empowering acts, and the President of the Reich, by his emergency legislation, strengthened a bureaucracy whose position was constitutionally secure in that the acquired rights of functionaries were made the subject of a constitutional guarantee. We have to add that the vote of censure, which is the final weapon of a Parliament against a government, could not be successfully applied in post-war Germany. Every government was a coalition government. The formation of a government was therefore so difficult, so complicated, and so intricate a task that a coalition partner, having finally set up a government, dared not endanger it by a vote of censure.

We have already seen that every fundamental right is equipped with the so-called reserve of the legislature, so that the bureaucracy can intervene in those fundamental rights on the basis of a law. The growing economic and political difficulties, especially after 1931, when the National Socialist Party entered Parliament with 107 members, brought about ever-increasing intervention in these constitutional rights. Freedom of meeting, freedom of the press, freedom of assembly, were more and more brought under the control of the bureaucracy. A bureaucracy is always stronger than the judiciary, as its commands (such as the banning of a paper) have to be executed at once.

15.3. The Change of the Legal System

To this changed economic and political structure there corresponded a rapid and decisive transformation of the legal structure.[16]

We have already shown that the conception of the generality of the law was abandoned by German legal theory under the influence of Laband's criticism. But suddenly this notion experienced a strange revival, mainly through the influence exercised by Carl Schmitt upon legal and constitutional thought.[17] Schmitt alleged that the word "law" used by the Weimar Constitution means only general laws, so that Parliament is only able to issue general laws. Individual commands therefore are in his view forbidden. The legislative power of Parliament is checked by the impossibility of issuing individual regulations. For proof of this assertion, on the one hand he has recourse to the ideological history of the notion of the law which we have followed up in the second part of our book, and on the other he finds his assertion proved by Art. 109 of the Weimar

Constitution, which says "All Germans are equal before the law". That the history of ideas does not support his assertion, we have already seen. We have attempted to prove that the postulate that the state may only rule through general laws is bound up with that of a certain social superstructure; and that it is indefensible to divorce the postulate of the generality of the law from the postulated social order. The political significance of that renaissance of the generality of the law is obvious. Carl Schmitt developed his theory for the first time in a publication intended to show that the suggested confiscation of the property of the former Kaiser and the other princes was unconstitutional because it violated the principle of equality before the law and the postulate of its generality. The generality of the law is asserted to be essentially for the economic as well as for the political sphere.

This assertion of Carl Schmitt's presupposes further that the postulate of equality is addressed not only to the executive but also to the legislature. That this fundamental principle is intended to govern the activities of executive organs and of the judiciary is not to be doubted. It means simply that civil service and judges must apply the law of the state equally without regard to any differences in the status of individuals, without hatred, without bias, so that the executive organs are subject only to a notion of duty.[18] Art. 109 of the Weimar Constitution obviously repeats this old notion of equality as expressed in every modern constitution as it is to be found, for instance, in Art. 4 of the old Prussian Constitution. Hänel, however, the liberal constitutional lawyer, brought in the Bismarckian period for the extension of the maxim of equality to the legislature; and asserted that the exceptional legislation against the Polish minority in Prussia, which made it possible to deprive Poles of their property, was in opposition to that extended principle of equality. Hänel's theory, however, was not accepted. It was universally rejected in pre-[1914] German constitutional theory.

Now, however, this old liberal idea was taken up by certain lawyers in order to protect private property. Now, after the Weimar Constitution had established Parliamentary sovereignty, the constitutional lawyers began to transform the principle of equality into a maxim intended to bind the legislative supremacy of Parliament. The beginning was made by Heinrich Triepel,[19] who asserted the new function of the maxim of equality, which did not allow the deprivation of shareholders of joint-stock companies of a part of the value of their shares on the occasion of the revaluation of the mark. An enormous literature was produced with the intention of proving that the Weimar Parliament could never violate the principle of equality, and the Association of German Constitutional Lawyers even devoted a meeting to the investigations of this question (Vol. 3 of their reports). We may be spared the particulars of these controversies.[20]

But even if the maxim of equality should bind the legislature, it does not necessarily follow that the principle of equality can only be realised through general laws. The assertion that equality can only be reached through such a structure of law is the fallacious conclusion of Rousseau, which we have already considered; that the general will, because it is general, can only express itself through general laws. As against such an assertion, it must be maintained that material equality can as well be established by means of individual interferences. Yet whether or not this is possible depends entirely upon the social structure to which the law is related. In a monopolistic economic organisation the legislature is very often confronted with only one individual case or with a limited number of monopolist undertakings. The legislature often can and must use individual regulations in order to do justice to these specific circumstances. Or should it be compelled to veil an individual regulation by having recourse to a general norm which is avowedly only intended to serve one particular case? If there is only one Kaiser, or if there are princes distinguished from the other strata of the population, must the state if it wants to provide for these particular persons use general norms without mentioning these particular persons?

As a matter of fact the President of the *Reich* enacted an emergency decree based on Art. 48 of the Constitution (Decree of 13th July, 1931), whose Art. VIII prohibits the application for bankruptcy against the Darmstädter Bank on the occasion of the onset of the banking crisis. Should he have been compelled to issue a law in abstract terms prohibiting such applications for all banks, if economically only the fate of this large bank was really decisive?

In the economic sphere, therefore, the postulate of the generality of the law becomes absurd if the legislature is no longer concerned with equal competitions, but with monopolies violating that principle of equality on the market which we have found to be essential to the theory of classical economy. So long as there are equal competitors, equal regulations can naturally be brought about only by general abstract laws.

Consequently the passionate attack of Hermann Heller against Carl Schmitt and against the postulated generality of the law in the Constitution of Weimar, is justified. Heller, however, overlooks the fact that the generality of the law has not only the function of rationalising and mechanising economic processes, but also an ethical function which becomes apparent in the political sphere.

The revival of the concept of the generality of the law and its indiscriminate application to the spheres of economic and political activities served therefore as a tool against the sovereignty of Parliament, which under the Weimar Constitution represented not only the interests of landlords and the bourgeoise but to a large extent those of the working class. The general law was intended to be applied as a means of maintaining the existing property order, and it was used as a factor designed to discredit the sovereignty of Parliament. By this the generality of the law took the place of a natural law. It was in fact nothing but a hidden natural law.

Whereas the controversies on the formal structure of the law were in pre-war times theoretical discussions, because, as we have seen, the judicial review of statutes was not accepted, these theoretical controversies became a political fact of the first order, owing to the fact that the German Supreme Court suddenly reversed its attitude as to its authority for reviewing enacted laws. By a decision of 28th April, 1921,[21] the *Reichsgericht* suddenly asserted that they had always regarded themselves entitled to review statutes as to their conformity with the Constitution. They maintain this attitude in later decisions.[22] The recognition of the right of the judges to review statutes constitutes a re-alignment of the strength of the state. The stronger the state the more the judges will submit to its authority; the weaker a state the more the judges will be inclined to attempt to assert their power. The recognition of the authority of judicial review is in fact an attempt on the part of the judiciary intended on the whole to protect the existing property order. That this is true may be seen by an analysis of the decisions recognising that right. All of them deal with intervention of the state in property, that is to say, with alleged violations of Art. 153 of the Weimar Constitution, which guaranteed property as conferred by the Constitution.[23] I refer for further particulars to the excellent work of Kirchheimer.*

At the same time the Supreme Court accepted the theory that the maxim of equality is directed also to the legislature so that the "arbitrary" decisions of Parliament are unconstitutional.[24] Art. 109 and Art. 153 rapidly became in legal theory and in legal practice the cover for the warding-off of any injury to the property order. The fundamental rights of the Weimar Constitution and the judicial review became in constitutional theory and in the jurisdiction of the Supreme Court the means of maintaining the existing state of political, cultural and economic life. German justice rapidly approached the American model. The final decision of the struggle between judiciary and Parliament was, however, prevented by the breakdown of Weimar democracy.

The constitutional theory and the judiciary, however, did not stop at the extension and the misinterpretation of fundamental rights and at recognising judicial review; they even began to revive the Natural Law which had been dead for more than a century. We have already mentioned the distinction between those fundamental rights which could be altered by the legislature and those which were beyond any change and which were therefore "inherent limitations upon the amending power".[25] The body of rules which in this connection was unchangeable and unalterable provided mainly for the maintenance of private property. This conservative and reactionary function of the new Natural Law is strikingly expressed by the resolution of the Association of the Judges of the Supreme Court, when the government of the *Reich* announced its intention of enacting a law dealing with the revaluation of the mark, and which in the opinion of the Association did not make enough concessions to mortgage holders. The resolution they adopted runs as follows:

> This idea of good faith [*Treu und Glauben*] stands outside the specific laws, outside the provisions of the positive law. No legal system, deserving this honourable name, can exist without this principle.
>
> Therefore the legislature may not frustrate by an arbitrary decision [*Machwort*], a result which is imperatively required by good faith.
>
> It would be severe violation of the honour of the government and of the feeling of right if somebody, who would invoke the new law, were to lose his case because the invocation of that law was against good faith.[26]

The Supreme Court hereby announced that it would deny legal protection to a mortgagee, who would invoke the new law, and James Goldschmidt[27] supported the Supreme Court and even revived the ancient right of resistance, forgetting only that the institution of democracy and the right of resistance are incompatible institutions. Hermann Isay even went so far as to assert that every judge is entitled to examine every statute on the basis of its compatibility with his feeling of right.[28] The development steered rapidly to the recognition of a natural law protecting the given property order.

Still more impressive is the change of front as to the theory of the function of the judge. The period from 1918 to 1930 is characterised by the acceptance of the theory of the school of free discretion. It implied the destruction of the rationality and calculability of the law. These ideas, which I have set out in previous publications, are formulated philosophically in an important contribution of Professor Max Horkheimer in *Zeitschrift fur Sozialforschung* who sums up the development as follows:[29]

> If in the last centuries it was essential for the maintenance of exchange to keep promises at least without continuous interference by might, this necessity has become less by the progressive accumulations of capital. The ruling stratum no longer consists of innumerable subjects who enter into contracts, but of large power groups controlled by a few persons competing with each other on the world market. They have transformed vast areas of Europe into enormous labour camps under iron discipline. The more competition on the world market develops into a struggle for power, the more rigid their internal and external organisation. The economic basis of the significance of the promises becomes weaker day by day. No longer the contract, but command and obedience, characterise increasingly the internal relations.

With regard to the formal structure of law this means the victory of the legal standards of conduct over the formal rational norms. These legal standards of conduct transform the whole legal system. They abolish formal rational law and replace it by material rational norms, and irrational decisions. The legal standards of conduct refer, as we have already seen, to extra-legal norms. Incidentally, the replacement of formal rational law by legal standards of conduct means that the boundary between jurisdiction and administration is shifting and that the realm of administration increases, but so that administrative decisions — which means political decisions — are taken in the form of judgments of ordinary civil courts.

In order to be able to decide the question whether legal standards of conduct endanger the calculability of exchange processes and the predictability of economic results, we have first to know where the legal standards are introduced and what rôle they are playing.

Legal standards of conduct fulfil their decisive function in any law which deals with the relations of monopolies. They appear wherever the legal system is confronted with the problem of private power.[30]

The problem whether a strike is legal or not, was mainly decided according to Sect. 826 of the German Civil Code. The strike was illegal if it was incompatible with the principles of good morals. The decisive formulation of the relation between employer and employee as class units was therefore based upon a moral norm, namely upon the question whether the dispute conformed to the feeling of "equity and justice" of the people. The question whether an employer is to pay wages if he cannot make use of the offered labour of an engaged employee put off on account of a strike in another trade, or of a fire or technical mischance in his factory, and so on, is clearly decided in Sect. 615 of the Civil Code in favour of the employee; but the Supreme Labour Court has continually disregarded this provision of the Court and has based its decisions on Sect. 242 of the Civil Code, a legal standard of conduct, showing that a debtor has to fulfil his obligations according to good faith. Whether an employee, who comes under the provisions of a collective agreement, but tacitly accepts less wages than the collective agreement provides for thereby lawfully waives his claim to the wages thus fixed, has been continuously decided with the help of Sect. 242; that is to say, that the decision was made dependent upon the particular circumstances of the case.

These are only a few examples from that realm of law which regulates the most decisive relations in a modern society. They show that rationality was abandoned for the sake of monopolists.

An equally dominating decision affected legal standards of conduct in the law relating to unfair competition, as we have already shown. They even altered the law relating to joint-stock companies and prevented the exercise of minority rights against the management of such companies. Legal standards of conduct pervaded the whole law relating to industrial combinations (Decree against the Abuse of Economic Power of 2nd November, 1923). According to that law the Minister of Economics was empowered to bring an action against any combination that "endangers the economic life of the community as a whole". According to Sect. 8, any party to an agreement or combination may withdraw without notice given for a substantial reason. And a substantial reason was "especially held to be established if the freedom of economic action in respect of such party be unfairly limited, particularly with regard to production, sale, and the fixing of prices". The legal standards of conduct altered even public law, administrative law and the law of civil proceedure. They transformed the whole legal system.

What are the reasons for the change in the attitude of the judges and the acceptance of the theory of free discretion? It was in the first place the economic motive of inflation which caused the Supreme Court to abandon the principle mark equal to mark in order to attempt the revaluation of devaluated claims on the basis of Sect. 242 of the Civil Code.[31] The second reason was the political attitude of the judiciary; their hostility to democracy.

From these reasons, and the instances indicated, the function of the legal standards of conduct can easily be discerned.

As far as the relationship of employers and workers is concerned the legal standards of conduct serve the compromise between the two classes, the settling of antagonistic interests;[32] but only until about 1930. Up to that date the Supreme Industrial Court carefully compromised between the two groups. This compromise was made possible by the changeable legal standards of conduct, which could be adjusted to any concrete situation.

But after 1930, with the beginning of the economic crisis and the political reaction, these norms became a weapon against social reform legislation. So long as the idea of parity was a reality, so long as collectivist democracy was functioning, the legal standards of conduct were a means of compromising between the two interests. Under that system of parity they were incalculable, and the result of an action was clearly unpredictable. The material rationality of such legal standards of conduct — in this we have to correct Max Weber — was in fact identical with irrationality. Sects. 826 and 242 of the Civil Code referred to extra-legal norms in the terminology of the Supreme Court, to those moral standards which are universally recognised by the people; but in a collectivistic democracy, which is clearly built upon antagonistic interests, such universal recognition of moral standards by the classes is clearly inconceivable. An agreement of the two classes as to whether a strike is legal or not is inconceivable. To the employer practically every strike is illegal, to the worker practically none. The relativity of the legal standards of conduct prevented practically any kind of rationality. So long as a judge wavers between the various possible interpretations of these norms, the material rationality becomes in fact material irrationality as the judge bases his decision on his individual evaluation.

This aspect has changed, however, since 1930. From that time on the material rationality of the legal standards of conduct is a rationality. The result of an action can confidently be expected by the monopolists. In the period of crisis and the beginning of political reaction the judge executes a series of identifications by which the objective structural change in the economic system leads to a psychological transformation in the outlook of the judge. The first step is a distinction of the undertaking as such from the ownership of the undertaking. As in other countries, so in Germany, in legal theory the institutionalist approach becomes predominant.[33] The undertaking is considered to be something different from the ownership of the undertaking. Further: monopolistic undertakings become identical with the economic system, and private economic units become identical with the nation. A monopoly such as the Chemical Trust appears in the judgments of the courts as a kind of national institution. The needs of monopolies even lead to an alteration of the law relating to unfair competition, which makes it possible to punish "economic betrayal of the country".

In the relationship between monopolies and consumers the law was never directed towards compromise, but only towards the production of monopolies.[34] Industrial combinations were conceived to be mere contracts admissible on the basis of the principle of freedom of contract, and not "a social organisation comparable to the State itself".[35] The misconception of the principle of freedom of contract is to be found in English judgment also. There, too, freedom of contract is asserted to imply the freedom to create monopolies.[36]

The decree against the abuse of economic power dated 2nd November, 1923, has never been effective. The *Reich* Minister of Economics has never brought any action based upon Sect. 4 of that decree, against an industrial combination. And the changes which the law against unfair competition underwent in the monopolistic economic system have already been mentioned.

In England, no better example can be found than in the decision in Hopwood v. Roberts,[37] where the provision of a statute of 1855, according to which local authorities may "pay such wages as they . . . may think fit", was interpreted in such a way that they were only made to pay "reasonable" wages. The court, therefore, deliberately inserted a legal standard of conduct into a statutory provision which did not know of it.

The insertion of the notion of reasonableness into abstract legal provisions is to be found in the English law relating to restraint of trade.[38] In the United States, the history of the interpretation of the Sherman Act of 1890 offers an excellent example. Art. I of that Act, clearly stated that "every contract . . . in restraint of trade . . . is hereby declared to be illegal". Whereas the first judgments based upon the statute rigidly applied that provision,[39] the latter decisions only declared illegal unreasonable restraint of trade.[40] It follows, therefore, that in the realm of monopoly law the legal standards of conduct throughout serve the interests of the monopolists. The irrational norms are calculable for the monopolists, as they are strong enough to dispense, if necessary, with formal rationality. The monopolist cannot only do without calculable law, formal rationality is even a fetter to the full development of his power. The rational law has, as we have tried to show, not only the function of rendering exchange processes calculable, it has an equalising function also. It protects the weak. The monopolist can dispense with the aid of the courts; he does not go to the courts. His power of command is a sufficient substitute for the coercive power of the state. By his economic power he is able to impose upon customers and workers, in the form of a free contract, all the conditions he thinks fit. The standard contracts of monopolists shift practically all conceivable risks on to the shoulders of the non-monopolist, whereas the latter has to fulfill all obligations of the law and the monopolist is able to compel him to do so without the help of the court. In such situations, the monopolist attempts to abolish freedom of contract, freedom of trade and the formal rationality of law. As the freedom of contract also includes the freedom for the workers to form organisations and to bargain collectively; as the freedom of contract implies the freedom of outsiders to keep away from industrial combination or to leave it whenever necessary; freedom of trade implies freedom to erect new undertakings thereby damaging established monopolistic possessions. The supplementary liberties of the freedom of contract and trade become fetters for the primary institution of monopolistic property. The productive relationships endanger the productive forces of the monopolists.

This victory of the school of free discretion, and thereby of irrationality, has endangered the legal protection enjoyed by the middle and poorer classes. This function of the school of free discretion had already been foreseen by Max Weber as early as 1911: "It is not sure whether the classes which are today negatively privileged, especially the working class, have to expect from an informal administration of justice, that which the ideology of the jurists [those belonging to the school of free discretion — *author's note*] alleges".[41] The legal standards of conduct establish the rule of the judges. A German judge of high position has expressed his views on the rule of judges, in the following way: "In the last resort therefore, the feeling of decency is decisive in the case of the older judges in high positions, who for the most part have never had any practical business experience".[42] Chief Justice Hughes, when he was Governor, expressed the same idea in a similar way: "We are under a constitution, but the constitution is what the judges say it is".[43]

This abandonment of formal rationality is the response of the judges to the challenge of formal rationality extended to the large masses of the populace. In spite of the political weakness of the Weimar democracy, the legal protection of the poor and of the working class, reached a very high standard. We need only look at the statistics of the industrial courts which were established by the law of 1927, and which set up special courts for the decision of litigation between workers and employers, between workers among themselves arising out of common work, and between trade unions and masters' organisations, to see that this is true. In the year 1931, 441,243 cases came before the courts of first instance, 20,633 before the courts of second instance, and 982 cases before the supreme industrial court. That is a legal protection not attained by any other country in the world. It shows that the boon of formal rationality was extended to the great masses of modern German society. It was made possible by the fact that the costs of litigation before industrial courts were extremely low, and poor persons' cases were preponderant in many spheres of the law.

This process of the disintegration of formal rationality was accompanied and made possible by a complete reversal in legal theory. We may distinguish between four types of judicial thinking: normative, institutional, decisionistic and functional thought.[44] The characteristic of normative thought has already been shown in previous chapters. Institutional thought is best made clear by some instances. Whereas the normativist considers jurisdiction as the mere application of given law which is asserted to have a prejudicial existence, for the institutionalist, the activity of the judge is entirely a creative one, as the law is not closed and the legal norms are open to interpretation. The normativist knows no difference between a positive and a negative state; the institutionalist, however, recognises such a distinction, and defines it in legal terms, namely, the positive state as a state intervening in liberty and property. The institutionalist sees a difference between case and statutory law, between autonomous law and that of the state, because he — rightly from his point of view — declares immaterial the ultimate attribution of case and autonomous law to that of the state.

Institutional thought has three sources: conservative socialism, catholic (Thomistic) Natural Law, and the idea of pluralism (syndicalism). The characteristic example was the Weimar Constitution, in which Catholic Solidarism, as, for instance, expressed in the Papal encyclical, *Quadragesimos anno* and trade union pluralism were fused into a whole, even if such unity proved to be unstable. Institutionalism is essentially a static theory which, however, believes in an evolution by an orderly process. It is conservative because it is opposed to any revolution, and it is progressive because it recognises the rights of the working class up to the limit of equal collaboration. It is a legal theory and not a sociological one, as it sees in the law an own value. Whereas the normativist jurist hates legal standards of conduct because they make him insecure and destroy calculability, the institutionalist acclaims them because they leave the exercise of discretion among the activities of the judge. The institutionalist accepts the positive state because it is positive, and the autonomous creation of law also because it is autonomous. He acclaims the evolution from contract to relation,[45] because he rejects the theory of the will, and alleges that rights and duties are not attached to will, but to objective facts. He accepts the reification of the undertakings, he regards the divorce of undertakings from ownership as an agreeable and progressive theory.

Institutional thought leads to one of two results: either to the ideology of collectivist democracy, or to that of the corporative state. It mystifies institution — and in this we accept the criticism of Bonnecase — by tearing them out of their social interdependence and by making them absolute. This mystic character of the notion of the institution can be found in the definition given by one of the leading exponents of institutional theory, Renard.[46]

Functional legal thought, which lies at the bottom of all our investigations, starts from the assumption that law is not a substance in itself, but a function of society. Law serves interests and ideas, but it is of no value in itself. Functional legal thought accepts neither the phonograph theory of the law, nor that of the school of free discretion. It does not believe that free discretion is always progressive, and the strict binding of the judge of the law always reactionary. Rather, it investigates the social conditions leading to the prevalence of the doctrine of the school of free discretion, and considers the reasons for the various theories. It does not believe that the reification of undertakings is always progressive, but takes into account the question whether such doctrines fulfill progressive social functions.

Decisionistic legal thought has, in fact, nothing to do with law. In this kind of legal thinking, law is nothing but a technique for transforming the political will into legal form. In decisionism law is nothing but an arcanum for the maintenance of power. It is an *arcanum dominationis*, and it is characteristic that in political theory the doctrine of the *arcana* arose at the time when theology lost its dominating influence.[47]

In accepting the functional approach to law, we do not reject the theories of normativism and institutionalism. We have rather to distribute the tasks between the various legal doctrines.

Judge and lawyer have, in the first place, to think in terms of normativistic theory. "The judge, as bound to the interpretation and the service of the positive legal order, can know no theory of the validity of the law but the juristic one."[48] The judge who has to apply laws, has to apply the provisions of those laws, and nothing else. The institutional and functional approaches are for him and for his task, of a secondary nature. He will think institutionally, so as to make understandable to himself the meaning and the significance of an institution; he will think functionally, if the interpretation of a legal provision is open to doubt, and he has therefore a choice between various interpretations. In such a situation, he will choose that interpretation which fits in the social system realised in the constitutional life.

CHAPTER 16

The Rule of Law Under National Socialism

The following chapter is not intended to deal exhaustively with the problem of law under National Socialism; it is, rather, intended to demonstrate the contrast between the liberal legal system, the transitional period of monopoly capitalism and collective democracy, and the legal system of National Socialism, so that the liberal principles, by thus contrasting them with later phenomena, may be made still clearer.[1]

16.1. The Doctrine of Fascism

The Italian doctrine of the totalitarian state is laid down clearly in two documents; the *Carta del Lavoro* of 30th April, 1927, and the contribution of Mussolini to the *Enciclopedia Italiana* (Vol. XIV).[2] According to Art. I of the *Carta*, the old and mighty Italian nation is an independent organism of higher value and with higher aims, standing above the individuals and the associations forming it. The nation is regarded in the Fascist state as a spiritual, economic and political entity. The Fascist state is a corporate state; that is to say, it is hostile to the idea of democracy, of majority rule, and to the idea of political equality. It abhors political and economic liberalism, but it still confesses its faith in private initiative in the sphere of production (*Carta*, Art. VII), because that initiative is the most valuable and the most efficient instrument for the realisation of the interests of the nation. State intervention is allowed only where private initiative is lacking (Art. IX). Although Fascism fights the nineteenth century, it does not seek to return to feudalism.[3] The basis of Italian

Fascism is the state, which is absolute in relation to the individual or to the social groups. It is asserted to be not a mere administrative machine, not a mere creation of politics, but a moral unity. The state is the embodied will to power, based upon discipline.

It is in the main the Hegelian idea of the state, and it is a corporate state. The corporations are the unified organisation of the productive forces and are asserted to represent all those interests (*Carta*, Art. VI). They are, however, not organs of self-government, but organs of the state (Art. 43 of the Royal Decree 1130 of July, 1926 — in execution of the Trade Union Law of 3rd April, 1926).

The corporations are centralised units operating between the syndicates, but they came into being only in February 1934, in spite of the fact that a Ministry of Corporations had been created by Royal Decree on 2nd July, 1926, and a National Council of Corporations by the law 206 of 30th March, 1930. The corporations themselves were created by the law of 5th February, 1934 (No. 163), as organs of the state. Their composition and activity is entirely subject to the decisions of the head of the government, and the activities of the syndicates have now almost ceased.

The accurate exposition of the ideology of National Socialism[4] is a far more difficult task, for its doctrine is laid down in two documents, claiming canonic character, both however, conceived before the accession to power of National Socialism: namely, the unchangeable Party Programme, and Hitler's autobiography — *My Struggle* [*Mein Kampf*].[5] Hitler's autobiography shows a grandiose contempt for the notion of the state, a contempt which still continues, as is shown in his two speeches at the Party Conference in Nüremberg in 1934 and 1935.

For him, the state is not a moral unit in the realisation of an absolute idea, but the servant of the idea of the "racial people". The state is "the organisation of a community of physically and mentally equal beings for rendering possible in a better way the maintenance of their species, and for the attainment of the aims of their existence designed by Providence" (p. 164). The state is not an aim in itself, but a means "for the maintenance of the racial existence of man" (p. 421). "For the task of the state is not to create abilities, but only to create free room for the existing forces. Therefore, the state can be considered as bad if, in spite of high cultural standards, it dooms to death the bearer of this culture in its racial composition." Hitler does not, therefore, recognise the absolute obedience of citizens.

According to his views, a citizen is only subject to the authority of the state if "it corresponds to the interests of his *Volkstum*, or at least does not damage them" (p. 104). The authority of the state is not an aim in itself. The standard of measurement for the evaluation of the state is "the quality of this institution of the *Volkstum* which is in question" (p. 435).

It is obvious that such a conception comes very near to that of liberalism. The state appears as a means, as a mere machine; Hitler's belief in "providence" performs a function similar to that of Natural Law in the liberal system of society, but is distinguished by the zoological formulation of the aims of the state; it appears as a means for the propagation of racially pure people.

This book (Hitler's autobiography) has somewhat embarrassed the German theory of the state. It compelled the constitutional lawyers to bring their teaching into line with that canonic document. Further, the attempt has even been made to give up the notion of the totalitarian state.[6]

The second difficulty lies in the social basis, in the conflict of the idea of the totalitarian state with the institution of private property, an antagonism which, however, is not specific to German National Socialism, but is also to be found in Italian Fascism. For its solution, one must first distinguish between the various kinds of totality and of totalitarian states. The German constitutional theory discriminates between the absolute totality of the absolute monarch; the totality of mass democracy, which is the totality of competing mass parties; the Bolshevist totality in which the state is conceived to be the mere instrument of the rule of the proletariat; the Fascist totality, which is the totality of the Italian state, and the National Socialist totality, whose spiritual basis is the idea of race. "This political idea is an objective external law of life, an unchangeable historical mission."[7] The *people* [are] the unit of life. [*They*] create the state and [they are] *not* created by it, as the theory of Italian Fascism teaches. The essential fact is therefore, "this totality of the political people".[8]

This totality is realised by the total movement (that is, the Party), which in its turn, is exclusively represented by the total leadership. The movement acts through the Leader who is penetrated by the idea. The Leader represents the people. The total movement is the dynamic force directed against the static force of the machinery of the state. The totalitarian state is therefore nothing but the form of the life of the people. The aims of the state are universal, but the racial state does not demand a total activity of the state as does the Bolshevist state, it is rather concerned with the total power of the Leader.

The law is the will of the Leader in the form of law. This is the new definition of law which is, in fact, a vicious circle. The principles of the legality of administration, of the subjection of the judge under the law, receive now a new "meaning", namely, the unconditional subjection of courts and administrative bodies under the politically unified will of the Leader. By this theory, the Hegelian theory of the state is finally rejected. The totalitarian state is therefore a "leadership" state, which is divided into three parts: the State, which is the static part; the Movement (the Party) which is the dynamic element; and the People.[9]

16.2. The Idea of Totality

The identification of the people with the movement, and of the movement with the Leader is a trick used by every dictator who intends to justify his rule immanently, and not by invoking transcendental justifications. That this is an unproved assertion, that actually the people are solely and exclusively the object of the rule and have no part in it, is expressly admitted by Schmitt, when he says "that the people are the unpolitical side growing in the protection and the shade of political decisions".[10] "Unpolitical" can only mean that the people, because they are not allowed to take part in any decision, are a mere object of leadership, that is to say, they must withdraw entirely into their private sphere.[11] Obviously, the referendum which the government can order at any time according to the law of 14th July, 1933, in order to learn whether the people assent to a law or not, is no substitute for the sovereignty of parliament. By this referendum the people do not become a political factor. Competing parties do not exist. The people cannot choose between two alternatives; it can say either yes or no.

The sociological reason for the fact that National Socialism stresses the supremacy of the movement and of the people, can in the first place be explained by the feeling of inferiority which the Party has towards the bureaucracy. For the German bureaucracy is numerically and functionally all-powerful. The constant complaints of the

Party, especially of its old guard, against the unwillingness of the bureaucracy to receive orders from the Party, has brought about passionate declarations by Hitler at the two Party Conferences in 1934 and 1935, that the state has not created the movement, but that the movement has created the state; that the state does not govern the movement, but the movement rules the state. This over-stressing of the claim of the Party for totality minimises ideologically at least the social importance of the bureaucracy and of the conservative and traditional forces.

The sociological, historical reason for the divergence of Italian and German ideas of the relation between state and nation can easily be determined. Italy is a colonial empire and can therefore have no use for the racial creed of National Socialism, whereas [in] Hitler's autobiography, colonial expansion is expressly rejected.[12] The intended eastern expansion of German National Socialism compelled the acceptance of the racial idea, in order to enable it to exclude the millions of eastern Jews. The stress laid upon the racial idea can further be explained by internal policy. According to Carl Schmitt — the Crown Jurist of National Socialism[13] — the state is the work of politics, and the notion of "the political" is not determined by the state. "The political" means, however, according to Schmitt, the relations between friend and foe. Only where such antagonism exists, only where people stand in the relation of friend and foe, are we able to speak of politics. Harmony, collaboration and competition have nothing to do with politics. The central idea of National Socialism is the abolition of the class war. The National Socialist ideology does not recognise the existence of classes; it does not recognise any antagonism between the various groups in the state. Its central idea is that of "the community of the people". Consequently, in Schmitt's terms, there could be no politics in Germany to-day, as there exists no constellation of foe and friend. But as the state is entirely the work of politics and politics are indispensable, an enemy must be created. This enemy is the alien race, which for all practical purposes, means the Jews. The existence of the Jews is the essential factor for the preservation of political life in Germany. The conception of the nation is valueless as it implies — as we have already pointed out — certain liberal and democratic consequences, and the idea of the race serves, therefore, as a means of integration of the National Socialist society. It further serves to differentiate that society from others, and finally, to preserve politics, apart from its function in foreign policy. The Nüremberg laws of 15th September, 1935, are the culmination of that development towards integration and differentiation of the National Socialist society.

On the other hand, the central position of the state in Italian fascism is explicable if one realises that the Italian state is a relatively recent creation. Bureaucracy, police, and an efficient army are mainly creations of Italian Fascism, whereas in Germany, the central machinery of the state was highly developed and completely intact when National Socialism came to power. The primary task of Italian Fascism was the creation of such an apparatus.[14]

Totality, however, means the universality of the aims of the state, the reversal of the liberal relationship between the state and the individual, the transformation of all important social spheres to public and political spheres. This totality, however, is opposed to a faith, as strongly expressed, in private initiative in the economic sphere. There is to-day, no more important realm than that of economics. The most important institution is undoubtedly that of property, particularly property in the means of production. If, therefore, one takes the idea of totality seriously, one ought to socialism. The converse, however, is true. The economic policy in Germany as well as in Italy[15] may not be actually liberal, but it is quite surely based on the institution of private property. In all National Socialist pamphlets and books dealing with this problem, the postulate of totality is immediately followed by that of private enterprise. How are these two postulates to be reconciled?

The key for the solution of this antinomy has been very ably found by Carl Schmitt. In an important lecture, delivered before the most powerful industrial organisation in north-west Germany[16] he distinguished between two kinds of totality — a quantitative and a qualitative one. The quantitative totalitarian state is a phenomenon of Romanism; it interferes in every sphere of activity. The qualitative totalitarian state is a specifically Germanic phenomenon. It is a strong state, but it does not intervene in all spheres of activity. The realm of economics is left free. It is satisfied with providing regulations for the "political" sphere. "Sound economics in a strong state" was the title of this lecture by Carl Schmitt, in which he gave legal expression to the unity between National Socialism and monopoly capitalism. It, in fact, is nothing but the doctrine of Pareto, who postulated the abolition of all political liberties and combined this with the postulate of a free economic system. It remains a mystery how the notion of totality can be qualitative. If something is total it must necessarily embrace the whole. The idea of totality can only be a quantitative notion.

In so far as National Socialism or Fascism seeks to realise corporative or an estate order, we must apply the same criticism as we have used against the mediaeval estate order. In the same way as the estates of the Middle Ages veiled the rôle of landed ownership, corporations and estates hide the domination of monopoly capitalism. The worker is fettered, and his rise as a class prevented, by any kind of estate organisation.

It is true that Fascism — Italian or German — was in the beginning a charismatic rule.[17] "Pure charisma is especially alien to economics. It constitutes a 'calling' in the emphatic sense of the word: as a mission or as an inner task. It scorns and rejects in its pure type, the economic use of *ex gratia* gifts as a means of income — this, however, is more often a postulate than a fact."[18] But charisma has become a matter of common usage, and what remains is feudal domination. In the political system of medieval feudalism, political rights were attached to landed property. *Beneficium* and *commendatio* are the two pillars, and the *commendatio* is the contract of faith — with unequal rights.[19] Consequently, this contract of faith between leader and followers, stands at the centre of German law.[20] Holdsworth describes feudalism in England at the beginning of the fourteenth and fifteenth centuries as follows: "The new feudalism compassed its ends, not by direct attack, but by a perversion of the machinery of centralised government. It was a bastard imitation of the old order of society founded upon the weakness of the crown and of the corruption of the ruling classes. Those ruling classes did not represent the great body of the nation".[21]

The society of National Socialism has become a static society, as any movement inside it might very well lead to its extinction. The sovereignty of parliament was abolished, because it gave to a labour party the opportunity of coming to power. The totality of the state is, in fact, the total domination over the state, exercised by the Leader for the sake of a feudal class, by transforming the people into serving estates.

16.3. The Law in the Totalitarian State

Is the National Socialist state a *Rechtsstaat?* This question is as passionately affirmed as it is denied.[22] According to Carl Schmitt,[23] *Rechtsstaat* is a mere liberal conception. The National Socialist state is a truly just state, but it is in no way a *Rechtsstaat.* On the other hand[24] *Rechtsstaat* character of the National Socialist state is as emphatically affirmed, so that under the pressure of these attacks, Carl Schmitt was compelled to abandon his views, to accept the official view, and to admit the *Rechtsstaat* character of the National Socialist state, even if the whole idea seemed to him superfluous.[25]

We have, therefore, to investigate whether the National Socialist state possesses the basic elements which in our view, constitute a *Rechtsstaat.* There is no doubt that National Socialist theory and practice reject the postulate of the rule of law. Law is nothing but the will of the Leader.[26] Innumerable individual laws have been enacted, such as the law of 2nd August, 1934, ordering a state funeral for the deceased President Hindenburg; of 3rd July, 1934, granting exemption from taxes for the National Socialist party; of 7th March, 1934, enabling the *Reich* Minister of Finance to reduce the taxes due on the occasion of the reorganisation of the Steel Trust; of 27th July, 1933, and 22nd October, 1935, granting exemption from taxes for the landed property of President Hindenburg and his descendants, and of Field-Marshal Mackensen; and of 3rd July, 1934, legalising all measures taken for the crushing of the Roehm revolt. There are further innumerable laws dealing with economic activities. It is characteristic that all individual commands grant privileges or regulate monopoly organisations. The renunciation of the general character of the law reveals at the same time, the feudal character of legislation.

The principle of non-retroactivity of law is no longer recognised.[27] In many cases, the law-giver has issued retroactive laws, such as the *lex* Van der Lubbe of 29th March, 1934, which extended the death penalty to certain crimes committed between 31st January and 28th February, 1933; the law of 14th July, 1933, empowering the Minister to repeal naturalisations and to deprive Germans of their citizenship; the law of 3rd July, 1934, retroactively making legal certain decrees and administrative acts; and finally, the law of

3rd July, 1934, legalising all measures undertaken for the crushing of the Roehm revolt, a law which for the first time in history did not declare a past action illegal, but made legal an already-committed crime. The characteristic of all these, and many other retroactive laws is either the annihilation of political opponents or the legalisation of illegal measures taken during the transitional period. The culmination of retroaction, however, is to be found in the new Section 2 of the German Penal Code, valid since the law of 28th July, 1935. According to this section: "He will be punished, who commits a crime which has been declared punishable by the law or which deserves punishment according to the principles of a penal statute and according to the sound feeling of the people. If no penal statute can directly be applied to such crime, the crime is punished according to that statute whose basic idea is best fitted for it". Wherever it is necessary for the security of the present rulers, National Socialism uses individual and retroactive laws; wherever monopolistic situations have to be dealt with, the monopolists are exempted from the universally valid laws.

By this transformation, however, the position of the judge has been fundamentally changed. It is true that Hitler has expressed himself in favour of the independence of judges in his speech before the Reichstag on 23rd March, 1933, and that the Reich Minister of Justice has also expressed the idea that a judge is bound by the law, and that the authoritarian idea implies the complete subjection of the judge under the law.[28] The judge, having fulfilled during the Weimar democracy his counter-revolutionary function, has now become once more, the absolute servant of the law, i.e., of the will of the Leader: "Right and the will of the Leader are the same".[29] The independence of the judge has now received a new "meaning".[30] Up to now, it served "to make secure the legal rights of a citizen against possible arbitrary action by a government which was hostile to him".[31] To-day, independence of judges means their subjection to the guiding principle of the National Socialist "leadership" state.[32] For the neutral state has gone. The guiding principles for the activity of the judge, must be the ideas of National Socialism, as laid down in the Party Programme and as expressed by the will of the Leader. The judge has to serve the Leader,[33] but at the same time he has to obey the written law.

We are only interested here in the question as to how it is technically possible to fulfil at one and the same time, the commands of the political leader and of the enacted law. Conflicts are naturally possible, and are sometimes reported. The synchronisation of the judicial machinery with the political leadership is not yet complete, but it has almost reached completion. The coordination is reached, in the first place, with the help of the new conception of law, and in the second, by means of legal standards of conduct; if we omit the discharging of judges based upon the law of 1st April, 1933, and of 15th September, 1935, and also omit all indirect interference in the activity of judges such as pressure by the Party, open or hidden terror, effects which cannot be controlled. We limit ourselves strictly to those constitutional means of interfering with the freedom of the judge which are open to control. The subjection of the law under individual commands makes the independence of judges illusory. The individual law is a measure, because it provides regulations for a concrete act. If the law does not state that any property belonging to a group hostile to the state has to be attached, but that property belonging to the Communist Party or to the Social Democratic Party has to be seized, and that the *Reich* Minister of the Interior finally decides whether or not property was intended to serve purposes hostile to the State,[34] then the judge in Germany to-day, no longer possesses the functions of a judge. He has become a mere bailiff, a mere policeman.[35] The retroactivity of law also partly abolishes the independence of judges, as retroactive laws always deal with already accomplished facts, and therefore, with individual cases.

Still greater is the significance of legal standards of conduct in the present legal system. Their main purpose is to bring into line the enacted law with the will of the Leader. "For the application and handling of the legal standards of conduct by the judge, the lawyer, the magistrate, and the law teacher, the principles of National Socialism are directly and exclusively decisive"; that is the thesis of Carl Schmitt's famous five leading principles for the practice of law.[36] The legal standards of conduct refer to moral norms outside the legal norms which prevail in the community. The declared view of the people is National Socialism. The constituent elements of National Socialism's view of life are solely determined by the Leader.[37] Although Carl Schmitt in his thesis No. 3 asserts that the legal standards of conduct in no way interfere with the independence of judges, even some National Socialist lawyers express dissatisfaction with his point of view.[38] But not only the transformation of the formal structure of law abolishes the independence of judges; the destruction of the principle of the separation of powers has its share also in their subjection. As a doctrine, it is emphatically and universally rejected in Germany, and in practice it is abolished. The Leader, by the empowering act of 24th March, 1933, and by the law relating to the rebuilding of the *Reich* of 30th January, 1934, has supreme legislative and executive power. Where the will of the political leader meets the resistance of already enacted law, he can change the substance of the law at any time and in any direction he likes.

But the last remnant of the independence of the judge disappears, if the Leader not only assumes legislative and executive powers, but also judicial functions; if he himself orders the death penalty, as happened in the famous Roehm revolt. According to the theory of the National Socialist leaders, as expressed by Hitler's Reichstag speech of 13th July, 1934 by Göring[39] and by the sensational article of Carl Schmitt, "The Leader protects the law",[40] the Leader is not only the supreme legislator, not only the supreme executive, he is also the supreme judge. "The deed of the Leader was, in fact, a genuine act of justice; it does not stand under the judicial machinery, it was highest justice."[41] The legal theory of Fascism is, therefore, "decisionistic". The whole machinery of the law stands exclusively at the service of the Leader, in order to transform, as rapidly as possible, his will into legal forms. We cannot, therefore, ascribe to the National Socialist State the basic principles of a *Rechtsstaat*. Whether the National Socialist state is a just state, is left entirely to the judgment of the reader.

16.4. The Economic System and the Calculability of the Law

We have already described the inroads into the formal rationality of the law during the transitional period of German collectivist democracy. We are not able to continue exhaustively with this exposition as it would entail a presentation of all the economic activities of National Socialism. It will suffice if we discuss one central problem. According to Max Weber's definition of capitalism, it is only possible on the basis of formally free labour. Exact calculation, according to him, depends entirely upon whether or not the worker is legally free to enter into contracts.[42] Free labour, however, no longer exists under National Socialism. The laws of 20th January, 1935, relating to the ordering of national labour,[43] the law of 15th May, 1934, prohibiting free migration of workers in Germany, the regulations concerning labour camps, land help and the prohibition of strikes, have transformed free labour into a legally-bound serving estate. Nevertheless, it cannot be doubted that the calculability of the exchange processes, in so far as it serves the interests of the monopolists, is still given, as their power is quite sufficient without the help of the state and without freedom of contract, to attain their economic ends. We do not propose to deal more exhaustively with this problem; it must suffice that we have indicated its existence.

16.5. The Ethical Function of the Law

Between the state and the individual there stands no collective organisation protecting the individual and realising his freedom. The fundamental sociological principle upon which National Socialism is built, is, in the first place, that of a complete *atomisation* of society. The German Workers' Front, an organisation of about twenty-five million members, is but another name for the German people, with the exception of the civil servants and peasants, who are not allowed to join it. It is a mass organisation of individuals and has no similarity whatever to any kind of trade union. It may not enter into collective agreements, and its property is administered by the Party. This atomisation and synchronisation of all social groups, this abolition of every democratic principle within corporations, and this supersession by the principle of leadership, leads to the complete atomisation of society, and therefore enables the State to control the individual effectively.

The second sociological principle of National Socialism, is that of *totality*, which is the control of private affairs by public power. This principle has found its most brutal expression in the drafting by the Academy of German Law, of a new divorce law, which gives the state the power to divorce marriages against the will of both parties, if such marriages are no longer in agreement with the principles of the state, so that the divorce becomes a kind of supplementary punishment for political offenders.

The third sociological principle is that of *differentiation* within the society, for the purpose of creating reliable élites, such as a certain stratum of peasants and the bureaucracy of the Party.

These three sociological principles are expressed by the rejection of the notion of the equality of all human beings. The idea of equality is considered to be merely abstract, a remnant revival of Roman law. Sect. I of the German Civil Code, which states that everybody, from the moment of birth, receives full legal rights, is still verbally in existence, and it is even formally suggested that it should be abolished and replaced by the maxim that legal rights can be enjoyed only by being a *Volksgenossen*.[44]

According to many definitions given, right is what is serviceable to Germany. No exception can be taken to such a definition any more than to definitions such as that law is that which aims at the attainment of common good. The fundamental problem is, what has to be understood by "Germany" and who is to decide what is serviceable and what is not.

We therefore sum up: That law does not exist in Germany, because law is now exclusively a technique of transforming the political will of the Leader into constitutional reality. Law is nothing but an *arcanum dominationis*.

Notes

PART I INTRODUCTION

1. Or — in other words — in such a period there is a prospect that sovereignty may emerge from free competition of the society.
2. For the concept of "rational" see pp. 27ff.
3. Other forms of justification are Traditionalism, by which the state is justified by its very existence; Charisma; and, of course, all divine theories.
4. Which is best presented in Harold J. Laski's, *Democracy in Crisis*, 1933.
5. Similarly see Bertrand Russell, "The Revolt against Reason", *Political Quarterly*, 1935, p. 5.
6. Kurt Wolzendorff, *Archiv für öffentliches Recht*, vol. XXXIV, p. 477.
7. "Eine staatstheoretische Form für jede politische Idee."
8. Cf. Max Horkheimer, "Zum Rationalismusstreit in der gegenwärtigen Philosophie", *Zeitschrift für Sozialforschung*, 1934, pp. 1ff; John Stuart Mill, "The danger of asking why? ", *Dissertations and Discussions*, vol. I, 3rd ed., p. 332.
9. General survey by Otto Gierke, *Natural Law and the Theory of Society 1500–1800*, ed. Ernest Barker, Cambridge, 1934, vol. I, pp. 111ff.
10. J. N. Figgis, *Studies of Political Thought from Gerson to Grotius*, Cambridge, 1916, pp. 157–8.
11. On the introduction of the notion of the natural state, see William A. Robson, *Civilisation and the Growth of Law*, 1931, p. 258.
12. See S. P. Gooch and H. J. Laski, *English Democratic Ideas in the Seventeenth Century*, Cambridge, 1927, p. 139.
13. Max Salomon, "Kants Originalität in der Auffassung der Lehre vom Staatsvertrage", *Archiv für öffentliches Recht*, vol. XXVIII, 1920, p. 97.

CHAPTER 1

1. Wilhelm Dilthey, *Einleitung in die Geisteswissenschaften*, vol. 1, Leipzig

and Berlin, 1922, p. 80.
2. Hegel, *Rechtsphilosophie*, §32, add.: "Die abstrakten Formen erweisen sich nicht als für sich bestehend, sondern als Unwahrheit".
3. Cf. Oliver Wendell Holmes, *Collected Legal Papers*, 1928, p. 170.
4. Dilthey, *Einleitung*, p. 80: "Die Rechtsordnung ist die Ordnung der Zwecke der Gesellschaft, welche von der äusseren Organisation derselben durch Zwang aufrecht erhalten wird. Und zwar bildet der Zwang des Staats. . . den entscheidenden Rückhalt der Rechtsordnung; aber äussere Bindung der Willen sehen wir durch die ganze organisierte Gesellschaft verbreitet und so erklärt sich, dàss in dieser auch andere Gesamtwillen neben dem Staat Recht bilden und aufrecht erhalten. Jeder Rechtsbegriff enthält also das Moment der äusseren Gesellschaft in sich. Anderseits kann jeder Verband nur in Rechtsbegriffen konstruiert werden".
5. Max Weber, *Verhandlungen des 1. Deutschen Soziologentages*, col. I. Tübingen, 1911, p. 75; J. Bentham, *Theory of Legislation*: "It is hence that we have the power of forming a general plan of conduct . . . , Expectation is a chain which unites our present existence to our future existence, and which passes beyond us to the generation which is to follow"; Holmes, *Legal Papers*, p. 169: Legal duty as a prediction, as a prophecy.
6. Max Weber, *Wirtschaft und Gesellschaft*, p. 369.
7. Gustav Radbruch, *Grundzüge der Rechtsphilosophie*, 2nd ed., p. 29: "Wirklichkeit, die den Sinn hat, der Rechtsidee zu dienen. Der Rechtsbegriff ist ausgerichtet an der Rechtsidee".
8. Dietrich Schindler, *Verfassungsrecht und Soziale Struktur*, Zürich, 1932, p. 35; Karl Mannheim, *Ideologie und Utopie*, pp. 110–11; Hermann Heller, *Die Souveränität*, Leipzig and Berlin, 1927, p. 128.
9. Karl Mannheim, "Ideologische und Soziologische Betrachtung der geistigen Gebilde", *Jahrbuch für Soziologie*, vol. II, Karlsruhe, 1926, pp. 424ff.
10. Hans Kelsen, *Reine Rechtslehre*, Leipzig and Vienna, 1934, p. 1.
11. H. J. Laski, "Law and the State", *Studies in Law and Politics*, London, 1932, p. 239.
12. Weber, *Wirtschaft*, p. 368.
13. Kitz, *Sein und Sollen*, Frankfurt, 1869, p. 74.
14. Hans Kelsen, *Hauptprobleme der Staatsrechtslehre*, Tübingen, 1911, p. 334.
15. In place of a reference to the whole of Kelsen's works, I refer the reader to his symposium, *Reine Rechtslehre*, Leipzig and Vienna, 1934, with its accompanying bibliography. For the English reader in particular, see his two articles in the *Law Quarterly Review*, 1934–5, transl. C. H. Wilson.
16. See Adolf Merkl, *Veröffentlichungen der Vereinigung der deutschen Staatsrechtslehrer*, vol. 4, Berlin and Leipzig, 1921, p. 200.
17. Here there seems to be a contradiction within Kelsen's theory. If a norm is a hypothetical judgment of the future behaviour of the state, the decision of the court cannot be itself a norm.
18. Here, characteristically of his Liberal starting-point, without any

proof, the legal norm is identified with the general norm and is therefore already given content.

19. Thomas Hobbes, *Leviathan*, ed. Molesworth, vol. VIII, chap. XXVI, p. 252.
20. Robert Filmer, "Observations upon H. Grotius" De Jure Belli ac Pacis", *Patriarcha and other Political Works*, ed. P. Laskett, Oxford, 1949, p. 267.
21. Thomas Hobbes, *A Dialogue*, ed. Molesworth, vol. VI, p. 15.
22. It follows, therefore, that Kelsen's "pure" theory of law is nothing but a purified theory of the British Absolutists: with Hobbes and Filmer, however, this theory had political significance, whereas it is reduced in the "pure" theory of law to a methodological principle.
23. Cf. Karl Renner, *Die Rechtsinstitute des Privatrechts u. ihre soziale Funktion*, Tübingen, 1929, p. 32;* also Max Huber, "Beiträge für Kenntnis der soziologischen Grundlagen des Völkerrechts", *Jahrbuch des öffentlichen Rechts*, 1910, vol. IV, p. 61.
24. Hegel, *Rechtsphilosophie*, p. 3, note: "abhänginges Moment einer Totalität im Zusammenhang mit allen übrigen Bestimmungen, welche den Charakter einer Nation und einer Zeit ausmachen . . . . Denn erst in diesem Zusammenhang erhalten sie ihre wahrhafte Bedeutung, sowie damit ihre wahrhafte Rechtfertigung".
25. By this, however, law is not an ideology, it is a real social relationship as Paschukanis rightly says.
26. F. Engels, *Ludwig Feuerbach*, pp. 49, 52–3: "Here the inter-connection between the ideas and their material conditions of existence becomes more and more complicated, more and more obscured by intermediate links. But the inter-connection exists".
27. Cf. criticism of this assertion by Max Weber, "Rudolf Stammler's Ueberwindung", *Gesammelte Aufsätze zur Wissenschaftslehre*, Tübingen, 1922, p. 309.
28. Hegel, *Rechtsphilosophie*, p. 2: "Der Begriff des Rechts (im philosophischen Sinne) fällt seinem Werden nach ausserhalb der Wissenschaft des Rechts".
29. Ibid., pp. 5ff.
30. *Verhandlungen des ersten deutschen Soziologentages 1910*, vol. I, Tübingen, 1911, pp. 209, 273.
31. John R. Commons, *Legal Foundations of Capitalism*, New York, 1924.
32. Karl Diehl, *Die rechtlichen Grundlagen des Kapitalismus*, Jena, 1929.
33. The clearest statement of the problem is to be found in Erwin Jacobi's *Grundlagen des Arbeitsrechts*, Leipzig, 1927, p. 397. My own views are expressed in *Koalitionsfreiheit und Reichsverfassung*, Berlin, 1932, pp. 33ff.
34. Ernst Forsthoff, *Die öffentliche Körperschaft im Bundesstaat*, Tübingen, 1931, p. 17.
35. Weber, *Wirtschaft*, p. 416.
36. Carl Schmitt, *Verfassungslehre*, Munich and Leipzig, 1927, p. 67, without acknowledgment to Max Weber whom he simply copies. Weber's formulation corresponds exactly to Sir H. Maine's famous generalisa-

tion, the validity of which cannot be contested. See idem, *Ancient Law* [London and New York, 1954, pp. 99–100].

37. *Elementorum Jurisprudentiae Universalis*, Oxford, 1927, p. 77.
38. Heller, *Souveranität*, p. 62.
39. In the same way H. J. Laski in his *Foundations of Sovereignty* (London, 1931) calls sovereignty an external power. Dietrich Schindler, however, does not recognise this clearly enough in his *Verfassungsrecht*. This chapter owes much to *Foundations*, as to all of Prof. Laski's work.
40. See also Heller, *Souveranität*, pp. 165ff.

CHAPTER 2

1. Austin's definition: "If a determinate human superior not in a habit of obedience to a like superior receives habitual obedience from the bulk of a given society, that determinate superior is sovereign in that society, and society (including the superior) is a society political and independent. . . . The part truly independent . . . is not the society but the sovereign portion of the society. . . . The State is usually synonymous with the sovereign". The first sentence is incomplete, as it is concerned with obedience. It is too narrow as for us only the actual fulfilment is of importance. The second and third sentences are unfortunately formulated, although in agreement with our definition. Just as in the first sentence, they lack the element of right. The connection with Bentham is stressed by C. E. Merriam, *History of the Theory of Sovereignty since Rousseau*, New York, 1900, pp. 131, 135.
2. Hans Kelsen, *Das Problem der Souveränität u. die Theorie des Völkerrechts*, Tübingen, 1920, and many other works.
3. See the essay by C. H. Wilson, "The Basis of Kelsen's Pure Theory of Law" (*Politica*, 1934, pp. 54ff.) for a criticism of the central postulates of the pure science of law.
4. Hermann Heller, *Die Souveränität, ein Beitrag zur Theorie des Staats- und Völkerrechts*, Berlin and Leipzig, 1927, p. 38.
5. Anton Menger, *Neue Staatslehre*, 3rd ed., Jena, pp. 166ff.
6. Carl Schmitt, *Politische Theologie, vier Kapitel zur Lehre von der Souveränität*, 2nd ed., Munich and Leipzig, 1934, p. 11; idem, *Die Diktatur*, 2nd ed., Munich and Leipzig, pp. x, 201, 272.
7. Heller, *Souveränität*, p. 62.
8. Karl Mannheim, *Rational ana Irrational Elements in Contemporary Society*, London, 1934, p. 14.
9. Weber, *Wirtschaft*, p. 12.
10. Mannheim, *Rational and Irrational*, p. 15.
11. Weber, *Wirtschaft*, p. 12.
12. See Max Weber, *Gesammelte Aufsätze zur Religionsoziologie*, Tübingen, 1920, vol. I, p. 11; Mannheim, *Rational and Irrational*, p. 29.
13. W. A. Robson, *Justice and Administrative Law*, London, 1928, pp.

189–90.

14. Weber, *Wirtschaft*, p. 396.
15. W. Holdsworth, *Some Lessons from our Legal History*, New York, 1928, pp. 20–3.
16. See an excellent exposition by A. L. Goodhart, *Essays in Jurisprudence and the Common Law*, Cambridge, 1931, p. 65; my own exposition in Chap. 14.3. of this book.
17. Thomas Hobbes, *Leviathan*, ed. Molesworth, vol. III, p. 116.
18. Rudolf Isay and Karl Geiler, *Die Reform des Kartellrechts*, Berlin, 1929, including their reports to the Salzburg Legal Congress; see also my *Koalitionsfreiheit u. Reichsverfassung*, Berlin, 1932, p. 51. My italics.
19. Ivor Jennings, *The Law and the Constitution*, London, 1933, p. 235.
20. H. J. Laski, *Liberty in the Modern State*, London, 1935, p. 76.
21. Edmund Burke, *Speeches*, I.
22. In *Some Legal Phases of Corporate Financing*, New York, 1927, p. 231.
23. J. N. Figgis, *Political Thought from Gerson to Grotius*, p. 156.
24. *Contrat Social*, II.
25. Hegel, *Rechtsphilosophie*, sect. 5, appendix: "Diese negative Freiheit . . . ist einseitig, aber dieses Einseitige enthält immer eine wesentliche Bestimmung in sich: es ist daher nicht wegzuwerfen, aber der Mangel des Verstandes ist, dass er eine einseitige Bestimmung zur einzigen und höchsten erhebt".
26. Karl Mannheim, *Mensch und Gesellschaft im Zeitalter des Umbaus*, Leiden, 1935, p. 109.
27. In addition to J. R. Commons, *Legal Foundations of Capitalism*, London and New York, 1934, p. 20, see also Weber, *Wirtschaft*, p. 454.
28. Neumann, *Koalitionsfreiheit*, pp. 20–63.
29. Lord Macnaghten, in the Nordenfeldt Case (1894) A.C. at 566: "It is obviously more freedom of contract between buyer and seller than between master and servant or between employer and a person seeking employment"; similarly, Lord Parker, in Morris v. Saxelby (1916) 1. A.C. 688 ad 708/9.
30. Hegel, *Rechtsphilosophie*, sect. 7, appendix.
31. Partial contributions in: Carl Schmitt, *Verfassungslehre*, pp. 161ff.; Anschütz-Thoma, *Handbuch des deutschen Staatsrechts*; Nipperdey (ed.), *Die Grundrechte u. Grundpflichten der Deutschen*, vol. I, Berlin, 1930, pp. 33ff.; Neumann, *Koalitionsfreiheit*, pp. 13ff. p. 13ff.
32. German literature: Schmitt, *Verfassungslehre*, pp. 99ff., 176. On the other hand: Richard Thoma in Nipperdey, *Grundrechte*, vol. I, pp. 40ff.; Franz Neumann, "Die Soziale Bedeutung der Grundrechte", *Die Arbeit*, 1930, pp. 570ff. — American literature: C. Groves Haines, *The Revival of Natural Law Concepts*, Harvard, 1930, pp. 336ff. taking into consideration the awakening of Natural Law — Further examples: W. A. Marbury, "The Nineteenth Amendment and After", *Virginia Law Review*, VII (1920). On the other hand: W. W. Willoughby, *The Constitutional Law of the USA*, 2nd ed., vol. I, pp. 598ff. (against the "inherent limitations upon the amending power").

33. Weber, *Wirtschaft*.
34. R. T. Ely, *Property and Contract in their Relation to the Distribution of Wealth*, 1914, I, pp. 94ff.; John Austin, *Jurisprudence*, 4th ed., 1873, vol. I, Lect. XIV, p. 382; Lect. XLVII, pp. 817ff.; W. H. Hohfeld, *Fundamental Legal Conceptions*, Newhaven, p. 28; Karl Renner, *Die Rechtsinstitute des Privatrechts u. ihre soziale Funktion*, Tübingen, 1930, p. 28; Menger, *Staatslehre*, p. 99.
35. Otto von Gierke, *Das deutsche Genossenschaftsrecht*, Berlin, 1868, Vol. 1, pp. 8ff.; Johannes Althusius, *Politica Methodica Digesta*, ed. C. J. Friedrich, Cambridge, Mass., 1932, pp. 21–2; Otto von Gierke, *Johannes Althusius*, 2nd ed., Breslau, 1902, pp. 48, 161, 197.
36. Hugo Sinzheimer, *Grundzüge des Arbeitsrechts*, 2nd ed., Jena, 1927.
37. Franz Neumann, "Gesellschaftliche u. staatliche Verwaltung monopolistischer Unternehmungen", *Die Arbeit*, 1928, p. 393.
38. Fundamental is Karl Renner, *Die Rechtsinstitute des Privatrechts und ihre soziale Funktion*, 2nd ed., Tübingen (1st ed. appeared under the pseudonym Josef Karner in vol. 1. of the Wiener Marx Studien); Menger, *Staatslehre*, Jena, 1903, pp. 99ff.; Ely, *Property and Contract*, pp. 94ff.; Neumann, *Koalitionsfreiheit*; Sinzheimer, *Grundzüge*.
39. "Free" in the sense of the dual freedom of the emancipated slave — legally free and free from property!
40. Fundamental: Renner, *Rechtsinstitute*; Carl Schmitt, *Freiheitsrechte, u. institutionelle Garantien in der Reichsverfassung*, Berlin, 1932; Neumann, *Koalitionsfreiheit*, pp. 86ff. Karl Renner's work presents property and all its auxiliary institutions, but unfortunately neglects to make a sufficiently sharp distinction between "Liberty" and "Institution".
41. Part IV of my *Koalitionsfreiheit* is devoted to this problem. The institutions auxiliary to the right of workers to associate are investigated with a view to finding out how far they share the fate of the main liberty, and how far they suffer an independent fate of their own.
42. See Renner, *Rechtsinstitute*, pp. 63–9.
43. See the paper by Prof. D. H. Parry, "Economic Theories in English Case Law", *Law Quarterly Review*, 1931, p. 199.
44. Karl Marx, *Lohnarbeit und Kapital*, *MEW*, vol. 6, p. 408.
45. Karl Marx, *Kapital*, *MEW*, vol. 3, pp. 789f.
46. Ibid., p. 885.
47. Karl Marx, *Theorien über den Mehrwert*, *MEW*, vol. 26, pp. 25ff. — i.e. in all essentials the data of modern economic theory apart from the subjective factor of individual wants.
48. Karl Marx, *Zur Kritik der politischen Ökonomie*, Foreword, *MEW*, vol. 13, p. 9.
49. Thomas Hobbes, *Philosophical Rudiments*, ed. Molesworth, vol. II, chap. XIV, p. 183.
50. Hobbes, *Leviathan*, vol. III, chap. XVI, p. 147; ibid., p. 185, the same Dialogue; ibid., vol. VI, p. 26: "Law is a command of him or them that have sovereign power given to those that be his or their subjects, declaring publicly and plainly, what every of them may do and what

they must forbear to do".

51. M. B. Foster, *The Political Philosophies of Plato and Hegel*, Oxford, 1935, p. 114.
52. See *State Trials*, III, pp. 1ff., Selden's defence, cols. 16ff; S. R. Gardiner, *Constitutional Documents of the Puritan Revolution*, 3rd ed., Oxford, 1906, p. 59; idem, *History of England from the Accession of James I*, vol. VI, pp. 213ff.
53. Transl. taken from McKechnie, *Magna Charta*, 2nd ed., 1914, pp. 375ff.

PART II INTRODUCTION

1. Telkamp, *Das Verhältnis des John Locke zur Scholastik*, Nünster, 1927.

CHAPTER 3

1. O. Dittrich, *Geschichte der Ethik*, vol. II, Leipzig, 1926, pp. 32–53; William A. Robson, *Civilisation and the Growth of Law*, 1931, p. 214.
2. See exposition by C. H. McIlwain, *The Growth of Political Thought in the West*, London, 1932, p. 111; Carlyle, vol. I, pp. 3ff.
3. All quotations from the Latin are taken from the edition of the Teubnerbibliothek, Leipzig: *De Legibus*, vol. II, and *Pro Cluentio*, vol. VIII.
4. Cf., on the controversy, Moritz Wlassak *Römische Prozessgesetze*, Leipzig, 1888–9, vol. II, pp. 5, 6, 108.
5. *Pro Cluentio*, pp. 55, 155.
6. Carlyle, vol. I, p. 9.
7. Robert Linhardt, *Die sozialen Prinzipien des hl. Thomas von Aquin*, Freiburg, 1932; Theodor Steinbüchel, *Christliches Mittelalter*, Leipzig, 1935; Wilhelm Schwer, *Stand und Ständeordnung in Weltbild des Mittelalters*, Paderborn, 1934; Martin Grabmann, *Mittelalterliches Geistesleben*, Munich, 1926; McIlwain, pp. 325ff.; Bede Jarrett, *Social Theories of the Middle Ages 1200–1500*, London, 1926; Carlyle, vol. I; E. Troeltsch, *Die Soziallehren der Christlichen Kirchen und Gruppen*, Tübingen, 1912 (transl. as *The Social Teaching of the Christian Churches*, 2 vols, London, 1931).
8. Linhardt, *Sozialen Prinzipien*, p. 94.
9. Linhardt, *Sozialen Prinzipien*, p. 104.
10. J. N. Figgis, *Studies of Political Thought from Gerson to Grotius*, Cambridge, 1916, p. 57.
11. Ibid., p. 20; Troeltsch, *Soziallehren*, p. 242 (*Social Teaching*, pp. 246ff.).
12. Albert Hauck, *Kirchengeschichte Deutschlands*, vol. IV, 4th ed., 1913, p. 714.
13. Schwer, *Ständeordnung* p. 20; Steinbüchel, *Mittelalter*, p. 274; Jarrett, *Social Theories*, p. 94; Carlyle, vol. I, pp. 111ff.

14. Figgis, *Political Thought*, p. 12; Schwer, *Ständeordnung* p. 9; Steinbüchel, *Mittelalter*, pp. 272ff.
15. Troeltsch, *Soziallehren*, pp. 252–302 (*Social Teaching*, vol. I, pp. 257–80) — Aquinas' system is here designated as one of reconciliation.
16. Linhardt, *Sozialen Prinzipien*, p. 207.
17. Jarrett, *Social Theories*, pp. 104ff; Carlyle, vol. I, pp. 109ff; Schwer, *Ständeordnung*, pp. 34ff.; Steinbüchel, *Mittelalter*, pp. 259ff.
18. Gierke, *Die Staats- und Korporationslehre des Altertums und des Mittelalters und ihre Aufnahme in Deutschland*, Berlin, 1881, p. 621.
19. E. Barker, *The Political Thought of Plato and Aristotle*, 1906, p. 366; similarly, Troeltsch, *Soziallehren*, p. 410 (*Social Teaching*, vol. I, p. 369).
20. Fritz Kern, *Humana Civilitas. Staat, Kirche und Kultur, eine Danteuntersuchung*, Leipzig, 1913, p. 15.
21. F. Kern, *Gottesgnadentum u. Widerstandsrecht*, p. 213; Figgis, *Political Thought*, p. 17.
22. Carl Schmitt, *Politische Theologie*, 2nd ed., Munich and Leipzig, 1934, p. 10.
23. Gierke, *Korporationslehre*, pp. 9ff.; Figgis, *Political Thought*, p. 57.
24. Gierke, *Korporationslehre*, p. 104, n. 9.
25. Idem, p. 105, n. 10; Figgis, *Political Thought*, p. 57.
26. Carlyle, vol. I, pp. 22ff.; Kern, *Gottesgnadentum*, App. XXIII, pp. 396ff.
27. Carlyle, vol. II, p. 203; McIlwain, *Political Thought*, p. 220.
28. Kern, *Gottesgnadentum*.
29. Troeltsch, *Soziallehren*, p. 283 (*Social Teaching*, vol. I, p. 269) — criticism of the Nominalists on the reconciliation ethics of Thomas Aquinas.
30. Cf. edition of C. P. Prévité-Orton, Cambridge, 1928.
31. Gierke, *Korporationslehre*, p. 46.
32. Translation from McIlwain, *Political Thought*, p. 303.
33. Figgis, *Political Thought*, p. 41.
34. Original text in ibid., p. 41; transl. by McIlwain, *Political Thought*, p. 34, as follows: "A general Council constituting and representing the Catholic Church, has authority immediately from Christ, which everyone in existence of whatsoever status and dignity, even of Papal, is bound to obey in those things which pertain to faith".
35. Figgis, *Political Thought*, p. 68.
36. Ibid.; McIlwain, *Political Thought*, p. 349.
37. As does also Borkenau, p. 43.

CHAPTER 4

1. William A. Robson, *Civilisation and the Growth of Law*, London, 1935, p. 169.
2. F. Kern, *Gottesgnadentum u. Widerstandsrecht*, p. 143; Stubbs, I, pp. 213, 290.

3. Kern, *Gottesgnadentum*, Appendix VIII, pp. 317, 325; Stubbs, pp. 158, 141; Pollock-Maitland, I, p. 41.
4. Kern, *Gottesgnadentum*, Appendices XX, XXI.
5. Pollock-Maitland, *The History of English Law before the Time of Edward I*, Cambridge, 1895, I, p. 524; Kern, *Gottesgnadentum*, p. 171; J. N. Figgis, *Studies of Political Thought from Gerson to Grotius*, Cambridge, 1916, p. 57.
6. Carlyle, II, p. 203.
7. Otto von Gierke, *Johannes Althusius*, 2nd ed., Breslan, 1902, pp. 71–2.
8. Kurt Wolzendorff, *Staatsrecht und Naturrecht.*
9. Gierke, *Althusius*, pp. 125ff.
10. Kern, *Gottesgnadentum*, p. 277; Theodore F. T. Plucknett, *A Concise History of the Common Law*, Rochester, NY, 1929, p. 23.
11. McKechnie, *Magna Carta*, p. 475.
12. Introduction to Harold J. Laski, *Junius Brutus, A Defense of Liberty against Tyrants*, London, 1924, p. 6.
13. On the problem see, above all: Charles Labitte, *De la democratie chez les prédicateurs de le Ligue*, 2nd ed. Paris, 1865; G. P. Gooch and Harold J. Laski, *English Democratic Ideas in the 17th Century*, 2nd ed., Cambridge, 1927, pp. 9–23; Laski, *Junius Brutus*; Wolzendorff, *Staatsrecht*.
14. This word "natural-rightly" has been created by Maitland in connection with Gierke's *Political Theory of the Middle Ages* and in accordance with the German "Naturrechtlich".
15. Gooch and Laski, *English Democratic Ideas*, p. 14.
16. Labitte, *De la democratie*, p. 366.
17. See: C. H. McIlwain, *The High Court of Parliament and its Supremacy*, New Haven, 1910; Gooch and Laski, *English Democratic Ideas*; C. G. Haines, *The Revival of Natural Law Concepts*, Cambridge, Mass., 1930; H. E. Malden (ed.), *Magna Carta Commemoration Essays*, 1917; Sir Frederick Pollock, *Essays in the Law*, London, 1922; idem, *The Expansion of Common Law*, n.d.; idem, "A Plea For an Historical Interpretation", *Law Review*, XXXIX, 1923, p. 165; William S. McKechnie, *Magna Carta*, 2nd ed.; Theodore F. Plucknett, "Bonham's Case and Judicial Review", *Harvard Law Review*, XL, 1926, p. 30; F. W. Maitland, *The Constitutional History of England*, Cambridge; William S. Holdsworth, *A History of English Law*, 4th ed.; idem, "Sir Edward Coke", *The Cambridge Law Journal*, 5, 1935, pp. 332ff.; Henri Lévy-Ullmann, *The English Legal Tradition*, London, 1935, p. 222.
18. Pollock, *Expansion*, p. 108; idem, *Essays*, pp. 63, 68, 69; Haines, *Natural Law Concepts*, pp. 39ff.
19. William A. Robson, *Civilisation*, 1935, p. 231.
20. McIlwain, *High Court*, pp. 42ff.
21. 8 Co. 114 a (C.P. 1610) and 2 Brown 1. 255 (C.P. 1610).
22. Holdsworth, *English Law*, V, p. 475.
23. McIlwain, *High Court*, p. 91.
24. Gooch and Laski, *English Democratic Ideas*, p. 99; McIlwain, *High Court*, p. 154.
25. Cf. Holdsworth, *English Law*, IV, p. 187.

26. A further example is offered by the French theory of the "souveraintè de raison", for instance in Quesnay, du Pont de Nemours and others. This theory justified the monarchy. Karl Marx (*Die Heilige Familie*, chap. VI, 1) has directed attention to the fact that "The doctrinaires who proclaim the sovereignty of reason in opposition to the sovereignty of the people [did this] in order to exclude the masses and to dominate alone". Today [1936] especially the revival of the sovereignty of reason against that of the people, which has become dangerous for private property, is very clearly shown in Barthélémy-Duaz, *Traité de droit constitutionel*, 1933, p. 78. Cf. also the very clear discussion by Kirchheimer, "Remarques sur la théorie de la souveraineté nationale en Allemagne et en France", *Archives de Philosophie du droit*, IV, nos. 3, 4, 1934, pp. 239ff.

CHAPTER 5

1. Roger Chauviré, *Jean Bodin, Auteur de la République*, Paris, 1914; J. W. Allen, *A History of Political Thought in the 16th Century*, London, 1928, p. 394; Friedrich Meinecke, *Die Idee der Staatsraison*, Munich and Berlin, 1924, pp. 70ff.; Carl Schmitt, *Die Diktatur*, 2nd ed., Munich and Leipzig, 1928, pp. 25ff.; J. N. Figgis, *Studies of Political Thought from Gerson to Grotius*, Cambridge, 1916, pp. 123ff.; Jean Bodin, *Les six livres de la République*, Lyons, 1588.
2. "La souveraineté est la puissance absolue et perpetuelle d'une République que les Latins appellent majestatem. . . .", Bodin, *Les six livres*, I.VIII.
3. "La loy n'est autre chose que le commandement du souverain, usant de sa puissance" and "La loy. . .prend sa vigeur de celuy qui a puissance de commander à tous", ibid., I.X; "Si donc le Prince souverain est exempt des loix de ses prédesseurs, beaucoup moins seroit-il tenu aux loix et ordonnances qu'il fait; car on peut bien recevoir loy d'autruy, mais il est impossible par nature de se donner loy . . .", ibid., I.VIII.
4. Allen, *Political Thought* pp. 415–16.
5. Borkenau, *Vom feudalen zum bürgerlichen Weltbild*, p. 119.
6. "République est un droit gouvernement de plusieurs ménages et de ce qui leur est commun, avec puissance souveraine", Bodin, *Les six livres*, I.I.
7. "Car si la justice est la fin de la loy, la loy oeuvre du Prince, le Prince image de Dieu, il faut par mesure suite de raison que la loy du Prince soit faicte au modelle de loy de Dieu", ibid., I.VIII.
8. "Mais quant aux loix divines et naturelles, tous les Princes de la terre y sont subjects, et n'est pas en leur puissance d'y contrevenir. Et par ainsi la puissance absolue des Princes et seigneuries souveraines, ne s'étend aucunement aux loix de Dieu et de nature", ibid., I.VIII.

9. Meinecke, *Staatsraison*, p. 64.
10. Cf. Chauviré, *Bodin*, pp. 304ff.
11. "Il est impossible que la République vaille rien les familles, qui sont les pilliers d'icelle sont mal fondées", Bodin, *Les six livres*, I.IV.
12. "En ôtant les mots Tien et Mien, on ruine les fondements de toutes Républiques", ibid., VI.IV.
13. "Aussi c'est mal parlé de dire que le Prince souverain a puissance de voler le bien d'autruy et de mal faire; veu que c'est plutost impuissance foiblesse et lascheté de coeur. Si donc le Prince souverain n'a pas puissance de franchir les bornes des loix de nature, que Dieu duquel il est l'image, a posées, il ne pourra aussi prendre le bien d'autruy, sans cause qui soit juste et raisonnable, soit par achat, ou exchange, ou confiscation légitime, ou traittant paix avec l'ennemi", ibid., I.VIII.
14. "Il n'est en la puissance de Prince du monde de lever impost à son plaisir sur le peuple, non plus que de rendre le bien d'autruy", ibid., I.VI; VI.II.
15. Allen, *Political Thought*, p. 421.
16. "Car quelquefois la loy civile sera bonne, iuste et raisonnable; et néanmoins le prince n'y doit etre suiet aucunement", Bodin, *Les six livres*, I.VIII.
17. "Le Prince souverain est tenu aux contracts par loy faicts, soit avec son subject soit avecques l'étranger", ibid., I.VIII.
18. "L'obligation est double: l'une pour l'équité naturelle qui veut que les conventions et promesses soyent entretenues: l'autres pour la foy du Prince", ibid., I.VIII.
19. "Or la plus noble différence du roy et du tyran est, que le roy se conforme aux loix de nature: et le tyran les foule aux pieds", ibid., II.IV.
20. "Qui, de sa propre auctorité, se faict Prince souverain, sans élection, ny droit successif, ny sort, ny iuste guerre, ny vocation speciale de Dieu", ibid., II.V; Chauviré, Bodin, p. 322.
21. "Loix qui concernent l'état du Royaume et de l'etablissement d'icelui . . . annexées et unies avec la couronne", Bodin, *Les six livres*, I.VIII.
22. This is one of the cases already mentioned, in which he already makes a distinction between sovereignty and the bearer of sovereignty.
23. Allen, *Political Thought*, p. 417.
24. Figgis, *Political Thought*, p. 126.
25. Chauviré, Bodin, pp. 148ff., 161ff.
26. This has since been published under several different titles.
27. Chauviré, *Bodin*, pp. 482–3.
28. As Chauviré remarked, Bodin assumed a loyalty on the part of the estates towards the crown.
29. C. J. Friedrich (ed.), *Politica Methodice Digesta of Johannes Althusius*, 1932; Figgis, *Political Thought*, pp. 230ff.; Otto von Gierke, *Althusius*, 2nd ed., Breslau, 1902; Borkenau, *Weltbild*, pp. 122ff.; Kurt Wolzendorff, *Staatsrecht u. Naturrecht*, pp. 180ff.

30. Friedrich, *Politica Methodice*, p. lix.
31. Ibid., pp. xxix, xxxvii; Figgis, *Political Thought*, pp. 218ff.; Borkenau, *Weltbild*, pp. 122ff.
32. Friedrich, *Politica Methodice*, p. lxx.
33. C. 9, 4 (p. 88): "Nam et regni proprietas est populi . . .".
34. Cf. Friedrich, *Politica Methodice*, p. xci.
35. C. 9, 16.
36. Borkenau, *Weltbild*, p. 131.
37. C. 18, 48 (p. 143).
38. C. 18, 91 (p. 151).
39. C. 18, 91 (p. 151); 29, 2 (p. 275).
40. 29, 4 (p. 275); 29, 5 (p. 276).
41. Roscoe Pound, *The Spirit of Common Law*, p. 1.
42. C. 10, 7 (p. 96).
43. C. 38 1 (p. 337): "Tyrannis igitur est justae et rectae administratione contraria, qua fundamenta et vinicula universalis consociationis obstinate, perseveranter insanabiliter contra fidem datam et praestitum juramentum, a magistratu summo tolluntur et evertuntur"; C. 39, 9.
44. C. 38, 28 (p. 382): "Cognita tyrannidis natura videndum nunc est de remedio, quo tempestive illa tollatur; quod consistit in resistentia et exauctoratione tyranni, solis optimatibus concessa"; C. 38, 65 (p. 390): "Quid vero de subditis et privatis ex populo sentiendu est? Nam quae hactenus diximus de ephoris, personis publicis dicta sunt. Plane hi privati, quando magistratus tyrannus est exercitio, quia non habent usum et jus gladii, neque co jure utentur . . . sed quiesent et injuriam patientes, jugum tyranni ferent . . . ".
45. Wolzendorff, *Staatsrecht*, p. 223.

CHAPTER 6

1. Grotius, *De jure belli ac pacis libri tres* (transl. F. W. Kelsey, Oxford, 1925); W. S. M. Knight, *The Life and Works of Hugo Grotius*, London, 1925; Erik Wolf, *Grotius, Pufendorf, Thomasius*, Tübingen, 1927; L. Neumann, *Hugo Grotius*, Hamburg, 1884.
2. *Prol.* 9, p. 13: "Long ago the view came to be held by many that this discriminating allotment is a part of law . . . nevertheless law . . . has a far different nature because its essence lies in leaving to another that which belongs to him, or in fulfilling our obligation to him".
3. Bk I, C.I.X.1, p. 38: "The law of Nature is a dictate of right reason which points out that an act, according as it is or is not in conformity with rational nature, has in it a duality of moral baseness or moral necessity; so that in consequence, such an act is either forbidden or enjoined by the author of nature, God".
4. Friedrich Meinecke, *Die Idee der Staatsraison*, Munich and Berlin, 1924, p. 261.

5. Bk I, C.III.XIV, p. 120: "Sovereignty must in itself be distinguished from the absolute possessor of it".
6. Samuel Pufendorf, *Elementorum Jurisprudentiae Universalis. Libri Duo*, 1660 (transl. W. A. Oldfather, Oxford, 1931); idem, *De Officio Hominis et Civis juxta Legam Naturalem, Libri Duo*, 1673 (transl. T. G. Moore, Oxford, 1927).
7. "Law . . . is a decree by which a superior obliges a subject to conform his acts to his own prescription."
8. "Man shares with all the animals that . . . he holds nothing dearer than himself, and is eager to preserve himself": *De Officio*, I, c.III.2 (p. 17).
9. "Those which teach how man should conduct himself, to become a good member of human society, are called natural laws . . . . The fundamental natural law is this: that every man must cherish and maintain sociability, so far as in him lies. From this follows that, as he who wishes an end, wishes also the means, without which the end cannot be obtained, all things which necessarily and universally make for that sociability are understood to be ordained by natural law, and all that confuse or destroy it forbidden. The remaining precepts are mere corollaries, so to speak, under this general law, and the natural light given to mankind declares that they are evident": *De Officio*, I, c.III.8, 9 (p. 19).
10. "That any one whatsoever should protect his own life and limbs, as far as he can, and save himself and what is his own."
11. "A man tends to promote the advantage of others indefinitely, if he thoroughly cultivates his own soul and body, so that useful actions may emanate from him to others."
12. "For, but for this, we should lose the greatest part of the advantage which is apt to arise for the race from the interchange of services and property. *And where there is not the necessity of keeping promises*, one could not build one's calculations firmly upon the *support of others*!"
13. "All onerous contracts. . .have this feature that equality must be preserved in them, in other words, that each of the contracting parties make an equal gain; and where an inequality arises, the one who has received less acquires a right to demand that this lack be made good, or the contract be broken off entirely. This, however, is particularly the case in states, where prices are fixed by the usage of the markets or by law."
14. "By the will of God, the consent of men in advance, and an agreement at least tacit, property in things, or ownership, was introduced."
15. "That he should not disturb human society, or in other words, that he should not do anything whereby society among men may be less tranquil."
16. "Natural law is not sufficient to restrain man from evil. Neither fear of the Divinity nor sting of conscience are sufficient."
17. "Genuine and principal reason why the patriarchs, abandoning their natural liberty, took to founding states, was that they might fortify

themselves against the evils which threaten man from man."

18. "A state is defined as a composite moral person, whose will intertwined and united by virtue of the compacts of the many, is regarded as the will of all, so that it can use the powers and resources of all *for the common peace and security.*"
19. "Wills of many can be united in no other way than if each subjects his will to the will of one man, or one counsel, so that henceforth, whatever such as one shall will *concerning things necessary to the common* security, must be accompted the will of all, collectively and singly."
20. *De Officio*, II, C.IX.1 (p. 116): "Every authority by which an entire state is ruled, in any form of government, has this quality, that it is supreme, that it is not dependent on its exercise on any man as a superior, but operating according to its own judgement and discretion so that its acts cannot be nullified by any man as a superior".
21. *De Officio*, II, C.IX.3 (p. 116): "Superior to human and civil laws as such and thus not directly bound by them. For those laws are dependent upon the supreme authority in origin as well as in duration."
22. *De Officio*, II, C.XII.1 (p. 124): "Civil laws which are decrees of the civil rulers by which it is enjoined upon the citizens what they ought to do in the civil life and what they should leave undone."
23. *Elementorum*, 1, def. XIII.19 (p. 162): "Objects of civil law is in general all that which can be effectively enjoined by a supreme human authority. The inner acts of the mind in regard of which laws are enacted in vain, are excluded because, forsooth, it is beyond the power of other men to know whether obedience has been rendered".
24. "To the civil law, in so far as they do not openly conflict with the divine law, the citizens owe obedience, not from mere dread of punishment, but from an intrinsic obligation, confirmed by the natural law itself; for among its precepts is this also that one must obey lawful rulers."

CHAPTER 7

1. Paul Johann Anselm Feuerbach, *Anti-Hobbes*, 1798; Ferdinand Toennies, *Thomas Hobbes, Leben und Lehre*, 3rd ed.; Richard Hönigswald, *Hobbes und die Staatsphilosophie*, Munich, 1924; Z. Lubiensky, *Die Grundlagen des ethisch-politischen Systems von Hobbes*, Munich, 1932; Julius Lips, *Die Stellung des Thomas Hobbes zu den politischen Parteien der grossen englischen Revolution*, Leipzig, 1927; John Laird, *Hobbes*, London, 1934; C. I. Vaughan, *Studies in the History of Political Thought before and after Rousseau*, vol. I, Manchester, 1925, pp. 25ff.; *The English Works of Thomas Hobbes*, ed. Molesworth, London, 1839 et seq.
2. Cf. Feuerbach, *Anti-Hobbes*, p. 3.
3. For example, Carl Schmitt, *Die Diktatur*, 2nd ed., Munich and Leipzig, 1928, pp. 22–3; M. B. Foster, *The Political Philosophies of Plato and Hegel*,

Oxford, 1935, p. 147.

4. Thomas Hobbes *Leviathan*, ed. Molesworth, III.XVI, p. 147.
5. Ibid., III.XVV, p. 117.
6. Ibid., III.XIV, pp. 117–18.
7. See his fragment, "L'Etat de Guerre", included by Vaughan, *Political Writings of Rousseau*, vol. I, p. 305.
8. Hobbes, *Leviathan*, III.XV, p. 145.
9. Ibid., III.XV, p. 145.
10. Lubiensky, *Grundlagen*, pp. 179–85; Georg Jäger, "Ursprung der modernen Staatswissenschaft und die Anfänge des modernen Staates", in *Archiv f. Geschichte der Philosophie*, VI.XIV, p. 570; Laird, *Hobbes*, p. 205.
11. Hobbes, *Leviathan*, III.XVIII, p. 165.
12. Laird, *Hobbes*, pp. 57–9.
13. Hobbes, *Leviathan*, III.XXI, p. 204.
14. Cf. Max Horkheimer, *Anfänge der bürgerlichen Geschichtsphilosophie*, Stuttgart, 1930, p. 56.
15. Otto von Gierke, *Althusius*, 2nd ed., Breslau, 1902, p. 70.
16. J. F. Horn, apparently the most important contemporary critic of Hobbes, is not even mentioned in the paper by J. A. Thomas, "Some contemporary critics of Hobbes", *Economica*, 1929, pp. 185ff.
17. F. J. Stahl, *Über die gegenwärtigen Parteien in Staat und Kirche*, Berlin, 1883, p. 23.
18. Thomas Hobbes, *Philosophical Rudiments*, ed. Molesworth, II.CXIV, p. 183.
19. Idem, *A Dialogue*, ed. Molesworth, VI, p. 26.
20. See Lips, *Stellung*.
21. Pp. 46–7.
22. Horkheimer, *Anfänge*, p. 39.
23. H. J. Laski, *State in Theory and Practice*, p. 18.
24. E. F. Carritt, *Morals and Politics*, pp. 32–3.
25. Hobbes, *Leviathan*, III.XVIII, p. 165.
26. Ibid., III.XIX, p. 175.
27. F. Atger, *Essai sur l'Histoire des Doctrines du Contrat Social*, 1906, p. 176.
28. *De Corpore Politico* (II.1.23.3); *De Cive* (II.5.6).
29. G. P. Gooch, *Political Theory*, p. 48.
30. Hobbes, *Leviathan*, III.XVIII, p. 160.
31. Idem, *Philosophical Rudiments*, II, p. 96.
32. Idem, *De Corpore Politico*, IV.II, p. 138.
33. Idem, *Leviathan*, III, p. 199.
34. Idem, *Elem.*, IV, p. 84.
35. Robert A. Duff, *Spinoza's Political and Ethical Philosophy*, Glasgow, 1903; Sir Frederick Pollock, *Spinoza, His Life and Philosophy*, London, 1899; W. Eckstein, *Zur Lehre vom Staatsvertrag bei Spinoza*, *Zeitschr. f. öffentl. Recht*, vol. XIII, 1933; W. Eckstein, *Die rechtsphilosophische Lehre des Spinoza im Zusammenhang mit seiner allgemeinen Philosophie*, Archiv f. Rechts- und Wirtschaftsphilosophie, vol. 26, 1933; Adolf Menzel, *Beiträge zur Geschichte der Staatslehre*, Vienna and Leipzig, 1929; C. F.

Vaughan, *Studies in the History of Political Thought Before and After Rousseau*, vol. 1, Manchester, 1925, pp. 62ff.; Spinoza, *Tractatus Teologico-Politicus* (TTP), 1670; idem, *Tractatus Politicus (TP) (Opera*, ed. van Vlooten & Land, 3rd ed., 1913).

36. Gierke-Barker, 1, p. 112.
37. Menzel, *Beiträge*, p. 375.
38. Pollock, *Spinoza*, p. 292.
39. Menzel, *Beiträge*, pp. 282ff.
40. Spinoza, *Opera*, vol. 3: "Et quia lex summa Naturae est, ut unaquaeque res in suo statu, quantum in se est, conetur persevare, idque nulla alterius, sed tantum sui habita ratione, hinc sequitur, unumquodque individuum jus summum ad hoc habere, hoc est (uti dixi) ad existendum et operandum prout naturaliter determinatum est. Nec hic ullam agnoscimus differentiam inter homines Ratione praeditos et inter alios, qui veram Rationem ignorant; neque inter fatuos, delirantes, et sanos. Quicquid enim unaquaeque res ex legibus suae naturae agit, id summo jure agit, nimirum quia agit, prout ex Natura determinata est, nec aliud potest . . . . Ex quibus sequitur, Jus et Institutum Naturae sub quo omines nascuntur, et maxima ex parte vivunt, nihil, nisi quod nemo cupit et quod nemo potest, prohibere; non contentiones, non iram, non dolos, nec absolute aliquid quod Appetitus suadet aversari. Nec mirum, nam natura non legibus humanae Rationis, quae non nisi hominum verum utile et conversationem intendunt, intercluditur, sed infinitis allis, quae totius Naturae, cujus Homo particula est, aeternum ordinem respiciunt; ex cujus sola necessitate omnia individus certo modo determinantur ad existendum et operandum".
41. *TP*, XI.30.11, pp. 9–11.
42. Menzel, as against Gierke's *Althusius* (2nd ed., p. 343; 3rd ed., pp. 379–80).
43. *TTP*, chap. XIV: "Quod si etiam consideremus, homines absque mutuo auxilio miserrime et absque Rationis cultu necessario vivere, ut in Cap. 5 ostendimus, clarissime videbimus, homines ad secure et optime vivendum necessario in unum conspirare debuisse, ac proinde affecisse, ut jus, quod unusquisque ex Natura ad omnia habeat, coolective haberent, neque amplius ex vi et appetitu uniuscujusque, sed ex omnium simul potentia et volumtate determinaretur. Quod tamen frustra tentassent, si, nisi quod appetitus suadet, sequi vellent (ex legibus enim appetitus unusquisque diverse trahitur); adeoque firmissime statuere et pacisci debuerunt, ex solo Rationis dictamine (cui nemo aperte repugnare audet, ne mente carere videatur) omnia dirigere, et appetitum, quatemus in damnum alterius aliquid suadet, fraenare, neminique facere, quod sibi fieri non vult, jusque denique alterius tanquam suum defendere".
44. *TTP*, chap. XIV: "Si. . .unus quisque omnem, quam habet, Potentiam in societatem transferat; quae adeo summum Naturae jus in omnia . . . Ex quo sequitur, summam Potestatem nulla lege teneri, sed omnes ad omnia ei parere debere: hoc enim taciti vel expresse pacisci debuerunt

omnes, cum omnem suam potentiam se defendendi, hoc est omne suum jus, in eam trastulerunt. Quippe, si aliquid sibi servatum volebant, debuerant simul sibi cavere, quo id tuto defendere possent; eum autem id non fecerint, nec absque imperii divisione, et consequenter destructione, facere potuerint, eo ipso se arbitrio summae potestatis absolute subriserunt. Quod cum absolute fecerint, idque (ut jam ostendimus) et necessitate cogente, et ipsa Ratione suadente; hinc sequitur, quod, nisi hostes Imperii esse velimus, et contra Rationem, Imperium summis viribus defendere suadentem, agere, omnia absolute summae potestatis mandata exequi etiam jubet".

45. *TTP*, chap. XIX: "At, ut verae Rationis documenta, hoc est . . . ipsa divina documenta, vim juris absolute haberent, necesse fuisse, ut unusquisque jure suo naturali cederet, et omnes idem in omnes, vel in aliquot, vel in unum transferrent; et tum demum nobis primum innotuit, quid justitia, quid injustitia, quid aequitas, quidque iniquitas esset. Justitia igitur, et absolute omnia verae Rationis documenta, et consequenter erga proximum charitas, a solo imperii jure, hoc est . . . a solo eorum decreto, qui jus imperandi habent, vim juris et mandati accipiunt. Et quia (ut jam ostendi) in solo justitiae et charitatis, sive verae Religionis, jure Dei Regnum consistit, sequitur, ut volebamus, Deum nullum regnum in homines habere, nisi per vim mandati a Deo immidiate non accipiunt, sed necessario ab iis, vel mediantibus iis, qui jus imperandi et decretandi habent; adeoque non, nisi mediantibus iisdem, concipere possumus, Deum in homines regnare, resque humanas secundum justitiam et aequitatem dirigere. Quod ipsa etiam experimenta comprobatur; nam nulla divinae justitiae vestigia reperiuntur, nisi ubi justi regnant".
46. *TP*, II.18; "Ex lui, quae in hoc capite ostendimus, perspicuum nobis fit, in statu naturali non dari peccatum".
47. *TP*, IV.5: "Videmus itaque, quo sensu dicere possumus, Civitatem legibus teneri, et peccare posse. Verum si per legem intelligamus Jus Civile, quod ipso Jure Civile vindicare potest, est peccatum id, quod Jure Civile fieri prohibetur, hoc est si haec nomina genuino senso sumantur, nulla ratione dicere possumus, civitatem legibus adstrictam esse, aut possere peccare . . . . At Jure civilis pendent a solo Civitatis decreto,. . . .".
48. *TP*, II.23: "Sed omnia omnium sunt, qui scilicet potestam habent sibi eadem vindicandi".
49. *TP*, III.16.
50. *TP*, IV.5.
51. *TP*, IV.5.
52. *TTP*, V.2: "Qualis autem cujuscunque Imperii sit status facile ex fine Status Civilis cognoscitur: qui scilicet nullus alius est, quam pax vitaeque securitas. Ac proinde illud imperium optimum est, ubi homines concorditer vitam transigunt, et cujus jura inviolata servantur".
53. *TTP*, V.4: "Civitas, cujus subditi, metù territi, arma non capiunt, potius dicenda est, quod sine bello sit quam quod pacem habeat. Pax

enim non bello privatio, sed virtus est, quae ex animi fortitudine oritur: est namque obsequimum constans voluntas id exequendi, quod ex communi Civitatis decreat fieri debit. Illa praetera Civitas cujus pax a subditorum inertia pendet, qui scilicet voluti pecora ducuntur, ut tuntam servire discant, rectius solitudo quam Civitas dici potest".

54. *TP*, I.6: "Imperium igitur, cujus salus ab alicuius fide pendit .... minime stabile erit".
55. *TTP*, V.
56. *TTP*, XX.
57. *TP*, VI.4.
58. *TP*, VII.1: "Ut omne jus sit regis explicata voluntas jus sit".
59. *TP*, VIII.1.
60. Cf. Duff, Spinoza, pp. 146ff., and *TTP*, XVI; *TP*, II.4: "Per Jus itaque Naturae intelligo ipsas Naturae leges seu regulas secundum quas omnia fiunt, hoc est ipsam naturae potentiam; atque adeo totius Nature, et consequenter uniuscujusque individui Naturale Jus eo usque se extendit, quo ejus potentia; et consequenter quicquid unusquisque homo ex legibus suae naturae agit, id súmmo Naturae Jure agit, tantumque in Naturam habet, juris quantum potentia valet".
61. For a similar formulation see Pufendorf, *Elementorum*, 1. def. XIII.19: "Objects of civil law are in general all that which can be effectively enjoined by a supreme human authority. The inner acts of the mind in regard to which laws are enacted in vain are excluded therefrom, because for sooth, it is beyond the power of other men to know whether obedience has been rendered".
62. *TP*, III.8.
63. *TP*, III.10.
64. *TTP*, VII.
65. *TTP*, VII.
66. Cf. Wolf (ed.), *The Correspondence of Spinoza*, London, 1928, Epist. 50.
67. *TTP*, XVII: "Contemplatii precedentis Capitis de jure naturali uniuscujusque in cardem translato, quamvis cum praxis ita instituti possit, ut ad candem magis ac magis accedat, umquam tamen fiet, quin in multis mere theoretica maneat. Nam nemo unquam suam potentiam et consequenter neque suum jus ita in alium transferre poterit, ut homo esse desinat".
68. *TP*, III.10.
69. *TP*, III.10.
70. Vaughan, *Studies*, p. 79.
71. *TP*, III.5: "Videmus itaque, unumquamque civem non sui sed Civitatis juris esse, cujus omnia mandata tenetur exequi".
72. *TP*, XI.3: "Ex dictis in praec. Art. patet, nos posse imperii Democratici diversa genera concipere; sed meum institutum non est de unoquoque sed de eo solumnodo agere, ni quos omnes absolute, qui solis legibus patriis tenentur, et *praetera sui juris* sunt, honesteque vivunt, jus suffrajii ni supremo Consilio habent, numeraque imperii subeundi".
73. *TP*, II.9: "Praeterea sequitur, unumquemque tamdia alterius esse

juris, quamdia sub alterius potestate est . . . . eatemus sui juris, quaetemus vim omnem repellere damnumque sibi illatum ex sui animi sententia vindicare, et absolute, quatemus ex suo ingenio vivere potest".

74. *TP*, VIII.21: ". . .quae prudentissimus belga v. H".
75. *TP*, VIII.4–6, 13–14.

CHAPTER 8

1. John Locke, *Of Civil Government, Two Treatises*; Charles Bastide, *John Locke*, 1907; H. R. Fox Bourne, *The Life of John Locke*, London, 1876; Harold J. Laski, *Political Thought in England from Locke to Bentham*; Pashal Larkin, *Property in the 18th Century with Special Reference to England and Locke*, Cork, 1930; C. E. Vaughan, *Studies in Political Thought*, vol. 1, pp. 130ff.
2. Cf. chapter on Thomas Aquinas.
3. Thomas Locke, *Essay Concerning Human Understanding*, Bk LV, chap. IX.
4. 11, chap. II, 6–8.
5. Vaughan, *Political Thought*, p. 131.
6. 11, chap. III, 19.
7. 11, chap. II, 11; also 11, chap. V, 34; 11, chap. XI, 134–7; 11, chap. XVI, 183.
8. 11, chap. V, 27.
9. 11, chap. XI, 134: "The great end of men's entering into society being the enjoyment of their properties in peace and safety, and the great instrument and means of that being the laws established in that society, the first and fundamental positive law of all commonwealths is the establishing of the legislative power, as the first and fundamental natural law which is to govern even the legislative. This legislative is not only the supreme power of the commonwealth, but sacred and unalterable in the hands where the community have once placed it".
10. "Through the legislative, whether placed in one or more, whether it be always in being or only by intervals, though it be the supreme power in every commonwealth, yet, first it is not, nor can possibly be, absolutely arbitrary over the lives and fortunes of the people."
11. 11, chap. XI, 135: "For nobody can transfer to another more power than he has in himself, and nobody has an absolute arbitrary power over himself, or over any other, to destroy his own life, or take away the life or property of another".
12. 11, chap. XI, 140: "But still it must be with his own consent - i.e., the consent of the majority, giving it either by themselves or their representatives chosen by them; for if any one shall claim a power to lay and levy taxes on the people by his own authority, and without such consent of the people, he thereby invades the fundamental law of property, and subverts the end of government".

13. 11, chap. XI, 139: "But yet we see that neither the sergeant that could command a soldier to march up to the mouth of a cannon, or stand in a breach where he is almost sure to perish, can command that soldier to give him one penny of his money".
14. 11, chap. XII, 144: "But because the laws that are at once, and in a short time made, have a constant and lasting force".
15. The quotation from Hooker occurs in chap. XI, 136.
16. 11, chap. XI, 137: "And therefore, whatever form the commonwealth is under, the ruling power ought to govern by declared and received laws, and not by extemporary dictates and undetermined resolutions, for then mankind will be in a far worse condition than in the state of Nature if they shall have armed one or a few men with the joint power of a multitude, to force them to obey at pleasure the exorbitant and unlimited decrees of their sudden thoughts, or unrestrained, and till that moment, unknown wills, without having any measures set down which may guide and justify their action".
17. 11, chap. XI, 134: "This legislative is not only the supreme power of the commonwealth, but sacred and unalterable in the hands where the community have once placed it".
18. 11, chap. XI, 141: "The legislative cannot transfer the power of making laws to any other hands, for it being but a delegated power from the people, they who have it cannot pass it over to others".
19. 11, chap. XII, 148: "Though, as I said, the executive and federative power of every community be really distinct in themselves, yet they are hardly to be separated and placed at the same time in the hands of distinct persons".
20. On the whole matter, see Laski, *Political Thought*, p. 40.
21. Vaughan, *Political Thought*, p. 169.
22. 11, chap. VIII, 111.
23. It must, however, be noted here that in certain circumstances he affirms the existence of such limitation of the prerogative by general rules: 11, chap. XVIII, 206.
24. 11, chap. XIV, 160: "This power to act according to discretion for the public good, without the prescription of the law and sometimes even against it, is that which is called prerogative".
25. 11, chap. XIV, 168: "And where the body of the people, or any single man, are deprived of their right, or are under the exercise of a power without right, having no appeal on earth they have a liberty to appeal to Heaven whenever they judge the cause of sufficient moment".
26. 11, chap. XIV, 168: "Between an executive power in being, with such a prerogative, and a legislative that depends upon his will for their convening, there can be no judge on earth".
27. 26, chap. XV, 172: "Despotical power is an absolute, arbitrary power one man has over another, to take away his life whenever he pleases".
28. 11, chap. XVI, summing up under 196: "The short of the case in conquest is this: The conqueror, if he have a just cause, has a despotical right over the persons of all that actually aided and con-

curred in the war against him, and a right to make up his damage and cost out of their labour and estates, so he injure not the right of any other. Over the rest of the people, if there were any that consented not to the war, and over the children of the captives themselves or the possessions of either he has no power".

29. 11, chap. XVIII, 199: "So tyranny is the exercise of power beyond right, which nobody can have a right to; and this is making use of the power any one has in his hands, not for the good of those who are under it, but for his own private, separate advantage".
30. 11, chap. XVIII, 202: "Wherever law ends, tyranny begins, if the law be transgressed to another's harm; and whosoever in authority exceeds the power given him by the law, and makes use of the force he has under his command to compass that upon the subject which the law allows not, ceases in that to be a magistrate, and acting with authority may be opposed, as any other man who by force invades the right of another".
31. 11, chap. XVIII, 204: "That force is to be opposed to nothing but to unjust and unlawful force. Whoever makes any opposition in any other case draws on himself a just condemnation, both from God and man; and so no such danger or confusion will follow, as is often suggested".
32. 11, chap. XVIII, 208–9.
33. 11, chap. XIX, 232, 233–9: "In whatsoever he has no authority, there he is no king, and may be resisted: for wheresoever the authority ceases, the king ceases too, and becomes like other men who have no authority".
34. 11, chap. XII, 146: "This, therefore, contains the power of war and peace, leagues and alliances, and all the transactions with all persons and communities without the commonwealth, and may be called federative if any one pleases; so the thing be understood, I am indifferent as to the name".
35. 11, chap. XII, 147: "And though this federative power in the well or ill management of it be of great moment to the commonwealth, yet it is much less capable to be directed by antecedent, standing, positive laws than the executive, and so must necessarily be left to the prudence and wisdom of those whose hands it is in, to be managed for the public good".
36. Cf. Fox Bourne, *Life*, vol. I, pp. 292, 311.
37. Cf. ibid., vol. II, p. 508.
38. Cf. Charles Bastide, *John Locke*, p. 132.
39. 11, chap. XIV, 161: "This power, whilst employed for the benefit of the community and suitable to the trust and ends of the government, is undoubted prerogative, and never is questioned".
40. Larkin, *Property* p. 67, and further, M. Beer, *History of British Socialism*, London, 1929, vol. I, pp. 192–3.
41. 11, IV.
42. Cf., on his contradictions as to slavery, Larkin, *Property*, pp. 76ff.
43. Larkin, *Property*, p. 65.
44. Quotation from Larkin, *Property*, p. 36.

CHAPTER 9

1. Ernst Cassirer, *Die Philosophie der Aufklärung*, Tübingen, 1928; "Das Problem Jean-Jacques Rousseau". *Archiv für Geschichte der Philosophie*, vol. 41, 1932, pp. 210ff.; C. E. Vaughan, *The Political Writings of J. J. Rousseau*, 2 vols., Cambridge, 1915; E. H. Wright, *The Meaning of Rousseau*, London, 1929; Harold J. Laski, *The Age of Reason: Studies in Law and Politics*, London, 1932; Georges Gurvitch, *L' Idée du Droit Social*, Paris, 1932; E. F. Carrit, *Morals and Politics*, Oxford, 1935, pp. 56ff.; Alfred Corban, *Rousseau and the Modern State*, London, 1934; Kurt Wolzendorff, *Staatsrecht und Naturrecht in der Lehre vom Widerstandsrecht des Volkes gegen rechtswidrige Ausübung der Staatsgewalt*, Breslau, 1916, pp. 351ff.; A. Schinz, *La Pensée de J. J. Rousseau*, Paris, 1919; Egon Reiche, *Rousseau und das Naturrecht*, Berlin, 1935.
2. See "Exposition of Interpretations", Corban, Rousseau pp. 28ff.
3. "Le cas de dissolution de l'État peut arriver de deux manières: Premièrement, quand le prince n'administère plus l'État selon les lois et qu'il usurpe le pouvoir souverain."
4. Rousseau, *Contrat Social*, III.18: "Les dépositaires de la puissance exécutive ne sont point les maîtres du peuple mais ses officiers".
5. Cf., as to the influence on the Revolution, Egon Zweig, *Die Lehre vom Pouvoir Constitutient*, Tübingen, 1909, p. 72.
6. "Economie Politique", in Vaughan, *Rousseau*, vol. I, p. 253.
7. Ibid., vol. 2, p. 317.
8. Ibid., vol. 1, p. 126.
9. Ibid., p. 14.
10. Ibid., p. 9.
11. Wright, *Rousseau*, p. 71.
12. Vaughan, *Rousseau*, vol. 1, p. 137: "Les modernes ne reconnaissent, sous le nom de loi, qu'une règle prescrite à un être moral, c'est à dire intelligent, libre et considéré dans ses rapports avec d'autres êtres . . . . Mais tant nous ne reconnaîtrons point l'homme naturel, c'est en vain que nous voudrons déterminer la loi qu'il a reçue".
13. Vaughan, Rousseau, vol. 1, pp. 158–9.
14. H. J. Laski, *Political Thought from Locke to Bentham*, p. 59.
15. Vaughan, *Discours*, I.169: "Le premier qui ayant enclos un terrain, s'avisa de dire: Ceci est à moi, et trouva des gens assez simples pour le croire, fit le vrai fondateur de la société civile".
16. Vaughan, *Rousseau*, vol. 1, p. 182.
17. Ibid., p. 181.
18. Cassirer, *Aufklärung*, p. 209.
19. "Si le rétablissement des sciences et des arts a contribué à épurer les moeurs." "Quelle est l'origine de l'inégalité parmi les hommes, et si elle est autorisée par la loi naturelle."
20. Otto von Gierke, *Althusius*, 2nd ed., Breslau, 1902, p. 117.
21. See note 1 to the *Discours*.
22. Cassirer, *Aufklärung*, p. 210.

23. Rousseau, *Contrat Social*, I.6: "Chacun de nous met en commun sa personne et toute sa puissance sous la suprème direction de la volonté générale et nous recevons encore chaque membre comme partie indivisible du tout".
24. Ibid., I.6: "Ces clauses, bien entendues, se réduisent toute à une seule: savoir, l'aliénation totale de chaque associé avec tous ses droits a toute la communauté".
25. Otto von Gierke, *Althusius*, 2nd ed., Breslau, 1902, pp. 116, 117.
26. Rousseau, *Contrat Social*, I.6: "Trouver une forme d'association qui défende et protège de toute la force commune la personne et les biens de chaque associé, et par laquelle chacun s'unissant à tous, n'obéisse pourtant qu'à lui même, et reste aussi libre qu'auparavant".
27. Vaughan, *Rousseau*, II.44: "On convient que tout ce que chacun aliène par le pacte social de sa puissance, de ses biens, de sa liberté, c'est seulement la partie de tout cela *dont l'usage importe à la communauté; mais il faut convenir aussi* que le souverain seul est juge de cette importance" (*Contrat Social*, II.6).
28. Ibid., II.4: "Comme la nature donne à chaque homme un pouvoir absolu sur tous les membres, le pacte social donne au Corps politique un pouvoir absolu sur tous les siens et c'est ce même pouvoir qui, dirigé par la volonté générale, porte, comme j'ai dit, le nom de souveraineté".
29. Cf. e.g. ibid., where he speaks of "la volonté générale ou la loi".
30. Wright, *Rousseau*, p. 78.
31. Rousseau, *Contrat Social*, II.2.
32. Ibid., II.2, note of 1762: "Pour qu'une volonté soit générale, il n'est pas toujours nécessaire qu'elle soit unanime, mais il est nécessaire que toutes les voix soient comptées; toute exclusion formelle rompt la généralité".
33. Vaughan, *Rousseau*, I.245.
34. Ibid., 246.
35. Ibid., 492.
36. Rousseau, *Contrat Social*, II.6: "Quand tout le peuple statue sûr tout le peuple, il ne considère que lui-même; et s'il se forme alors un rapport, c'est de l'objet entier sous un point de vue à l'objet entier sous un autre point de vue, sans aucune division du tout. Alors la matière sûr laquelle on statue est générale comme la volonté qui statue. C'est cette acte que j'appelle un loi.

    Quand je dis que l'objet des lois est toujours général, j'entends que la loi considère les sujets en corps et les actions comme abstraites, jamais un homme comme individu ni une action particulière. Ainsi la loi peut bien statuer qu'il y aura des privilèges, mais *elle n'en peut donner nommément à personne*; . . . en un mot, toute fonction qui se rapporte à un objet individuel n'appartient point à la puissance legislative".
37. Vaughan, *Rousseau*, II, p. 343: "Mais ni les lois agraires, ni aucune loi ne peuvent jamais avoir l'effet rétroactif; et l'on ne peut confisquer nulles terres, acquises légitimement, en quelque quantité qu'elles

puissent être, en vertu d'une loi posterieur, qui défende d'en avoir tant".

38. *Economie Politique*, in Vaughan, *Rousseau*, I.241.
39. Rousseau, *Contrat Social*, III.15.
40. Vaughan, *Rousseau*, II.313.351.
41. Friedrich Julius Stahl, *Die Philosophie des Rechts*, 1847, vol. I, p. 303.
42. Vaughan, *Rousseau*, I, pp. 237–41: "Je prie meș lecteurs de bien distinguer entre l'économie politique, dont j'ai à parler et que j'appelle *Gouvernement*, de l'autorité suprême que j'appelle Souveraineté: distinction qui consiste en ce que l'une a le droit législatif, et oblige, en certains cas, le Corps même de la nation, tandis que l'autre n'a que la puissance exécutrice, et ne peut obliger que les particuliers".
43. Rousseau, *Contrat Social*, II.10.
44. Ibid., III.4.
45. Ibid., II.313.
46. Laski, *Political Thought*, p. 60.
47. *Economie Politique*, in Vaughan, *Rousseau*, I.242: "Toute société politique est composée d'autres sociétées plus petites de différents espèces, dont chacune a ses intérêts et ses maximes . . . tous les particuliers qu'un intérêt commun réunit en composant autant d'autres . . . . Ce sont toutes ses associations tacites ou formelles qui modifient de tant de manières les apparences de la volonté publique par l'influence de la leur".
48. "La volonté de cette société particulière a toujours deux relations: pour les membres de l'association, c'est une volonté générale; pour la grande société, c'est une volonté particulière."
49. Vaughan, *Rousseau*, I.169.
50. V.I.259: "Il est certain que le droit de propriété est le plus sacré . . . et plus important, à certains égards, que la liberté même".
51. Rousseau, *Contrat Social*, I.1; I.9.
52. *Emile* (livre 5), in Vaughan, *Rousseau*, vol. 2, p. 152: "Il est inviolable et sacré pour elle *tant qu'il demeure un droit particulier et individuel: sitôt qu'il est considéré comme commun à tous les citoyens, il est soumis à la volonté générale, et cette volonté peut l'anéantir. Ainsi le souverain n'a nul droit de toucher au bien d'un particulier, ni de plusieurs. Mais il peut legitimement s'emparer du bien de* tous . . .".

    "This right is inviolable and sacred for the State, so long as it remains private and individual. But directly it is considered as a right common to all citizens, it is subordinated to the general will, and the general will can annul it. The sovereign has no right to touch the possessions either of one individual or of several. But it has every right to appropriate the possessions of all . . . ."
53. *Lettres de la Montagne*, in Vaughan, *Rousseau*, II, p. 284, letter 9, ". . . qui craint les exceptions aime les lois".
54. V.2.342.343: "Tous veulent que les conditions soient égales pour tous et la justice, n'est que cette égalité".
55. Vaughan, Rousseau, II, p. 337.

56. Vaughan, *Rousseau*, vol. 2, p. 355: "Car la propriété particulière étant si faible et si dépendante, le Gouvernement n'a besoin que de peu de force et *conduit pour ainsi dire les peuples avec un mouvement du doigt*".

CHAPTER 10

1. Wilhelm Metzger, *Gesellschaft, Recht und Staat in der Ethik des deutschen Idealismus*, Heidelberg, 1917; Emil Lask, *Rechtsphilosophie* (Die Philosophie im Beginn des 20. Jahrhunders), Heidelberg, 1907; Friedrich Julius Stahl, *Die Philosophie des Rechts in geschichtlicher Darstellung*, Heidelberg, 1847; Victor Basch, *Les Doctrines Politiques des Philosophes Classiques de l'Allemagne*, Paris, 1927, pp. 60ff.; E. F. Carritt, *Morals and Politics*, Oxford, 1935, pp. 80ff.; Edward Caird, *A Critical Account of the Philosophy of Kant*, Glasgow, 1877; Kurt Lisser, *Der Begriff des Rechts bei Kant* (Kantstudien, Ergänzungsheft, no. 58), Berlin, 1922; Werner Haensel, *Kants Lehre vom Widerstandsrecht* (Kantstudien, Ergänzungsheft, no. 60), Berlin, 1926.
2. In *Über den Gemeinspruch*, p. 131.
3. Morris Ginsberg, *Modern Theories of Law*, London, 1933, p. 51.
4. The decision is mainly dependent upon the interpretation of his conception of ethics. If with Lisser (*Kant*, p. 4) one construes a broader sense of ethics, law is subordinated to ethics. Further, according to Lisser, ethics as a system of ends comprises the law. Finally, according to Lisser, all obligations belong, as obligations, to ethics. The opposite interpretation, which seems to me to have more foundation, is to be found in Metzger, *Gesellschaft*, p. 83.
5. Ibid., pp. 17–21.
6. Ibid., p. 47.
7. *Grundlegung zur Metaphysik der Sitten, 2. Abschnitt*, transl. J. W. Semple, 3rd ed., 1871, p. 34: "Weil die Allgemeinheit des Gesetzes, wonach Wirkungen geschehen, dasjenige ausmacht, was eigentlich Natur im allgemeinsten Verstande (der Form nach), das ist das Dasein der Dinge heisst, sofern es nach allgemeinen Gesetzen bestimmt ist, so könnte der allgemeine Imperativ der Pflicht auch so lauten: Handle so, als ob die Maxime Deiner Handlungen durch Deinen Willen zum allgemeinen Naturgesetz werden sollte".
8. Ibid., p. 43.
9. Ibid., p. 44.
10. Ibid., pp. 36, 37.
11. *Metaphysik der Sitten, Rechtslehre, Einteilung der Rechtslehre*, A, transl. W. Hastie, 1887, p. 54.
12. Ibid., (Einleitung II), pp. 15–16, 20ff. (transl. Hastie, p. 15).
13. From the *Lose Blätter*, ed. Reicke, quoted Metzger, *Gessellschaft*, p. 71: "Die Rechtslehre enthält den Inbegriff der Pflichten, die unabhängig von allen Bewegursachen zu ihrer Beobachtung stattfinden, die

Tugendlehre aber den Inbegriff der Pflichten, die sich selbst zur Bewegursache machen".

14. *Rechtslehre*, Einleitung III: "Die ethische Gesetzgebung (die Pflichten mögen allenfalls auch äussere sein) ist diejenige, welche nicht äusserlich sein kann; die juridische ist, welche auch äusserlich sein kann. So ist es eine äusserliche Pflicht, sein vertragsmässiges Versprechen zu halten; aber das Gebot, dieses bloss darum zu tun, weil es Pflicht ist, ohne auf eine andere Triebfeder Rücksicht zu nehmen, ist bloss zur äusseren Gesetzgebung gehörig" (transl. Hastie, p. 23).
15. *Metaphysik der Sitten, Tugendlehre*, Einleitung II: "Aller Pflicht korrespondiert ein Recht als Befugnis (facultas moralis generatim) betrachtet, aber nicht aller Pflicht korrespondieren Rechte eines Anderen (facultas juridica), jemanden zu zwingen, sondern diese heissen besonders Rechtspflichten" (transl. Semple, p. 197).
16. Ibid., *Einleitung* IV, "Ebenso ist es ein Widerspruch, eines anderen *Vollkommenheit* mir zum Zweck zu machen und mich zu deren Beförderung für verpflichtet zu halten. Denn darin besteht eben die *Vollkommenheit* eines anderen Menschen als einer Person, dass er *selbst* genügend ist, sich seinen Zweck nach seinem eigenen Begriff von Pflicht zu setzen, und es widerspricht sich, zu fordern (mir zur Pflicht zu machen), dass ich etwas tun soll; was kein anderer als er selbst tun kann" (transl. Semple, p. 201).
17. *Idee zu einer allgemeinen Geschichte*, 5. Satz: ". . . die die grösste Freiheit, mithin einen durchgängigen Antagonismus ihrer Glieder, und doch die genaueste Bestimmung und Sicherung der Grenzen dieser Freiheit hat, damit sie mit der Freiheit anderer bestehen könne".
18. *Rechtslehre*, I.3, p. 41: "Rechtmässige Gesetze (z.B. eheliche, vaterliche, häusliche überhaupt und beliebige mehr)" (transl. Hastie, p. 156).
19. Ibid., p. 41: "Der nicht rechtliche Zustand, das ist derjenige, in welchem keine austeilende Gerechtigkeit ist, heisst der natürliche Zustand (status naturalis)" (transl. Hastie, p. 156).
20. Ibid., I Teil, 1. Hauptstück, p. 9.
21. Ibid., I.2, p. 15: "Die bürgerliche Verfassung, obzwar ihre Wirklichkeit subjektiv zufällig ist, ist gleichwohl objektiv, das ist als Pflicht notwendig. Mithin gibt es in Hinsicht auf dieselbe und ihre Stiftung ein wirkliches Rechtsgesetz der Natur, dem alle àussere Erwerbung unterworfen ist" (transl. Hastie, p. 90).
22. Ibid., I.3, p. 42: "Aus dem Privatrecht im natürlichen Zustand geht nun das Postulat des öffentlichen Rechts hervor: Du sollst im Verhältnis eines unvermeidlichen Nebeneinanderseins mit allen anderen aus jenem heraus in einen rechtlichen Zustand, das ist den einer austeilenden Gerechtigkeit übergehen. Der Grund davon lässt sich analytisch aus dem Begriff des Rechts im äusseren Verhältniss im Gegensatz der Gewalt (violentia) entwickeln" (transl. Hastie, p. 157).
23. Lisser, *Kant*, p. 18.
24. *Rechtslehre*, II.1, p. 47: "Der Akt, wodurch sich das Volk selbst zu

einem Staat konstituiert, eigentlich nur aber die Idee desselben, nach der die Rechtmässigkeit desselben allein gedacht werden kann, ist der ursprüngliche Kontrakt, nach welchem alle (omnes et singuli) im Volk ihre äussere Freiheit aufgeben, um sie als Glieder eines Gemeinwesens, das ist des Volks als Staat betrachtet (universi) sofort wieder aufzunehmen" (transl. Hastie, p. 169).

25. Ibid., p. 45: "Ist die Vereinigung einer Menge Menschen unter Rechtsgesetzen. Sofern diese als Gesetze a priori notwendig, das ist aus Begriffen des äussern Rechts überhaupt von selbst folgend (nicht statutarisch) sind, ist seine Form die Form eines Staats überhaupt, das ist der Staat *in der Idee*, wie er nach reinen Rechtsprinzipien sein soll, welcher jeder wirklichen Vereinigung zu einem gemeinen Wesen (also im inneren) zur Richtschnur (norma) dient" (transl. Hastie, p. 165).
26. Ibid., *Einleitung*, Einteilung B: Denn die "Freiheit" (Unabhängigkeit von einer anderen nötigenden Willkür), "sofern sie mit jedes anderen Freiheit nach einem allgemeinen Gesetz zusammen bestehen kann", das "einzige ursprünglich jedem Menschen kraft seiner Menschheit zustehende Recht" (transl. Hastie, p. 56).
27. Ibid., II.1, Abschnitt, Allgemeine Anmerkung A: "Denn der, welcher die Staatsgewalt einschränken soll, muss doch mehr oder wenigstens gleiche Macht haben als derjenige, welcher eingeschränkt wird; und als ein rechtmässiger Gebieter, der den Untertanen beföhle, sich zu widersetzen, muss er sie auch schützen können und in jedem vorkommenden Falle rechtskräftig urteilen, mithin öffentlich den Widerstand befehligen können. Alsdann ist aber nicht jener, sondern dieser der oberste Befehlshaber; welches sich widerspricht" (transl. Hastie, p. 175).
28. Haensel, *Kants Lehre*, p. 61.
29. *Rechtslehre*, II.1 Abschnitt, allgemeine Anmerkung A. (transl. Hastie, p. 181).
30. Ibid., II.1, Abschnitt, allgemeine Anm. E: "Richterliche Strafe (poena forensis) von der natürlichen Strafe (poena naturalis), wodurch sich das Laster selbstbestraft und auf welche der Gesetzgeber gar nicht Rücksicht nimmt". Diese richterliche Strafe "kann niemals bloss als Mittel, ein anderes Gute zu fördern, für den Verbrecher selbst oder für die bürgerliche Gesellschaft, sondern muss jederzeit nur darum über ihn verhängt werden, weil er verbrochen hat . . . . Das Strafgesetz ist ein kategorischer Imperativ" (transl. Hastie, p. 195).
31. Ibid., "Wenn die Gerechtigkeit untergeht, so hat es keinen Wert mehr, dass Menschen auf Erden leben . . . . Wenn die Menschheit heute untergehen sollte, müsste vorher der letzte im Gefängnis befindliche Mörder sterben . . . Der Mörder muss sterben . . . . Hat er gemordet, so muss er sterben. Es gibt hier kein Surrogat zur Befriedigung der Gerechtigkeit. Es ist keine Gleichartigkeit zwischen einem noch so kummervollen Leben und dem Tode, also auch keine Gleichheit des Verbrechens und der Wiedervergeltung als durch den am Täter gerichtlich vollzogenen Tod" (transl. Hastie, pp. 196, 198).

32. *Grundzüge der Rechtsphilosophie*, 1st ed., p. 112.
33. *Rechtslehre*, II.1, Abschnitt, allgemeine Anm. E.: "Ich als Mitgesetzgeber, der das Strafgesetz diktiert, kann unmöglich dieselbe Person sein, die als Untertan nach dem Gesetz bestraft wird; denn als ein solcher, nämlich als Verbrecher, kann ich unmöglich eine Stimme in der Gesetzgebung haben. Der Gesetzgeber ist heilig" (transl. Hastie, p. 201).
34. Stahl, *Die Philosophie des Rechts*, p. 701.
35. Thus Lask, "Rechtsphilosophie", p. 289.
36. Georg Simmel, *Kant*, p. 254.
37. Idem, *Probleme der Geschichtsphilosophie*, Munich and Leipzig, 1919.
38. *Rechtslehre*, Anhang zur Einleitung I: "Stumme Gottheit, die nicht gehört werden kann. . . . Hieraus folgt auch, dass ein Gerichtshof der Billigkeit (in einem Streit anderer über ihre Rechte) einen Widerspruch in sich schliesse" (transl. Hastie, p. 51).
39. *Kritik der praktischen Vernunft*, I.I.1, p. 4 (note).
40. *Rechtslehre*, II.1, Abschnitt, p. 45 (transl. Hastie, p. 165).
41. Ibid., p. 46: "Der Geselle. . .der Dienstbote (der nicht im Dienst des Staats steht); der Unmündige, alles Frauenzimmer und überhaupt jedermann, der nicht nach eigenem Betriebe sondern nach der Verfügung anderer (ausser der des Staats) genötigt ist, seine Existenz (Nahrung und Schutz) zu erhalten, entbehrt der bürgerlichen Persönlichkeit, und seine Existenz ist gleichsam nur eine Inhärentz" (transl. Hastie, pp. 167, 168).
42. Ibid., I.2.1, p. 15: "Wie weit erstreckt sich die Befugnis zur Besitznehmung eines Bodens? Soweit, als das Vermögen, ihn in seiner Gewalt zu haben, das ist als der, so ihn sich zueignen will, ihn verteidigen soll, gleich ob der Boden spräche: wenn Ihr mich nicht beschützen könnt, so könnt Ihr mir auch nicht gebieten" (transl. Hastie, p. 91).
43. Emil Lask, *Fichtes Idealismus und die Geschichte*, 1914 (new ed., annotated); Marianne Weber, *Fichtes Sozialismus und sein Verhältnis zur marxschen Doktrin*, 1900; Metzger, *Gesellschaft*; Basch, *Les Doctrines Politiques*, pp. 72ff.; H. C. Engelbrecht, *Johann Gottlieb Fichte*, New York, 1933; Reinhard Strecker, *Die Anfänge von Fichtes Staatsphilosophie*; Fichte, *Sämtliche Werke*, ed. J. H. Fichte, 8 vols, Berlin, 1845–6, quoted as *GW*; idem, *Fichtes Nachgelassene Werke*, 3 vols, Bonn, 1834, quoted as *NW*.
44. *GW*, VI, p. 300, 1794.
45. *GW*, VI, p. 72.
46. "System der Sittenlehre", *GW*, IV, p. 166, 1798.
47. *GW*, VI, pp. 58ff.
48. *GW*, IV, p. 256.
49. "Beitrag zur Berichtigung der Urteile des Publikums über die französische Revolution", *GW*, VI, pp. 86ff., 1793.
50. *GW*, VI, pp. 297ff.
51. *GW*, IV, p. 329.
52. *GW*, VI, p. 306.

53. *GW*, IV, p. 234.
54. *GW*, IV, p. 230.
55. Metzger, *Gesellschaft*, p. 125.
56. *GW*, IV, p. 253.
57. "Vorlesungen über die Grundzüge des gegenwärtigen Zeitalters", GW, VII, pp. 26, 188.
58. *GW*, VII, p. 38.
59. *GW*, VII, p. 35.
60. *GW*, VI.
61. *GW*, VI, p. 81.
62. *GW*, VI, p. 178.
63. *GW*, VI, p. 111.
64. *GW*, VI, p. 121.
65. *GW*, VI, p. 132.
66. *GW*, VI, p. 90.
67. "Bestimmung des Gelehrten", *GW*, VI, p. 306.
68. Cf. esp. "Grundlage des Naturrechts", *GW*, III, 1796.
69. Ibid., p. 160.
70. *GW*, III, p. 112.
71. *Grundlage des Naturrechts*, *GW*, III, p. 159, 1796.
72. *GW*, III, p. 160.
73. *GW*, III, p. 182.
74. *Die Grundzüge des gegenwärtigen Zeitalters*, *GW*, VII, p. 3.
75. *GW*, VII, p. 157.
76. *GW*, VII, pp. 143, 157, 162.
77. *Grundlage des Naturrechts von 1796*, *GW*, III, p. 202.
78. *GW*, IV, p. 236.
79. See Engelbrecht, *Fichte*, pp. 95–107.
80. "Über Macchiavelli als Schriftsteller und Stellen aus seinen Schriften", 1807, *NW*, III, p. 401.
81. *NW*, III, p. 428, transl. Engelbrecht, *Fichte*, pp. 110–11.
82. *Angewandtes Naturrecht*, *GW*, III, p. 235.
83. *Der geschlossene Handelsstaat*, *GW*, III, p. 510, 1800.
84. *Handelsstaat*, *GW*, III, p. 399.
85. Friedrich Meinecke, *Die Idee der Staatsraison*, Munich and Berlin, 1924, p. 466.
86. Ibid., p. 465.
87. *GW*, VII, p. 181.
88. *GW*, VII, p. 166.
89. Engelbrecht, *Fichte*, p. 158.
90. *Reden an die deutsche Nation*, *GW*, VII, p. 436.
91. F. Meinecke, *Weltbürgertum und Nationalstaat*, Bk. I, chap. 6.
92. *NW*, II, p. 493.
93. *NW*, II, p. 515.
94. *NW*, II, p. 514.
95. *NW*, II, p. 548.
96. *NW*, II, p. 568.

97. *NW*, II, p. 537.
98. *NW*, II, p. 540.
99. *NW*, II, p. 629.
100. *NW*, II, p. 633 (transl. in Engelbrecht, *Fichte*, p. 137.)
101. *GW*, IV, p. 369.
102. *GW*, IV, p. 450.

CHAPTER 11

1. Franz Rosenzweig, *Hegel und der Staat*, 2 vols., Berlin, 1920; R. Haym, *Hegel und seine Zeit*, 1857; Wilhelm Dilthey, "Die Jugendgeschichte Hegels", *Gesammelte Schriften*, vol. IV, 1921; Wilhelm Metzger, *Gesellschaft. Recht und Staat in der Ethik des deutschen Idealismus*, Heidelberg, 1917; Hermann Heller, *Hegel und der nationale Machtstaatsgedanke in Deutschland*, 1921; Paul Vogel, *Hegels Gesellschaftsbegriff und seine geschichtliche Fortbildung durch Lorenz Stein, Marx, Engels und Lassalle* (Kantstudien Ergänzungsheft, no. 59,) 1925; Julius Löwenstein, *Hegels Staatsidee, ihr Doppelgesicht und ihr Einfluss im 19. Jahrhundert*, Berlin, 1927; Victor Basch, *Les Doctrines Politiques des Philosophes Classiques de L'Allemagne*, Paris, 1927, p. 111; E. F. Carritt, *Morals and Politics*, Oxford, 1935, pp. 105, 159; M. B. Forster, *The Political Philosophies of Plato and Hegel*, Oxford, 1935; Hegel, *Vorlesungen über die Philosophie der Geschichte*, ed. von Lasson, 1922; idem, *Grundlinien der Philosophie des Rechts*, ed. von Lasson, 1921 (English transl. by Dyde); idem, *Schriften zur Politik und Rechtsphilosophie*, ed. von Lasson, 1913, containing "Über die wissenschaftlichen Behandlungsarten des Naturrechts", p. 396.
2. "Wo die Grenze zwischen dem Zufälligen und Notwendigen gehe, was also im Chaos des Naturzustandes oder in der Abstraktion des Menschen bleiben und was weggelassen werden müsse."
3. Rosenzweig, *Hegel*, I.159.
4. Metzger, *Gesellschaft* p. 302; Rosenzweig, *Hegel*, I, p. 191; Löwenstein, *Staatsidee*, p. 32.
5. Hegel, *Schriften* p. 450.
6. Löwenstein, *Staatsidee*, p. 40.
7. "Der freie Wille ist es, der alles vermittelt. Und so geschieht die Vermittlung ebenso gut durch den individuellen Vorteil wie durch allgemeine Interessen. Die Individualität soll nicht mehr aufgeopfert werden", *Lectures on the Philosophy of History*, p. 497.
8. For Montesquieu's influence on Hegel, see Metzger, *Gesellschaft*, p. 317; Dilthey, "Jugendgeschichte", pp. 8, 17, 31.
9. "Ob das Individuum sei, gilt der objektiven Sittlichkeit gleich, welche allein das Bleibende und die Macht ist, durch welche das Leben der Individuen regiert wird", *Philosophy of Right*, sect. 145, addition.
10. "Die Weltordnung, sondern für sie, denn es ist die List der Idee, dass sie die Leidenschaften für sich wirken lässt", *Lectures*, p. 83.

11. *Philosophy of Right*, sect. 260. We should like to draw attention to an important observation of Metzger's (*Gesellschaft*, p. 313, n. 1): Metzger points out that in the first edition of the *Encyclopedia* (1807) the people still played the principal rôle; that it is only in Hegel's *Philosophy of Right* of 1821, that is, after his removal to Berlin, that the people are superseded by the state. Since this observation of Metzger's is undoubtedly true, the construction of the state from the two elements, "freedom" and "the people", appears to be no longer possible. It cuts, however, at the root of Löwenstein's interpretation which, precisely on the ground of Hegel's conception of the people, sees in the state created by Bismarck an embodiment of the Hegelian idea. It appears, therefore, that Hegel does not apply the dialectical method to the construction of the state. The state is not deduced from the two [elements] individual and people, as the [element] people disappears in the *Philosophy of Right*, and is replaced by the state. It follows, therefore, that the state is a philosophical and political *a priori* concept.
12. *Grundzüge*, p. 928.
13. "Der Staat ist die Wirklichkeit der sittlichen Idee", *Philosophy of Right*, sect. 257.
14. "Der zur vorhandenen Welt und zur Natur des Selbstbewusstseins gewordene Begriff der Freiheit", ibid., sect. 142.
15. "Die Person muss sich eine äussere Sphäre ihrer Freiheit geben, um als Idee zu sein", ibid., sect. 41.
16. "Es ist wohl an die anderthalbtausend Jahre, dass die Freiheit der Person durch das Christentum zu erblühen angefangen hat und unter einem übrigens kleinen Teil des Menschengeschlechts allgemeines Prinzip geworden ist. Die Freiheit des Eigentums aber ist seit gestern, kann man sagen, hier und da als Prinzip anerkannt worden", ibid., sect. 62, note last para.
17. Ibid., sect. 200.
18. Ibid., sect. 270, note.
19. Esp. ibid., sect. 319, note.
20. ". . . denn solches Reden gehört der noch ganz ungebildeten Roheit und Oberflächlichkeit des Vorstellens an."
21. ". . . die Differenz, welche zwischen die Familie und den Staat tritt", addition. ibid., sect. 182.
22. "Die Individuen sind als Bürger dieses Staats *Privatpersonen*, welche ihr eigenes Interesse zu ihrem Zwecke haben. Da dieser durch das Allgemeine vermittelt ist, das ihnen somit als *Mittel* erscheint, so kann er von ihnen nur erreicht werden, insofern sie selbst ihren Willen, Wollen, Tun auf allgemeine Weise bestimmen und sich zu einem *Gliede* in der Kette dieses *Zusammenhanges* machen", ibid., sect. 187.
23. "Die Industrie und Gewerbe sind nunmehr sittlich geworden", *Lectures*, p. 888.
24. "In dieser Abhängigkeit und Gegenseitigkeit der Arbeit und der Befriedigung der Bedürfnisse schlägt die subjektive Selbstsucht in den Beitrag zur Befriedigung der Bedürfnisse aller Anderen um — in die

Vermittlung des besonderen durch das allgemeine als dialektischer Bewegung, sodass indem jeder für sich erwirbt, produziert und geniesst, er eben damit für den Genuss der Übrigen produziert und erwirbt", *Philosophy of Right*, sect. 199.

25. Rosenzweig, *Hegel*, II, pp. 120–1.
26. *Philosophy of Right*, sects. 244, 253.
27. Vogel, *Gesellschaftsbegriff*, p. 107.
28. Forster, *Political Philosophies*, p. 160.
29. *Philosophy of Right*, sect. 230.
30. ". . . doch nur in Existenz, weil es nützlich für die Bedürfnisse", *Philosophy of Right*, sect. 209, addition.
31. Forster, p. 121.
32. Here — section 211 — he criticises the English Common Law, but rightly observes that the Common Law is written law. Here is also to be found the criticism of Savigny and the defence of Thibaut, without mention of their names.
33. ". . . ohne die subjektive Empfindung des besonderen Interesses", (sect. 219).
34. Rosenzweig, *Hegel*, II, p. 154.
35. ". . . die Gewalt, das Allgemeine zu bestimmen und festzusetzen"; "die Subsumption der besonderen Sphären und einzelnen Fälle unter das Allgemeine"; "in der die unterschiedenen Gewalten zur individuellen Einheit zusammengefasst sind, die also die Spitze und der Anfang des Ganzen — der konstitutionellen Monarchie ist" (sect. 273).
36. Rosenzweig, *Hegel*, II, p. 144.
37. Forster, *Political Philosophies*, p. 162.
38. "die in das einzelne Benehmen nicht reichende Kontrolle von oben, von unten ergänzt" (sect. 295).
39. "ihrem Inhalt nach ganz allgemeinen inneren Angelegenheiten" (sect. 321).
40. "Hegel macht sich einer. . .Halbheit schuldig. . ., indem er die Philosophie für das Dasein des absoluten Geistes erklärt und sich zugleich dagegen verwehrt, das wirkliche philosophische Individuum für den absoluten Geist zu erklären", Karl Marx, *Die Heilige Familie*, 6; idem, *Kapital*, 1a.
41. Rosenzweig, *Hegel* ii, pp. 161ff.
42. Haym, *Hegel* p. 391.
43. As does Löwenstein, *Staatsidee*, p. 62.

PART III INTRODUCTION

1. Ernst Krieck, *Nationalpolitische Erziehung*, 1933, p. 68.
2. Ernst Forsthoff, *Der totale Staat*, Hamburg, 1933, p. 13.
3. Ibid., p. 14.

4. Hans Gerber, *Staatsrechtliche Grundlagen des neuen Reichs*, Tübingen, 1933, p. 16.
5. For example, Ernst Rudolf Huber, "Die Totalität des völkischen Staats", *Die Tat*, 1934, pt. 1, p. 30.
6. Julius Binder, *Der Deutsche Volksstaat*, Tübingen, 1934, p. 17.
7. Otto Koellreuter, *Vom Sinn und Wesen der nationalen Revolution*, Tübingen, 1933, p. 17.
8. Dr von Leers (Deutsche Hochschule für Politik), in the Introduction to Karl Lohmann, *Hitlers Staatsauffassung*, Berlin, 1933, p. 10.
9. Carl Schmitt, *Hüter der Verfassung*, Tübingen, 1931.
10. Friedrich Schaffstein, *Politische Strafrechtswissenschaft*, Hamburg, p. 8.
11. Ibid., p. 9.
12. Heinrich Lange, *Liberalismus, Nationalsozialismus und bürgerliches Recht*, Tübingen, 1933, p. 5.
13. Carl Schmitt, *Staat, Bewegung, Volk*, Hamburg, 1933, p. 13. Schmitt means F. J. Stahl and Hugo Preuss, the creator of the Weimar Constitution and Carl Schmitt's predecessor in the chair of constitutional law in the Handelshochschule, Berlin. Carl Schmitt raised a beautiful memorial to him in a speech which has also been published as a pamphlet (Carl Schmitt, *Hugo Preuss, sein Staatsbegriff und seine Stellung in der deutschen Staatslehre*, Tübingen 1930). I quote two extracts showing how Carl Schmitt changed his opinion of Hugo Preuss, the "racially alien" theorist — who by the way was the favourite disciple of Otto von Gierke — after Hitler's access to power. In his speech on Preuss, Schmitt praised the "independent spirit of a man whose life and work have proved the connection of free bourgeois education with the Constitution of the State", and he continued: ". . . the history of the German bourgeoisie shows that this connection is not incidental but essential, *and the fate of the German intelligentsia and education will therefore be inseparably linked with the fate* of the Weimar Constitution". (My italics.)
14. Quoted from the new German edition edited by Ludwig Fischer, *Der Staat Gottes*, Karlsruhe, 1933, p. 293.

CHAPTER 12

1. Otto Bähr, *Der Rechtsstaat*, 1864; J. C. Bluntschli, *Allgemeine Staatslehre*, 6th ed., 1886, vol. I; A. V. Dicey, *Introduction to the Study of the Law of the Constitution*, 8th ed., London, 1915; idem, *Lectures on the Relation between Law and Public Opinion in England during the Nineteenth Century*, 2nd ed., London; John Dickinson, *Administrative Justice and the Supremacy of Law in the United States*, Cambridge, Mass., 1927; Peter Drucker, *Friedrich Julius Stahl*, Tübingen, 1933; Fritz Fleiner, *Institutionen des deutschen Verwaltungsrechts*, 8th ed., Tübingen, 1928; Rudolf Gneist, *Der Rechtsstaat und die Verwaltungsgerichte in Deutschland*, 2nd ed., Berlin, 1879;

Hermann Heller, *Rechtsstaat oder Diktatur?*, Tübingen, 1930; C. G. Haines, *The Revival of Natural Law Concepts*, Cambridge, Mass., 1930; idem, *The American Doctrine of Judicial Supremacy*, 2nd ed., Berkeley, 1932; W. Ivor Jennings, *The Law and the Constitution*, London, 1933; Harold J. Laski, *The State in Theory and Practice*, London, 1935; Gerhard Masur, *Friedrich Julius Stahl. Geschichte seines Lebens 1802–1830*, 1930; Otto Mayer, *Deutsches Verwaltungsrecht*, 3rd ed., Munich and Leipzig, 1924; Robert von Mohl, *Geschichte der Literatur der Staatswissenschaften*, vol. I, 1855; idem, *Encyklopädie*, Tübingen, 1859; idem, *Politik*, vol. I, Tübingen, 1862; Franz Neumann, *Koalitionsfreiheit und Reichsverfassung. Die Stellung der Gewerkschaften im Verfassungssystem*, Berlin, 1932; Dietrich Schindler, *Über den Rechtsstaat* in *Festgabe für Max Huber*, Zürich, 1934; Carl Schmitt, *Verfassungslehre*, Munich and Leipzig, 1926; Friedrich Julius Stahl, *Die Philosophie des Rechts*, vol. II, *Rechts- und Staatslehre auf der Grundlage christlicher Weltanschauung*, 3rd ed., Heidelberg, 1856; Lorenz von Stein, "Rechtsstaat und Verwaltungsrechtspflege", *Zeitschrift für das Privat- und öffentliche Recht*, ed. von Grünhut, vol. 6, 1879, pp. 399ff.; Richard Thoma, "Rechtsstaatsidee und Verwaltungsrechtswissenschaft", *Jahrbuch des öffentlichen Rechts (1910)*, IV, p. 196; C. T. Welcker, "Staatsverfassung", in Rotteck-Welcker, *Staatslexikon*, vol. XV, 1843.

2. Laski, *State*, pp. 177–8.
3. Gneist, *Rechsstaat*, p. 333, n. 2.
4. Von Mohl, *Geschichte*, vol. 1, pp. 296ff.
5. Von Stein, *Rechtsstaat*, p. 350.
6. Stahl, *Philosophie*, vol. II, p. 137.
7. Gneist, *Rechtsstaat*, p. 33.
8. Bähr, *Rechtsstaat*, pp. 1–2.
9. Masur, *Stahl*, p. 211.
10. Stahl, *Philosophie*, vol. II, p. 88.
11. Bähr, *Rechtsstaat*, pp. 2, 5.
12. Gneist, *Rechtsstaat*, pp. 24–5.
13. Heller, *Rechtsstaat*, p. 8.
14. Von Mohl, *Encyklopädie*, Tübingen, 1859, pp. 106, 328ff.
15. Drucker, *Stahl*, p. 8.
16. Thoma, 'Rechtsstaatsidee', p. 204.
17. Blackstone, *Commentaries*, vol. I, p. 160, with the quotation from Coke's *Fourth Institute*, p. 31; Dicey, *Constitution*, p. 39. Further, see G. Haines, *The American Doctrine*, p. 9.
18. R. Pound, *Spirit of Common Law*, p. 60.
19. Dicey, *Constitution*, p. 402.
20. Ibid., p. 403.
21. Ibid., p. 406.
22. Ibid., p. 409.
23. Ibid., p. 409.
24. In *Commentaries*, vol. I, p. 87.

CHAPTER 13

1. Max Weber, *Gesammelte Aufsätze zur Wissenschaftslehre*, p. 176.
2. Ibid., p. 194.
3. Cf. Morris Ginsberg, *Sociology*, 1934; Hermann I. Grab, *Der Begriff des Rationalen in der Soziologie Max Webers*, Karlsruhe, 1927; Karl Mannheim, "Historismus", *Archiv für Sozialwissenschaft*, 1924; idem, *Mensch und Gesellschaft in Zeitalter des Umbaus*, Leiden, 1935, pp. 125–49.
4. Mill, *A System of Logic*, book. IV, chap. X, paras. 2–6.
5. Bolingbroke, *Works*, vol. I, p. 319.
6. Ibid., vol. IV, p. 319; also Walter Sichel and W. Ludwig.
7. Adam Smith, *An Enquiry into the Wealth of Nations*, Cannan ed., Oxford; idem, *A Theory of Moral Sentiments*, 6th ed., 2 vols., 1790; idem, *Lectures on Justice, Police, Revenue and Arms*, Cannan ed., Oxford, 1896; Walter Hasbach, *Die allgemeinen philosophischen Grundlagen der von Quesnay begründeten politischen Ökonomie*, Leipzig, 1890; Leslie Stephen, *History of English Thought in the 18th Century*, 2 vols, London, 1927; James Bonard, *Philosophy and Political Economy*, London, 1922; Gunnar Myrdal, *Das politische Element in der nationalökonomischen Begriffsbildung*, Berlin, 1932; Eduard Heimann, *Soziale Theorie des Kapitalismus*, Tübingen, 1929; Adolf Loewe, *Economics and Sociology*, London, 1935; Franz Böhm, *Wettbewerb und Monopolkampf*, Berlin, 1933.
8. Smith, *Moral Sentiments*, vol. II, pt. VIII, sect. II, chap. III, pp. 286, 305.
9. Smith, *Wealth of Nations*, vol. I, bk. IV, chap. II, p. 421.
10. Stephen, *English Thought*, vol. II, pp. 70, 73.
11. Smith, *Moral Sentiments*, vol. I, pt. IV, chap. I, p. 466.
12. Cf. Heimann, *Kapitalismus*, pp. 8, 9.
13. Loewe, *Economics*, p. 40.
14. Smith, *Moral Sentiments*, vol. I, pt. III, chap. III, p. 339.
15. Ibid., vol. I, pt. II, sect. II, chap. II, p. 206.
16. Cf. Lobe, *Die Bekämpfung unlauteren Wettbewerbs*, Leipzig, 1907; C. H. Nipperdey, "Wettbewerb und Existenzvernichtung", *Kartell Rundschau*, 1930, pp. 128ff; Böhm, *Wettbewerb*.
17. Böhm, *Wettbewerb*, p. 274.
18. Loewe, *Economics*, pp. 66, 88.
19. Loewe, *Economics*, p. 68.
20. Smith, *Wealth of Nations*, vol. I, bk. I, chap. VII, p. 63; chap. XI, pt. I, p. 148; vol. II, bk. IV, chap. VII, pt. III, pp. 109, 127, 129; chap. VIII, p. 146.
21. Ibid., vol. II, bk. V, chap. I, pt. III, p. 245.
22. Ibid., vol. II, bk. IV, chap. VIII, p. 146.
23. Idem, *Lectures*, p. 177.
24. Quoted by Granville Stapleton, *Intervention and Non-intervention or the Foreign Policy of Great Britain from 1790 to 1865*, London, 1866, p. 15.
25. Smith, *Wealth of Nations*, vol. II, bk. V, chap. I, part III, art. I.
26. F. H. Knight, *Risk, Uncertainty, and Profit* (No. 16 of the Reprints of

Scarce Tracts of the London School of Economics), p. 291.

27. Knight, *Risk*, p. 298.
28. Smith, *Wealth of Nations*, vol. II, bk. IV, chap. IX, p. 184.
29. Heimann, *Kapitalismus*, p. 19.
30. Max Weber, *Wirtschaft und Gesellschaft*, p. 610.
31. Trade Union Amendment Act of 1876, cf. Slesser and Baker, 12, 132.
32. Franz Neumann, *Koalitionsfreiheit und Reichsverfassung*, 1932, pp. 20ff.
33. H. Sidgwick, *Elements of Politics*, 1891, chaps. IV, IX.
34. R. H. Tawney, *The Sickness of an Acquisitive Society*, London, 1920, p. 7.
35. Sorrell v. Smith (1925) A.C. 700.
36. Ratcliffe v. Evans (1892) 2 Q.B. 524.
37. South Wales Miners' Federation v. Glamorgan Coal Co. Ltd. (1905) A.C. 239.
38. Jethro Brown, *The Underlying Principles of Modern Legislation*, 1912, chap. IV.
39. Heimann, *Kapitalismus*, p. 135.
40. Nassau-Senior, *Political Economy*, p. 75.
41. In addition to both the nationalistic and the bourgeois liberal interpretations of German Prussian history of the nineteenth century, I should like to mention especially the following works: S. Cavaignac, *La formation de la Prusse Contemporaine*, 2 vols, 1891, 1898; Max Lehmann, *Freiherr v. Stein*, 2 vols, 1902, 1905; Franz Mehring, "Zur preussischen Geschichte von Tilsit bis zur Reichsgründung", *Gesammelte Schriften und Aufsätze*; Ferdinand Lassalle, *Gesammelte Schriften und Reden*, ed. Eduard Bernstein, Berlin, 1915, esp. vol. 2; articles by Karl Marx, esp. those in the *Rheinische Zeitung*; Walter Koch, *Volk und Staatsführung vor dem Weltkriege*, Stuttgart, 1935.
42. Stephen, *English Thought*; Walter Sichel, *Bolingbroke and His Time*, London, 1912; Walter Ludwig, *Lord Bolingbroke und die Aufklärung*, Heidelberg, 1928.
43. Bolingbroke, "Remarks on the History of England", *Works*, XI, pp. 82–3.
44. Sichel, *Bolingbroke*, p. 332.
45. Cf. L. E. Schücking, *Die Reaktion in der inneren Verwaltung Preussens*, 2nd ed., Berlin, 1908.
46. Cf. statistics and maps in Koch, *Staatführung*, p. 10, Appendix.
47. Otto Bauer, *Die Nationalitätenfrage und die Sozialdemokratie* (Marx-Studien, Vol. 2), Vienna, 1924; Ernest Barker, *The National Character and the Factors of its Formation*, London, 1917; Morris Ginsberg, *Sociology*, London, 1934; R. G. Hawtry, *Economic Aspects of Sovereignty*, London, 1930; Hermann Heller, *Staatslehre*, Leiden, 1934, pp. 178ff.; Friedrich Hertz, "Wesen und Werden der Nation", *Ergänzungsband der Jahrbücher für Soziologie*, Karlsruhe, 1927; René Johannet, *Le principe des nationalités*, Paris, 1923; Harold J. Laski, *Nationalism and the Future of Civilization*, London, 1932; R. Carré de Malberg, *Contribution à la théorie générale de l'Etat*, 2 vols., Paris, 1920; Friedrich Meinecke, *Weltbürgertum und Nationalstaat*, 6th ed., Münich and Berlin, 1922; F. J. Neumann, *Volk*

und Nation, Leipzig, 1888; Ernst Renan, *Qu'est-ce qu'une nation*, Paris, 1882; Karl Renner, *Das Selbstbestimmungsrecht der Nationen in besonderer Anwendung auf Österreich*, I, *Nation und Staat*, Leipzig and Vienna, 1918, Heinz O. Ziegler, *Die moderne Nation*, Tübingen, 1931.

48. Renner, *Nationen.*
49. Ginsberg, *Sociology*, p. 56.
50. Bauer, *Nationalitätenfrage*, p. 114.
51. Renan, *Qu'est-ce qu'une nation*, p. 27.
52. The political basis of Renan's theory is the relation of France to Alsace-Lorraine (cf. Hertz, "Wesen und Werden", p. 56).
53. Cf. Benjamin Disraeli in "The Spirit of Whiggism", 1836, reprinted in *Whigs and Whiggism: Political Writings by B. Disraeli*, London, 1913, p. 343: "The phrase 'the people' is sheer nonsense. It is not a political term. It is a phrase of natural history. A people is a species; a civilised community is a nation. Now, a nation is a work of art and a work of time. A nation is gradually created by a variety of influences . . .".
54. Bauer, *Nationalitätenfrage*, pp. 165–6.
55. Ziegler, *Nation*, p. 75.
56. Important are: Montesquieu's *Esprit des Lois*, 1748, bk. XIX; Voltaire's *Essai sur les Moeurs et l'Esprit des Nations*, 1769.
57. Only in this sense can we agree with Professor Barker's statement: "It is possible for nations to exist, and even to exist for centuries, in unreflective silence" (*National Character*, p. 116). Until reflection has begun, we can only speak of a people and not of a nation.
58. The discussions on the concepts of people and nation in the deliberations of the Third Estate of 1789 are set out by Neumann (*Volk und Nation*, p. 123) and Meinecke (Weltburgertum, p. 24).
59. Cf. de Malberg, *La Théorie . . . de l'Etat*, vol. 2, p. 168.
60. Cf. Neumann, *Volk und Nation*, p. 124; de Maistre's statement runs as follows: "Qu'est-ce qu'une nation? c'est le souverain et l'aristocratie".
61. Bauer, *Nationalitätenfrage*, p. 177.
62. The distinction between the sovereignty of the people and the sovereignty of the nation even has its legal consequences, according to the view held by French constitutional lawyers; the Senate is reconcilable with the sovereignty of the nation but not with that of the people. Cf. de Malberg, *La théorie . . . de l'Etat*, vol. II, p. 175.
63. Laski, *Nationalism*, pp. 26, 27.
64. Hawtrey, *Sovereignty*, pp. 15, 27.
65. Hertz, "Wesen und Werden", pp. 9ff.
66. Meinecke, *Weltbürgertum*, p. 39.
67. Treitschke, *Politik*, vol. I, p. 28.

CHAPTER 14

1. Michael B. Foster, *The Political Philosophies of Plato and Hegel*, Oxford, 1935, p. 115.

2. "Une prescription qui ne vise ni un cas particulier et actuel, ni telles personnes déterminées, mais qui est édictée d'avance pour s'appliquer à tous les cas et à toutes les personnes rentrant dans les prévisions abstraits du texte régulateur", R. Carré de Malberg, *La Loi, expression de la volonté générale, étude sur le concept de la loi dans la Constitution de 1875*, Paris, 1931, p. 4; and similarly idem, *Contribution à la théorie générale de l'état*, vol. I, Paris, 1920, p. 289.
3. On the three functions, cf. 14.4.1., below.
4. Cf. E. Buss, "Montesquieu and Cartesius", *Philosophische Monatshefte*, vol. IV, 1869–70, p. 5.
5. Merlin, *Répertoire universel et raisonné de jurisprudence*, 5th ed., 1827, p. 384.
6. Joseph Barthélmy Duez, *Traité de droit constitutionel*, Paris, 1933, pp. 224, 225; Duguit, *Manuel de droit constitutionel*, Paris, 1923, p. 97; idem, *Traité de droit constitutionel*, vol. II, 3rd ed., Paris, 1921, p. 160.
7. du Malberg, *La Loi*, p. 54.
8. Idem, *La théorie . . . de l'Etat*, pp. 276, 314.
9. Examples are to be found in Duguit, *Traité de droit*, vol. II, p. 168; de Malberg, *La théorie . . . de l'Etat*, vol. I, p. 295.
10. Robert von Mohl, *Politik*, vol. I, Tübingen, 1862, p. 420.
11. Idem, *Encyklopädie*, 1859, p. 139.
12. Lorenz von Stein, *Verwaltungslehre*, vol. I, p. 78.
13. Johann Ludwig Klüber, *Öffentliches Recht des Teutschen Bundes und der Bundesstaaten*, Frankfurt, 1846, pp. 363, 558.
14. A predecessor is von Stockmar, in *Zeitschrift für deutsches Staatsrecht*, 1867, p. 201. Laband's works are: *Deutches Reichsstaatsrecht*, 7th ed., ed. Otto Mayer, Tübingen, 1919, p. 114, and *Das Staatsrecht des deutschen Reiches*, 5 vols, Tübingen, 1911 — here, specifically, 2nd vol., p. 27.
15. Gerhard Anschütz, *Kritische Studien zur Lehre vom Rechtssatz und formellen Gesetz*, 2nd ed., Halle, 1911; Georg Meyer. Gerhard Anschütz, *Lehrbuch des deutsches Staatsrecht*, 7th ed., Munich and Leipzig, 1919, pp. 637, 638; Hans Kelsen, *Hauptprobleme der Staatsrechtslehre*, Tübingen, 1911, p. 538; Georg Jellinek, *Gesetz und Verordnung*, Freiburg, 1887, p. 228; their chief opponent is Albert Hänel, *Studien zum deutschen Staatsrecht*, II, 2, Leipzig, 1888; see also Hermann Heller, "Der Begriff des Gesetzes in der Reichsverfassung", *Veröffentlichungen der Vereinigung der deutschen Staatsrechtslehrer*, vol. 4, Berlin and Leipzig, 1928, p. 98 (on the whole repeating the criticism of Carré de Malberg).
16. Laband, *Staatsrecht*, vol. II, p. 2.
17. Anschütz, *Kritische Studien*, p. 33.
18. Meyer-Anschütz, p. 654.
19. C. K. Allen, *Legal Duties and Other Essays in Jurisprudence*, Oxford, 1931, p. 124; W. A. Robson, *Civilisation and Growth of Law*, London, 1935, p. 47.
20. Sir Frederick Pollock, "A Plea for Historical Jurisprudence", *Law Quarterly Review*, vol. XXXIV, p. 145; Ernest Barker, "Introduction", in Otto Gierke *Natural Law and the Theory of Society*, vol. I, Cambridge,

1934, xlvi.
21. Jeremy Bentham, *Comment on the Commentaries*, Oxford ed., p. 152.
22. Blackstone, vol. I, p. 41.
23. Ibid., p. 37.
24. Ibid., p. 46.
25. Ibid., p. 44.
26. Ibid., p. 53.
27. Austin, *Lectures*, 4th ed., vol. I, p. 94.
28. Sir Courtenay Ilbert, *Methods of Legislation*, London, 1912, p. 28.
29. (1910) 2 K.B. 576, approved by the Judicial Committee of the Privy Council (1926) A.C., p. 518.
30. Ferdinand Lassalle, "Das System der erworbenen Rechte", in Eduard Bernstein (ed.), *Gesammelte Schriften und Reden*, vols IX, X,XI.
31. *Moniteur*, 1er juin, 1828, p. 755; quoted Lassalle, *Das System*, vol. IX, p. 53.
32. Duguit, however, in his *Traité de Droit* (p. 230), asserts that the principle of non-retroactivity applies also to laws issued by the legislative body, because he still affirms the validity of the Declaration of 1789.
33. Cf. J. Barthélmy, *Sur l'interpretation de lois par le législateur*, Paris, 1909.
34. See *Decisions of the Reichsgericht in Penal Matters*, vol. 29, p. 11.
35. For USA, cf. Caldor v. Bully 3 Dall: 386 (U.S. 1798).
36. Esp. Dr Nicolai in *Juristische Wochenschrift*, 1933, p. 2315, and even the memorandum of the Prussian Minister of Justice for the reform of the penal law, p. 127.
37. Lassalle, vol. XI, p. 520.
38. Blackstone, vol. I, p. 46, where he invokes Coke's formulation: "Nova constitutio futuris formum imponere debit, non praeteritis".
39. Craies, *Statute Law* p. 324; Edward Beal, *Cardinal Rules of Legal Interpretation*, 3rd ed., 1924, p. 468.
40. Moon v. Durden (1848) 2 Es. 22, 42.
41. Smithies v. Nat. Assoc. of Plasterers (1909) 1 K.B. 310, 319.
42. *Reine Rechtslehre*, p. 79.
43. Ibid., p. 90.
44. Ibid., p. 98.
45. Heller, "Der Begriff", p. 98.
46. Jennings, p. 19.
47. Morris R. Cohen, *Law and the Social Order*, p. 112.
48. Le juge a "de faire un syllogisme dont la loi est la majeure; un fait plus ou moins générale la mineure; et la conclusion l'application de la loi", *Rapport sur le projet girondin*, *Archives parlamentaires*, LVIII, quoted in Joseph Barthélemy, *Le rôle du pouvoir exécutif dans les républiques modernes*, Paris, 1906, p. 489.
49. Montesquieu, *Esprit des Lois*, XI.6.
50. Archives parlementaires, 1re série, vol. XV, p. 892.
51. Ibid.
52. No. LXXVIII, Hamilton.

53. Hobbes, *Leviathan*, chap. 26.
54. Hale, *History of the Common Law*, ed. Runnington, 1820, chap. IV, p. 90.
55. Roscoe Pound, *An Introduction to the Philosophy of Law*, New Haven, 1924, p. 48; similarly Max Weber, *Wirtschaft und Gesellschaft*, p. 395.
56. Lord Esher, M. R., in Willis & Co. v. Baddeley (1892) 2, Q.B. 324/326.
57. Farwell, L. J., in Baylis v. Bishop of London (1913) 1 Cl. at 137; cf. also Mirehouse v. Rennell 1 Cl. and F. 527, p. 46; and Dicey's observations in *Law and Opinion*, pp. 336, 367.
58. *American Law Review*, 1911, p. 275.
59. Jeremy Bentham, *General View of a Complete Code of Laws*, Bowring ed., vol. III, p. 210.
60. Francois Gény, *Méthode de l'Interprétation et Sources du Droit Privé positif*, 2nd ed., Paris, 1919, pp. 77, 84; de Malberg, *La théorie . . . de l'Etat*, vol. I, p. 719.
61. *Archives parlementaires*, 1er série, vol. XX, p. 516; similar formulations are used by Chapelier.
62. Gény, *Méthode*, vol. I, pp. 92ff.
63. Quoted Fenet, *Recueil Complet des Travaux préparatoires du Code civil*, I–XIV, Paris, 1836, vol. I, pp. 467–76.
64. Gény, *Méthode*, vol. I, pp. 17–60; Julien Bonnecase, *La Pensée juridique française de 1804 à l'heure présente*, 2 vols, Bordeaux, vol. I, p. 246.
65. Similarly, in Austria, Joseph II introduced, in Art. XIII of his Code of 1786, the *référé legislatif* if no clear decision could be found in a statute.
66. Gustav Radbruch, *Feuerbach*, Vienna, 1934, p. 85.
67. Savigny, *System des heutigen römischen Rechts*, vol. I, Berlin, 1840.
68. Cf. for instance the following decisions of the German Supreme Court in civil matters: vol. 95, p. 35; vol. 97, p. 312; vol. 98, p. 124.
69. Zachariah, *Archiv für civilistische Praxis*, vol. 16, p. 170; Schulze-Gävernitz, *Das Preussische Staatsrecht*, vol. II, 2nd ed., Leipzig, 1881, p. 40.
70. F. J. Stahl, *Rechts- und Staatslehre*, vol. II, p. 508.
71. *Decisions of the Supreme Court in Civil Matters*, vol. 24, p. 3; vol. 40, p. 69; vol. 48, p. 87.
72. Ibid., vol. 77, p. 231; also in *Juristische Wochenschrift*, 1916, p. 596.
73. Cf. Chih-Mai Chen, *Parliamentary Opinion of Delegated Legislation*, Columbia, 1923, p. 20; John Willis, *The Parliamentary Powers of English Government Departments*, Cambridge, Mass., 1933, p. 91; William A. Robson, *Justice and Administrative Law*, chap. III; and the following decisions: Sands v. Child 3 Lev. 532 (1693); Raleigh v. Goschen 1 Ch. 73 (1898); Re Petition of Rights (1915) 3 K.B. 649; Att. Gen. v. De Keyser's Hotel (1920) A.C. 508.
74. John Chipman Gray, *The Nature and Sources of Law*, New York, 1916; K. N. Llewellyn, "A Realistic Jurisprudence", *Columbia Law Review*, 1930, p. 431; idem, "*Some Realism about Realism*", *Harvard Law Review*, 44, 1931, p. 31; idem, *Präjudizienrecht und Rechtsprechung in Amerika*, Leipzig, 1933; Underhill Moore, "Rational Basis of Legal Institutions", *Columbia Law Review*, 1923, p. 609; Jerome Frank, *Law and the*

Modern Mind, New York, 1930; A. L. Goodhart, "Some American Interpretations of Law", *Modern Theories of Law*, London, 1933, pp. 1ff.; Cohen, *Social Order*, New York, 1933; Hermann Kantorowicz, "Some Rationalism about Realism", *Yale Law Review*, 43, 1934, p. 1240.

75. Gray, *Nature and Sources*, p. 191.
76. Ibid., p. 21.
77. Llewellyn, *Jurisprudence*, p. 442.
78. Frank, *Law*, pp. 5–6.
79. Ibid., p. 46.
80. Ibid., p. 98.
81. Ibid., p. 130.
82. The selection is very strange. It is certain that Dean Pound and Cardozo are "brilliant legal thinkers"; but it is equally certain that this term cannot be applied to Jhering, Demogue, and Wurzel. The most influential legal thinkers of the Continent are missing, such as Gény, Duguit, Hauriou, Lambert, in France, and Max Weber, Eugen Ehrlich, and Radbruch, in Germany.
83. Frank, *Law*, p. 250.
84. Eugen Ehrlich, *Freie Rechtsfindung*, 1903; *Grundlegung der Soziologie des Rechts*, Munich and Leipzig, 1913; Gnaeus Flavius [Hermann Kantorowicz], *Der Kampf um die Rechtswissenschaft*, 1906; idem. *Rechtswissenschaft und Soziologie*, Tübingen, 1911; idem, *Tat und Schuld*, Zürich, 1933; idem, *Aus der Vorgeschichte der Freirechtsschule*, 1925; idem, "Some Rationalism about Realism", *Yale Law Review*, 43, 1934, p. 1240; Franz Neumann, "Richterliches Ermessen und Methodenstreit im Arbeitsrecht", *Arbeitsrecht*, 1929, pp. 321ff.; idem, *Die politische und soziale Bedeutung der arbeitsgeschichtliche Rechtsprechung*, Berlin, 1929; Bonnecase, *La Pensée juridique*; Gény, *Méthode*; Ignaz Kornfeld, *Soziale Machtverhältnisse*, Vienna, 1911; Ernst Fuchs, *Juristischer Kulturkampf*, Karlsruhe, 1912; *Was will die Freirechtshule?*, Rudolfstadt, 1929.
85. Ernst Fuchs, *Die Justiz*, vol. 1, p. 349.
86. Hegel, *Philosophy of Right*, sect. 211, addition.
87. Gustav Radbruch, *Rechtsphilosophie*, 3rd ed., Leipzig, 1932, p. 111.
88. Karl Mannheim, "Wissenssoziologie", in *Handwörterbuch der Soziologie*, p. 659; Morris Ginsberg, *Sociology*, pp. 216ff.
89. Kelsen, *Allgemeine Staatslehre*, p. 231.
90. Mannheim, *Wissensoziologie*, p. 662.
91. Idem, *Mensch und Gesellschaft im Zeitalter des Umbaus*, Leiden, 1935, p. 93.
92. Ernst Fraenkel, *Zur Soziologie der Klassenjustiz*, Berlin, 1927, p. 27.
93. Scrutton, "The Work of the Commercial Courts" in *Cambridge Law Journal*, 1921, vol. I, p. 8.
94. Gneist, *Der Rechtsstaat*, p. 259.
95. Benjamin N. Cardozo, *The Nature of the Judicial Process*, New Haven, 1921; idem, *The Growth of Law*, New Haven, 1924.
96. Goodhart, "Some American Interpretations of Law", *Modern Theories of Law*, pp. 1ff.

97. Cardozo, *Judicial Process*, p. 31; idem, *Growth of Law*, p. 61; Goodhart, "American Interpretations", p. 76.
98. Cardozo, *Judicial Process*, p. 43.
99. Cf. Fritz Fleiner, *Institutionen des deutschen Verwaltungsrecht*, 8th ed., Tübingen, 1928; Kelsen, *Staatslehre*; Adolf Merkl, *Allgemeines Verwaltungsrecht*, Tübingen, 1927; John Dickinson, *Administrative Justice and the Supremacy of the Law in the United States*, Cambridge, Mass., 1927; Robson, *Justice*; Ivor Jennings, *The Law and the Constitution*.
100. Kelsen, *Staatslehre*, p. 238.
101. Dickinson, *Administrative Justice*, p. 11; similarly Kelsen, *Staatslehre*, p. 238.
102. Jennings, *Constitution*, pp. 45ff.
103. C. K. Allen, *Law in the Making*, 2nd ed., Oxford, 1930; idem, "Case Law, an Unwarrantable Intervention", *Law Quarterly Review*, 51, 1935, p. 33; idem, *Legal Duties and other Essays in Jurisprudence*, Oxford, 1931; Ashburner, *Principles of Equity*, 2nd ed. by Denis Brown, London, 1933; Beal, *Cardinal Rules*; C. H. S. Fifoot, *English Law and its Background*, London, 1932; A. L. Goodhart, *Essays in Jurisprudence and the Common Law*, Cambridge, 1931; idem, "Precedent in English and Continental Law", *Law Quarterly Review*, 50, 1934, p. 40; idem, "Case Law — A Short Replication", *Law Quarterly Review*, 50, 1934, p. 196; Sir William Holdsworth, *History of English Law*, 5th ed., Oxford, 1925; idem, *Some Lessons from our Legal History*, New York, 1928; idem, "Case Law", *Law Quarterly Review*, 50, 1934, p. 180; Georg Jäger, *Das englische Recht zur Zeit der Klassischen Nationalökonomie*, Leipzig, 1919; D. M. Kerley, *An Historical Sketch of the Equitable Jurisdiction of the Court of Chancery*, Cambridge, 1890; Henri Levy-Ullmann, *The English Legal Tradition, its Sources and History*, London, 1935; H. S. Maine, *Ancient Law* (Oxford Classics); F. W. Maitland, *Equity*, ed. A. H. Chaylor and W. J. Whitaker, Cambridge, 1929; Herman Oliphant, *A Return to Stare Decisis*, 1928; Theodore Plucknett, *A Concise History of the Common Law*, Rochester, NY, 1929; Sir Frederick Pollock, *Essays in the Law*, London, 1922; idem, *A First Book of Jurisprudence*, 6th ed. London, 1929; *Essays in Jurisprudence and Ethics*, London, 1912; Pollock-Maitland, *The History of English Law before the Time of Edward I*, 2 vols, Cambridge, 1895; Roscoe Pound, *The Spirit of the Common Law*, Boston, 1925; idem, *An Introduction of the Philosophy of Law*, New Haven, 1924; idem, *Interpretations of Legal History*, Cambridge, 1923; Sir Paul Vinogradoff, *Common Sense in Law* (Home University Library); Percy H. Winfield, *The Chief Sources of English Legal History*, Cambridge, Mass., 1925.
104. Quinn v. Leatham (1901) A.C. 495 at 506.
105. Goodhart, "Precedents", p. 50.
106. Weber, *Wirtschaft*, p. 663; Jeremy Bentham, *Rationale of Judicial Evidence*, bk VIII, chap. III, para. 4.
107. R. v. Denyer (1926) 2.K.B., p. 258.
108. Vinogradoff, *Common Sense*, p. 177; Goodhart, "Precedents", p. 43.
109. Goodhart, *Essays*, chap. I, p. 4.

110. Earl of Halsbury, in Quinn v. Leatham (1901) A.C., p. 506.
111. Vinogradoff, *Common Sense*, p. 182.
112. Allen, "Case Law", p. 336.
113. Vinogradoff, *Common Sense*, p. 177.
114. Goodhart, *Essays*, chap. III, p. 53; Allen, *Law in the Making*, p. 150; idem, "Case Law", p. 337.
115. Allen, *Law in the Making*, p. 150.
116. Especially Jones v. Randall (1774) 1 Cowp. 37.
117. Levy-Ullmann, *Legal Tradition*, p. 54.
118. Cf. pp. 226ff., above.
119. Blackstone, chap. I, p. 70: "This doctrine of the law is then this: that precedents and rules must be followed unless manifestly absurd or unjust".
120. Idem, vol. I, p. 71.
121. Holdsworth, "Case Law", p. 185.
122. Ibid., p. 197.
123. Jäger, *Das englische Recht*, p. 38.
124. Blackstone, vol. II, p. 258.
125. Ibid., p. 405.
126. Ibid., p. 400.
127. Ibid., p. 405.
128. Goodhart, *Essays*, chap. III, p. 55.
129. Levy-Ullmann, *Legal Tradition*, pp. 222ff.; Blackstone, vol. I, p. 87.
130. Holdsworth, "Case Law", p. 188.
131. Vinogradoff, *Common Sense*, p. 177.
132. Lord Truro, LC, Tommey v. White (1850) 3 H.L.Cas. 48 at 69; Lord Cranworth, *ex parte*, White & others v. Tommey (1853) 4 H.L.313 at 333; and, especially, Lord Campbell, Attorney General, v. Dean of Windsor (1860) 8 H.L. Cas. 369 and 391; Beamish v. Beamish (1859) 9 H.L. Cas. 274 at 338; Lord Halsbury, L.C., London Street Tramways Co. v. London County Council (1898) A.C. 375 at 379/380.
133. Holdsworth, "Case Law", p. 180; Allen, "Case Law", p. 333; Goodhart, "Case Law".
134. Who is not considered to be a typical common law judge. Goodhart, *Essays*, chap. III, p. 53.
135. (1866) L.R.2 E. at 339.
136. Allen, *Law in the Making*, p. 181.
137. Rawlings v. General Trading Co. (1921) 1.K.B.635 (App. C.); Montefiore v. Monday Motor Components Co. Ltd. (1918) 2 K.B. 241; Hartley v. Hymans (1920) 3 K.B. 475; Gayler & Pope Ltd. v. Davies & Son Ltd. (1924) 2 K.B. 75; Aktieselskabet Reidar v. Arcos (1927) 1.K.B. 352, 362 (App.C.)
138. An exception is not even to be found in Lord Abinger's arguments in Priestley v. Fowler (1837, 3 M. and W.1), where he says: "It is admitted that there is no precedent for the present action by a servant against a master". Here, Lord Abinger denied (probably wrongly) the existence of a precedent and thereby created the doctrine of common

employment. It is worth while to note that the German Supreme Court, in interpreting section 278 of the Civil Code (which expressly provides for the contractual liability of the master for any *culpa* of his servant) denied the applicability of that section to common employment! Even in the revolutionary judgment in Donoghue v. Stevenson (1932, A.C. 562) Lord Atkin denies (on p. 582) that the Court creates new rule; and in Lord Macmillan's view (p. 595) the court simply applies "standards of a reasonable man".

139. Goodhart, "Precedents", p. 50.
140. Vinogradoff, *Common Sense*, pp. 203, 204.
141. Blackstone, vol. I, p. 62.
142. Pollock-Maitland, *History*, vol. I, p. 189.
143. Winfield, *Sources*, p. 129; Levy-Ullmann, *Legal Tradition*, p. 296.
144. Blackstone, vol. I, p. 62.
145. Maitland, *Equity*, p. 1.
146. Ibid., p. 20.
147. Smith v. Clay (1767) 3 Bro. C.C. 640; Knight v. Simmonds (1896) 2 Cl. 294.
148. *Decisions of the Reichsgericht* in civil matters, vol. 144, p. 22; *Decisions of the Reichsarbeitsgericht*, in the collection of Bensheimer Publishing Co., vol. III, p. 58.
149. (1615) 1 C.L. Rep. 1.
150. Holdsworth, [sic], vol. V, p. 39; Blackstone, vol. III, p. 54; Kerley, *Chancery*, pp. 113, 115.
151. Selden, *Table Talk and Blackstone*, vol. III, p. 432.
152. Gee v. Pritchard (1818) 2 Swanst. 402; Kerley, *Chancery*, p. 181.
153. Mr. Justice Buckley (later Lord Wrenbury) in Re Telescriptor L.R. (1903) 2 C.L. at p. 195.
154. Ashburner, *Equity*, pp. 34ff.
155. In re Hallett (1879) L.R. 13 Ch.D at p. 710.
156. Fifoot, *English Law*, p. 252.
157. Lord Cranworth, Young v. Robertson (1862) 4 Macq.H.L. 314 at 345.
158. Lord Hardwicke, Ellis v. Smith (1751) 1 Ves. Jnr. at p. 17.
159. Thesiger, L. J., in Pugh v. Golden Valley Railway Co. (1880) 15 Ch.D. 330 at 334 and 49 L.J. Ch. 721 at 723.
160. Brett, M. R., in Palmer v. Johnson (1884) 13 Q.B.D. 351 at 354. 53 L.J. Q.B. 348 at 349.
161. Lord Esher, M. R., in Phillips v. Rees (1889) 24 Q.B.D. 17 at 21. 59 L.J. Q.B. 1 at 4.
162. Lindley, L. J., in Andrews v. Gas Meter Co. (1897) 1 Ch. 361 at 371.
163. Weber, *Wirtschaft*, p. 174.
164. Jäger, *Das englische Recht*, p. 30.
165. Weber, *Wirtschaft*, p. 174.
166. Ibid., p. 174.
167. Pound, *Common Law*, pp. 46, 47.
168. Weber, *Wirtschaft*, p. 3; idem, *Gesammelte Aufsätze zur Religionssoziologie*, vol. I, p. 1 (transl. as *The Protestant Ethic and the Spirit of Capitalism*).

169. Weber, *Protestant Ethic*, p. 17.
170. Idem, *Wirtschaft*, p. 166.
171. Fraenkel, *Klassenjustiz*, Berlin, 1927; Gneist, *Rechtsstaat*; Eduard Kern, *Der gesetzliche Richter*, Berlin, 1927; Johann Ludwig Klueber, *Die Selbstständigkeit des Richteramts und die Unabhängigkeit seines Urteils im Rechtsprechen*, Frankfurt, 1832; Johann Jakob Moser, *Von der Landeshoheit in Justizsachen*, Frankfurt and Leipzig, 1773; Neumann, *Bedeutung*; Carl von Pfizer, *Ueber die Grenzen zwischen Verwaltungs- und Ziviljustiz*, Stuttgart, 1818; Carl Schmitt, *Verfassungslehre*, Munich and Leipzig, 1928; idem, *Unabhängigkeit der Richter, Gleichheit vor dem Gesetz und Gewährleistung des Privateigentums nach der Weimarer Verfassung; ein Rechtsgutachten*, Berlin, 1926; idem, *Ueber die drei Arten des rechtswissenschaftlichen Denkens*, Hamburg, 1934; von Staff, "Commentary to articles 102–104 of the Weimar Constitution", in H. C. Nipperdey (ed.), *Die Grundrechte und Grundpflichten der Deutschen*; Adolf Stoelzel, *Die Entwicklung des gelehrten Richtertums in den deutschen Territorien*, Stuttgart, 1872; idem, Brandenburg–Preussens Rechtsverwaltung und Rechtsverfassung, Berlin, 1888; idem, *Karl Gottlieb Suarez*, Berlin, 1885.
172. Fleiner, *Institutionen*, p. 133.
173. Schulze-Gävernitz, *Staatsrecht*, p. 22.
174. Leband, *Reichstaatsrecht*, p. 117.
175. Stölzel, *Suarez*, p. 385.
176. Instances of such interference are to be found in Stölzel, *Brandenburg–Preussen*, vol. II, pp. 317, 324.
177. Idem, *Suarez*, p. 381.
178. Idem, *Brandenburg–Preussen*, vol. II, p. 355.
179. Kern, *Richter*, p. 97.
180. Stölzel, *Brandenburg–Preussen*, vol. II, p. 741.
181. Ibid., p. 359.
182. Ibid., pp. 521, 522.
183. Instances of such courts to be found in Kern, *Richter*, p. 102. The case of the brothers Karl and Gottlieb Welcker and E. M. Arndt, Professors at the University of Bonn, might be mentioned.
184. Compare the controversy centering on Section 99, II, 17 and Section 103, II, 10, of the Prussian Allgemeine Landrecht in Stölzel, *Brandenburg–Preussen*, vol. II, p. 396.
185. Gneist, *Rechtsstaat*, p. 228.
186. Hedemann, [sic], p. 4.
187. Fraenkel, *Klassenjustiz*, p. 14.
188. Neumann, *Trade Unionism, Democracy, Dictatorship*, pp. 22ff.; idem, *Koalitionsfreiheit*, pp. 1ff.
189. Maitland, *Constitutional History*, pp. 220, 221.
190. Robson, *Justice*, p. 16; Pound, *Common Law*, p. 73; F. W. Maitland, *Collected Papers*, vol. I, *The Shallows and Silences of Real Life*, pp. 470, 478; Holdsworth, *History*, pp. 502, 508.
191. Ibid., pp. 187, 188.
192. Blackstone, vol. III, p. 83.

193. Bentham, *Judicial Evidence*, bk. VIII, chap. III, para. 4.

CHAPTER 15

1. Otto Bauer, *Kapitalismus und Sozialismus nach dem Weltkrieg*; vol. I, *Rationalisierung-Fehlrationalisierung*, Vienna, 1931; Herman Levy, *Industrial Germany; A Study of its Monopoly Organisations and their Control by the State*, Cambridge, 1935; Robert A. Brady, *The Rationalisation Movement in German Industry*, Chicago, 1933; Thorsten Veblen, *Imperial Germany and the Industrial Revolution*, 1915; Neumann, *Koalitionsfreiheit*, idem, *Trade Unionism*; Rudolf Hilferding, *Das Finanzkapital*, Vienna; Paul Sering, "Die Wandlungen des Kapitalismus", *Zeitschrift für Sozialismus*, 22/23, 1935, p. 704; A. A. Berle and G. C. Means, *Corporation and Private Property*, New York, 1933; Karl Renner, *Die Rechtsinstitute des Privatrechts und ihre soziale Funktion*, Tübingen, 1929.
2. Karl Marx, *Kapital*, vol. 1, p. 555 (German edition).
3. Hilferding, *Finanzkapital*, p. 455; Neumann, *Trade Unionism*, p. 45.
4. Gerhard Leibholz, *Die Auflösung der liberalen Demokratie in Deutschland und das autoritäre Staatsbild*, Munich and Leipzig, 1933; Harold J. Laski, *Democracy in Crisis*, London, 1932; idem, *The State in Theory and Practice*, London, 1935; idem, "The Pluralistic State", *The Foundations of Sovereignty*, London, 1931, pp. 232ff.; Otto Kirchheimer, *Weimar — und was dann?*, Berlin, 1930; Carl Schmitt, *Die geistesgeschichtliche Lage des Parliamentarismus*, 2nd ed., Munich and Leipzig, 1926; idem, *Legalität und Legitimität*, Munich and Leipzig, 1932; idem, *Der Hüter der Verfassung*, Tübingen, 1931; idem, *Verfassungslehre*; Hermann Heller, *Rechtsstaat oder Diktatur?*, Tübingen, 1930; Neumann, *Koalitionsfreiheit*; Arthur Rosenberg, *The Birth of the German Republic*, Oxford; idem, *Geschichte der Deutschen Republik*, Prague, 1935; R. T. Clark, *The Fall of the German Republic*, London, 1935; Tatarin-Tarnheyden, *Berufsverbände und Wirtschaftsdemokratie*, Berlin, 1930.
5. Schmitt, *Verfassung*; Laski, "The Pluralistic State".
6. Gröner, *Der Dolchstoss-Prozess in München — Oktober–November*, 1925, Munich, 1925, p. 223.
7. Tatarin-Tarnheyden, *Berufsverbände*; Neumann, *Koalitionsfreiheit*, pp. 39ff.
8. Lederer, *Grundriss des oesterreichischen Sozialrechts*, 2nd ed., Vienna, 1932.
9. Paul Pic, *Traité élementaire de législation industrielle*, Paris, 1922; report by Ignace Bessling, *Internationales Handwörterbuch des Gewerkschaftswesens*, I, pp. 504ff.
10. W. Milne Bailey, *Trade Unions and the State*, London, 1934, pp. 298ff.
11. Heller, *Rechtsstaat*; Neumann, *Koalitionsfreiheit*, pp. 53ff.
12. Karl Mannheim, *Rational and Irrational Elements in Contemporary Society*, London, 1934, p. 39.

13. Ibid., p. 10.
14. Kirchheimer, *Weimar*, p. 20.
15. Schmitt, *Verfassungslehre*, p. 30, and many others.
16. Bonnecase, *La pensée juridique*; Friedrich Dessauer, *Recht, Richtertum und Ministerialbürokratie*, Mannheim, 1928; Fraenkel, *Klassenjustiz*; A. L. Goodhart, "Some American Interpretations of Law", *Modern Theories of Law*, London, 1933; Georges Gurvitch, *L'Idée du droit social*, Paris, 1932; idem, *L'Experience juridique*, Paris, 1935; Justus Wilhelm Hedemann, *Die Flucht in die Generalklauseln*, Tübingen, 1933; Heller, "Der Begriff", Hermann Isay, *Rechtsnorm und Entscheidung*, Berlin, 1929; W. J. Jennings, "The Institutional Theory", *Modern Theories of Law*, London, 1933; Otto Kahn-Freund, *Das soziale Ideal des Reichsarbeitsgerichts*, Mannheim, 1931; Kirchheimer, *Weimar*; idem, *Grenzen der Enteigung*, Berlin and Leipzig, 1930; Neumann, *Bedeutung*; idem, "Gegen ein Gesetz über Nachprüfung der Verfassungsmässigkeit von Reichsgesetzen", *Die Gesellschaft*, 1929, p. 517; Georges Renard, *L'Institution*, Paris, 1933; Schmitt, *Verfassungslehre*; Heinrich Triepel, *Goldbilanzenverordnung und Vorzugsaktien*, Berlin and Leipzig, 1934.
17. Schmitt, *Verfassungslehre*, p. 138; idem, *Unabhängigkeit*, p. 9.
18. Weber, *Wirtschaft*, p. 128.
19. Triepel, *Vorzugsaktien*, p. 26.
20. Cf., on this discussion, Neumann, *Koalitionsfreiheit*, p. 41.
21. *Decisions of the Reichsgericht in Civil Matters*, vol. 102, p. 161.
22. Idem, vol. 107, p. 139; idem, vol. 111, p. 323; *Decision of the Reichsfinanzhof* . . ., vol. 5, p. 333; Neumann, "Gegen ein Gesetz".
23. Vol. 102, p. 161: the court investigates whether a statute which restricts the rights of the owners of premises is valid; vol. 111, p. 320: the court examines whether the law relating to the revaluation of the Mark is valid; vol. 103, p. 200: the court denies the validity of a statute of a federal state which abolishes the payment of state grants to princes; vol. 107, p. 370: the court examines the validity of revaluation decree; vol. 109, p. 310p: the court examines the question of whether a tax of a federal state laid upon the output of a mind is valid.
24. Ibid., vol. III, p. 329.
25. See on Chap. 2.2 above — "Classification of Liberties".
26. *Juristische Wochenschrift*, 1924, p. 90.
27. Ibid., p. 245.
28. Ibid., p. 213; also Charles Groves Haines, *The Revival of Natural Law Concepts*, p. 246, for international law.
29. Max Horkheimer, *Zeitschrift für Sozialforschung*, vol. IV, 1935, pp. 14–15.
30. Cf. Neumann, *Bedeutung*; Hedemann, *Die Flucht*.
31. *Decision of the Reichsgericht in Civil Matters*, vol. 104, p. 122; *Juristische Wochenschrift*, 1925, p. 1377. Cf. Fraenkel, *Klassenjustiz*.
32. Cf. Neumann, *Bedeutung*; Kahn-Freund, *Das soziale Ideal*.
33. Cf. pp. 284ff., below.
34. Franz Boehm, *Wettbewerb und Monopolkampf*, Berlin, 1933, pp. 168, 353.

35. A. A. Berle, "Corporation", *Encyclopaedia of Social Sciences*, vol. 4, p. 422; Berle and Means, *Corporation.*
36. United Shoe Machinery Company of Canada v. Brunet (1909), A.C. 330; Attorney General of Australia v. Adelaide Steamship Company (1913) A.C. 781; North West Salt Company v. Electrolytic Alcali Company (1914), A.C. 461.
37. (1924) 1 K.B. 514, and (1925) A.C. 578; also, for a critical view, Harold J. Laski, *Studies in Law and Politics*, chap. IX, London, 1932.
38. Compare A. L. Haslam, *The Law Relating to Trade Combinations* (London, 1931), the decisions in Wittacker v. Howe (1841) 3, Bead., 383, and the Nordenfeldt case (1893) 1 Ch. 630, (1894) A.C. 535 — esp. Lord Macnaghtan's statement on p. 574: "It is sufficient justification . . . if the restriction is reasonable, that is, in reference to the interests of the parties concerned, and reasonable in reference to the interests of the public".
39. For example, U.S. v. Trans-Missouri Freight Assoc. (1897) I, 166, U.S. 290; U.S. v. Joint Traffic Assoc. (1898) 171, U.S. 503; Northern Securities Corp. v. U.S. (1904), 193 U.S. 197.
40. Standard Oil Co. of New Jersey v. U.S. (1911) 191, 221, U.S. 1; U.S. v. American Tobacco Co. (1911) 221, U.S. 106.
41. Weber, *Wirtschaft*, p. 511.
42. Senatspräsident Baumbach, in a commentary on the Wettbewerbsgesetz (Berlin, 1929, p. 174).
43. Quoted in Edward S. Corwin, *The Twilight of the Supreme Court*, New Haven, 1935, p. xxviii.
44. The following pages contain a criticism of Carl Schmitt's *Über die Drei Arten des Rechtswissenschaftlichen Denkens*, Hamburg, 1934.
45. Pound, *Common Law*, p. 31.
46. Renard, *L'Institution*, pp. 174, 178: "Toute institution est une structure juridique rationellement ordonnée à quelque Bien commun, et cet ordonnement est sa loi constitutive. . . . L'institution n'est point une simple relation, c'est un être: une 'tout' aux parties intégrées dans sons être, un 'tout' constitué par un agencement de postes ordonnés à un fin; un 'tout' au regard duquel chaque partie est investée d'un certain titre juridique . . . la relation institutionelle est une intériorisation, consortium, invicem membra".
47. Carl Schmitt, *Die Diktatur*, 2nd ed., Munich and Leipzig, 1928, p. 13.
48. Radbruch, *Rechtsphilosophie*, p. 83.

CHAPTER 16

1. Julius Binder, *Der deutsche Volksstaat*, Tübingen, 1934; Georg Dahm, *Nationalsozialistisches und faschistisches Strafrecht*, Berlin, 1935; Ernst Forsthoff, *Der totale Staat*, Hamburg, 1933; Hans Gerber, *Staatsrechtliche*

Grundlinien des neuen Reiches, Tübingen, 1933; Herman Göring, *Die Rechtssicherheit als Grundlage der Volksgemeinschaft*, Hamburg, 1935; Heinrich Henkel, *Die Unabhängigkeit des Richters in ihrem neuen Sinngehalt*, Hamburg, 1934; Reinhard Höhn, *Die Wandlung im staatsrechtlichen Denken*, Hamburg, 1934; E. R. Huber, *Vom Sinn der Verfassung*, Hamburg, 1935; "Die Totalität des völkischen Staates", *Die Tat*, 1934, p. 30; Otto Köllreuter, *Vom Sinn und Wesen der nationalen Revolution*, Tübingen, 1933; idem, *Grundriss der allgemeinen Staatslehre*, Tübingen, 1933; idem, *Der deutsche Führerstaat*, Tübingen, 1934; idem, *Volk und Staat in der Weltanschauung des Nationalsozialismus*, Berlin, 1935; Heinrich Lange, *Liberalismus, Nationalsozialismus und bürgerliches Recht*, Tübingen, 1933; idem, *Vom Gesetzesstaat zum Rechtsstaat*, Tübingen, 1934; Karl Larenz, *Deutsche Rechtserneuerung und Rechtsphilosophie*, Tübingen, 1934; idem, *Rechts- und Staatsphilosophie der Gegenwart*, 2nd ed., Berlin, 1935; idem, *Rechtsperson und subjektives Recht*, Berlin, 1935; Karl Lohmann, *Hitler's Staatsauffassung*, Berlin, 1933; Gerhard Maunz, *Neue Grundlagen des Verwaltungsrechts*, Hamburg, 1934; Karl Michaelis, *Wandlungen des deutschen Rechtsdenkens*, Berlin, 1935; H. Nicolai, *Der Neuaufbau des Reiches*, Berlin, 1934; idem, *Grundlagen der kommenden Verfassung*, Berlin, 1933; Wolfgang Siebert, *Vom Wesen des Rechtsmissbrauchs*, Berlin, 1935; Karl Siegert, *Grundzüge des Strafrechts im neuen Staat*, Tübingen, 1934; Friedrich Schaffstein, *Politische Strafrechtswissenschaft*, Hamburg, 1934; Carl Schmitt, *Fünf Leitsätze für die Rechtspraxis*, Berlin, 1933; idem, *Staat, Bewegung, Volk*, Hamburg, 1933; idem, *Staatsgefüge und Zusammenbruch des zweiten Reiches*, Hamburg, 1934; idem, *Drei Arten des rechtswissenschaftlichen Denkens*, idem, "Was bedeutet der Streit um den Rechtsstaat?", *Zeitschrift für die gesamte Staatswissenschaft*, 1935, p. 189.

2. Published in England as *The Political and Social Doctrine of Fascism* by the Hogarth Press, London.
3. Mussolini, "Fascism", p. 19.
4. Cf. Herbert Marcuse, "The Doctrine of National Socialism", *Zeitschrift für Sozialforschung*, vol. III, 1934, p. 161. The trend is the heroization of man (Stephan George, Möeller van der Bruck), Vitalistic Philosophy, Irrationalism and Universalism (Othmar Spann).
5. The author uses the German unabridged single-volume 16th edition of 1932.
6. Roland Freisler, *Deutsche Justiz*, 1934, p. 43.
7. Huber, Die Totalität, p. 35.
8. Ibid.
9. Schmitt, *Staat*, p. 12.
10. Ibid., p. 12.
11. This careless admission by Carl Schmitt has provoked biting criticism by his intimate enemy Köllreuter, in the various pamphlets and books mentioned in n. 242 above. It has also caused Schmitt's disciple, Huber, to speak continually of "a political people". What, however, constitutes "people" as a political entity if they have no share in the political power, remains a mystery.

12. That, however, does not mean that this rejection is definite. On the contrary, for we know now that owing to the difficulty of Eastern expansion, Germany has officially claimed the restoration of her colonial possessions.
13. Carl Schmitt, *Der Begriff des Politischen*, Hamburg, 1933.
14. By this we do not mean that an Italian democratic state could not have built up this central machinery; on the contrary, we believe that democratic integration is an even better means of building up such machinery than is a dictatorial one. It may be true that under democratic conditions, its formation would have needed more time.
15. For Italy, see Rosenstock-Frank, *L'Economie corporative fasciste en doctrine et en fait*, Paris, 1934.
16. Carl Schmitt, *Mitteilungen des Langnam Vereins*, 1932, p. 18.
17. Weber, *Wirtschaft*, p. 140.
18. Ibid., p. 142.
19. Ibid., p. 142.
20. Göring, *Grundlage*, p. 8.
21. Holdsworth, *History*, vol. II, p. 417.
22. The same controversy is taking place in Italy.
23. Carl Schmitt, *Nationalsozialismus und Rechtsstaat in Juristische Wochenschrift*, 1934, p. 17; idem, *Leitsätze*.
24. According to Köllreuter, Frank, Lange and Göring.
25. Schmitt, "Was bedeutet".
26. Compare the writings of Köllreuter, Schmitt, Huber, Gerber, Lange, Binder, Henkel, Schaffstein and Forsthoff, for which see n. 242, above.
27. Henkel, *Unabhängkeit*, p. 11.
28. *Deutsche Justiz*, 1934, p. 370.
29. Idem, p. 881: Göring, at a meeting of the Prussian Public Prosecutors after the Roehm revolt.
30. Henkel, *Unabhängkeit.*
31. Cf. *Decisions of the Reichsgericht in Penal Matters*, vol. 66, p. 386.
32. Henkel, *Unabhängkeit*, p. 21.
33. Huber, "Die Totalität", p. 30.
34. Cf. laws of 23rd May 1933 and 14th July 1933.
35. In his earlier period, Carl Schmitt expressed this connection between the generality of law and the independence of judges: see Schmitt, *Legalität*, p. 84.
36. Idem, *Leitsätze*; idem, *Drei Arten*, p. 59; also Lange, *Liberalismus.*
37. Schmitt, *Drei Arten*, pp. 56, 63.
38. Köllreuter, *Grundriss*, p. 254.
39. Göring, *Grundlage*, p. 17.
40. Carl Schmitt, "Deutsche Juristenzeitung", 1934, p. 945.
41. Ibid., p. 947.
42. Weber, *Gesammelte Aufsätze*, vol. I, p. 4 (English transl., p. 22).
43. Cf. the present author's article on "The State and Labour in Germany", *Contemporary Review*, 1935, p. 713.
44. Larenze, *Rechtsperson*, p. 21; Göring, *Grundlage*, p. 12.

EDITORIAL FOOTNOTES, marked * in text [M.R.]

Page 12 Neumann often uses 'right' when translating *Recht*. This should however not be confused with the present-day use of the concept 'right'. Often, it would have been more appropriate to use 'law'.

Page 15 One theory in German law distinguishing public and private insists on public law having a higher validity, i.e. *Mehrwert*, without in any way being linked to Marx's theory of surplus value. Neumann explains this legal theory on p. 20 below.

Page 34 *Polizeigewalt* in German law indicates a much broader scope of powers than 'police powers' — 'interventionist state power' would possibly be the more accurate translation.

Page 39 *Betrieb* could also be translated as 'plant' or 'works'.

Page 218 This ought not to be confused with the present use of the concept 'right' in British or American legal theory. *Rechtssatz* refers to the attempt to delimit an *internal* sphere of the state from an external sphere. It was only in the latter sphere that rules were described as *Rechtssatz*. It is only recently that this notion of a non-legal *forum internum* of the state has come under strong attack, and traces of this theory can still be identified in present day (West) German legal practise.

Page 226 Here and below Neumann presumably means judicial decision making when he talks about 'jurisdiction'.

Page 228 'Judicial review' is used here in a narrow sense to refer to judicial control of *legislative* acts.

Page 276 Kirchheimer published two major works on Art. 153 of the Weimar Constitution: 'Eigentumsgarantie in Reichsverfassung und Rechtsprechung', VII (1930), *Die Gesellschaft* 166; and *Die Grenzen der Enteignung*, Berlin/Leipzig, de Gruyter, 1930. The latter has recently been published in a translation by K. Tribe in *Economy and Society* 12 (1983), 69.

Page 301 In English as *The Institutions of Private Law and their Social Functions*, London, 1942, repr. 1976.